DATE D

WITHDRAWN

The handicapped child
in the regular classroom

The handicapped child in the regular classroom

BILL R. GEARHEART
Professor of Special Education,
University of Northern Colorado,
Greeley, Colorado

MEL W. WEISHAHN
Associate Professor of Special Education,
University of Northern Colorado,
Greeley, Colorado

Illustrated

The C. V. Mosby Company
Saint Louis   1976

Copyright © 1976 by The C. V. Mosby Company

All rights reserved. No part of this book may be reproduced in any manner without written permission of the publisher.

Printed in the United States of America

Distributed in Great Britain by Henry Kimpton, London

Library of Congress Cataloging in Publication Data

Gearheart, Bill R
  The handicapped child in the regular classroom.

  Bibliography: p.
  Includes index.
  1. Handicapped children—Education. I. Weishahn, Mel W., 1940-   joint author. II. Title.
LC4015.G38   371.9   75-31543
ISBN 0-8016-1764-2

Cover photo by Craig DeRoy
with special thanks to the
Blind Children's Center

CB/CB/B 9 8 7 6 5 4 3 2 1

PREFACE

Since the beginning of public education, classroom teachers have been involved in the education of children with various handicapping conditions. Crippled children often missed out on certain physical activities, but otherwise were educated with all other children. Children with moderate hearing or visual impairments were educated along with nonhandicapped peers, often repeating a grade or two, but children who were blind or those with severe hearing loss were usually referred to state residential schools. The mildly mentally handicapped were allowed to move through the educational system at a slower-than-normal pace, but those who just could not learn to read or do arithmetic were eventually "counseled" out of school. Many of the moderately mentally handicapped and most of the more severely retarded were eventually sent to residential settings.

Beginning shortly after the turn of the century (1900–1910), a number of public schools in the United States started special classes for children with various handicapping conditions. The development of Binet's individual test of intelligence made it more practical to "sort out" children with different degrees of mental ability and, to some extent, permitted educators to determine whether deaf children were deaf *and* mentally handicapped or simply deaf, with ability to learn if appropriately educated. (Throughout the years, many deaf children have been thought to be mentally retarded when, in fact, they had normal intelligence.) It was discovered that orthopedically handicapped children in proper specialized educational settings could benefit greatly, and as a result, a number of special schools for the orthopedically handicapped were opened throughout the nation,

leading to further promotion of the special class–special school concept.

There is little question as to the value of some of these programs *for some children,* but the concept promoted by general educators (who were happy to get problems out of the regular classroom), by parents of more severely handicapped children (for whom the special class or special school seemed the only answer), by special educators (who had a considerable vested interest), and by well-intentioned legislators, parent groups, and considerable emotional appeal has been overdone and misused. By midcentury a move to return blind and deaf children to the public schools was under way. At first, most were served in self-contained special classes, but it became obvious that they could profit from more contact with "normal" children. The resource-room and the itinerant-teacher concepts for these children with sensory losses became accepted, with the nonspecial education teacher providing the majority of the child's instructional program. The special education teacher assisted the regular classroom teacher in planning, obtained specialized instructional materials, and provided needed specialized educational programming (such as braille and language development), which the nonspecial education teacher could not be expected to provide.

During the last half of the 1960s, two events occurred that were destined to place even greater responsibility on the regular classroom teacher. It was discovered (or verified) that a number of children who had been earlier diagnosed as educable mentally retarded had potentially greater ability than had earlier been believed. This related particularly to bilingual and bicultural children and those who lived in extreme poverty. Court decisions throughout the land accelerated what might have otherwise been a very slow evolutionary movement. These children were returned to regular classrooms in large numbers. In a somewhat different type of movement, children who had experienced serious educational problems but had been denied any type of special educational help because they were not visually impaired, hard of hearing, or mentally handicapped were recognized as learning disability children and became eligible for special educational assistance. But they remained in the regular classroom for most of the day, and the teacher now felt the need to provide some sort of special assistance for this newly recognized group.

The purpose of this text is to briefly overview the various types of handicapping conditions and to focus on the "what to do" and "how to do it," as these questions relate to the regular classroom teacher. Since 1970, some states have added requirements to teacher training and certification programs, either through direct legislative enactment or through regulation, so that all teachers must receive some formal training in this important area. The question is no longer one of "Should all teachers learn how to deal with handicapped children?" but rather "What should they learn?" This text has been prepared to answer this question and is designed for both in-service and preservice programs.

The Handicapped Child in the Regular Classroom was developed in response to a strongly expressed need from practitioners and students, and much of the content is the result, at least indirectly, of suggestions made by these individuals. We do, however, wish to acknowledge the contributions of a number of specific individuals. We hope that their expenditure of personal time and effort has helped to make the content of this text more meaningful. These include Robert Bliler, Carolyn Boyd, Pamela Brand, David Kappan, John Sansone, Woodrow Schrotberger, Sarah Sonier, and Steven Sweek. In addition, certain other individuals made unique contributions that we wish to acknowledge in relation to that contribution. Ronald Stewart took the majority of photographs used as illustrations in this text. His personal interest in the concerns of special education undoubtedly led to more meaningful photographic efforts. Clifford Baker has prepared an instructor's manual that should be of considerable practical value to college instructors. We sincerely appreciate his efforts in this endeavor. The chapter prepared by Barbara Coloroso provides strategies for working with troubled students in her own unique style, a style that we could not imitate. Finally, typing and manuscript assistance by Ruth Perkins have been consistently invaluable throughout.

To all of these individuals and to students and professional colleagues who provide continued inspiration and challenge, we express our gratitude.

Bill R. Gearheart
Mel W. Weishahn

A special note on terminology

We have attempted to use a minimum of special terminology, and when such is used, we have tried to define or explain it in simple terms. Nevertheless, the use of certain words in this text may deserve special comment.

Mainstreaming is discussed and defined, but throughout the text it is used interchangeably with the word *integration*. Mainstreaming is the more popular word, perhaps the more commercial word, but we have some concern that children may be placed in the mainstream and never really become a part of it. Integration (to us) means becoming a part of the mainstream and implies joint efforts on behalf of special and general educators to assist in meaningful integration. However, because of the frequent use of the word mainstreaming and the necessity of its use when quoting others who use it repetitively, these two terms are used interchangeably and should be construed to mean the same process.

The terms *regular classroom teacher, general educator,* and *nonspecial educator* are meant to indicate the same group of beautiful people to whom we have attempted to relate in this text. What we really mean are *educators who are not specially trained special educators.* Readers are asked to understand that we do not intend to imply ordinariness or to indicate that regular classroom teachers are "just" regular classroom teachers. The regular classroom teacher is—in our eyes—the most important person in the integration process.

Handicapped and *handicapping conditions* are terms used regularly in every chapter. Our special education colleagues sometimes engage in long debates as to whether and when the words *handicapped, disabled, deficient,* or some other choice adjective should be used. We would be delighted to find a more satisfactory descriptive adjective, but until then, we hope that the reader will understand that we have used handicapped and handicapping conditions because we felt they would be generally understood.

Finally, we had to relate to the current concern with the use of pronouns. In a recent professional text we found an instance in which the woman who wrote the text used the masculine pronoun and indicated at the start that "he" refers equally to "she" in all cases. Thus, logically, we might use the feminine pronoun and indicate that "she" refers equally to "he" in all cases. However, after considerable soul-searching and long and intensive consideration, we have elected to use "he" and "she" in whatever manner it first occurred to us to use them in each instance (undoubtedly this related in many cases to a real individual—an actual "he" or "she") and hope that the reader might understand.

CONTENTS

8 Strategies for working with troubled students, 143

9   The importance of good personal interaction (or what it's really all about), 175

Appendices

CHAPTER 1
A historical and philosophic
base for education of the handicapped

Ronald Stewart

The emphasis on education of handicapped children in the regular classroom and the related trend toward requiring that all teachers have some training to better prepare them to fulfill this function became nationally evident between about 1970 and 1975. As with all such movements, the specifics of implementation within the fifty states have varied, but the end results are similar. It would appear likely that by 1980 nearly all geographic areas of the United States—progressive or conservative and urban, suburban, or rural—will have felt the force of this movement.

The effects on various segments of the educational community have been considerable. A number of states will apparently now require that all teachers who are to be newly certified after some target date (1978 to 1980 appears to be a popular time period) have some formal college training in education of the handicapped. Some states have allocated significant sums of money for in-service programs for teachers who are presently teaching but who have no such special training. Larger colleges and universities that have a major role in teacher education are including a requirement for such coursework even before state legislatures or other state agencies involved in licensing or certifying teachers complete work on new regulations. These institutions usually have a department or division of special education, and special education staff previously involved in training teachers to work full time with the handicapped are now involved in providing information and orientation to the regular classroom teacher. Smaller colleges, which provide many good teachers but are less likely to have full-time professors or instructors in the area of education of the handicapped, are busy finding a way to meet this new challenge. Some confusion and misunderstanding have inevitably resulted, with some nonspecial educators feeling they may be asked to do more than they can possibly do, whereas others seem to be simply resigned to "one more fad."

A term to describe the integration of handicapped children with nonhandicapped children in the regular classroom came into common use during the early 1970s. That term is *mainstreaming* and has numerous definitional variations (for expanded discussion see Chapter 2). To some it apparently means the return of all handicapped children (now served through other types of educational efforts) to the regular classroom. It may also indicate to some that *no* child should be served in a totally segregated setting. The reasons for the mainstreaming emphasis are many, ranging from evidence of lack of effectiveness of various special educational efforts or indications that members of various ethnic groups have been improperly placed in special education programs (another type of racial segregation) to the fact that special education has sometimes been used as a place for any child who does not "fit" existing programs or cannot adjust to a particular teacher, regardless of whether the available special education program is appropriate for the child's special needs. It was also recognized that many handicapped students, namely, the visually impaired, crippled, and other health impaired, had been successfully integrated for many years. This success led to increased recognition that other handicapped children could also be successfully educated in regular classrooms.

We believe that all of the preceding factors are real and provide justification for much greater emphasis on retention in regular classrooms rather than special education placement for children who seem to have different educational needs than the others with whom school authorities have grouped them. We further believe that many children now in special classes could function as well, or better, in regular classrooms if the teacher is provided with meaningful information, materials, and assistance. However, our concept of mainstreaming is that of maximum integration in the regular class, coupled with concrete assistance for the nonspecial education teacher. The role of many special educators may be that of a helping or assisting teacher—one who works cooperatively by sharing unique skills and competencies with general educators who also have a great deal to contribute to the education of handicapped students.

The remainder of this chapter is devoted to a statement of our philosophy of education for the handicapped, plus a historical account of the development of special education. The statement of philosophy is the basic point of view from which this text has been developed. (If the reader disagrees vehemently, he or she may wish to read no further.) The historical account is provided so that the reader may better understand the basis for present programs and practices and also to attempt to "tie together" the total fields of general and special education and the major forces that have shaped their development. We believe this will promote better understanding of the various handicapping conditions and the manner in which we should modify or adapt educational materials, methods, and (in some cases) goals, due to the nature of the handicap.

Although it is recognized that there are serious limitations imposed by classifying or labeling children on the basis of medically derived systems, it is also recognized that state legislatures, state departments of education, colleges and universities, and local school districts are still providing for these students on a categorical basis.

It is not our intent to promote the use of labels or categories; however, from a practical viewpoint, teachers and administrators are currently identifying and serving students on the basis of the most identifiable behavior, for example, a vision problem, a behavior disorder, or a hearing difficulty. When considering the practices in the field today, we believe that a common entry must be established that will most closely approximate the child's behavior. As a result, this text is organized on the basis of categorical entry. Regular classroom teachers will, in all likelihood, continue to initially identify students on the basis of observable behavior.

In this text we will call hearing impaired children *deaf, hard of hearing,* or *hearing handicapped* even though we are fully aware that some members of the special education fraternity might view these as old fashioned terms. They could be called children with "receptive problems," but this is just another label, and we believe that although the public has some misunderstandings of deafness or hearing problems, even after decades of efforts at public education, the introduction of a new term serves no useful purpose. We will also persist with the idea that there is such a thing as mental retardation (mental handicap or limited intellectual ability) even though errors have been made in assessment of mental ability, particularly with children who are culturally different from the majority middle-class population. Our major effort has just one central goal—to assist teachers to more effectively work with these handicapped children in their classrooms. We will attempt to attain this goal in the most simple, straightforward manner possible.

A PHILOSOPHY OF EDUCATION FOR THE HANDICAPPED

The handicapped, like all other members of society, must be provided an opportunity to fully develop their abilities. This means that the public, tax-supported educational systems of the nation must adjust and adapt existing educational programs and offerings so as to make this possible. Educational planning should emphasize the learning strengths and abilities of the handicapped, and "labeling" children according to handicap should be avoided whenever possible. On the other hand, children who are hearing impaired or visually impaired must have certain specific assistance that relates directly to their sensory loss, and thus it will often be advantageous to the child and to his educational programming to think of him and at times call him visually impaired (handicapped or disabled) or hearing impaired. Too often in the past, we have not recognized moderate hearing losses or visual impairments to the serious detriment of the child. We believe it would be a professionally unforgivable error to be so concerned about labeling that we permit or encourage teachers to overlook hearing losses or other disabilities because we are afraid to use the term *hearing impaired.*

Handicapped children and youth should be served in the regular classroom whenever possible, and additional efforts should be directed toward increasing the effectiveness of such programming. (This is the major purpose of this text.) If a child must receive specialized assistance in a small, separate grouping of children with special needs, we should provide such help but keep him in the normal classroom setting as much as possible. If the child has been removed for all or part of the school day, careful attention should be given to ensure that he is returned to the regular classroom at the earliest possible time, consistent with his social and educational well-being.

Special educators are needed because (1) the child's needs may be so unusual that the regular classroom teacher cannot adequately meet them, and thus they must be met through direct special educational service; (2) the child and the regular classroom teacher may require the support provided through specialized or adapted materials and equipment; and (3) assistance in assessment or direct consultive efforts may spell the difference between success and failure.

Certain principles closely related to the preceding philosophy are of prime importance. These include

1. Early intervention is highly desirable in most cases.
2. Minority or low socioeconomic status may present unusual problems in assessment, and special care must be taken where this may be a factor.
3. Some disabilities may be more appropriately viewed as symptoms rather than as specific physical disorders and may exist at one time in life and not exist at another.
4. Even in the case of a specific, irreversible disability, the need for special educational services may vary from full-time, special class service at one time in the child's life to little or no service at another time.
5. A wide variety of services and the total spectrum of service delivery capabilities is essential.

6. Services for a broad age range, preschool through high school, are essential.
7. A broad, flexible assessment program including provision for initial and ongoing assessment and formal and informal evaluation is required.

EDUCATION OF HANDICAPPED CHILDREN—HISTORICAL PERSPECTIVE

The manner in which we have arrived at our present state of evolution and development in any arena of human endeavor has relevance to the understanding of that area of interest. Though the history of early efforts to assist (or to eradicate) the handicapped can be documented in great detail, and such documentation might be of considerable interest to some, we will examine only the skeletal outline; hopefully this will be sufficient to permit understanding of the present form and structure of educational provisions for the handicapped.

Other writers have subdivided the history of societal treatment of the handicapped into six or seven major eras, with as many as three or four occurring prior to 1800. For the sake of brevity, we will consider all events prior to 1800 as early history and review total historical development as follows:

Early history	Origin of man to 1800
Era of institutions	1800 to 1900
Era of public school–special classes	1900 to 1960/70
Era of accelerated growth	1960 to present

It must be noted that these eras overlap to a considerable extent; no fine line of demarcation exists. Quite often we find that although a new "era" may have begun in some parts of the nation, the older era is far from over in others. With this limitation in mind, we will proceed with our historical outline.

Early history—origin of man to 1800

The early history of societal involvement with the handicapped is primarily one of misunderstanding and superstition. It would seem likely that blindness, deafness, and mental retardation have existed since the beginning of the human race, and early references clearly document such practices as abandonment of handicapped infants in an attempt to become free of the burden of their care. Roman history repeatedly refers to "fools" kept by the wealthy for entertainment, and the belief that individuals who were considerably "different" from normal in appearance or behavior were possessed by demons or evil spirits was almost universal.

Historical writers such as Zilboorg and Henry (1941), Pritchard (1963), and Kanner (1964) have provided comprehensive accounts of the manner in which we have related to the handicapped, mainly accounts of inhumanity that developed as a result of fear and ignorance.

The early historical origins of present-day programs for the handicapped will be reviewed without the cumbersomeness of repeated references to specific source data. The majority of documentation of the following information may be found in the preceding three references or in Gearheart and Litton (1975) and Gearheart (1972).

Most early records refer to handicapped or defective individuals in such a manner as to make it quite difficult to determine whether those referred to were mentally retarded, mentally ill, or perhaps deaf and unable to communicate. In many societies a father could determine whether he wanted a newborn infant; if he indicated he did not, it might be thrown off a cliff, left in the wilderness, or perhaps simply left by the roadside. Such infanticide was supported by the common belief that individuals who were unusually different were possessed by demons or evil spirits and that the actions taken were not directed against the human infant but against the demon. At one time the Romans even extended this absolute rule of the father over infants to include the possibility that any female infant might be so disposed of, with general public acceptance.

There were, of course, short periods of time during which specific rulers imposed more humane practices, but the foregoing, repugnant as it may seem today, was the general practice in much of the "civilized" Western world for centuries.

The Middle Ages and the rise and further development of Christianity brought about varied effects, depending on the type of handicap, the geographic location, and the specific era. Though the idea of love and concern for others gained some headway, the handicapped were variously viewed as fools, nonhuman, or perhaps witches, witches being an obvious throwback to earlier demonology. The belief that the mentally ill or retarded were possessed by demons or evil spirits at times led to the offering of prayers or in some instances the practice of exorcism. On many occasions this exorcism was somewhat rigorous, but not nearly so final as the later treatment of witches, such as burning at the stake.

Although there were some bright spots, all the more bright for their infrequent appearance, until the sixteenth century the general picture was very bleak. The handicapped were not accepted as totally human and were misunderstood, mistreated, and in many cases put to death. Leading philosophers, national governments, and the organized church all shared responsibility for this attitude.

Then, slowly and with frequent backsliding, the picture began to change. During the latter part of the sixteenth century a Spanish monk, Pedro Ponce de León, was successful in teaching a small group of deaf pupils to speak, read, and write. This was a major breakthrough and led to a reversal of the official position of the church that the deaf could not speak and were uneducable, a position based on the writings of Aristotle. In the following century an early version of finger spelling for the deaf was developed by Juan Bonet, and in 1760, the Abbé de l'Epee opened a school for the deaf in Paris. Organized education for the deaf became a reality.

An associate of the Abbé de l'Epee became interested in the blind and by 1784 had established a school for the blind, also in

Paris. This man, Valentin Huay, had also associated with such intellectuals as Voltaire and Rousseau, and after a traumatic personal experience, in which he witnessed ten blind men being exploited for public entertainment, he vowed to improve the lot of the blind. The National Institution for Young Blind People was the result of this resolve.

Only a few years later, in 1798, an event took place near Aveyron, France, that was to lead to educational programs for the retarded. A boy of 11 or 12 years of age was found roaming "wild" in the woods. Discovered by hunters, this boy was unable to speak, bore the scars of years of encounters with wild animals, and himself was most animal-like in appearance. He bit and scratched all who approached, chose his food by smell, and was in nearly all respects more animal than human. This boy (eventually named Victor) was taken to the Central School in Aveyron, where he came to the attention of Professor Bonaterre, who was interested in the potential value of scientific study of such an unusual "wild boy." (It should be noted that Victor was not the first such "wild person" discovered in Europe, undoubtedly due, at least in part, to the policy of abandonment of children, particularly those who were seen as defective. Although abandoned infants were almost certain to die, older children were sometimes abandoned, and if sufficiently healthy, they literally grew up wild.)

Victor was eventually taken to Paris to be observed by students who were studying the development of primitive faculties. There, Phillipe Pinel, a renowned scientist, declared him to be an incurable idiot, but Jean Marc Gaspard Itard, who also saw him there, thought otherwise. He obtained custody of Victor and launched an involved program to civilize and educate him, hoping to make him normal. The record of Itard's work, *The Wild Boy of Aveyron* (Itard, 1962), is an important classic in the education of the retarded. Though Itard despaired of efforts he saw as fruitless (his expectations were far too high), one of Itard's students, Edouard Seguin, became a major force in the development of educational programs for the retarded.

Thus we see that educational programs for the deaf, blind, and retarded had their beginnings within less than half a century, all in or near Paris, France.* Perhaps the most fitting comment on the long era brought to a close by these new efforts is that the change, the opening of a new chapter in the history of treatment of the handicapped, was long overdue. May we never again see these "good old days."

Era of institutions—1800 to 1900

Historical documentation of the nineteenth century as the era of institutions is conclusive; the obviousness and consistency of this trend is in marked contrast to the variability of treatment and care of the handicapped in all of the preceding centuries. The beginnings of this movement were outlined previously, but the total effort and the manner in which it swept Europe and the United States is a reflection of the combination of a critical need on the part of the population of handicapped persons, an awareness of this need on the part of professionals (both physicians and educators), and changing attitudes among the general population permitting its popular acceptance.

Some of the motivations of the general public may seem less than desirable in light of accepted philosophy of today. Considerable support for institutionalization seems to have come from the fact that this kept these undesirable and physically unattractive persons out of the public eye and thus off the public conscience; however, this was certainly much better than encouraging beggary, using prisons as holding centers, or putting infants to death.

*The work of Pedro Ponce de León with the deaf had come over a century earlier and had set the stage for the later efforts of Abbe' de l'Epee, but the later time period represents more formalized efforts, efforts that led to development of similar programs in Germany and England in a matter of a very few years. Programs in the United States came shortly thereafter.

Institutions for the handicapped were initially developed for the blind, the deaf, and the mentally retarded, with those for the blind and deaf initiated at about the same time and those for the retarded coming some fifty to sixty years later.*

The first institutional programs for the handicapped were initiated in Europe, with France, Germany, Scotland, and England leading the way. By 1800, recognized programs for the blind existed in France, England, and Scotland; for the deaf, in France, Germany, Scotland, and England. Institutions specifically for the mentally retarded were not begun until 1831, when the first such program was initiated in France, but multipurpose institutions such as the Bicetre and Salpetriere, in Paris, had housed a variety of societal outcasts, the blind, senile, mentally ill, prostitutes, and mentally retarded, since the seventeenth century. Perhaps one reason for the later start of institutional programs for the retarded was the fact that until the early nineteenth century there was little differentiation made between the mentally ill and the mentally retarded, and until the work of Itard and Seguin, there was little hope for those of this retarded or mentally ill category.

A great deal might be said about the multiplicity of factors that encouraged the development of publicly supported institutions

for the blind, deaf, and retarded during the nineteenth century. Sociopolitical changes throughout the world, expansion of the concept of individual worth, and a general increase in the level of education, led by the ideal of free public education, all contributed significantly. The development of psychiatry as a distinct subdiscipline of medicine and the differentiation between the mentally ill and mentally retarded also played a major role in developing programs for the mentally retarded. The effectiveness of braille in teaching the blind and the success of both oral and manual methods with the deaf were major factors in these two areas of development. Better communication systems, particularly between Europe and the United States, and the formation of national and international interest groups, formal and informal, led to a rapid exchange of new ideas and success stories that, although sometimes slightly exaggerated, were nevertheless quite effective in the promotion of new programs.

Although there was a definite trend toward institutional programs for the handicapped, several leaders of the time advocated that wherever possible, handicapped students should attend educational programs along with their nonhandicapped peers in the public schools. In 1810, Johann Wilhelm Klein began to promote the principle of education of blind children in local schools for nonhandicapped children, and in 1819, Klein prepared a guide to assist regular class teachers who had blind children enrolled in their classes. In 1842, the government of Lower Austria took an official stand on this matter and issued the following formal statement, a decree (undoubtedly written by Klein [1845]), cited in Lowenfeld (1973):

According to experiences the existing institutions for the blind are insufficient to accept all the blind who are in need of education. Those who are accepted must as a rule be removed from their home conditions and be transferred into an environment strange to them until then. There they become acquainted with desires and habits of a kind which they cannot satisfy in their future lives. Therefore, the need is obvious that

*The reader who further pursues the question of where and when various programs for the deaf, blind, or retarded were established will find, in various source materials, apparently contradictory data. This is due to the fact that some authorities may refer only to public institutions, meaning those for which all persons were eligible, whereas others use private or semipublic program initiation as their point of reference. Some may use the date when, for example, a school for the blind was incorporated; others will use the date when a director was employed; and still others the date when the first individuals were institutionalized in the school. Thus, with reference to the same school or institution, we may find three dates—all supportable through historical documents. Where dates are used in this historical narrative, we have used commonly accepted dates, but variations do exist for the reasons indicated.

education of blind children according to their needs be provided in their parental home and in the school of their community, and that education of the blind be whenever possible incorporated into the regular institutions for the people's education, the public schools [translation by Lowenfeld, p. 14].*

Other leaders in the field of education of the blind voiced similar views, but for the most part, except for Klein's efforts, institutions for the handicapped were the accepted means of providing educational service during the 1800s.

The principle of institutions for the blind, the deaf, the retarded, and the mentally ill was now well established. In institutions for the blind and deaf (these included a limited number of partially seeing, who were not totally blind, and hard of hearing, who were not profoundly deaf) the emphasis was on the teaching of skills that would permit adjustment to the sensory loss and return to the world of the nonhandicapped. In institutions for the mentally retarded and the mentally ill the hope was for a "cure" for the condition, and the success rate here was much less than in programs for the deaf and blind. Particularly in the case of the mentally retarded (this usually meant the more severely retarded), the rate of return to society was so low that it soon became a basic assumption that few would return—the institution became a place of residence until death.

A new trend was just beginning at the end of the century, a trend toward public school classes for children with various handicapping conditions. Alexander Graham Bell, in an address to the National Education Association in 1898, suggested that an "annex" to the public schools should be formed to provide special classes for the deaf, the blind, and the mentally deficient. Then, in 1902, he further urged that this "special education" should be provided so that these children would not have to leave their homes (to attend institutions) and that the National Education Association should actively pursue

---

*From Lowenfeld, B. *The Visually Handicapped Child in School,* copyright © John Day Publishers.

such educational provisions. As a result, the N.E.A. officially formed a Department of Special Education, thus originating a name that remains to this day (Gearheart, 1974). These efforts by Bell and the actions of the public schools, which soon followed, ushered in a new era.

Era of public school–special classes— 1900 to 1960/70

Direct educational programming designed specifically for handicapped children had its origins slightly before the turn of the century (1900), but such efforts were sporadic and met limited acceptance and success. The order of introduction of special programs in the public school was reversed as compared to that of institutional programs, with public school classes for the retarded coming before those for deaf or blind. Such classes had been attempted in New York, Cleveland, and Providence (Rhode Island) before 1900, but they tended to be classes provided for "problem children" and probably included more acting-out, nonretarded than retarded. Then, early in the twentieth century, several cities tried gathering in groups of children who had been previously unschooled and who, for the most part, were definitely mentally retarded. Like the institutions, the schools were interested in a return to normalcy, including normal learning ability, and were for the most part unsuccessful. Thus these early classes for the mentally retarded were often unsatisfactory and many were dropped soon after initiation. Later in the century, particularly after the appearance of a more adequate way to determine degree of mental retardation (Lewis Terman's revision of the Binet test of intelligence—the Stanford-Binet), classes for the more mildly retarded were started and were successful enough to warrant continuation.

Day-school classes for the visually impaired and hearing impaired were slower in starting but did not tend quite so much to the start-and-stop pattern that characterized early classes for the retarded. With institutions for the deaf and blind, the institutional setting was more truly a school, and parents were more likely to accept and support this residential school setting. Thus there was not the kind of urgency that was felt regarding the mentally retarded.

With the enactment of compulsory school attendance laws in the early part of the century came the problems involved in providing for *all* children, including the handicapped. It should be noted that since most states provided state residential schools for the blind and deaf and the more severely mentally retarded were often institutionalized at an early age, the real problem for school officials was that of provision for the more mildly retarded.

It is fairly safe to assume that most school districts first attempted to educate the mildly retarded within the regular class setting. Because many educators visualized these children as learning almost exactly the same way as all other children, the practice of "failing" children, holding them in a given grade until they could do most of the work of that grade, was first attempted. This was common practice with other children, so it was reasoned that it should work with these children whose main difference was that they were *much* slower than normal rather than just a little slower than normal. The only problem was that it did not work; there were often related behavior problems, and so the special class evolved and flourished. Though there were some special classes for children with visual and hearing handicaps and special programs for children with speech defects or unusual physical or orthopedic problems, the major early thrust in the public schools was for special classes for the mildly retarded, with a few children whose major problem was behavioral (resulting in low academic performance) included in classes for the retarded for good measure.

Though there were a few who may have felt that these mildly retarded should stay in the regular class, their dismal academic record soon led to popular acceptance of the special class model for the low- or borderline-IQ child who experienced failure in the regular classroom. Few regular classroom teachers complained when they lost (to the special class) those children who were experiencing the most academic problems. In fact, they were often tempted to send along another child or two, those without the prerequisite low IQ but with academic problems similar to those with lower intelligence. In some cases, for a variety of reasons, these children who actually were not eligible for such placement were placed in the special class, perhaps on a so-called trial placement, which sometimes lasted for years.

After about 1920, as special classes for the mentally retarded (these soon became more popularly named classes for the *educable mentally handicapped* to differentiate from the few programs existing for the trainable mentally retarded) continued to grow in popularity, there was also a slower but measurable growth in special programs for children with less than normal visual acuity (called classes for the blind, visually handicapped, visually impaired, or partially seeing) and classes for those with less than normal hearing (called classes for the deaf, hearing handicapped, aurally handicapped, or acoustically handicapped). In addition, there were special programs for children with speech problems, and often a special room for children with heart problems, orthopedic handicaps, or crippling conditions. Some classes for children whose major problems related to unacceptable or antisocial behavior were also initiated, but as often as not, if the problem was not too severe such children were placed in the class for the retarded, and those who could not get along in this obviously special setting were expelled from school on the basis of their bad effect on other children.

Commencing during the 1920s, an inaccurate but nevertheless widely accepted practice led to the use of the terms *special education classes* and *special education teacher* to refer to classes and teachers of the educable mentally handicapped, with any other type of special education program or service named in relation to the specific handicap involved, that is, for example, class for hard of hearing, crippled, and speech therapy program. This practice continues in some locations and is important to note because the term *special education* is meant to include all handicapping conditions and in many states also includes programs and services for the talented, gifted, or creative child. The teacher of nonhandicapped, the so-called regular class teacher, should remember that providing for handicapped children in the regular class, with or without specialized assistance, means *all* handicapped children, not just the educable mentally handicapped.

We should indicate at this point just how and why the definition of special education differs in various areas of the United States. For all practical purposes, special education is defined on a state-by-state basis in relation to two factors: (1) specific legislation defining special education for purposes of special state reimbursement to those districts providing such programs or services and (2) legislation relating to mandatory education of the handicapped.

In many states both of the preceding types of legislation have been enacted, but in some only the first exists.

There is some acceptance of a national definition of special education, but due to the fact that education is primarily a state function, a degree of variation continues. Two national groups have, in effect, defined special education, and it seems predictable that with one exception (that exception is gifted, talented, or creative children), there will be much more agreement between the states in the near future. The two national definitions are primarily operational in nature and are provided by the Council for Exceptional Children, an organization of professionals who work with exceptional children, and the Bureau of Education for the Handicapped, a major component of the United States Office of Education. These two national entities have provided definitions through the scope of their efforts, definitions actually more meaningful than theoretically oriented verbalizations, which find limited application in practice.

The Council for Exceptional Children has eleven divisions, seven of which relate to recognized categories of exceptionality. These seven are (1) the Association for the Gifted, (2) the Council for Children with Behavioral Disorders, (3) the Division for Children with Communication Disorders, (4) the Division for Children with Learning Disabilities, (5) the Division on Mental Retardation, (6) the Division on the Physically Handicapped, Homebound, and Hospitalized, and (7) the Division for the Visually

Handicapped, Partially Seeing, and Blind. Thus we see that in addition to the three areas of handicap having a well-established historical base, special education now includes the gifted, behavioral disorders, learning disabilities, and physically handicapped.

The Bureau of Education for the Handicapped was established in 1966 after an unusually comprehensive round of hearings conducted by congressional committees into the effectiveness of then existing federal programs for the handicapped. A variety of internationally recognized special educators, plus representatives from the Council for Exceptional Children, the National Association for Retarded Citizens, the United Cerebral Palsy Associations, Inc., and others gave consistent testimony to the effect that an earlier reorganization within the Office of Education had seriously limited the effectiveness of federal dollars spent on behalf of the handicapped. Their recommendation was the establishment of an office to coordinate all educational activities directly established to benefit the handicapped and funded by Congress. The Bureau of Education for the Handicapped was established through legislative enactment and became the focal point of the efforts of special educators from throughout the nation and, to some extent, spokesmen for the field.

The Bureau of Education for the Handicapped fulfills a variety of responsibilities as dictated through federal legislation, which brought it into being and continues to provide funding for specific congressional concerns. Because it is responsible for keeping the Congress informed as to needs of the handicapped, the bureau must periodically make estimates as to numbers of school-age children in the various categories of handicap, which in turn provides another type of definition of scope of special education as it relates to the handicapped. Though some members of the bureau might like to avoid talking about categories of handicap, their estimates of needs have been traditionally made in the following categories: (1) visually disabled, (2) deaf, (3) hard of hearing, (4) speech handicapped, (5) crippled and other health impaired, (6) emotional disturbed, (7) mentally retarded, and (8) learning disabled. Thus we see the same handicapping conditions as those recognized by the Council for Exceptional Children, except that for purposes of estimating needed personnel for the nation, the bureau has often used two subcategories deaf and hard of hearing, rather than a single category.

We view special education as a subsystem of the total educational system, responsible for the joint provision of specialized or adapted programs and services (or for assisting others to provide such services) for exceptional children and youth. We must remember that exceptional children may be defined in a variety of ways, depending on the state in which one is involved in special educational programming. We should also note that the emphasis of this text is on the handicapped, not the gifted, but the classroom teacher would be well advised to plan for those gifted or creative children who will sooner or later make their presence known.

This section of the historical review has been called the era of special classes and indicated as spanning the time interval of 1900 to 1960/70. The dual dating of the close of this era is due to the fact that although there was a considerable increase in the utilization of service delivery plans other than the special class during the 1960s, many special classes remained in 1970. By calling this the era of special classes, we do not mean that other means of serving the handicapped were not in use during this time. Many children with physical disabilities and those with visual or hearing impairments were integrated with excellent success.

It must also be recognized that "special class" may mean either full-time or part-time special class. For example, speech therapy has been conducted for years in small groups of two to four children, in a totally segregated special setting, usually for time periods of only thirty to forty minutes per day, two or three days per week. Programs for the visually impaired have sometimes been segregated special classes, at the preschool level and while learning special skills such as braille, but these same children may be almost totally integrated in the regular classroom from second grade on through school.

This first sixty to seventy years of the twentieth century is properly called the special class era because this was the *major* means whereby handicapped children were served and it represented definite evolution beyond the institutional era. It was characterized by general educators happily sending problem children to the special class for mentally handicapped and by special educators accepting children who should not have been so placed. Toward the end of the era it became a time of contradictory and inconclusive efficacy studies, and claims—verified in court—that special classes were sometimes "dumping grounds," other times a vehicle of segregation, and in certain geographical areas a convenient way to do something about culturally different, bilingual children without actually initiating a bilingual program.

As the era came to a close a generally negative feeling was left in the minds of many whenever the words "special class" were uttered, particularly when the reference was to a self-contained special class. It is possible that the self-contained special class for *preschool* hearing impaired or retarded children may be the best possible program, given the lack of publicly supported preschools and the specialized needs of such children. We should further note that special classes, not necessarily totally segregated, but certainly segregated for a major part of the day, may be the best program for many severely handicapped children, regardless of age. The misuse and overuse of the special class is a generally accepted fact, but misuse and overuse do not automatically indicate there is no value or benefit to the special class when properly used.

Era of accelerated growth—1960 to the present

Commencing in the early 1960s, a series of separate but related events took place that were, in their total effect, to literally change the face of special education. The federal government played a major role in these events, starting slowly in 1958 with a law to provide captioned films for the deaf, and another, much further-reaching enactment, Public Law 85-926, which provided funds to states and to institutions of higher learning to train college instructors who would in turn train teachers of the mentally retarded. This law and the National Defense Education Act, passed at about the same time, established the principle of federal support for college students whose training was seen to be essential to established national priorities. Public Law 85-926 also established the principle of support of specific categories of handicap.

The next major step in federal support of special education came in 1963 with Public Law 88-164, hailed by many as the ultimate in assistance for handicapped children and youth. President Kennedy, himself a strong personal advocate of assistance to the handicapped, signed this bill into law and soon afterward established the Division of Handicapped Children and Youth to administer all programs for the handicapped. This act indicated federal interest in all categories of handicap and firmly established the responsibility of the federal government with respect to this interest.

In addition to the establishment of important precedent, it appeared that Congress found a unique degree of satisfaction in passing legislation benefiting a group that did not contribute to campaigns, picket or demonstrate, or even possess any great power through control of voting blocs. It apparently "felt good" to do something beneficial just because it was beneficial. The next Congress, the Eighty-ninth, passed ten highly important laws, nine expressly for the handicapped and one, Public Law 89-10 (the Elementary and Secondary Education Act), that had profound effects on education in general, including education of the handicapped. Special education, as far as federal support was concerned, had arrived.

A number of factors contributed to this deluge of positive congressional action. The following are among the most important:

1. A number of major political figures, including President Kennedy, had an unusual personal interest in the handicapped because of handicapped individuals in their immediate families. Twenty years earlier the existence of handicapped family members might have been hidden, but increased objectivity about the handicapped, public relations efforts by major organizations concerned with the handi-

capped, and national concern about minority populations made it socially and politically acceptable to promote such causes.

2. Organizations such as the National Association for Retarded Children and the United Cerebral Palsy Associations, Inc., had become increasingly active in the preceding years, and leading national figures, particularly those in show business, had supported their efforts and had given the cause of the handicapped unusually high national visibility.

3. Professional organizations, led by the Council for Exceptional Children but including many more, had grown in power, recognition, and lobbying expertise.

4. Congress was venturing into new fields of involvement, and this appeared to be a fruitful one. Few would criticize efforts to assist the handicapped.

5. It is our personal knowledge that two or three individuals who were among the most influential in the world of business, banking, and economics and who knew each of the presidents, starting with President Eisenhower, well enough to call them on the phone and receive immediate personal attention, were promoting the cause of the handicapped. This was not a matter of party politics but of power and influence with Congress and the President, regardless of party.

In total, the federal government, through meaningful legislation and relatively adequate funding, gave special education an impetus (in the late 1960s) that few would have dared predict possible ten years earlier.

Along with this flood of emphasis at the federal level came efforts at the state and local level to encourage state legislators to pass more comprehensive legislation for the handicapped. These efforts included a wide variety of emphases, depending on the state of evolution of programming for the handicapped within each state. In some states it took the form of broad-scale permissive legislation; in others, mandatory legislation; and in still others, it meant inclusion of a hitherto excluded category of handicap (for example, the trainable mentally retarded). Whatever the emphasis, things seemed to be going well for proponents of better, more complete educational provisions for the handicapped. Special education was riding the crest of a wave of success.

Then, somewhere in the background new voices were heard. For the most part these were voices of professional special educators, and their message seemed to run counter to the prevailing mood of the day. They were saying "Are these special efforts really doing any good? Is special education really effective, in terms of actual achievement, or is much of it a waste?" Specifically, they were asking if special education classes for the mildly (educable) mentally retarded were even *as* effective as retention in the regular class. Lloyd Dunn asked this question in such a manner as to shake some of the foundations of special education (Dunn, 1968). Because of Dunn's stature in special education, wide scale reevaluation began soon thereafter and is still taking place. Dunn's comments were directed primarily at self-contained classes for the educable mentally retarded, but many confused the message and generalized his words to a broader scope of programs for the handicapped. Thus, for at least a few years, we seemed to have one group of special educators encouraging lawmakers at the state and federal level to pass laws and provide funds for special programs for the handicapped, whereas in the opposite corner we found those who said (or were interpreted as saying) that what we had was essentially negative and children would be better off without it.

Now, add to this confusion a series of court actions, specific litigation regarding special education classes and services to and for handicapped children. This litigation began to appear in earnest in the early 1970s, and although it took many forms, we will consider two major thrusts here. The first may be characterized as litigation in which it was alleged that special education classes (usually classes for the educable mentally retarded) lead to stigma, inadequate education, and irreparable injury. These were usually class-action suits; that is, suits brought on behalf of specific plaintiffs and "all others similarly situated." A majority of these suits were brought on behalf of black or Mexican-American children and were in part the result of placement of children in special classes on the basis of grossly inadequate evaluation. One example is the case of *Diana* v. *State Board of Education (California)*. This suit, used as the basis for many other similar suits, alleged that the intelligence tests used for placement were culturally biased and that class placement based on these inadequate tests led to an inadequate education. In addition, this suit claimed that as a result, the stigma of mental retardation was suffered by children who were not mentally retarded. In the *Diana* case the plaintiffs sought relief from existing practices of identification and placement. They also sought compensatory damages.

Diana v. *State Board of Education* was settled out of court with the following points of agreement: (1) children whose primary language is not English must be tested in their primary language and in English; (2) verbal questions, which by their very nature are unfair to children whose primary language is not English, cannot be used in testing such children; (3) all Mexican-American and Chinese children already enrolled in special education classes must be retested in accordance with the preceding two principles; (4) every school district in the state must develop and submit to the court the school district plan for retesting and reevaluating Mexican-American and Chinese children presently in classes for the educable mentally retarded, and as a part of this plan they must show how they will place back into regular classes those children whom this reevaluation indicates were misplaced; (5) school psychologists must immediately begin the development of more appropriate testing devices and measures that will reflect Mexican-American culture and norm these instruments on Mexican-Americans; and (6) any school district that has a significant disparity between the percentage of Mexican-American children in regular classes and this percentage in classes for educable mentally retarded must submit an acceptable explanation for this discrepancy.

The *Diana* case is similar to many filed against the schools. Most were settled in a manner similar to that of the *Diana* case.

A second type of major litigation appeared to be going in a different direction, that of demanding more special education classes and services for the handicapped in the public schools. The following description of two cases, one in Pennsylvania and the other in Washington, D.C., illustrates this effort (Gearheart and Litton, 1975, pp. 15,16). Although the first affected only the mentally retarded, the second specifically related to all handicapped and, because it was based on the United States Constitution, has ramifications for all areas of the United States.

Two major cases appear to have established the right of free access to public education for the school age trainable mentally retarded. The first, *The Pennsylvania Association for Retarded Children* v. *the Commonwealth of Pennsylvania,* questioned educational policies of the state of Pennsylvania, which led directly to practices that denied an appropriate education at public expense to retarded children of school age. This case was filed on January 7, 1971, by the Pennsylvania Association for Retarded Children on behalf of fourteen specifically named children and all other children similarly situated. This was a typical *class action* suit, filed in such a manner as to affect those fourteen children named, all others of a similar "class" now residing in the state, and all children similarly situated who will be living in Pennsylvania in the future.

Pennsylvania, like a number of other states, had compulsory school attendance laws, provided certain types of special classes for handicapped children within the public schools, and provided residential schools for some handicapped children. But within the Pennsylvania School Code, there were two specific ways in which the trainable mentally retarded child could be excluded from public education. First, if a qualified psychologist or personnel from a mental health clinic certified that a given child could no longer profit from public school attendance, the child could be excluded. Second, because the law provided that the local board of directors could refuse to accept or retain children who had

not reached the mental age of 5 years, most trainable retarded were never admitted to the public schools. Even if a child were not excluded under either of these two provisions, there was a third provision that permitted the local board to provide training outside the public schools, "If an approved plan demonstrates that it is unfeasible to form a special class."

The Pennsylvania Association for Retarded Children (PARC) set out to establish three main points in their case: (1) Mentally retarded children can learn if an appropriate educational program is provided, (2) "education" must be viewed more broadly than the traditional academic program, and (3) early educational experience is essential to maximize educational potential.

After considerable testimony by the state and by a variety of "expert witnesses," the case was won by the PARC. In a finalization of earlier decrees, the court ordered (on May 5, 1972) that each of the named plaintiffs be immediately reevaluated, and that each be provided free access to public education and training appropriate to his learning capabilities. It further ordered that all retarded persons between the ages of 6 and 21 years be provided such access and programming as soon as possible but in any event, no later than September 1, 1972.

The order and agreement also contained a number of added benefits for the retarded of Pennsylvania. The state department was made responsible for supervision of educational programs in state institutions, children served through homebound programs must now be automatically reevaluated every 3 months, and any district providing preschool education for other children must now provide preschool for the retarded.

The Pennsylvania Association for Retarded Children v. *Pennsylvania* suit, like many which were to follow, was settled on the basis of a *consent agreement*. This is an out-of-court agreement, usually formally approved by the court. In this suit, the state was ordered to provide free public education, appropriate to the learning capabilities of retarded children, and the consent agreement provided the working framework. To make certain that the consent agreement was carried out, the court established a time schedule for implementation and appointed two "masters" to oversee the total process.

A second case, *Mills* v. *the Board of Education of the District of Columbia,* is of unusual significance because it applied to *all* handicapped children. To a certain extent, it established a principle that was to tend to lead to the inclusion of all handicapped children in future class action suits. This case, like the PARC versus Pennsylvania suit, led to a court order that required the public schools to provide for handicapped children, even if they did not fit the educational mold. As in the Pennsylvania case, the court appointed masters to oversee the operation.

Unlike the Pennsylvania case, which resulted in a consent agreement between the parties, the Mills versus District of Columbia case was decided through a judgment of the court and was based on a constitutional holding.

These two cases, plus a number of less publicized cases, have firmly established the rights of handicapped children to appropriate, free public education. They have led to the existence of a number of parent groups that are ready to assist other parents throughout the nation in this cause. In nearly every case when litigation is actually initiated the public schools have been found to be neglecting their responsibility and have been ordered to assume full responsibility for education of the handicapped.

SUMMARY

The handicapped child, like all other children in American society, deserves an opportunity to develop whatever abilities he may possess. Since each of the fifty states provides tax-supported public education for other boys and girls, it seems only consistent with nationally accepted philosophical statements of equal opportunity to provide appropriate educational opportunities for the handicapped. The philosophy of education for the handicapped presented in this chapter supports an emphasis of learning strengths and abilities and a deemphasis of labeling of handicapped children. On the other hand, education for many handicapped children *must* be adapted (that is, braille for the blind, adapted language systems for the severely hearing impaired, and others), and to provide such adaptations, we must speak objectively of the type and degree of handicap; thus some "labels" must be used at times. However, most handicapped children can be served effectively in the regular classroom *if*

materials and consultive assistance are provided. All possible efforts should be directed toward such participation in the regular class.

Historically, the handicapped have been eliminated, ignored, made to work as indentured servants, and institutionalized in that approximate order. There have been variations in different parts of the world and differences between the various types of handicapping condition, but these were the most common societal reactions to the handicapped until about 1900. Commencing soon after the beginning of the twentieth century, public school special classes became popular and commonly accepted. They represented a significant step in the right direction but before long were misused and overused, and thus some reform was needed. This reform began to take shape in the 1960s and was given a boost by court rulings that directed the public schools to educate the handicapped, but to do so in a manner that permitted them to be in the most nearly normal setting possible.

Thus, as we bring this historical account up to the present, we can see that educational efforts on behalf of the handicapped have been greatly expanded in recent years, with the federal government playing a significant role. State governments have followed suit (sometimes reluctantly), and when their action has been too slow, they have been ordered by the courts to provide for all children, even those who have been traditionally viewed as uneducable. At the same time the value of the self-contained special class for the handicapped has been questioned, and a variety of alternate educational strategies have been suggested. The following chapter will further examine this recent trend, some of the more popularly accepted alternate strategies, and the effect of all of these events on the teacher of the nonhandicapped, often called the regular classroom teacher.

References and suggested readings

Abeson, A. *A Continuing Summary of Pending and Completed Litigation Regarding the Handicapped.* Arlington, Va.: Council for Exceptional Children. (These summaries are issued periodically by the Council for Exceptional Children. Those issued after 1973 may be of particular interest in relation to topics discussed in this chapter.)

Ashcroft, S. C. "The Handicapped in the Regular Classroom." *N. E. A. Journal,* November 1967, *56,* 33-34.

Birch, H. G., and Gussow, J. *Disadvantaged Children.* New York: Harcourt Brace Jovanovich, Inc., 1970.

California State Department of Education. *An Investigation of Spanish-speaking Pupils Placed in Classes for the Educable Mentally Retarded.* Sacramento: The Department, 1969.

Christoplos, F., and Renz, P. A. "A Critical Examination of Special Education Programs." *Journal of Special Education,* 1969, *3,* 371-379.

Cruickshank, W., Paul, J., and Junkala, J. *Misfits in the Public Schools.* Syracuse, N. Y.: Syracuse University Press, 1969.

Dunn, L. M. "Special Education for the Mildly Retarded: Is Much of it Justifiable?" *Exceptional Children,* 1968, *35,* 5-22.

Gearheart, B. R. (Ed.). *Education of the Exceptional Child: History, Present Practices and Trends.* Scranton, Pa.: Intext Publishers Group, 1972.

Gearheart, B. R. *Organization and Administration of Educational Programs for Exceptional Children.* Springfield, Ill.: Charles C Thomas Publisher, 1974.

Gearheart, B. R., and Litton, F. *The Trainable Retarded: A Foundations Approach.* St. Louis: The C. V. Mosby Co., 1975.

Itard, J. M. G. *The Wild Boy of Averyon.* New York: Appleton-Century-Crofts, 1962.

Kanner, L. *A History of the Care and Study of the Mentally Retarded.* Springfield, Ill.: Charles C Thomas, Publisher, 1964.

Kott, M. G. "The History of Mental Retardation." In Rothstein, J. (Ed.). *Mental Retardation: Readings and Resources.* New York: Holt, Rinehart and Winston, Inc., 1971.

Lilly, S. "Improving Social Acceptance of Low Sociometric Status, Low Achieving Students." *Exceptional Children,* January 1971, *37,* 341-348.

Lowenfeld, B. *The Visually Handicapped Child in School.* New York: The John Day Company, Inc., 1973, (A translation by Lowenfeld from Klein's *Guide to Provide for Blind Children the Necessary Education in the Schools of Their Home Communities and in the Circle of Their Families;* 1836; revised edition, 1845.)

Pritchard, D. G. *Education and the Handicapped: 1760-1960.* London: Routledge & Kegan Paul Ltd., 1963.

Weintraub, F. "Recent Influences of Law Regarding the Identification and Educational Placement of Children." *Focus on Exceptional Children,* 1972, *4*(2), 1-11.

Wolfensberger, W. *Normalization: The Principle of Normalization in Human Services.* Toronto: National Institute on Mental Retardation, 1972.

Wright, R. G. "Special—But Not Separate." *Education,* May 1967, *87,* 554-557.

Zilboorg, G., and Henry, G. W. *A History of Medical Psychology.* New York: W. W. Norton & Company, Inc., 1941.

CHAPTER 2
Present framework for services
for the handicapped — vectors and influences

Ronald Stewart

As we entered the last half of the 1970s it became increasingly clear that the integration-mainstreaming trend was well established. Although the variables discussed in the previous chapter served to provide the basic framework for this trend, there were several more recent vectors of influence that provided the needed force and direction. These included:

1. Prevalence-need studies, which established the number of handicapped students being served and those in need of service
2. State and federal legislative declarations, which mandated that handicapped students be educated in regular classrooms wherever possible
3. Changes in teacher certification requirements
4. Changes in delivery systems adopted by school districts

There were a number of other factors that had an indirect influence on this trend. Open schools and the availability of a variety of new instructional materials, which were developed for all levels of ability and functioning, had an influence. The concepts of equalizing educational opportunity and humanizing the educational process and content have played a significant role. The belief that regular classroom teachers and nonhandicapped students have been disadvantaged by not having experience with individuals who are different has also gained growing acceptance.

PREVALENCE OF HANDICAPPED CHILDREN

The prevalence of handicapped children has been estimated and reported by a variety of agencies over the past fifty years. The important data is that which is generated when we convert the percent of population into the number of school-aged children in need of service.

Table 1 reflects a range of prevalence derived from a composite of federal reports and other generally accepted published estimates.* It indicates the lowest percent usually reported as the minimum of this range and a median figure as the upper limit.

NEEDS STUDIES

In an attempt to determine the extent to which handicapped students are adequately served, federal and state agencies have conducted a number of needs studies. These studies were initiated for the purpose of de-

*It must be concluded that it is difficult to know precisely the number of handicapped students, but this table is consistent with estimates provided by government agencies, such as the Bureau of Education for the Handicapped (United States Office of Education).

Table 1. Prevalence of handicapped children in the United States

	Percent of population	Number of children ages 5 to 18*
Visually impaired (includes Blind)	0.1	55,000
Hearing impaired (includes Deaf)	0.6 to 0.8	330,000 to 440,000
Speech handicapped	3.5 to 5.0	1,925,000 to 2,750,000
Crippled and other health impaired	0.5	275,000
Emotionally disturbed	2.0 to 3.0	1,100,000 to 1,650,000
Mentally retarded (both educable and trainable)	2.5 to 3.0	1,375,000 to 1,650,000
Learning disabilities	2.0 to 4.0	1,100,000 to 2,200,000
	11.2 to 16.4	6,160,000 to 9,020,000

*Number of children based on 1978 population estimates.

termining more accurately the number of students served by special education programs and the number of students in need but not receiving specialized services. Table 2 relates the findings of surveys conducted by the Bureau of Education for the Handicapped (United States Office of Education), and a variety of state and regional studies to the prevalence data reflected in Table 1. The resulting data (Table 2) reflects the approximate percent and number of children receiving services and those in need but not receiving services.

It is important to note that a large percent of children (approximately 60%)—though mildly handicapped and thus not "labeled" for purposes of receiving services—would benefit from supportive assistance from specialized personnel. In many cases this service could be most efficiently provided through the regular class teacher, *assisted by* the appropriate special educator.

Several state departments of education, in an effort to determine the number of students in their state who were in need of special services, conducted similar studies. Often these studies were mandated by state legislatures for purposes of accountability and for budgetary projections. The Colorado legislature, for example, directed that such a study be conducted. The findings of the Colorado Needs Assessment supported the findings of the earlier BEH study in that more than sixty percent of the handicapped students were being served in regular classrooms without the needed support or assistance from special education. Table 3 presents the findings of this survey.

Table 2. Handicapped children receiving service and those in need but not receiving service*

	Total number of children†	Percent receiving service	Number receiving service	Percent remaining in need of service	Number remaining in need of service
Visually impaired	55,000	35	19,250	65	35,750
Hearing impaired	330,000	25	82,500	75	247,500
Speech handicapped	1,925,000	55	1,058,750	45	866,250
Crippled and other health impaired	275,000	20	55,000	80	220,000
Emotionally disturbed	1,100,000	15	165,000	85	935,000
Mentally retarded	1,375,000	55	756,250	45	618,750
Learning disabled	1,100,000	‡	330,000	‡	770,000
	6,160,000		2,466,750		3,693,250

*We have elected to use the more conservative prevalence data from Table 1 and to round off recent estimates of those receiving services to the nearest five percent, rounding upward (increasing the percent presumed to be receiving services) to reflect a slow increase in the percent of children served owing to mandatory legislation. This will tend to result in a conservative estimate of children remaining in need of services.
†Number of children based on 1978 population estimates (see Table 1).
‡Services to children with learning disabilities have been increasing rapidly and any estimate of number and percent of children served may quickly become inaccurate. In addition, much of the reported data in state studies reflects a definition of learning disabilities that includes more moderate and mild learning problems than those indicated by the two percent (1,100,000 children) figures used to reflect the total number of children who should receive service. However, information from a variety of sources leads us to estimate that thirty percent of the 1,100,000 children were receiving some service as of 1976.

Table 3. Colorado needs assessment*

Type of handicap	Number of children	Percent receiving services	Percent in need of services
Visually impaired	1813	32	68
Hearing impaired	2854	18	82
Crippled and other health impaired	5885	44	54
Limited intellectual capacity	27,944	43	57
Learning disabilities and behavior problems	49,963	13	87

*This needs assessment did *not* include children with impaired speech because sufficient information existed (in Colorado) concerning the numbers of children being served.

LEGISLATIVE CHANGES

As a direct result of these and similar needs studies and as a part of the trend toward educational normalization, state legislatures have placed emphasis on the placement of handicapped students in regular classrooms by stating that these students should be served in the "most normal" educational program possible.

The Colorado Forty-ninth General Assembly endorsed the following legislative declaration:

State of Colorado House Bill 1164, Sec. 123, 22, 2, 1973: Legislative declaration: The general assembly, recognizing the obligation of the state of Colorado to provide educational opportunities to all children which will enable them to lead fulfilling and productive lives, declares that the purpose of this article is to provide means for educating those children who are handicapped. It is the intent of the general assembly, in keeping with accepted educational principles, that handicapped children shall be educated in regular classrooms, insofar as practicable, and should receive supplementary services only when the nature of the child's handicap makes the inclusion of the child in a regular classroom impractical. To this end, the services of special education personnel shall be utilized within the regular school programs to the maximum extent permitted by good educational practices, both in rendering services directly to children and in providing consultative services to regular classroom teachers.

The state of Tennessee has also established regulations concerning placement of the handicapped in regular classrooms.

Tennessee Laws, Sec. 2B, Ch. 839, 1972. To the maximum extent practicable, handicapped children shall be educated along with children who do not have handicaps and attend regular classes. Impediments to learning and to the normal functioning of handicapped children in the regular school environment shall be overcome by the provision of special aids and services rather than separate schooling for the handicapped. Special classes, separate schooling, or other removal of handicapped children from the regular school environment shall occur only when and to the extent that the nature and severity of the handicap is such that education in the regular classroom, even with the use of supplemental aids and services, cannot be accomplished satisfactorily.

Florida law specifies that in providing for the education of handicapped students, educational personnel shall use the regular school facilities and adapt them to the needs of exceptional students whenever possible. No student shall be segregated and taught apart from normal students until a careful study of the student's case has been made and evidence obtained indicating that segregation would be for the student's benefit or is necessary because of difficulties involved in teaching the student in a regular class.

Wisconsin law states that "preference is to be given, whenever appropriate, to education of the child in classes along with children who do not have exceptional educational needs."

These legislative statements clearly reflect the belief that educational programs for handicapped students must be provided in the least restrictive setting. Although only four legislative declarations have been reviewed here, it appears that this trend will be maintained, since several other states have implemented similar statements and others are in the process of drafting this type of legislation.

On August 21, 1974, Public Law 93-380 was signed into law. An extension of the earlier Elementary and Secondary Education Act of 1965, Part B of Title VI, ended the question of federal feelings on a number of topics. Henceforth, for states to receive federal funds for handicapped children the provisions of this act must be followed. Note the specific references to (1) full educational opportunity for *all* handicapped children, (2) procedural safeguards in identification, evaluation, and placement, and (3) assurances that children will be educated to the maximum extent appropriate, with children who are *not* handicapped.*

(12) (A) establish a goal of providing full educational opportunities to all handicapped children, and (B) provide for a procedure to assure that funds expended under this part are used to accomplish the goal set forth in (A) of this paragraph and priority in the utilization of funds under this part will be given to handicapped children who are not receiving an education; and (13) provide procedures for insuring that handicapped children and their parents or guardians are guaranteed procedural safeguards in decisions regarding identification, evaluation and educational placement of handicapped children including, but not limited to (A) (i) prior notice to parents or guardians of the child when the local or State educational agency proposes to change the educational placement of the child, (ii) an opportunity for the parents or guardians to obtain an impartial due process hearing, examine all relevant records with respect to the classification or educational placement of the child, and obtain an independent educational evaluation of the child, (iii) procedures to protect the rights of the child when the parents or guardians are not known, unavailable, or the child is a ward of the State including the assignment of an individual (not to be an employee of

the State or local educational agency involved in the education or care of children) to act as a surrogate for the parents or guardians, and (iv) provision to insure that the decisions rendered in the impartial due process hearing required by this paragraph shall be binding on all parties subject only to appropriate administrative or judicial appeal; and (B) procedures to insure that, to the maximum extent appropriate, handicapped children, including children in public or private institutions or other care facilities, are educated with children who are not handicapped, and that special classes, separate schooling or other removal of handicapped children from the regular education environment occurs only when the nature or severity of the handicap is such that education in regular classes with the use of supplementary aids and services cannot be achieved satisfactorily; and (C) procedures to insure the testing and evaluation materials and procedures utilized for the purposes of classification and placement of handicapped children will be selected and administered so as not to be racially or culturally discriminatory.

TEACHER PREPARATION

Legislatures, while recognizing that the majority of handicapped students were being served in regular classrooms without the needed assistance, also recognized that if these students were to be served more effectively, efforts must be initiated to provide regular classroom teachers with the necessary skills and competencies to work with them.

The 1972 Colorado legislature earmarked two million dollars for the in-service training of regular teachers to acquaint them with the recently enacted mandatory legislation and to provide them with the necessary understanding, skills, and competencies to work with handicapped students in their classrooms. This appropriation was followed by similar amounts for two subsequent years to ensure that a large number of general educators would have the opportunity to participate in in-service offerings.

Other states have enacted specific legislation requiring that all teachers, to become certified, must receive specific preparation in techniques of how to work with handicapped students in regular classrooms. The following bills from the states of Missouri and

---

*P.L. 93-380, Title VI, Part B, Section 612 (d).

Georgia are examples of legislation requiring that all general educators receive preparation in this area.

House Bill No. 370
77th General Assembly of the State of Missouri

Be it enacted by the General Assembly of the State of Missouri, as follows:

Section 1. 1. After July 1, 1976, no person shall be granted a certificate of license to teach in the public schools of this state as provided by section 168.021, RSMo, unless he has satisfactorily completed a course of two or more semester hours in the psychology and education of the exceptional child.

2. The course shall include instruction on identification of children with learning disabilities caused by neurological disorders, mental retardation and sociological factors. The course shall provide information on methods and techniques for teaching exceptional children, sources of referral and assistance to teachers and parents.

*The State of Georgia**

Section 8A. Course in Education of Exceptional Children. (a) After July 1, 1976, any person granted a certificate as a teacher, principal, or guidance counselor, pursuant to Section 8 of this Act, shall have satisfactorily completed a course of five or more quarter hours, approved by the State Board of Education, in the education of exceptional children, or participate in a local system's staff development program designed to

*Only the applicable section is quoted.

assist teachers in the identification of students with special needs.

Other states have adopted similar positions concerning the need for specific preparation at either the preservice or in-service level to provide general educators with the needed understanding of students who are different and with the necessary skills to work more effectively with them.

Colleges and universities have been called on to develop specific courses and units or modules of instruction to meet this challenge. The way in which these offerings are provided must ensure that these teachers in training will be provided with the best possible preparation for this important responsibility. It will not be effective to attempt to use existing introductory courses in special education to provide needed understandings and competencies to this population of regular class teachers. Rather, a specific offering tailored to the unique needs of general educators must be provided; this is our interest and purpose in preparing this text.

SERVICE DELIVERY

As a direct outgrowth of the interaction of the various factors mentioned previously, school districts have reorganized their methods of service delivery. There is considerable debate concerning how and where handi-

Table 4. A continuum of alternative educational provisions for handicapped children

	1	2	3	4
Regular class No assistance needed	Regular class and consultive assistance from special education	Regular class and consultation plus special materials from special education	Regular class and itinerant teacher service from special education	Regular class and resource room, source teacher vice from speci education
	Regular class teacher—primary responsibility			
		Consultant, itinerant, resource room, special education teacher responsibility		

*Regular class teacher may (1) assist homebound/hospital teacher, (2) teach the child through tele electrical-electronic mode, direct and indirect service may be provided by special education.

capped students should be served. For example, some professionals believe that all but the most seriously handicapped should be mainstreamed into regular classrooms, whereas others advocate continued special class placement for the majority. It is our opinion that a continuum of services must be offered —a continuum that provides all required services at any particular time during the child's educational program. In years past, school districts have offered as few as two or three service delivery systems for their handicapped students. Such an approach obviously demanded that the student be "fit into" the organizational plans offered. A program continuum provides a full spectrum of services that may be tailored to the individual needs of each student at any given time during his educational career. A program continuum for handicapped students is shown in Table 4.

Closer examination of the continuum of alternative educational provisions for handicapped children (Table 4) indicates that a full range of services is offered, a range from regular classroom placement to very intensive special education programming. In the first four plans the student remains in a regular classroom for all or a majority of the school day, and his regular classroom teacher has primary responsibility for his program. In the first two plans the regular classroom teacher receives consultative assistance or special instructional materials from special education personnel, but the student does not work directly with special educators. In the third and fourth plans the regular classroom teacher retains primary responsibility, but special education personnel provide supportive or supplemental assistance to *both* the child and his teacher or teachers. The services provided by special education personnel may take place in the regular classroom or in a designated work area, such as a resource room.

In plans five and six the student attends a regular classroom part time and a special class part time. The amount of time spent in the regular classroom is dependent on the individual's ability to profit from regular classroom instruction. In plan five, the student may spend a near equal amount of time in each setting, whereas in plan six the student spends the majority of his day in a special class and is selectively included in regular classroom activities.

The last three plans (seven, eight, and nine), reflect comprehensive services needed by the more seriously involved or multiply handicapped. Plan seven involves service by specialized personnel in a school in which all students are receiving special assistance

5	6	7	8	9	
ular class half-time) nd special ass (half- ne)	Special class in regular school some integration for at least some children	Special class in separate special day school	Hospital and homebound service	Residential or boarding school	No educational provision (This "no-service" condition is rapidly disappearing owing to recent court decisions.)
			*		
	Special class teacher—primary responsibility				

up or electronic equipment, (3) not be involved at all. If child is taught by regular class teacher through due to handicapping conditions. Plan eight may involve the regular class teacher, and instruction may be provided through electrical-electronic hookup with the regular classroom. Plan nine is for children with severe problems who require twenty-four-hour programming.

Although we agree that placement in regular classrooms is desirable for the majority of students, there are and will be students whose needs must be met through placement in special education programs. The alternative program continuum does not assume that one type of program is better for *all* students. *An important basic assumption is that each and every student must be considered individually.* For one student, special class placement may be the best alternative, whereas another may be most effectively served in a regular classroom with or without special education services. Still another student may be best served in a residential or boarding school.

To be effective, such a continuum must be flexible. It must be recognized that students' needs may change over time or as a result of corrective work (such as glasses, prosthesis, and hearing aid) or educational remediation. Students should be reevaluated routinely to determine if they are able to move to another program. It is also possible that a student may make large skips from one type of program to another. Hopefully, most moves will be in the direction of less restrictive settings.

OVERVIEW OF NATURE OF SERVICES
Regular class placement with observation and consultation from special education personnel

In this type of program the student is enrolled in the regular class on a full-time basis. Supportive assistance from special education personnel may involve observation of a student in his regular classroom, followed by consultation with the teacher to relate specific suggestions or procedures that may be helpful. The services of the special educator may be needed for only a limited time, or some problems may require repeated observations and consultation.

The special educator must be a master diagnostician to be able to analyze the problem and to develop meaningful educational recommendations. The key to this type of service is open communication between the regular teacher and the special educator. The regular teacher must feel comfortable in asking for assistance from this outside person and in trying out the recommendations offered. The special educator, by nature of his or her experience and preparation, should be competent in analyzing problems and offering tentative solutions to the identified problem.

Regular class placement with observation and consultation from special educators, plus recommendation or provision of special materials, or both

The nature of services at this level may be essentially the same as the previous level except that specific materials may be recommended and tried. For example, the regular classroom teacher and special educator may agree on an approach that involves special resource materials. It is possible in this instance that the special educator may provide the needed materials on a trial basis.

Regular class placement plus itinerant services

In this type of service the student is enrolled in his neighborhood school, but he and his teachers receive direct assistance from special education personnel. The itinerant-teacher plan with which most educators are familiar is that followed by public school speech therapists. This plan has also been used quite extensively by teachers of the visually impaired and hearing impaired where there is only a limited number of students in a school district.

Though there are variations in the manner in which this plan is implemented, generally the itinerant or traveling teacher will work with the students on a regularly-scheduled basis (two or three times a week) or whenever necessary, depending on the child's needs at that particular time. The itinerant teacher will provide instruction in a designated area outside of the classroom or may meet with the student in his classroom. Many itinerant teachers use a van or station wagon, filling much of the cargo space with equipment and materials, and some occasionally use the van for instructional purposes. The itinerant teacher may also assume a helping or assisting teacher role by working with a small group of students who are in need of the same remedial work as the handicapped child.

Certain conditions lead to adoption of the itinerant-teacher plan, and in some of these situations it appears to be the best method of service delivery. In sparsely populated areas of the country, where schools tend to be quite small in total pupil enrollment, it is difficult to justify a full-time resource room program at one school, and because of long distances between schools, it is equally difficult to justify busing children into a specific school so as to enlarge the population of children requiring special services. As mentioned previously, this plan seems to be a viable service delivery system for many of the low incidence handicaps such as the visually impaired, the hearing impaired, and children with crippling conditions or health impairments. The itinerant-teacher plan does not seem to be as practical as the resource-room plan (see following paragraphs) for children with learning disabilities, behavior problems, or for children with limited intellectual ability because it does not provide intensive services on a daily basis.

Regular class placement plus assistance in the resource room

In this plan the student is enrolled in a regular classroom but receives supplemental or remedial instruction in a resource room. The resource-room plan differs from the itinerant-teacher plan in that the student is provided more specific assistance on a regularly scheduled basis (probably daily) from the resource teacher, and he has a specific room in which he receives this assistance.

There are many variations in the way resource rooms operate. In some instances the resource teacher may serve the student on a temporary basis while completing assessment techniques and planning instructional strate-

gies that may be carried out in the child's regular classroom. In this situation the child may go to the resource room for a brief period of time each day until assessment procedures have been completed and a program plan has been implemented. In most school systems, however, a placement or program planning committee will have reviewed a variety of information about any child referred for possible assistance in the resource room, and programming will be initiated only as this committee has indicated its feasibility (for the child) and its consistency with local school district policy. In all cases the parents should have been involved in such placement-planning committee deliberations and must have given express permission for resource-room intervention.

The resource-room teacher should have the time, the materials, and the specific training to find more effective ways to teach children with special needs. Her function becomes a dual one—to initiate alternative strategies and help the child find success in the resource room, and to provide suggestions to the regular classroom teacher that may increase the odds that the child will find success in that setting.

Often the resource room teacher will provide valuable "unofficial" assistance to various teachers, sometimes in terms of general instructional ideas, but often in relation to a specific child. This is one of the more highly effective functions of the resource-room teacher, but in some states it must be done unofficially due to state reimbursement guidelines and restrictions on the number of children who may be served.

In recent years some resource teachers have been providing their services in regular classrooms rather than "pulling out" the students. By assisting the child in the regular classroom, it is assumed that there will be greater transfer and maintenance than if programming is provided only in a special setting. Although this practice is presently being employed on a limited basis, it should be given serious consideration if the nature of the problem is not so significant that it calls for very intensive work in the resource room.

Cooperative plan

Under this plan the student is enrolled in a special class but attends a regular classroom for part of the school day. The basic difference between this plan and the resource-room plan is that the child's home room is the special class. In the resource room plan, the child's home room is in the regular classroom. The amount of time spent in the regular class would depend on his ability to profit from regular class instruction. This plan has been popular in past years; however, there is a definite movement toward resource rooms. Under this plan, both the regular teacher and the special education teacher have instructional responsibilities for these students. It is necessary to establish close lines of communication to ensure maximum carryover from one situation to the other.

Special class in regular school

Under this plan, the student receives his academic instruction from a special education teacher but may attend school-wide activities, such as assemblies, concerts, clubs, and athletic events, and probably would share luncheon facilities. In a few instances some children may attend classes such as industrial arts, physical education, and home economics.

In the past, students classified as educable mentally retarded or educable mentally handicapped have often been served on this basis. There has been a definite move away from such programming except for the more seriously involved or multiply handicapped. This type of service delivery has been seriously criticized since it has served to segregate these students.

Special day school

The special day school plan is generally designed for students who are very seriously involved or multiply handicapped and need comprehensive special education services for their entire school day. They return to their homes at the end of the day to be with their families. Often this type of facility will offer all of the needed services for these students,

such as physical and occupational therapy, counseling, special vocational workshops, and the needed adapted equipment. Although this type of service delivery has been criticized, there remains a need for such services for some students. A variation of this plan, which meets some of the criticism just mentioned, is a specially designed wing, attached to a regular elementary or secondary school building.

Hospital and homebound

Students with chronic conditions requiring long-term treatment in a hospital or in their homes receive special instruction from homebound-itinerant special education personnel. The nature of the educational program is dependent on the student's ability, level of achievement, prognosis of the condition, and likelihood of the student returning to school. Some students who are hospitalized or homebound because of a short-term illness may also be served on this basis. In this instance, the instruction would be closely related to the programming in his regular classroom and would be planned in conjunction with teachers of the classes to which he will return. In situations in which the child requires long-term care, a two-way communication system between the child's home and regular classroom may be set up. This system may employ a telephone or a videotelephone to reduce the isolation of being at home or in a hospital. This two-way telephone or videotelephone system provides an opportunity for full-time educational programming and maximum interaction with other students.

Residential or boarding school

Residential and boarding schools are the oldest type of educational delivery system. These schools were generally established for students who were visually impaired, hearing impaired, emotionally disturbed, or mentally retarded because local school districts did not offer the needed services. In these programs the students may attend only during the nine-month school year or on a year-around basis, depending on the extent of the handicap. Because of the trend toward main-streaming/integration of mildly to moderately handicapped students, these programs have begun to serve the more seriously involved and multiply handicapped. In addition to educational programming they can also provide the needed twenty-four-hour-a-day comprehensive services required by many of these students.

VARIABLES THAT MAY ASSIST IN DETERMINING PLACEMENT

As mentioned previously, there are a number of variables that would be considered when determining the best possible educational placement for a particular student. The following, although not inclusive, would be considered by professionals concerned with placement decisions for a particular student.

A. Chronological age
B. Type and degree of impairment or disability
C. Age at onset (birth or acquired)
D. Level of achievement
E. Measured intellectual ability
F. Social maturity
G. Presence of multiple handicapping conditions (thus the need for related, non-educational services)
H. Ambulation or mobility (particularly important when considering crippled and other health impaired and visually impaired)
I. Success of past and present placement
J. Speech and language
K. Wishes of student and student's parents
L. Availability of services

In the next few paragraphs we have provided three hypothetical cases illustrating the use of the preceding variables. We have also established tentative recommendations concerning placement, based on these variables. Actual placement decisions in real cases would likely have considerably more information than provided here, but we believe these cases may serve as illustrations of the use of significant variables in the placement decision.

MINICASE A

Jerry is a 9-year-old, totally, congenitally blind student who is achieving at the third grade level. His measured intellectual ability is within the normal range. He relates quite well with his peers and is quite mature socially. He has no multiple handicapping conditions, and orientation and mobility (travel) skills are adequate for his age. He has attended regular classrooms and received assistance from a resource teacher during his entire school career. He and his parents prefer that he be maintained in regular classrooms.

Where and how would this student be most effectively served at this time in his educational program assuming that his district has available all of the services depicted in Table 4?

It is our opinion that Jerry would be most effectively served in a regular classroom coupled with concrete assistance from a resource teacher in a resource room. However, consideration should also be given to itinerant services as he develops the necessary skills in braille reading and the use of other equipment and materials.

MINICASE B

John, 9 years old, is having difficulty both academically and behaviorally in his third grade classroom. His reading achievement is middle first grade, and his math scores indicate first grade level achievement. He acts out frequently during class time and gets into fights with his classmates. An individually administered test of intelligence places him in the bright-normal range of intellectual ability. He has had extensive medical examinations and there is no indication of any physical or mental difficulty.

His achievement and behavior during kindergarten and first grade were slightly below average but within the normal range. He began to fall farther and farther behind during the second grade.

The parents blame his difficulty on his past teachers and feel strongly that he should remain with his peers rather than be placed in a special class for children with behavior and learning disorders.

Where would John be most effectively served, assuming a full continuum of services?

It is our recommendation that John remain in his regular classroom and also be served in a resource room by a resource teacher for at least 1 to 1½ hours each day. Remedial efforts by the special education resource teacher should be directed at reading and math. In addition, the resource teacher must assist the classroom teacher to incorporate successful procedures in the regular classroom. The final goal is assistance to the regular classroom teacher so that she may work with John in her classroom as much as possible.

MINICASE C

Karen is a 12-year-old, severely mentally retarded child. Her achievement level is at approximately the first grade level. Her IQ has been variously indicated to be 41, 44, and 47. Although she is socially immature, she is very outgoing and friendly and enjoys being with almost anyone. In addition to her retarded mental development, she has cerebral palsy, a serious speech disorder, and uses a wheelchair to get around. She attended a special school for retarded, cerebral palsied students for several years. Her parents would like her to attend a school closer to their home.

Where would this student be most effectively served, assuming that a full continuum of services was available?

The most effective program for Karen at this time would be in a special class for severely retarded children. Ideally, this classroom would be in a regular building so that she would have some interaction with non-disabled students.

EMPHASIS OF INDIVIDUALIZATION

There has been increased emphasis on individualizing instruction for all children, regardless of whether they are handicapped, during the past several years. The use of individual behavioral objectives, considerable concern over the use of intelligence tests, and the increasing popularity of diagnostic-prescriptive teaching are a few examples of today's emphasis on the individual child. Open classrooms are gaining popularity throughout the United States, and it is interesting to note that many instructional practices and strategies being promoted today are

similar to those used in better special education programs. These include (1) learning centers, (2) programming and self-instructional materials, (3) encouragement that each child move at his own learning rate, and (4) continuous evaluation as part of a diagnostic prescriptive teaching model. It has finally been recognized that there are considerable differences between children who are placed in a common room under the assumption that the group is, in fact, homogeneous.

These changes in educational procedures and the emphasis on individualized instruction will obviously facilitate the integration of children who learn at disparate rates. Several years ago, when educational programs offered a "lockstep" approach, handicapped students would have failed, but today it is possible that many of these children can achieve the needed success in regular classrooms.

ADVANTAGES TO NONHANDICAPPED STUDENTS

Often regular classroom teachers are concerned that if a handicapped child is enrolled in their classroom this will detract from the education of the nonhandicapped students. On the contrary, there are indications that the nonhandicapped children learn as much if not more when a handicapped child is in their classroom. An obvious advantage of educating the handicapped children in regular classrooms is that children need to be exposed to differences in individuals—not for purposes of "feeling sorry for" another individual but to gain respect for and appreciate the differences in individuals. Children must be exposed to racial and ethnic, intellectual, and psychological differences if they are to reach their personal potential.

It is our opinion that perhaps today's adults were "disadvantaged" to some extent because when they were in school they did not have the opportunity to know classmates who were handicapped or different. This disadvantagement may be observed in many ways. For example, why are there so many prevalent misconceptions about disabled individuals expressed by adults today? Could it be that they were not exposed to differences in individuals? Is it possible that they never sat next to a braille-reading classmate or a classmate in a wheelchair? Are the often less-than-desirable attitudes reflected by today's society an indication of our lack of experience with different persons? We owe nonhandicapped students the opportunity to work and play with individuals who are different if we are to provide them with the best possible education—an education that must include more than purely academic skills.

ADVANTAGES TO TEACHERS

Teachers must have challenges to grow personally and professionally. A handicapped child does present that challenge. We have had considerable experience with regular classroom teachers who expressed concern when they were informed that they would have a handicapped student in their classroom. Certainly this situation may present a serious threat to a teacher who has not had previous experience or preparation in how to work with such students. However, it has been very encouraging to observe these same teachers grow both personally and professionally and at the end of the year indicate that it was one of the most exciting and challenging experiences of their teaching career. Often such teachers ask if they may have another handicapped student the following year. What initially may be seen as a serious threat often turns into a very positive growth experience. Teachers benefit from such growth experiences, and they need to work with students who are different. Very often the methods and instructional techniques used with a handicapped student may be used with many other students. The challenge of working with students with different ability, intellectual or physical, or both, may keep teachers from "teaching at" students. With only minimal help they may learn to serve as a facilitator who will provide each student with the opportunity to reach his fullest potential.

ADVANTAGES TO HANDICAPPED STUDENTS

Although we have briefly reviewed the relative advantages to nonhandicapped students and regular classroom teachers, our discussion would not be complete if we did not consider the obvious advantages to the handicapped student. Although questions still exist about the most effective way to educate handicapped students, it seems obvious that to physically isolate handicapped students for educational purposes is to do a serious disservice to these students except as such isolation is absolutely necessary. Does it seem reasonable to educate these students in a physically isolated setting during their school career and upon completion of their education ask them to compete in a nonhandicapped society? Would we ask an individual learning to drive an automobile to complete his driver training without actually driving on the streets with other automobiles? Perhaps this is not an appropriate analogy, but in some respects it is very similar to our past educational practices with handicapped students. If our purpose is to provide handicapped students with the opportunity to reach their maximum potential and to become contributing members of society, we must provide them with an *equal* educational opportunity—an opportunity to be educated with their nonhandicapped peers whenever possible.

SUMMARY

There is little question that the trend to educate handicapped children in regular classrooms whenever possible is clearly established. Federal and state government agencies have conducted need studies in an attempt to determine the number of handicapped students in need of services and have established legislative declarations that indicate their intent. There is, however, a lack of agreement among professional educators as to the best way to implement this trend. Some have argued that nearly all handicapped students should be placed in regular classrooms and that general educators have primary responsibility for their programs, whereas others believe that handicapped children are most effectively served in special programs. It is our opinion that it is not an "either-or" situation but that a full range or continuum of services must be offered and that *each child* must be considered individually. We further believe that the responsibility should be shared by both general and special education personnel. When regular classroom teachers and special education personnel share their unique skills, competencies, insights, and attitudes, it is not only an advantage to all students but a very positive growth experience for them—an experience that teachers must have if they are to continue to grow professionally and personally.

Although it is too early to measure the effects of mainstreaming/integration, it is exciting to consider the effects of this trend on the handicapped, their nonhandicapped peers, their teachers, and on society.

References and suggested readings

Adamson, G., and Van Etten, G. "Zero Reject Model Revisited: A Workable Alternative." *Exceptional Children*, 1972, *38*, 735-738.

Alexander, M. "Let Me Learn With the Other Kids." *Learning*, March 1973, *1*, 18-21.

Ashcroft, S. C. "The Handicapped in the Regular Classroom." *N. E. A. Journal*, November 1967, *46*, 33-34.

Beery, K. *Models for Mainstreaming.* San Rafael, Calif. Dimensions Publishing Co., 1972.

Birch, J. W. *Mainstreaming: Educable Mentally Retarded Children in Regular Classes.* Leadership Training Institute/Special Education, University of Minnesota, 1974.

Brenton, M. "Mainstreaming the Handicapped." *Today's Education*, March-April 1974, 20-25.

Chaffin, J. D. "Will the Real 'Mainstreaming' Program Please Stand Up! (or . . . Should Dunn Have Done It?)." *Focus on Exceptional Children*, October 1974, *6*, 1-18.

Christopherson, J. "The Special Child in the 'Regular' Preschool: Some Administrative Notes." *Childhood Education*, December, 1972, 138-140.

Christoplos, F., and Renz, P. A. "A Critical Examination of Special Education Programs." *Journal of Special Education*, 1969, *3*, 374-379.

Cormany, R. B. "Returning Special Education Students to Regular Classes." *Personnel and Guidance Journal*, April, 1970, *48*, 641-646.

Deno, E. N. (Ed.). *Instructional Alternatives for Exceptional Children.* Council for Exceptional Children.

Deno, E. N. "Special Education as Developmental Capital." *Exceptional Children*, 1970, *37*, 229-237.

Dunn, L. M. "Special Education for the Mildly Retarded—Is Much of It Justified?" *Exceptional Children*, 1968, *35*, 5-22.

Dunn, L. M. *Exceptional Children in the Schools: Special Education in Transition.* New York: Holt, Rinehart and Winston, Inc., 1973.

Gallagher, J. J. "The Special Education Contract for Mildly Handicapped Children." *Exceptional Children*, 1972, *38*, 527-535.

Grosenick, J. K. "Integration of Exceptional Children Into Regular Classes: Research and Procedure." *Focus on Exceptional Children*, October 1971, *5*, 1-8.

"Handicapped and Normal Children are More Alike than Different." *N. E. A. Journal*, November 1961, *50*, 48-50.

Iano, R. P. "Shall We Disband Special Classes?" *Journal of Special Education*, 1972, *6*, 167-177.

Klein, J. W. "Mainstreaming the Preschooler." *Journal of the National Association for the Education of Young Children*, 1975, *30*, 317-326.

Kolstoe, O. P. "Programs for the Mildly Retarded: A Reply to the Critics." *Exceptional Children*, 1972, *39*, 51-56.

Kreinberg, N., and Chou, S. (Eds.). *Configurations of Change: The Integration of Mildly Handicapped Children into the Regular Classroom.* Far West Laboratory for Educational Research and Development, 1973.

Lilly, S. "Special Education: A Teapot in a Tempest." *Exceptional Children*, 1970, *37*, 43-49.

Lilly, S.: "A Training Based Model for Special Education." *Exceptional Children*, 1971, *37*, 745-749.

Martin, D. L. "Are Our Public Schools Really Ignoring the Very Children Who Need the Schools Most?" *The American School Board Journal*, 1975, *162*, 52-54.

Martin, E. W. "Some Thoughts on Mainstreaming." *Exceptional Children*, November 1974, *41*, 150-153.

Molloy, L. "The Handicapped Child In The Everyday Classroom." *Phi Delta Kappan*, January 1975, 337-340.

Reger, R. "What is a Resource Room Program?" *Journal of Learning Disabilities*, December 1973, *6*, 15-21.

Russo, J. R. "Mainstreaming Handicapped Students: Are Your Facilities Suitable?" *American*

School and University, October 1974, *47,* 25-32.

Van Etten, G., and Adamson, G. "The Fail-Save Program: A Special Education Continuum." In *Instructional Alternatives for Exceptional Children.* Council for Exceptional Children, 1973, 156-165.

Weininger, O. "Integrate or Isolate: A Perspective on the Whole Child." *Education,* November-December 1973, *94,* 139-146.

Weintraub, F. J. "Recent Influences of Law Regarding the Identification and Educational Placement of Children." *Focus on Exceptional Children,* 1972, *4*(2), 1-11.

Weintraub, F. J., and Abeson, A. "New Education Policies for the Handicapped." *The Education Digest,* September 1974, 13-16.

Wright, R. G. "Special—But Not Separate." *Education,* May 1967, *87,* 554-557.

CHAPTER 3
Strategies and alternatives
for educating the hearing impaired

Ronald Stewart

Every classroom teacher should have a basic understanding of the nature of hearing impairment and its relationship to learning. Classroom teachers may not realize that some of the problems students are having may be caused by hearing impairments. In other instances in which a hearing impairment has been identified, there are a number of methods and techniques the regular classroom teacher can use that may be beneficial to the hearing impaired child.

This chapter will briefly overview (1) the nature of a hearing impairment, (2) methods of identifying a child with a hearing impairment, (3) referral procedures, (4) appropriate classroom modifications and adaptations for the hearing impaired child in the regular classroom, and (5) the specific role and responsibility of special education resource/itinerant personnel.

From the time a child is born he learns through listening. An infant learns to discriminate between loud and soft, high and low, and disturbing and pleasant sounds. He also learns to determine the direction, distance, and meaning of sounds. He analyzes the human voice and differentiates his babbling and crying from the sounds of others. Sometime between the ages of 12 and 24 months, as a result of his previous language experiences, he begins to learn to speak and develop his own language. It is obvious that if the child has a hearing impairment his speech and language development will be delayed. This underdeveloped speech and language is the greatest limitation imposed by a hearing impairment. The child's delayed speech and language will have an influence on his ability to develop communication skills such as reading, writing, listening, and speaking. As a result, these skills will develop at a slower rate than those of the normally hearing child (see pp. 94-96).

At both elementary and secondary levels the hearing impaired child will have the most difficulty in the language arts areas, such as reading, English, spelling, and writing, because of their relationship to speech and language development. The extent of difficulty will depend on the child's

language level or command of the language, degree of hearing loss, and age at onset.

The child is not necessarily handicapped in acquiring concepts; however, he may have difficulty learning the label or language used to describe the concept. For example, the concept of buoyancy can be understood by the child; however, he may have difficulty in writing, saying, or spelling the word *buoyancy*. He may have much less difficulty with science, math, or other nonlanguage arts programs. Math, with the exception of story problems, is conceptual in nature. Science may also be thought of as conceptual rather than primarily related to the language arts. In contrast, the reading process involves associating meaning with sounds and written symbols. A hearing impairment seriously limits the association between sounds and written symbols; therefore, reading may be an area of considerable difficulty for these children, particularly for the young child who is in the process of acquiring reading skills. He *can* learn to read; however, a very well planned program must be offered—a program that reflects close cooperation between the regular teacher and the special education resource/itinerant teacher. Although language development is very important to success in school, the hearing impaired child is able to learn and profit from instruction in the regular classroom.

TYPES OF HEARING LOSS

There are two major types of hearing impairment, and different degrees of hearing loss are associated with each of these two types. One type of hearing impairment affects the loudness or intensity with which a person hears speech. The other type affects the frequency, intelligibility, or clarity of the sounds the person hears.

An example that roughly illustrates the two types of hearing loss and with which most are familiar is the radio. One dial on the radio controls the volume or loudness of the sounds. By turning the volume down, we can simulate what it is like to have a hearing loss affecting the loudness with which we hear sounds. If we can hear the sounds, we can understand them—they are not distorted.

The tuning dial controlling the frequency of the sounds may be used to illustrate the second type of hearing loss. If the radio is not tuned in correctly, the sounds are not clear and are difficult to understand (often words are not complete). A sentence such as "He sat at his desk at recess" may sound like "e a a iz de."

HOW HEARING IS MEASURED

Hearing acuity is measured by an instrument known as a *pure tone audiometer.* An audiometer produces sounds at varying intensities (loudness) and varying frequencies (pitch). An *audiologist,* when administering an audiometric examination, systematically presents a series of carefully calibrated tones that vary in loudness and pitch. The results are charted on a graph called an *audiogram,* which provides an indication of the person's ability to hear each tone at each of the presented frequencies. The *audiometric evaluation* assists in determining the extent and type of hearing loss so that the proper remedial or medical steps may be taken to overcome the hearing problem.

The unit of measurement used to express the intensity of sound is the *decibel* (dB), and the frequency is expressed in *hertz* (Hz). If an individual has a hearing loss, it is indicated in dB; the more significant the

loss, the larger the number value. For example, a 60 dB loss is a greater loss than a 25 dB loss. In addition to information concerning the extent of the loss in decibels, it may be helpful to have information concerning the frequency at which the loss occurs. The preceding audiogram indicates a severe hearing loss of an 11-year-old student.

To better understand the nature of hearing loss, we have presented the following common environmental sounds expressed in intensity (decibels):

Decibels	Sounds
140	Threshold of pain
120	Threshold of feeling
100	Riveting machine at thirty feet
80	Loud radio or phonograph music in a home
60	Average restaurant sounds or normal conversation
40	Outdoor minimum in a city
20	Very quiet conversation
0	Threshold of hearing

DEGREES OF HEARING IMPAIRMENT

Systems that attempt to classify hearing acuity in relation to actual hearing efficiency or functional ability generally do not account for a number of outside factors such as motivation, intelligence, social maturity, and family background. These variables may have a definite influence on the individual's functional ability. No two individuals with the same measured hearing loss will function in an identical manner.

Although it is difficult to classify degrees of hearing impairment on the basis of severity, it is necessary to have a classification system that provides some insight into the degree of loss and the resulting implications. The following system is quite commonly used by educators:

Mild	27 to 40 dB
Moderate	41 to 55 dB
Moderately severe	56 to 70 dB
Severe	71 to 90 dB
Profound	91 dB+

Mild: 27 to 40 dB

A person who has a hearing loss between 27 dB and 40 dB has a mild hearing loss and

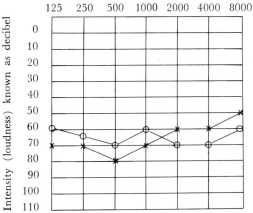

Audiogram

Frequency (pitch) known as hertz

is likely to have difficulty with faint or distant speech. Children with mild losses may need favorable seating; may benefit from speechreading instruction, vocabulary, or language instruction, or a combination of these; and may need speech therapy.

Moderate: 41 to 55 dB

The moderately hearing impaired individual has a hearing loss in the 41 to 55 dB range. He can understand conversational speech at a distance of three to five feet. This child will probably need a hearing aid, auditory training, speechreading, favorable seating, speech conversation, and speech therapy. The extent of services provided by the resource/itinerant specialist may vary considerably, depending on the child's actual achievement in the regular classroom.

Moderately severe: 56 to 70 dB

A hearing loss in the 56 to 70 dB range is usually classified as moderately severe. For the child with a moderately severe loss, conversation must be loud to be understood. His speech will probably be defective, and he may have a limited vocabulary. This child will have difficulty in group and classroom discussion, can use all of the services usually provided children with mild and moderate losses, and in addition, will require specific assistance from the resource/itinerant teacher in the language arts areas.

Severe: 71 to 90 dB

A person who has a hearing loss between 71 and 90 dB has a severe loss and may hear a loud voice at about one foot. He may be able to distinguish some environmental sounds and will have difficulty with vowel sounds but not necessarily consonants. He will need all of the services required by hearing impaired students with less severe losses and many of the techniques used with deaf children.

Profound: 91 dB+

Individuals with a hearing loss of more than 91 dB have a profound impairment. Although this individual may be able to hear some loud sounds, he probably will not rely on hearing as the primary learning channel. This child will likely need all of the previously mentioned services and possibly more intensive services from the resource/itinerant teacher of the hearing impaired. The profoundly hearing impaired child will require special assistance with emphasis on speech, auditory training, and language; however, he may be able to attend regular classes on a part-time basis or attend classes that do not require language skills.

As mentioned previously, a great deal of caution must be exercised in using a classification system, because children with nearly identical losses may function differently. In addition to using caution with classification systems, educators must also exercise care in predetermining the extent of special education services needed in relation to the degree of loss. Instead the characteristics of need may be defective speech, with substitutions, omissions, or distortions; reading problems; immature language patterns; a lower level of abstraction; and perhaps lower interpersonal relationships (Northcott, 1972). Some children with severe losses may be readily integrated into regular classrooms, whereas a child with a less severe, or moderate, loss may need extensive special education services for the majority of his school day.

A wide continuum of services must be provided to meet the needs of the hearing impaired, ranging from self-contained classes to full-time regular classes (see Table 4, pp. 22-23).

IDENTIFICATION OF CHILDREN WITH HEARING LOSS

Often the classroom teacher is not aware that a particular child's learning problems or behavior problems might be due to a hearing loss. The teacher could misjudge the child as mentally retarded, emotionally disturbed, or as having some type of specific learning disability. In other instances the teacher *may* feel the child's problems are due to some failure in her methods of teaching. Until the teacher recognizes that the child's problem may be due to a hearing loss, she could waste a great deal of time on fruitless remedial measures. Therefore, it is very important for the regular classroom teacher to be aware of some common behaviors that are indicators of a hearing loss. The following are the most commonly found behaviors and medical symptoms that *may* indicate a hearing loss.

Lack of attention

One such behavior is an apparent lack of attention. If the child does not pay attention, it is possible that he cannot hear what is being said. Another possibility may be that the child hears sounds but that they are so distorted it is difficult for him to understand. Consequently, he tunes them out or does not make the effort to attend to them.

Turning or cocking of head

Another behavior that may indicate the child has a hearing loss is an unusual amount of cocking the head to one side. The child may need to turn one ear toward the speaker to hear more adequately. In addition, the child with a hearing loss may make frequent requests for repetitions.

Difficulty in following directions

Another behavior that may indicate hearing impairment is when the child is having an unusual amount of difficulty in following oral directions. The child who has little difficulty with written directions and considerable difficulty with oral directions may have a hearing loss. Also, if a child often loses his place in oral reading assignments, it could be because he has difficulty hearing what the others are reading.

Acting out, stubborn, shy, or withdrawn

Have you ever tried to listen to a speaker who was talking so softly you had difficulty hearing him? You could see his lips move but were unable to hear what was being said. Remembering that frustrating experience may help the teacher understand why a child with a hearing loss may be stubborn, disobedient, shy, or withdrawn. If the child is unable to hear, personality and behavior problems may arise. He may be compensating for his inability to hear by acting out in the classroom. Other hearing impaired children may compensate by withdrawing, acting stubborn, or being shy.

Reluctance to participate in oral activities

A less extreme behavior sometimes characteristic of the hearing impaired child may be a reluctance to participate in oral activities. Another possible identifying characteristic of the child with a hearing loss is a lack of a sense of humor. The child who often does not laugh at a joke may not be hearing the joke.

Dependent on classmates for instructions

Another indication of which the teacher should be aware is the child who watches his classmates to see what they are doing before he starts working. He may not have fully heard or understood the directions given and will look for a cue from his classmates or teacher.

Small-group achievement best

If the child seems to do his best work in small groups or in a relatively quiet working area, this may be an indication of a hearing loss. More success with tasks assigned by the teacher at a relatively close distance or in an uncluttered auditory area (as compared with tasks assigned at a distance or in a noisy situation) may also be an indication.

Disparity between expected and actual achievement

Another possible indication of a hearing loss is a disparity between expected and actual achievement. Obviously, there may be many reasons for a child not achieving in a manner consistent with his ability, but the teacher should be aware that one of the reasons may be a hearing loss.

Medical indications

So far we have been concerned only with *behavior* that may indicate a child has a hearing loss. There are also medical indications of a hearing loss that should not be ignored by the teacher. These include frequent earaches, fluid running from the ears, frequent colds or sore throats, and recurring tonsilitis. These physical characteristics must be brought to the attention of the school nurse and the parents. The parents should be urged to contact their physician.

A LOSS IS SUSPECTED— WHAT IS NEXT?

The teacher who suspects a child has a hearing loss should refer the child to the school nurse, speech therapist, or audiologist. The teacher should be certain to describe the specific behavior (or behaviors) or medical indications that led her to believe there may be a hearing loss. Any of these professionals will be able to do preliminary screening. If there is an indication from the preliminary screening that a child has a hearing impairment, the child should next be referred to a physician (otologist) who specializes in diseases of the ear.

If the direct services of a school nurse, speech therapist, or audiologist are not available, refer the child to the school counselor, principal, or directly to the child's parents. The teacher may have to assume a leadership position in the referral process; she may have to check to be certain that subsequent referrals have been made. Often a referral will be made, but for any of a variety of reasons, no further action is taken. The teacher has an important role to ensure that services have been provided.

In a hypothetical case, let us assume the teacher observed some behavior that made her suspect a child had a hearing loss. The teacher referred the child to the nurse, speech therapist, or audiologist, who found that a hearing loss was present. The child was then referred through the parents to an expert for a more extensive examination. The otologist may find an accumulation of wax or some other obstruction in the ears, infected tonsils or adenoids, or some other abnormality that may be medically corrected. In this instance the hearing can be restored, and the child returned to school without any educational modifications or adaptations. However,

many referrals do not result in medical correction, and as a result, a hearing aid may be recommended. Now what happens to the child? Should he be placed in a special class, or can he continue in his regular class? Every effort should be made to keep the child in the regular classroom. The advantages of regular classroom placement far outweigh the disadvantages. Of course, recommendations regarding placement must be very carefully considered during individual staffing of the child. The following are some advantages offered by regular classroom placement:

1. An opportunity to continue relationships with hearing children, which will reinforce the feeling that he is more like other children than not like them. He will gain, or maintain, a feeling of belonging.
2. An exposure to a greater variety of language styles.
3. The need to keep his speech and language patterns at a more intelligible level. Often when hearing impaired children are grouped together in the same class, they do not develop or maintain a high level of speech and language.
4. The need to establish a wider variety of communication techniques. The hearing impaired child may have to modify his communication skills if he is not understood by his classmates. This may necessitate a reexamination and modification of his communication skills.
5. An opportunity for the child to compete academically with hearing children.

Another advantage of regular classroom placement, although not directly related to the hearing impaired, is that the hearing children have an opportunity to become acquainted with someone who is different. This must be seen very positively, particularly today when many children do not have the opportunity to mix with children of different ethnic backgrounds, different races, or children who are disabled. It is our opinion that children, all children, are tremendously advantaged when they have the opportunity to meet and associate with individuals who are different from themselves.

SUGGESTIONS FOR THE REGULAR CLASSROOM TEACHER

If the hearing impaired child is to remain in the regular classroom, there are certain classroom modifications and adaptations the teacher can use that may be beneficial to the hearing impaired child.

Obtain complete information about the child

Before taking a hearing impaired child into the class, be certain that there is sufficient information concerning (1) the nature of the loss, (2) the amount of residual hearing, and (3) the ways in which the child communicates. Arrange for a few brief private sessions with the child so a comfortable relationship and communication process can be established. Because the speech of a hearing impaired child may be defective, these brief sessions may be used to familiarize the teacher to the child's unique speech patterns. The teacher may also find it most helpful to discuss the child's speech needs with his speech therapist or special education resource person. Most of this information concerning the child can be obtained from the special education resource personnel in the school or school district.

Use a "listening helper" or "buddy"

The teacher may wish to use a listening helper or buddy. This peer may sit next to the hearing impaired child to ensure his turning to the correct page, taking notes, or for other appropriate assistance in areas such as adjusting to a new class or school or participating in activities such as physical education. At the upper elementary and secondary levels the listening helper or buddy may assist in note taking by simply making a carbon copy of his notes.

The listening helper or buddy may be rotated weekly or monthly, or a few classmates may volunteer for an extended period of time. Some caution must be exercised in this area so that the helper or buddy provides assistance only when needed; otherwise, the very purpose of the integrated educational experience may be defeated. If the helper provides assistance when it is not necessary, the hearing impaired child may become overly dependent on his classmates—a dependency that must be carefully avoided.

Care of hearing aid

It is important for the teacher to have a basic understanding of the use and limitations of the child's hearing aid. A hearing aid is not a complicated piece of equipment. The aid helps compensate for the hearing loss by amplifying sound. It cannot replace the natural ability of the ear. Do not expect the child who wears an aid to hear "normally."

There are several things than can be checked by the regular classroom teacher if the child does not seem to be hearing well because of a malfunction in the hearing aid. Although it is not the primary responsibility of the regular classroom teacher to troubleshoot hearing aid problems, it may be helpful to be aware of a few minor factors that may be causing the malfunctions so that the resource teacher or the parents may be alerted. Check the following:

1. Check to make sure the battery is not dead.
2. Determine if the battery is in properly, with the positive and negative terminals in the proper position.
3. Check the cord to see if it is worn or broken or if the receiver is cracked.
4. Check to be sure the plug-in points are not loose. Check both the hearing aid and the receiver.
5. Check the ear mold to make sure it is not obstructed by wax and that it is inserted properly. An improperly fitted ear mold can cause irritation and feedback (squeaky sounds).
6. Keep a fresh battery at school (changed at least monthly, even though it may not have been used) so the child does not have to go without his hearing aid on the day the battery goes dead. Often the resource/itinerant teacher will have an extra supply of batteries and will assist in determining where other problems might exist.

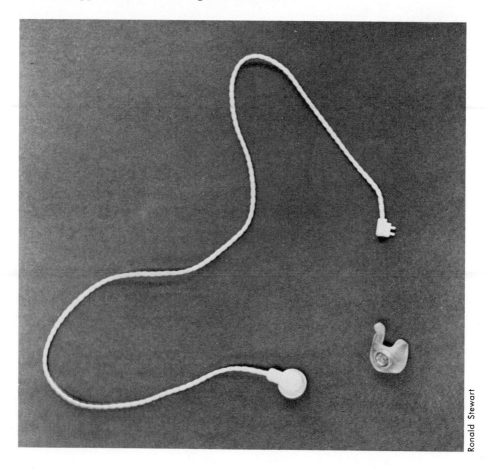

Ronald Stewart

There are some additional considerations that the regular teacher must be aware of with respect to proper care and maintenance of hearing aids.

1. Do not get the hearing aid wet.
2. Serious damage may result from leaving it in extremely hot or cold places.
3. Always turn the aid off before removing it from the ear. (Removing the aid without turning the aid off will cause a squeal.)
4. Do not allow the child to wear the hearing aid microphone too close to the receiver; if this is done, the aid will make unusual noises. If the child has a unilateral loss (one ear), the hearing aid should be worn on the opposite side of the receiver.
5. Do not take the aid apart and attempt to repair it. This should be done by a hearing aid dealer.

Facilitate speechreading

Although most hearing impaired children have some remaining or residual hearing, special efforts must be made to facilitate speechreading because the child may not hear all of the sounds in his environment. The child must learn to closely observe lips, facial gestures, body gestures, and other environmental clues to fully understand what his teacher and classmates are saying. The following factors should be considered by the regular teacher:

1. Allow the child to sit where he can make the most of what he hears and sees; sometimes a younger child will need guidance in this area. Remember, the hearing impaired child listens with his eyes as well as his ears. The child should be within five to ten feet of the speaker. Do not, however, have him sit so close that he con-

stantly has to look up. To aid the child in becoming a more proficient speech-reader, change the child's seating arrangement from time to time to give him practice in watching different speakers in the classroom from different positions. Seating arrangements must be flexible to facilitate speechreading and communication. However, be sure the child is able to observe and participate in class activities.

2. Seating should be arranged so that the child does not have to look into a light source—do not stand in front of windows—this makes speechreading very difficult. Do not stand in a dark area or an area where there may be shadows. Generally, speechreading is easier when the light source is behind the child.

3. Do not exaggerate gestures. Exaggerated gestures may cause considerable confusion. Use gestures, but keep hands and any objects away from the face whenever possible. Beards and mustaches sometimes distract from the lips or make them difficult to see.

4. Provide a good pattern of speech for the child; distinct articulation is more helpful to the hearing impaired child than speaking louder. Speech patterns should not be exaggerated.

5. Try to face the group when speaking, and when members of the class are speaking, encourage them to face the hearing impaired child. Many of us frequently turn our back to the class and talk when writing on the board. Overhead projections and transparencies work extremely well for all children. In general, visual aids are effective with the hearing impaired child.

6. Ask questions of the child occasionally to make certain he is following the discussion. When presenting a new word or asking a question, repeat it if it is not understood the first time, speaking directly at the child. If he seems to miss the term or request, rephrase what was originally said and ask him a question; for example: "This is a stapler." "How could you use a stapler?" "Who would use a stapler often?"

7. Certain words are not easily understood through speechreading; therefore, encourage the child to ask questions or have statements repeated if he doesn't understand.

8. When isolated words are presented, such as in spelling, the words should be used in context. Spelling tests may also be given by providing the contextual words of the sentence on a sheet of paper and replacing the spelling word with a blank space. In this way the child will have the necessary contextual clues. Remember, many words appear alike on the lips and sound alike, for example, beet and bead. Other examples are meal and peal, safe and save, and pie and buy.

9. When presenting new vocabulary words, present the multiple meanings for these words; some words have more than five meanings. This can be very difficult for the hearing impaired child because his vocabulary may not be sufficient to understand the multiple meanings.

Facilitate desirable speech habits

As mentioned previously, speech training is an essential component of educational programming for the hearing impaired child. The child's ability to monitor his expressive language may be seriously limited by his hearing impairment, limiting his expressive language abilities.

Often the speech therapist working with the child will have clearly established goals and objectives related to the child's speech patterns and general articulation. The regular classroom teacher plays an important role in facilitating good speech habits. Reinforcement of therapy goals and objectives in the child's classroom is essential if the needed carry-over and maintenance in everyday situations are to be expected. The following suggestions may facilitate this carry-over and maintenance:

1. Encourage the child to use the dictionary to aid in pronunciation when difficult words are encountered. (This would naturally depend on the age and reading level of the child.)

2. Encourage the child to participate in oral discussions, and expect him to use complete sentences when speaking. Be careful, however, not to "emotionally load" the situation. If proper speech is insisted on and the child is demeaned in front of the entire class for incorrect usage or incomplete sentences, the child may be discouraged from participating in any oral discussion. Be careful not to "nag" the child. Often, correction of a mispronounced word may be accomplished by a brief conference at the end of the period or day. Some teachers have had success with keeping a list of words, with the correct pronunciation, and giving them to the child without any verbal mention. He should also be encouraged to participate in conversation, reading, storytelling, and creative dramatics.

3. The teacher should not be afraid to talk with the child about his hearing loss. Hearing impaired children need to be told when they are speaking too loudly or too softly. The teacher can do a great deal to keep the child from developing dull or expressionless speech habits by speaking with the child honestly and openly.

4. Praise and encourage the child when he has correctly pronounced a previously difficult word. The child will need a great deal of encouragement and success if he is to accomplish this very difficult task.

5. Provide a relaxed language environment. The more relaxed and casual the speech and language styles of the teachers and students, the better the opportunity for language acquisition.

Discuss new materials or assignments ahead of class time

Whenever possible, the teacher should briefly discuss topics ahead of time that are to be presented later in class. This may also be accomplished by providing the child with an outline of the material to be discussed. Sometimes, prereading of assignments is very helpful. Another suggestion worthy of consideration is to provide a list of key vocabulary words on the board or a piece of paper that deals with the new material. When giving an assignment, write it on the board rather than only giving it orally. The child's "listening helper" may check with him to see that he has the correct assignment.

Be aware of student fatigue

The teacher should be aware that the hearing impaired child may fatigue more readily than other children. This may be noticeable particularly in young children near the end of the day, but it will be a factor for all hearing impaired children. Do not interpret the fatigue as boredom, disinterest, or lack of motivation. The fatigue is due in part to the continuous strain from speech-reading, using residual hearing, and the constant watching required to keep up with the various speakers while participating in the activities of the classroom. It may be helpful to vary the daily schedule so that the child is not required to attend to academic subject areas for an extended period of time. However, he should be expected to complete all assignments.

Facilitate participation

The hearing impaired child may have a tendency to be very shy and withdrawn if he is not fully aware of what is going on in the class. Provide the opportunity for him to interact; however, the child should not be pushed into peer group relationships.

Discuss nature of hearing impairment

Hearing children often do not understand the nature of a hearing impairment or the limitations imposed by a hearing loss. Mini-in-service sessions may be held to explain the exact nature of a hearing loss through simulation activities or discussions. The resource/itinerant teacher or speech therapist are valuable persons to consider when such activities are being planned. They may bring to the class a variety of hearing aids and allow the children to listen through them to gain a better understanding of how they work.

The child should be encouraged to participate in these mini-in-service sessions, but it is generally a good idea to consult with the hearing impaired child prior to the actual demonstration to be certain he does not feel that he is being exploited. The time spent in such activities often can do a great deal to clear up many misconceptions and possible misunderstandings concerning the child's abilities and limitations.

Consider district audiovisual personnel and equipment

A valuable asset for all teachers is the school district's audiovisual department. The audiovisual department or personnel can be of particular value to the teacher who has a child with a hearing impairment in her class. Overhead projectors can greatly enhance the achievement of the hearing impaired child. As the teacher lectures she may put important notes or key vocabulary words or phrases on the overhead projector. An overhead projector allows the teacher to maintain eye contact with the children while writing on the projector. Filmstrips and captioned films may also facilitate the learning process. Many educational films have been captioned (words placed at bottom of picture—subtitles) so they may be used by the hearing impaired child in the regular classroom (see Appendix A). The resource or itinerant teacher of the hearing impaired may provide the teacher with a detailed listing of available materials.

The use of these modified and adapted instructional materials will not interfere with the education of the normally hearing children; in fact, they will facilitate their achievement.

Grading

The teacher need not use special grading techniques or grade the hearing impaired child differently than the other class members. The resource/itinerant teacher may want to add a special note to the report card to indicate his progress on resource-room activities, such as speechreading and auditory training.

These suggestions to regular classroom teachers are certainly not all-inclusive, but

they do represent the areas of greatest concern. It would be helpful to periodically review these suggestions and discuss these and others with the resource/itinerant teacher. It is the classroom teachers' use of ingenuity and creativity that is instrumental in modifying and adapting curriculum, materials, and teaching strategies to make this a successful experience for everyone.

Above all other suggestions or techniques, the overriding factor is the attitude of the teacher. The teacher is the single most important variable. She must be understanding, but not sympathetic. She should treat the hearing impaired child as near as possible like any other child in the classroom, being fair and truthful, not lenient, in reporting his progress. *The handicapped child should be treated as a child who is able, who is an individual, and who, incidentally, has impaired hearing.*

ROLE OF RESOURCE/ITINERANT TEACHER

The roles and responsibilities of special education resource/itinerant personnel will vary extensively, depending on the age or grade level of the hearing impaired children served, number of children, geographic area (number of teachers or buildings served by itinerant teacher), and the local school district policy concerning specific responsibilities. In some school districts the resource teacher's responsibilities relate only to a limited number of children in one building and their role is well established, whereas in other districts the resource personnel may serve a number of buildings and their role may be quite varied.

In the following paragraphs we will briefly review a few of the responsibilities of special education resource/itinerant personnel.

Cooperation is the key

The key to a successful educational program for the hearing impaired is a cooperative working arrangement between the regular teachers and the resource teacher. They must establish a working relationship that will enhance the education of the hearing impaired child. The ability of the resource teacher to relate to other staff members in a meaningful way is paramount. The regular teacher must feel free to ask for assistance, whenever needed, without reservation. The resource teacher should be allowed to observe in the regular class at any time, not in a judgmental manner but as a helper. If the working relationship between the regular classroom teachers and the resource teacher is one of mutual respect and understanding, the child's education will be greatly enhanced. They should jointly plan educational strategies, modify and adapt materials, and have an ongoing dialogue centering around the hearing impaired child's unique needs. They must recognize that there are no "experts," that neither is self-sufficient, and that when working with each other, open communication is the key.

Placement

The resource teacher often shares in the responsibility for placement of the hearing impaired child. In most programs a child is studied and staffed by a team. The team is generally composed of the principal, the resource teacher, speech therapist, school psychologist, school social worker, audiologist, director of special education (or a representative from his office), a member of the medical profession, the regular classroom teacher, and often the child's parents. The staffing team carefully studies past performance and problem areas and makes recommendations concerning educational programming and placement.

Although the staffing team makes recommendations concerning placement, the ultimate decision as to which teacher the child should be placed with often rests with the principal and resource teacher. The principal has information concerning the unique competencies of each teacher, their willingness and attitude toward accepting a child with a hearing loss and their ability to work cooperatively with resource personnel. The principal knows which teachers will see this experience as a new and exciting challenge.

The principal may recommend several teachers who would meet the preceding criteria; however, the next step would be for the resource teacher to informally interview these teachers, observe in their classrooms, and discuss in greater detail the nature of the new challenge. The resource teacher must observe carefully to determine the general position of the teacher in the room, lighting, the teacher's rate of speech and type of voice, visibility of lip movements, and visual aids used. These factors must be carefully reviewed prior to placement because they are important in facilitating the speech and language of the hearing impaired child.

Orientation/in-service

Depending on the geographic area to be served (one or more schools), resource/itinerant teachers may be responsible for the in-service education of regular classroom teachers in their building or outside of their building. Often the resource/itinerant teacher is called on to acquaint a building staff with the rationale underlying integrated placement of the hearing impaired. The nature of the in-service may be quite general and relate only to the philosophy of integrated education, or it may be specifically related to techniques of how to modify and adapt curriculum, materials, and teaching strategies.

Another role often assumed by the resource teacher is to provide select journal articles, readings, or topics of special interest in relation to a particular child's problem or specific teaching techniques (see Appendix B). The orientation and in-service efforts of the resource personnel are an ongoing responsibility that must be taken seriously. The way in which the resource personnel sell themselves, the program, and the children will have a tremendous influence on the program.

Demonstration teaching

Special educators have traditionally served their students in what might be termed "pull-out" programs. That is, they pull the children out of the classroom and work with them in a special resource room. This practice, although it may be necessary in some instances, is totally unnecessary and even undesirable in some situations.

If we are to fully appreciate the potential of integration or mainstreaming, we should attempt to involve special educators in regular classrooms wherever possible. This practice can greatly facilitate the communication between special and general educators and overcome many of the misunderstandings between them. The expertise held by both professions can be shared in the most meaningful way through the actual teaching of children. Special educators can increase their knowledge concerning large group instruction and the limitations imposed in modifying and adapting materials, curricula, and teaching strategies. Regular classroom teachers can increase their competency in working with the hearing impaired child by observing the resource person work with large and small groups. At times, the resource teacher could assume an aide or tutor role not only with the hearing impaired child, but also with small groups of students who are having problems with a difficult concept or assignment. This is not a new concept; some resource teachers have been assuming a helping or assisting role with regular teachers for some time. Unfortunately, the number has not been significantly large.

The resource teacher may also demonstrate a particular teaching strategy. For example, if the resource teacher has asked the regular teacher to use an overhead projector to teach a science or social studies lesson, it would be desirable for the resource teacher to actually demonstrate the use of the overhead by teaching the lesson. This method may be employed in giving a spelling test, or any other teaching technique. It is also possible for the resource teacher to assist in teaching a unit on the anatomy and physiology of the ear or a unit on hearing as one of the senses to acquaint the students with the nature of a hearing loss. The resource teacher may actually conduct or assist in conducting mini-in-service sessions with the students concerning the nature of a hearing loss, the benefits of a hearing aid, or any other topics that may be of interest to the hearing students.

Procuring, modifying, and adapting materials

The resource teacher may assist the regular teacher in modifying or adapting materials for the hearing impaired child. For example, this person may provide outlines or vocabulary lists that are about to be introduced into the regular classroom. Many times the regular teacher does not have time to modify materials, and this service can be a tremendous help. If neither the regular teacher nor resource teacher has the necessary time, volunteers or teacher aides may be most helpful in this area.

If activities are planned far enough in advance, many times the resource teacher may obtain captioned films, slide-tape presentations, or other tangible teaching materials to be used by the regular teacher.

Serve as liaison between medical personnel, therapists, and regular teacher

The resource teacher, by nature of her professional preparation and experience, generally has a very good understanding of medical aspects, audiology, and speech therapy. She may serve as the liaison between these disciplines and the regular teacher. She may interpret the exact nature of the hearing loss in relation to medical and audiological evaluations and provide specific suggestions related to the unique characteristics of hearing efficiency for a particular child. It is hoped that information concerning the child's functional ability would be emphasized rather than medical/quantitative information. In addition, she may interpret the child's development of language and its influence on learning. She may also serve as an extension of the speech therapist by reinforcing those speech sounds that may reasonably be expected of the child and those that are in need of further therapy. In some instances the resource teacher may serve as the follow-up agent for the hearing impaired child or for

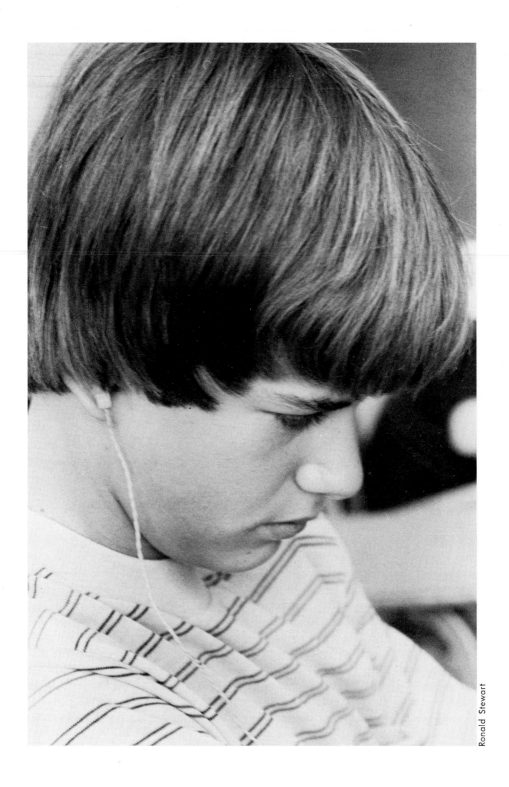

children who have been referred for medical examinations.

Assessing hearing aid effectiveness

The resource teacher can assist in evaluating many aspects of hearing aid problems and hearing aid effectiveness. She can routinely check all aspects of hearing aid operation by checking and replacing worn out batteries and, in general, troubleshooting any other problems. Many resource teachers obtain a tester for use in the building or make arrangements for assistance from a local hearing aid dealer.

A more important role of the resource teacher is to assess hearing aid effectiveness in the actual classroom situation, particularly if the child has just recently been fitted with an aid. She can appraise the effectiveness of the aid by evaluating changes in the manner in which the child handles everyday situations. She should look very carefully for the following: (1) increased social interactions, (2) changes in voice quality and articulation, (3) increased language skills, (4) reactions to sound and amplification, and (5) increased educational achievement. In addition, she should observe to see if the child is turning the volume down or completely turning it off; this may be an indication of an improperly fitted aid. The need for systematic longitudinal evaluation of a child's hearing and hearing aid effectiveness is an important role of the special education resource teacher.

Teaching special skills

There are a number of special skills that should be routinely provided by resource personnel. The specific skills will vary, depending on the grade level of the children. At the primary level the resource teacher may have responsibility for reading instruction or she may supplement the material presented in the child's regular class. The reading material used by the resource teacher may be the same as that used in the regular class, except the resource teacher will spend considerably more time on comprehension, questioning, and related language activities. At the intermediate level the resource teacher will probably supplement the regular classroom instruction by emphasizing phonetic and comprehension skills or by introducing new vocabulary words prior to their introduction in class.

In addition to supplemental instruction, the resource teacher may work on a number of other areas such as individual and small-group auditory training, vocabulary development, comprehension, questioning, speech-reading, and speech correction.

The exact nature of the resource teacher's role will depend on the age or grade level of the children, the number of children, and the extent of hearing impairment. Generally, the role involves tutoring or supplemental instruction, the introduction of new materials or skills, and instruction in highly specialized skills related to hearing impairment.

Counseling

The resource teacher, by nature of her specialized preparation and experience, may assist the regular teachers in counseling the hearing impaired child and the child's parents. This counseling may relate to routine academic matters, such as parent-teacher conferences, or to specific problems imposed by a hearing impairment, such as interpersonal relationships, language and speech problems, or vocational interests.

Assist with vocational education programs

The resource teacher will assist in planning and implementing work-study, vocational education, and vocational rehabilitation services for hearing impaired students in secondary school. The resource/itinerant teacher may be responsible for actually initiating these services or may contact others who will initiate them.

As mentioned previously, the role and responsibility of resource personnel will vary considerably. The key to successful resource services is communication between the regular teachers and the resource personnel.

SUMMARY

The education of hearing impaired children in regular classrooms has only recently gained momentum, and the number who have been integrated/mainstreamed has been relatively small. There have been integrated programs for children with mild and moderate losses for several years, but children with more severe and profound losses have most frequently been served in separate special education classes or state residential schools. It has not been until very recently that professionals have given serious consideration to integrating children with all degrees of hearing loss into regular educational programs.

It is not clearly established which variables (such as age, intelligence, speech, language, and degree of loss) contribute more to the successful integration of hearing impaired students. There has been a feeling among educators of the hearing impaired that if a child has a severe or profound loss he could not be effectively served in regular classrooms. There have been, however, children with profound losses who have been very successful in regular programs.

It is very probable that younger children and children with severe and profound losses will need greater amounts of special education service during their early school years and may attend regular classes on a very limited basis. After they have acquired the necessary skills, they may attend regular classrooms for increasing amounts of time, but nearly all will need the supportive assistance from special education resource/itinerant personnel during their entire school career.

Recent improvements in hearing aids and the increased use of these aids have led to an increase in the number of children who can successfully participate in regular programs. In addition, the development of captioned films and other media has had a very positive influence on the education of the hearing impaired. As a larger number of hearing impaired students are integrated into regular classrooms, as professionals continue to improve the effectiveness of their efforts, and as general and special educators begin to work together and to analyze and share information and expertise about these students, integration/mainstreaming may reach its fullest potential for these students.

This chapter has overviewed the nature of a hearing loss, the limitations imposed by such a loss, techniques of identification, and methods of referral. Several very specific suggestions to regular classroom teachers were offered that should facilitate the education of hearing impaired children. In addition, the role and responsibility of special education resource/itinerant personnel was reviewed, and it was emphasized that the key to successful programming for these students is a cooperative working arrangement between regular classroom teachers and special education personnel.

The child with impaired hearing must be exposed to different language styles. He must establish a variety of communication techniques, and reexamine and modify these communication skills to keep his speech and language at a more intelligible level. Perhaps most important is the opportunity for these children to establish and continue relationships with hearing children. Naturally, this may best be accomplished by these students in the least restrictive setting—a regular classroom.

References and suggested readings

ABC's in Ways the Regular Classroom Teacher Can Aid the Hard of Hearing Child. Salem, Oregon: State Department of Education, Division of Special Education, 1967.

Alexander Graham Bell Association for the Deaf. "Guidelines for an Integrated Program." *Volta Review,* Parent's Section, February 1964, *66,* 87-88.

Alexander Graham Bell Association for the Deaf. "Guidelines for Pre-School Programs for Hearing Impaired Children, 3-6 Years." Washington, D. C.: Volta Bureau, 1967.

Ashcroft, S. C. "The Handicapped in the Regular Classroom." *N. E. A. Journal,* November 1967, *56,* 33-34.

Bitter, G. B., Johnston, K. A., and Sorenson, R. G. *Integration of the Hearing Impaired: Educational Issues.* Washington, D. C.: U. S. Office of Education, Bureau of Education for the Handicapped, 1973.

Bitter, G. B., and Mears, E. G. "Facilitating the Integration of Hearing Impaired Children into Regular Public School Classes." *Volta Review,* 1973, *75,* 13-22.

Bothwell, H. "What the Classroom Teacher Can Do for the Child With Impaired Hearing." *N. E. A. Journal,* November 1967, *56,* 44-46.

Braddock, M. J. "Integrating the Deaf and Hard of Hearing Student." *Volta Review,* October 1962, *64,* 500-501.

Bruce, W. "Social Integration and Effectiveness of Speech." *Volta Review,* September 1960, *62,* 368-372.

Bruininks, R. H., and Kennedy, P. "Social Status of Hearing Impaired Children in Regular Classroom." *Exceptional Children,* February 1974, *40,* 336-342.

Carruth, K. J., Kryeger, A. H., Lesar, D. I., and Redding, A. J. "Possible Effects of Integration of the Deaf Within a Typical Vocational School Setting." *Journal of Rehabilitation of the Deaf,* 1971, *4,* 30-41.

Carver, R. L. "A Parent Speaks Out on Integration in the Schools." *Volta Review,* 1966, *68,* 580-583.

Classroom Teacher's Guide for the Hard of Hearing. Garden Grove Unified School District, 10331 Stanford Ave., Garden Grove, Calif., 17 pages.

Cohen, O. P. "An Integrated Summer Recreation Program." *Volta Review,* April 1969, *71,* 233-237.

"Community College of Denver Provides Integrated Programs." *Volta Review,* 1971, *73,* 190.

Connor, L. E. "The Oral Education of Deaf Children." *Voice* (Montreal Oral School), November 1968, *11,* 3-12.

Connor, L. E. "Integration." *Volta Review,* 1972, *74,* 207-209.

Dale, D. M. *The Deaf Child at Home and at School.* London: University of London Press, 1967.

Delaney, P. A. "Is It a Hearing Problem?" *Grade Teacher,* March 1972, *89,* 17-19.

Dixon, C. C. "Integrating . . . a Positive Note." *Hearing and Speech News,* 1968, *36,* 16, 18.

Elser, R. P. "The Social Position of Hearing Handicapped Children in the Regular Grades." *Exceptional Children,* 1959, *25,* 305-309.

Ford, F. C. "Reactions of the Hearing Impaired Child to School Situations." *Peabody Journal of Education,* November 1968, *46,* 177-179.

Formaad, W. "Help for the Child with Impaired Hearing." *N. E. A. Journal,* December 1965, *54,* 45-47.

Freeman, G. G. "Innovative School Programs: The Oakland School's Plan." *Journal of Hearing and Speech Disorders,* August 1969, *34,* 220-225.

Frick, E. "Adjusting to Integration: Some Difficulties Hearing Impaired Children Have in Public Schools." *Volta Review,* 1973, *75,* 36-46.

Garrett, C., and Stovall, E. M. "A Parent's Views on Integration." *Volta Review,* 1972, *74,* 338-344.

Gildston, P. "Hard of Hearing Child in the Classroom: A Guide for the Classroom Teacher." *Volta Review,* 1962, *64,* 239-245.

Gonzales, B. R. "Breaking the Fear of Placement for the Hearing Impaired." *Journal of the Rehabilitation of the Deaf,* October 1969, *3,* 22-28.

Hedgecock, D. "Facilitating Integration at the Junior High Level." *Volta Review,* March 1974, *76,* 182-188.

Johnson, A. L. "Supportive Instruction for Hearing Impaired Students." *Volta Review,* March 1968, *70,* 184-188.

Johnson, J. C. *Educating Hearing Impaired Children in Ordinary Schools.* Washington, D. C.: Volta Bureau, 1962.

Kennedy, P. "Social Status of Hearing Impaired Children in the Regular Classroom." *Exceptional Children,* February 1974, *40,* 336-341.

Kodman, F., Jr. "Educational Status of Hard of Hearing Children in the Classroom." *Journal of Speech and Hearing Disorders,* August 1963, *28,* 297-299.

Kowalsky, M. H. "Integration of a Severely Hard of Hearing Child in a Normal First Grade Program: A Case Study." *Journal of Speech and Hearing Disorders,* 1962, *27,* 349-358.

Leckie, D. J. "Creating a Receptive Climate in the Mainstream Program." *Volta Review,* 1973, *75,* 23-27.

Leigh, D. "The Deaf Child Enrolled in a Hearing School." *Volta Review,* 1963, *65,* 312.

Lewis, D. N. "Lipreading Skills of Hearing Impaired Children in Regular Schools." *Volta Review,* 1972, *74,* 303-311.

Lexington School for the Deaf. "Giving Deaf Children Needed Experience with the Hearing World." *Audiovisual Instruction,* November 1969, *14,* 98-99.

Lloyd, L. L. "Have You a Pupil with a Hearing Handicap?" *Instructor,* 1962, *72,* 62, 136.

McGee, D. I. "The Benefits of Educating Deaf Children with Hearing Children." *Teaching Exceptional Children,* 1970, *2,* 133-137.

Mecham, S. R., and VanDyke, R. C. "Pushing

Back the Walls Between Hearing and Hearing Impaired Children." *Volta Review,* 1971, *73,* 359-364.

Miller, A. S. "Academic Preparation to Insure Adjustment into Classes with Hearing Students." *Volta Review,* 1964, *66,* 414-425.

Monagham, A. "Educational Placement for the Multiply Handicapped Hearing Impaired Child." *Volta Review,* September 1964, *66,* 383-387.

Northcott, W. H. "Candidate for Integration: A Hearing Impaired Child in a Regular Nursery School." *Young Children,* 1970, *25,* 367-380.

Northcott, W. H. "An Experimental Summer School: Impetus for Successful Integration." *Volta Review,* 1970, *72,* 498-507.

Northcott, W. H. "Integration of Young Deaf Children into Ordinary Education Programs." *Exceptional Children,* 1971, *38,* 29-32.

Northcott, W. H. "A Hearing Impaired Pupil in the Classroom." *Volta Review,* 1972, *74,* 105-108.

Northcott, W. H. (Ed.). *The Hearing Impaired Child in a Regular Classroom: Preschool, Elementary, and Secondary Years.* Washington, D. C.: The Alexander Graham Bell Association for the Deaf, 1973.

O'Connor, C. D. "The Integration of the Deaf in Schools for the Normally Hearing." *American Annals of the Deaf,* 1961, *106,* 239-245.

O'Connor, C. D., and Connor, L. E. "Study of the Integration of Deaf Children in Regular Classrooms." *Exceptional Children,* 1961, *27,* 483-486.

Paul, R. L. "Resource Room for Hard of Hearing Children in the Public Schools." *Volta Review,* 1963, *65,* 200-202.

Paynter, D. H. *The Role of the Principal Assigned to Hard of Hearing Classes.* Garden Grove, Calif.: Garden Grove Unified School District, 1971.

Pollock, M. B., and Pollock, K. C. "Letter to the Teacher of a Hard of Hearing Child." *Childhood Education,* January, 1971, *47,* 206-209.

Regular Classroom Teacher's Manual for Aurally Handicapped Children. Garden Grove, Calif.: Stanford Elementary School, 1969.

Rister, A. "Deaf Children in a Mainstream Education." *The Volta Review,* 1975, *77,* 279-290.

Roberts, W. "Regular School Teachers' Views on Integration." *Voice* (Montreal Oral School), November, 1968, *11,* 13-17.

Rosenthal, C. "Social Adjustment of Hearing Handicapped Children." *Volta Review,* 1966, *68,* 293-297.

Rudy, J. P., and Nace, J. G. *A Transitional Integrative Program for Hearing Impaired Students.* Newark, Del.: Sterck School for the Hearing Impaired, 1973.

Salem, J. M. "Partial Integration at the High School Level." *Volta Review,* January 1971, *73,* 42-46.

Scheeline, A. "Integrating Deaf Children into Public Schools." *Volta Review,* 1971, *73,* 370-373.

Schwartz, M. G. "Deaf Child in My Hearing Class." *Volta Review,* 1964, *66,* 627-630.

Silverman, S. R. "The Hard of Hearing Child: How the Classroom Teacher Can Recognize and Help Him." *N. E. A. Journal,* 1950, *39,* 136-137.

Stuckless, E. R. *A Notetaking Procedure for Deaf Students in Regular Classes.* Rochester, N. Y.: National Technical Institute for the Deaf, 1969.

Sykes, G. "Tips on Note-Taking." *Volta Review,* April 1965, *67,* 307-309.

Tudyman, A. "Public School Problems in Educating Hard of Hearing Children." *Hearing News,* October 1952, *20,* 5-8.

VanWyk, M. K. "Integration, Yes, if . . ." *Volta Review,* February 1959, *61,* 59-62.

Vaughn, G. R. *Education of Deaf and Hard of Hearing Adults in Established Facilities for the Normally Hearing.* Pocatello, Idaho: Idaho State University Press, 1967.

Watson, F. J. "Use of Hearing Aids by Hearing Impaired Pupils in Ordinary Schools." *Volta Review,* 1964, *66,* 741-744.

Weiss, J. T. "Integrating the Hearing Handicapped." *Instructor,* 1968, *78,* 102.

CHAPTER 4
Strategies and alternatives
for educating the visually impaired

Ronald Stewart

The visually impaired child may be considered on the basis of medical, legal, educational, or functional definitions, but our emphasis will relate to educational and functional ability rather than numerical or medically derived definitions. For our purposes the visually impaired child may be defined as one whose vision is limited to such an extent that it may require educational modifications and adaptations. If the child can read printed material, either enlarged print or standard print with the use of special magnification devices, he will be classified as partially seeing or a print-reader. Children whose visual impairment is so severe that they must use materials other than print (such as braille and taped materials) are classified as educationally blind or as a braille-reader.

Although there is a trend toward educational or functional definitions, there are a number of state and local school programs that continue to define children on the basis of medical or legal aspects. Generally these definitions are used for eligibility for services or materials from state or federal agencies or for reimbursement purposes from state departments of education. The most common classification used relating to visual acuity (measurement of visual ability) divides the visually impaired into two groups, the partially seeing and the legally blind. The definition for legally blind, given by the National Society for the Prevention of Blindness (1957), is as follows:

A legally blind child is one who has central visual acuity of 20/200 or less in the better eye after correction; or visual acuity of more than 20/200 if there is a field defect in which the widest diameter of the visual field subtends an angle distance no greater than 20°.

Visual acuity is generally expressed by two numbers, such as 20/20, 20/70, or 20/200. These numbers correspond to the size of symbols or letters on the Snellen chart, each relating to the standard distance at which a person with normal vision can comfortably read the symbols or letters. For example, if an individual can read the twenty-foot-size symbol or letter on the chart at twenty feet, the measured acuity would be 20/20, or normal vision. If an individual can only read the seventy-foot letter or larger, his distance visual acuity would be indicated as 20/70. If the only letter that can be read is the largest, the two-hundred-foot letter, then the individual's measured distance visual acuity is 20/200.

These figures are indications of an individual's distance visual acuity, but they do not provide information concerning near-point vision (the ability to see at close distances, such as while reading). Not only do these definitions exclude information about near-point vision, but there is considerable variance between individuals with the same measured acuity. For example, two children may have 20/200 measured acuity, but one may be able to read printed material, whereas the other may have to read braille.

IDENTIFICATION OF CHILDREN WITH IMPAIRED VISION

Children with severe visual impairments are usually easily identified prior to enrollment in school. There are, however, a large number of children whose impaired vision has gone undetected for many years. The child's impairment may be detected by routine visual screening during the primary grades, or it may not be detected until the child is in the fourth or fifth grade. It is common for a visual defect not to be identified until the upper elementary years when the nature of the subject matter requires extensive visual work, such as reading and map study skills. This delay in identification may be attributed to the nature of academic tasks required up to this level or to poor vision screening procedures conducted during the child's early elementary years. Many screening programs are carelessly conducted; the procedures may be inaccurate or not carried out on a routine basis. In addition, tests for near vision (tests of the child's ability to read at twelve to eighteen inches) are required by only a very few states. Most screening programs are concerned with the child's distance vision (ability to see at twenty feet). Although vision screening procedures are improving, it must be recognized that these procedures, at best, are only a screening process and will not identify all children with impaired vision.

When considering the relative problems associated with vision-screening procedures, the role of the regular classroom teacher in identifying children with vision problems cannot be overemphasized. The teacher has the opportunity to observe the child in a variety of settings, under a variety of conditions, and may be in the best position to identify visual difficulties. Therefore, it may be helpful for the regular classroom teacher to have a list of common signs and behaviors that could indicate a visual problem.

Observable signs
1. Red eyelids
2. Crusts on lids among the lashes
3. Recurring styes or swollen lids
4. Watery eyes or discharges
5. Reddened or watery eyes
6. Crossed eyes or eyes that do not appear to be straight
7. Pupils of uneven size
8. Eyes that move excessively
9. Drooping eyelids

Visual behavior
1. Rubs eyes excessively
2. Shuts or covers one eye; tilts head or thrusts head forward
3. Sensitivity to light
4. Difficulty with reading or other work requiring close use of the eyes
5. Squinting, blinking, frowning, facial distortions while reading or doing other close work
6. Holds reading material too close or too far or frequently changes the distance from near to far or far to near
7. Complains of pain or aches in the eyes, headaches, dizziness, or nausea following close eye work
8. Difficulty in seeing distant objects (preference for reading or other academic tasks rather than playground or gross motor activities)
9. Tendency to reverse letters, syllables, or words
10. Tendency to confuse letters of similar shape (*o* and *a, c,* and *e, n* and *m, h* and *n,* and *f* and *t*)
11. Tendency to lose place in sentence or page
12. Poor spacing in writing and difficulty in "staying on the line"

If a child demonstrates any of these signs or behaviors, he should be referred immediately to the school nurse, principal, or individual responsible for vision problems. This individual may conduct additional tests to determine if the child should be referred to an eye specialist for a more extensive evaluation. After some determination is made concerning needed services, the teacher may have to serve as the catalyst or advocate to ensure that the recommendations are not lost in a file somewhere and that the needed services are provided.

To assist in the identification and treatment of children with vision problems, it may be helpful to have information concerning the role and capabilities of the various eye specialists found in a community. Occasionally, the classroom teacher may need to confer with one of these specialists; therefore, a brief description is provided as follows:

ophthalmologist (or oculist) a medical doctor who has specialized in the diagnosis and treatment of diseases of the eye. This physician is also licensed to prescribe glasses.
optometrist a highly trained person who has specialized in eye problems but does not possess a medical degree. This individual is licensed to measure visual function and prescribe and fit glasses. If disease is suspected, a referral will be made to an ophthalmologist.
optician a craftsman who makes glasses and fills the prescriptions of ophthalmologists and optometrists.
orthoptist a nonmedical technician who directs prescribed exercises or training to correct eye muscle imbalances and generally works under the direction of an ophthalmologist.

EDUCATIONAL PROGRAMMING

Although the integration of children representing other handicapping conditions is a relatively recent trend, children with vision impairments have been integrated or mainstreamed into regular classrooms for more than half a century. Early professionals

Ronald Stewart

recognized that children with vision impairments could be educated with their sighted peers with only minor modifications and adaptations and that the limitations imposed by a visual disability did not require a special curriculum.

Materials are modified or adapted so the child will be able to learn through sensory channels other than vision. For example, if the student is not able to read printed material, this material would be provided through the tactual (touch) or auditory channels. If the student can read printed material but only with considerable difficulty, the material may be enlarged. The child may use magnification devices, or material may be presented through the auditory channel. The primary nature of special education services for visually impaired students relates to the modification and adaptation of educational materials.

As suggested, the curriculum for children who are visually impaired is the same as it is for their sighted peers; however, in addition to the regular curriculum they require many "plus factors." In other words, the student will have, for example, reading, math, and social studies, but in addition, he may need braille instruction, orientation and mobility (travel) training, typewriting, training in the use of the abacus, and many other areas of instruction. Generally, the "plus factors" are taught by the resource/itinerant teacher and are not the responsibility of the regular classroom teacher (see pp. 66-70 for a more complete discussion of this topic).

NEED FOR CONTINUUM OF SERVICES

As mentioned in Chapter two, there is a very definite need for a full range or continuum of services for children with impaired vision. The following variables should be considered when placement options are being studied: (1) age, (2) achievement level, (3) intelligence, (4) presence of multiple handicapping conditions, (5) emotional stability, (6) nature and extent of eye condition, (7) wishes of students and parents, (8) recommendations of staffing team, and (9) availability of services. Naturally each child should be considered individually, but there are some general placement considerations that should be taken into account. For example, there seems to be a relationship between the age of the child, the nature and extent of the visual impairment, his level of achievement, and the amount of direct special education service and instruction needed. If the child is a young braille-reader (age 5 to 9), resource/itinerant assistance will be needed on a routinely scheduled daily basis to provide the needed instruction in braille reading and other areas requiring the specialized services of the resource/itinerant teacher. During the child's early education, he may spend as much as an hour to an hour and a half each day with his resource teacher. When he has developed braille-reading skills and a familiarity with all of the necessary tangible apparatus, he may attend his regular classroom for increasing amounts of time. If the child is able to read printed materials, with or without an aid, it would

not be necessary to spend as much time with the resource/itinerant teacher. The student at the secondary level probably would not receive a great deal of direct service from the resource/itinerant teacher.

SUGGESTIONS TO REGULAR CLASSROOM TEACHERS

The following suggestions may be used for the child who is either a braille- or print-reader, as many of the techniques and modifications are the same for either group. These suggestions fall into five categories: (1) adapted educational materials and equipment, (2) the educational environment, (3) orientation and mobility, (4) alternative teaching strategies, and (5) general considerations. Although it was difficult to determine proper placement for some suggestions, we believe they will be more easily conceptualized if grouped into general areas.

Adapted educational materials and equipment

It is not practical to review all of the adapted material and special equipment available for children with impaired vision since there are several hundred different types. Most of these materials are directed at increasing the child's learning through sensory channels other than vision. The following listing of materials indicates the many different types:

Geography aids
  Braille atlases
  Molded plastic dissected and undissected relief
    maps
  Relief globes
  Landform model (a set of three-dimensional
    tactual maps illustrating forty geographic
    concepts)
Mathematics aids
  Special slates to be used in computation
  Abacuses
  Raised clockfaces
  Geometric area and volume aids
  Wire forms for matched planes and volumes
  Braille rulers
Writing aids
  Raised-line check books
  Signature guide

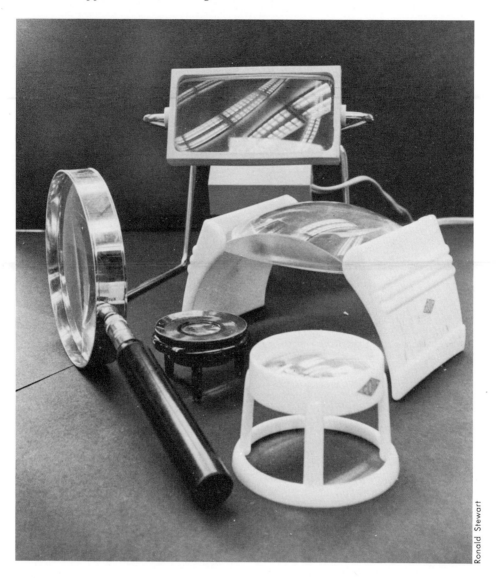

Ronald Stewart

Raised-line writing paper
Longhand writing kit
Script letter sheets and boards
Miscellaneous aids
  Audible goal locators, which can be used as a
    goal, base, object locator, or warning device
  Special braille or large-type answer sheets
  Science measurement kits (containing such
    items as thermometers, spring balances, gram
    weights, and gravity specimens)
  Sports field kit (raised drawings of various
    sports playing fields or courts)
  Simple machine kits, including working models
    of simple machines such as pulleys and levers,
    including plane, wheel and axle

Childrens games, such as rook, Rack-O, Scrab-
  ble, bingo, cards, checkers, and Parcheesi
Adapted sports equipment (audible balls)
Braille clocks, wristwatches, and timers

The American Printing House for the Blind* has a very extensive offering of adapted materials and educational equipment. In addition, the American Foundation† has an "Aids and Appliances Catalog"

*American Printing House for the Blind, 1839 Frankfurt Avenue, Louisville, Ky. 40206.
†American Foundation for the Blind, 15 West Sixteenth Street, New York, N. Y. 10011.

from which materials may be ordered. There are several other agencies that also have special materials available. More than half of the states have established instructional materials centers serving as a registry and depository for materials, loaning materials to school districts as needed. These state instructional materials centers will assist in locating specific materials and may even reproduce them in the desired format, that is, large type, tape recording, or braille (see Appendix C for list of instructional materials centers).

Generally, it is not the responsibility of the regular classroom teacher to obtain materials, since the resource/itinerant teacher is already familiar with all the agencies that have adapted materials and equipment and with the procedures used to acquire these materials. In the event selected materials are not available from any of the agencies, it would be necessary for the resource/itinerant teacher to reproduce these materials or make some provision for them to be prepared by community volunteers. For example, a particular reading text may not be available because it is of a very recent copyright. After all agencies have been queried, including the state instructional materials center for the visually impaired, the resource/itinerant teacher may have the text reproduced in large type, tape recorded, or transcribed into braille by community volunteers or a paid aide who has the necessary special skills.

In addition to textbooks and special adapted materials that may be available from an agency, there is always a need for teacher-made materials used on a day-to-day basis, such as teacher-made tests, worksheets, and special games or activities. These must be reproduced in the desired format by the resource/itinerant teacher or specially trained aides or volunteers because it is essential that the child's materials be the same as those of his peers. Advanced planning and a special communication system must be implemented with the resource/itinerant teacher, which will provide for an explanation of the nature of the needed materials and allow sufficient time for their reproduction. This is usually accomplished by leaving the desired materials in the resource/itinerant teacher's mailbox, establishing a routine conference between the regular teacher and resource/itinerant teacher, or by sending the material with the child when he meets with the resource/itinerant teacher.

At times it may be necessary for the regular classroom teacher to modify needed materials. For example, if mimeographed materials are being prepared for class distribution, it may be necessary to darken the letters or figures with a felt-tipped pen so they can be seen more easily by the partially seeing child. Usually, materials duplicated in purple cause considerable difficulty; therefore, if possible, use black stencils to ensure the desired contrast. It may also be of value to consider preparing handout materials in primary or enlarged type for all students, since they too are able to read enlarged materials more easily.

Educational environment

There are several environmental or classroom modifications that will facilitate the education of children with impaired vision. Preferred or open seating allows the child to sit wherever he is most comfortable. When the teacher is using the chalkboard, when a movie or filmstrip is being shown, and when the teacher is demonstrating a particular concept using tangible materials, the child should be allowed to move as close as necessary.

Arrange seating for the best possible lighting conditions. This does not imply that all partially seeing children should be in bright or highly lighted areas. Some visual impairments require no special lighting, whereas others require lower levels of illumination. The resource/itinerant teacher or the report from the child's eye specialist should be of particular value in this area. The teacher should not stand with his back to a bright light source such as a window since the child will then be looking directly into the light. Writing on a chalkboard where there is considerable glare should also be avoided.

Safety while traveling independently in

the classroom can be a problem if doors are not completely open or closed. Often the visually impaired child may think the classroom door is open, because of auditory and other cues, only to find that it was only partially open. Keeping the door completely open or closed is generally difficult to accomplish with thirty other students in the classroom, but it should be attempted.

Some teachers who have a visually impaired student in their class are reluctant to change the classroom seating or position of desks, tables, and other items because they are afraid the child may become disoriented or sustain an injury. The physical arrangement of the room should be changed as often as necessary, but the visually impaired child must be oriented to the changes. This should only take a few minutes of formal orientation and a few minutes of independent exploring by the child, followed by a brief question-and-answer session concerning the new arrangement. Other children in the class could be of some assistance by directing or telling the visually impaired child the new arrangement. The noise level of the classroom should be kept reasonably low since the visually impaired child must depend on his auditory skills for a great deal of his educational program. Braille-reading students need open space and shelves at the side of the room since braille materials are very large and bulky, and they may need room for their braille writer, typewriter, books, and other materials. The extent of classroom or environmental modifications are quite minimal and depend on the age of the student, the amount of time spent in a particular room, and the degree of visual loss.

Independent travel (orientation and mobility)

The ability of a visually impaired student to move about independently is one of the most important factors in his total education program. Programming efforts should be directed toward academic and social development, but if the area of travel is neglected, the student may be denied the opportunity to move freely and independently in his school and community. In view of the relative importance of independent travel, an overview of the nature of training, the major modes of mobility, and the role of the regular classroom teacher will be reviewed.

The terms *orientation* and *mobility* are interrelated since a person must be oriented to become mobile and mobility cannot be achieved unless the individual is oriented. *Orientation* refers to an individual's use of his remaining senses to establish his position and relationship to objects in his environment. *Mobility* refers to the individual's movement from one point in his environment to another. In other words, mobility is getting from point *A* to point *B*, whereas orientation involves knowing his location, the location of his objective, and knowing the most efficient way to reach the objective.

The regular classroom teacher is not responsible for formal training in orientation and mobility. The nature of this training is very specialized and should be conducted by an orientation and mobility specialist or by the resource/itinerant teacher. It is important, however, that the regular classroom teacher understand the nature of the training and the major methods or modes of independent travel. The five modes of travel used by visually impaired individuals are (1) the sighted guide, (2) the long cane, (3) dog guides, (4) electronic devices, and (5) independent travel without any assistance or devices.

The *sighted guide technique* is one of the first taught to most visually impaired students. It is an efficient way to "orient" an individual to an unfamiliar area and is also a viable mobility technique. This technique involves the visually impaired individual grasping a sighted person's arm just above the elbow. He will place his thumb on the outside and his fingers on the inside of the guide's arm and will walk about one-half step behind the guide. In effect, the visually impaired person is "reading" the sighted individual's arm or elbow, and any movement of the guide's body and arm will be communicated to the student. By following

Ronald Stewart

approximately one-half step behind, the student will know when the guide is stepping up or down, turning left or right, and so on. There are some additional methods related to the efficient use of this technique that would be taught by the resource/itinerant teacher or orientation and mobility specialist but will not be reviewed here.

The second and the most common systematic method of travel is the use of the *long cane*. The age at which a child is introduced to and provided formal training in the use of a cane is dependent on the student's maturity, need for more independent travel, and ability to profit from rather extensive one-to-one training. The decision to initiate this formal training in the use of a cane is made after careful consideration of the aforementioned factors. Generally, instruction in the use of the cane is not started until age 14 or 15, but some children have succeeded in learning cane techniques as early as 11 or 12. The reasons for waiting until the student is 14 or 15 generally relate to his ability to profit from instruction and, more importantly, his need for a more independent mode of travel. There are many types of canes, but the most common are made of aluminum or fiberglass and are approximately one-half inch in diameter. Some have a crook for balance and easy placement, and others have a golf-club-type grip. The tip of the cane is usually made of steel or nylon.

The third mode of independent travel is the *dog guide*. Like the long cane, a dog guide is not recommended until the student is at least 17 or 18. Prior to this age the student may not have the maturity to handle a dog properly nor the need for more independent travel. Often young visually impaired children indicate an interest in obtaining a dog guide as a pet or companion but not necessarily for independence in traveling. For obvious reasons the dog guide should not be considered a pet, but rather a partner in achieving independent travel. Contrary to popular opinion, less than two percent of the visually impaired population use dog guides. Although there may appear to be many advantages to using a dog, the dis-

advantages outweigh the advantages for all but a very few. Specific information concerning dog guide agencies, such as cost, and nature of training, may be provided by either the resource/itinerant teacher or the orientation and mobility specialist.

The fourth mode of independent travel is the use of an *electronic mobility device*. There are a number of electronic devices available; they are used as a primary mobility device or as a supplement to other devices such as the long cane. Although it is encouraging to see research being conducted in this most important area, it does not seem that any one device will meet the needs of all individuals. Some of the devices enhance hearing efficiency, some detect obstacles, others enable the individual to walk in a straight line, whereas others are directed at revealing the specific location of obstacles in the environment. Most of these devices are still in the field-testing stage, and it is difficult to predict when they will be available for general use.

The fifth method of travel, *independent travel* without any assistance or device, is probably the most commonly used, considering that most school age children do not use a cane, dog, or electronic device. There are, however, certain basic skills that are prerequisite to other modes and are designed to achieve efficient and safe travel. These basic skills are taught at a very early age and are essential if the child is to achieve independent travel in his school and community. A few of the basic techniques that would be taught by the resource/itinerant teacher or orientation and mobility specialist are as follows:

1. Upper hand and forearm—protection for head and upper body from half-open doors, walls, and so on
2. Lower hand and forearm—protection for lower body and location of desks, tables, and so on
3. Trailing—follow lightly over a straight surface with back of fingertips to locate specific objects or to get a parallel line of direction
4. Direction taking—using an object or

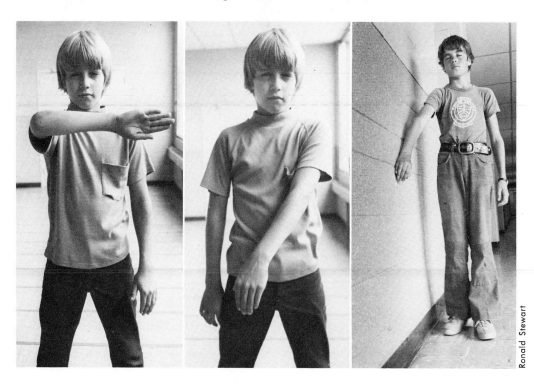

Ronald Stewart

sound to establish a course of direction toward or away from an object

Patterns of familiarization, geographical directions, hearing acuteness for travel, sound localization, and the use of residual vision would also be provided by the resource/itinerant teacher or orientation and mobility specialist.

The type of mobility aid or device to be used, whether it be cane, dog, or electronic device, is totally an individual matter and should be given very careful consideration by the student, his parents, and others after careful thought and planning in cooperation with the resource/itinerant teacher or orientation and mobility specialist.

Suggestions to regular teachers concerning orientation and mobility

The regular classroom teacher should be aware of the nature of training provided by special education personnel so that she can reinforce concepts and specific techniques being taught. The teacher is generally able to observe the child in a variety of settings, under a variety of conditions, and at differ-

ent times of the day, as well as being able to provide information to special education personnel concerning the transfer and maintenance of a desired concept or skill. It is not uncommon for a student to demonstrate efficiency with a particular skill when working with the resource/itinerant teacher, but be unable to transfer this skill when he returns to his classroom.

Be as specific as possible when giving directions to the student. For example, do not say to the child "Go down to Mr. Jones' office, which is about halfway down corridor number three." Instead, provide very specific directions such as "Go to Mr. Jones' office, which is on the right side of corridor number three, two doors past the water fountain." Directions in the classroom should also be specific. It would not be sufficient to say "Your science project is on the shelf in the back of the room." Instead, you might say "Your science project is on the shelf in the back of the room, three feet to the left of the sink, at the back of the shelf."

Acquaint all of the students with the proper procedures used in serving as a sighted guide.

The resource/itinerant teacher or orientation and mobility specialist may want to attend or actually conduct this type of mini-in-service session. The students may want to wear blindfolds to gain a better understanding of traveling without sight. Some caution should be exercised here so that the students do not develop a sympathetic attitude but rather an objective understanding of travel techniques used by the visually impaired.

Alternative teaching strategies

Although it is not necessary for the regular classroom teacher to change her teaching strategies to any great extent, it may be helpful to consider certain suggestions and strategies. Whenever possible begin instruction at a concrete level, include concrete materials, and move to the abstract as the child develops the concept. The use of manipulative, tangible, or auditory materials is preferred to totally verbal and abstract instructions or lessons. Although a model of an object may be necessary, the real object or situation is much preferred. For example, if a science lesson is concerned with simple pulleys, an actual pulley should be provided if possible. The resource/itinerant teacher is a valuable asset in this area since this individual may be able to assist in obtaining the actual object or may make a model similar to the one needed.

The concepts of "learning by doing" and "teaching by unifying experiences" are certainly not new concepts to regular classroom teachers. These concepts, however, are particularly important to the student with impaired vision because he may not have the same experiential background as other students of the same age. Whenever possible allow the visually impaired child to actually experience "doing it" rather than just verbally explaining the process. Closely related to this is the need to unify or integrate experiences and concepts as often as possible. A young child may not be able to relate one isolated concept to another because he may not have had any previous experience with the particular concept.

When writing on the chalkboard, be certain to explain verbally the concept or actual writing being presented. In general, any highly visual instructions or lessons should be supplemented with verbal explanation. This can become routine with a little effort and practice.

Lessons in physical education or gross motor activities should be demonstrated by physically taking the child through the activity. For example, if a particular tumbling routine is being taught, the instructor may want to actually "move the child through the correct movements" rather than merely explain the process.

In art, emphasis should be placed on tactual activities such as clay, finger painting, weaving, paper sculpture, and collage whenever possible. It is important that the child have the experience of carrying out the process involved in an art project while de-emphasizing the end product. By completing the process, in whatever medium, the student can achieve the same objectives as his peers.

Modifications in testing procedures may have to be made for the visually impaired student. Reading braille or large type takes considerably longer than reading standard print, and it may be necessary to either extend the amount of time for completion of the test or reduce the number of items. Of course, this would depend on whether the purpose of the test was speed or power; if speed, the visually impaired child may have considerable difficulty. The actual test administration may also have to be modified; for example, it may be necessary to (1) administer the test orally, (2) tape the test in advance and ·have the student type his answers, or (3) send the test home with the student and have the parent read the test while the student either types or brailles his answers. Of course, some students would require little or no modifications and would be able to take the test with the other students. Achievement tests administered at the beginning and end of the school year, because of their relative importance and amount of time needed for completion, may have to be adminstered by the resource/itinerant teacher or an aide. The regular teacher should be certain to consult with the resource/itinerant teacher in advance to consider these and other options for testing.

Vary classroom activities as much as possible. The visually impaired child who is partially seeing may become fatigued if tasks involving close visual examination are required for long periods of time. This can be accomplished by alternating listening activities, close visual activities, and motor activities. The child should be encouraged to take short breaks from activities requiring prolonged periods of visual work whenever possible.

Teachers who cannot read braille often express considerable concern when informed that they will have a braille-reading student in their classroom. Actually, it is not necessary for the teacher to know braille because the resource/itinerant teacher will write or print directly above the braille dots whatever the student has written. For example, if the student completes an assignment and turns the assignment in to the regular teacher, the teacher in turn should give it to the resource/itinerant teacher, who will "write in" the student's responses and return it to the regular teacher. At the upper elementary, middle school, and secondary levels, the child may complete his assignment on a conventional typewriter (discussed on p. 67).

As mentioned previously, there are few special teaching techniques required of the regular classroom teacher, and we believe that for most teachers an understanding of techniques used with the visually impaired will tend to improve teaching competency with all children.

General considerations

A number of general suggestions exist that are not specific to the preceding discussion; these will be briefly reviewed here.

When speaking to the visually impaired student during class discussion, the teacher should be certain to use his name because he may not know that the teacher is looking at him. For example, "Don, what is the answer to problem 16?" This would also be true when the teacher enters a room. The teacher should address the student by name and identify herself to let him know who has entered the room. Similarly, if the child enters a room where the teacher is alone, she should provide some indication that she is there, either by speaking to him directly or by some other auditory clue.

Established standards for grading or discipline should not be altered for the visually impaired student. When an assignment has been given or a classroom rule established, the visually impaired child should be expected to adhere to the same procedures as the other students. If the teacher employs a double standard, one for the class and another for the visually impaired student, the other children will be quick to recognize the difference and may resent the visually impaired student. This resentment may have a very adverse effect on their interpersonal relationships; the other students may identify the visually impaired student as the "teacher's pet" and subsequently reject him.

The child with impaired vision may not be able to see the teacher's facial gestures or smile when he has completed an assigned task successfully or look of displeasure when he has not. Physical contact such as a pat on the back or a touch on the arm may be necessary. Of course, the teacher should only praise the child when the job has been well done, not just because it was done by a visually impaired student.

If the visually impaired student has some remaining or residual vision, encourage him to use it to the fullest extent possible. Unless the eye specialist has indicated that the child should not use his vision, every effort must be made to increase the student's visual efficiency. It is well established that if we encourage a child to use his residual vision its efficiency can be increased. It is not unusual for a child's measured visual acuity to remain the same over a period of years while his visual performance may actually increase.

Somewhat related to this area is the use of low-vision or optical aids (such as magnifiers and special glasses). Students who use these aids should be encouraged to do so whenever appropriate. The regular classroom teacher should observe whether the device seems to be helpful, how often it is used, and under what conditions. Naturally, this information should be shared with the resource/itinerant teacher who, in turn, may share this information with the child's doctor or low-vision aids specialist.

The regular classroom teacher may want to assign a "buddy" to assist the visually impaired child with, for example, highly visual assignments, orientation to a new school building, and emergencies such as fires. The use of a "buddy system" is a desirable approach to peer teaching or assistance regardless of whether or not there is a disabled child in the classroom.

The regular teacher should reinforce concepts taught by the resource/itinerant teacher, orientation and mobility specialist, or any other personnel working with the child. Communication is essential between disciplines if we are to see the needed transfer to every possible situation. Often one individual in the child's school environment may be emphasizing a particular skill (such as using a particular magnification device, traveling independently, and typing), and another individual, who may assist in reinforcing and ensuring the transfer and maintenance of the particular skill, may be unaware of it. Be certain to establish an open and ongoing communication system with other professionals working with the student.

The need for independence, freedom of movement, and play are as important for the student with impaired vision as for his sighted classmates. Approximately 130 years ago Samuel Gridley Howe, a noted educator of the visually impaired, offered the following general rules in working with these children (Buell, 1950):

Never check the actions of the child; follow him, and watch him to prevent any serious accidents, but do not interfere unnecessarily; do not even remove obstacles which he would learn to avoid by tumbling over them a few times. Teach him to jump rope, to swing weights, to raise his body by his arms, and to mingle, as far as possible, in the rough sports of the older boys. Do not be apprehensive of his safety. If you should see

him clambering in the branches of a tree, be assured he is less likely to fall than if he had perfect vision. Do not too much regard bumps on the forehead, rough scratches or bloody noses; even these may have their good influences. At the worst, they affect only the bark, and do not injure the system like the rust of inaction.

It is not unusual for a teacher to overprotect visually impaired students, to expect less of them than their sighted classmates. Every effort should be made *not* to underestimate their capabilities. The teacher's responsibility to the child with impaired vision is the same as for other students—to assist him in developing socially, emotionally, physically, morally, and educationally.

ROLE AND RESPONSIBILITY OF THE RESOURCE/ITINERANT TEACHER

The role and responsibility of the resource/itinerant teacher varies considerably from school district to school district and at times within a single district. The exact nature of the resource/itinerant teacher's assignment will be dependent on the following factors:

1. The geographic distance to be traveled between schools may vary greatly. Some teachers are responsible for only one school, whereas others may have responsibilities extending to two or three schools. In some rural areas the resource/itinerant teacher may travel to several communities.
2. Number of students and teachers to be served.
3. Age of students (generally, the younger the student, the more need for direct service).
4. The number of braille-readers and print-readers can vary extensively (generally, the braille-reading student will require considerably more direct services).
5. Availability of orientation and mobility instruction. If an orientation and mobility specialist is not available, the resource/itinerant teacher may be responsible for this instruction.
6. Availability of paid or volunteer braille transcribers, large-print typists, and tape transcribers.

7. The availability of adapted and special materials. (In states in which an instructional materials center for the visually impaired is available, the acquisition and distribution of educational materials can be greatly facilitated.)

Services provided by the resource/itinerant teacher can generally be classified on the basis of direct or indirect service. Direct service involves working directly with the visually impaired student on a one-to-one basis or in small groups. Indirect service involves working with individuals other than the student, such as the child's teacher, administrators, medical personnel, and parents. The extent to which the resource/itinerant teacher works directly with the student would depend on the preceding variables. Most resource/itinerant personnel will provide both direct and indirect services.

Although it is difficult to clearly establish that one type of service is direct and another indirect, the following discussion of specific responsibilities will be related to the type of service provided.

DIRECT SERVICE TO STUDENTS

As mentioned previously, there are a number of "plus factors" that must be provided in addition to regular curricular offerings such as reading, math, and social studies. These plus factors would be provided by the resource/itinerant teacher.

Specialized instruction in reading

The resource/itinerant teacher will provide the needed instruction in braille reading and writing and the use of slate and stylus. The amount of time required for instruction in these special skills will depend on the age of the student. More time will be required for a younger braille-reading student because

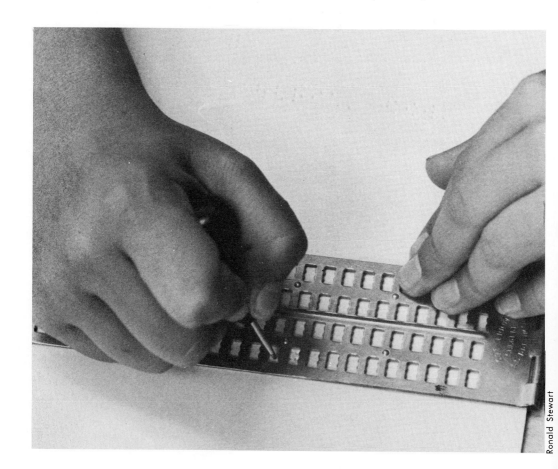

Ronald Stewart

he will be developing these specialized skills during his elementary school years, whereas the student at the secondary level may have already developed these skills. Braille instruction should be provided on a daily scheduled basis for the first three years of the student's education or until he develops the necessary competency. After the student is relatively proficient at braille reading and writing, it may not be necessary for the resource/itinerant teacher to work with the student on a daily basis.

If a student is a print-reader, the amount of instruction will usually not be as great as for a braille-reader. However, if the student uses low-vision aids (magnification devices), it may be necessary to provide specific instruction in their use.

Instruction in the use of adapted or special equipment and aids

Specialized instruction in the use of equipment and aids such as tape recorders, tape players, and talking-book machines will be necessary for the visually impaired. Special mathematic computation devices such as the abacus and instruction in the use of special maps will also be required. Generally, instruction in the use of this equipment will be introduced as the need arises rather than systematically scheduled as with braille instruction.

Instruction in listening skills

It has been estimated that forty-five percent of our time in communication is spent in listening activities and that approximately two-thirds of a student's school day is spent in activities related to listening. Listening is one of the most significant avenues of learning for the visually impaired student. He must rely on his auditory channel more than his sighted classmates. As a result, systematic instruction in listening activities must be provided. Instruction in listening should include a variety of listening situations, such as environmental, formal presentations, informal conversations, and audio reading required by using talking books and tape recorded materials.

Instruction in writing

Instruction in handwriting for a partially seeing student should be initiated at the same time as it is introduced to his sighted classmates. It may be necessary, however, for the resource/itinerant teacher to provide supplemental assistance in this area. The braille-reading student will want to gain some proficiency at handwriting so that he can sign his own name and make brief notations. Special handwriting aids and instruction will be necessary to achieve this skill.

Typing, using an electric typewriter (if available), is routinely taught to visually impaired students. Since their handwriting may be difficult to read and braille writing can only be read by a few individuals, typing can be a boost to their written communication skills. Instruction is generally initiated at about the fourth grade level. Often, typing instruction is taught to the student along with spelling assignments because there is considerable repetition in both subject areas. As the student increases his typing proficiency he can complete more and more assignments with the aid of the typewriter. The adapted approach to instruction is known as "touch typing" and employs a special system that does not require vision. Naturally, accuracy is emphasized rather than speed, since it will be difficult for the student to check his work. Instruction in this area would be continuous throughout the student's upper elementary and secondary school years.

Development of visual efficiency

Through systematic instruction the visual efficiency of a low-vision student can be increased. Special techniques and materials to determine the amount of visual efficiency and specific techniques to increase visual ability are available. Constant visual stimulation provided through a sequentially planned program can increase the visual efficiency of many students. This instruction should be provided by the special resource/itinerant teacher on a routine basis. The resource/itinerant teacher may also observe the student in the regular classroom to determine if the student is using his vision as much as possible.

Instruction in orientation and mobility

The extent to which the resource/itinerant teacher is responsible for direct instruction in orientation and mobility will depend on whether an orientation and mobility specialist is available. If available, the specialist will be responsible for formal instruction; if not, the resource/itinerant teacher will assume this responsibility. There are, however, certain basic or "precane" skills that may be taught by the resource/itinerant teacher. In addition, the resource/itinerant teacher will be responsible for familiarizing or orienting the student to a new classroom or school building and supplementing the instruction of the orientation and mobility specialist. Throughout the student's educational program, orientation and mobility should be systematically provided.

Instruction in techniques of daily living

To function effectively as a responsible and contributing member of society requires more than just being able to complete the required academic tasks such as reading and writing. Often a visually impaired individual does not know how to carry out all of the activities of independent living such as personal grooming, housecleaning, cooking and serving food, and home repair. These specific techniques of daily living must be part of the visually impaired student's school curriculum. Many of these activities could be provided in a home economics course at the secondary level, but often the home economics teacher is not familiar with the ways in which these activities should be modified or adapted or with the special equipment available. Often these activities are taught after school, in the evening, or in Saturday programs; but in the event they are not offered at these times, they may have to be provided during school hours by the resource/itinerant teacher independently or in cooperation with others.

Supplementary or introductory instructions

Because it may take longer for the student to complete an assignment or the assignment may be highly visual, it is often necessary for the resource/itinerant teacher to supplement the instruction of the regular classroom teacher. For example, if the process of "carrying" in mathematical addition is being introduced, the resource/itinerant teacher may want to introduce the use of a special mathematics aid that would be of assistance, or she may want to supplement the regular classroom teacher's instruction by using a special "mental mathematics" technique.

Often the resource/itinerant teacher will want to introduce a particular concept prior to its actual introduction in the regular classroom. For example, a unit on the solar system may have considerably more meaning to the visually impaired student if the resource/itinerant teacher provides a model of the solar system and actually introduces the unit to the student. In physical education it is often necessary to orient the student to special equipment, games, or activities prior to the physical education period so the student acquires a basic understanding of the concept and so that the physical education instructor will not have to take a disproportionate amount of time to introduce the concept. Supplemental or introductory instruction can play a very important role in the education of the visually impaired child in a regular classroom.

Child and parent counseling

Many resource/itinerant teachers assume responsibility for child and parent counseling and for seeking appropriate professional counseling when needed. They may work with the student for several years, whereas the student's regular teachers may only be in close contact with the student for one year. Resource/itinerant teachers are acquainted with the unique problems imposed by impaired vision and their relationship to adjustment, social and emotional growth. They may also be in the best position to discuss personal problems, interests, and projected vocational plans.

Although the primary responsibility for reporting student progress rests with the regular classroom teacher, the resource/itinerant teacher should attend parent-teacher conferences to report the student's progress in the special areas. Often it is necessary for the resource/itinerant teacher to meet separately with the student's parents to interpret special programming efforts or other special problems that may be related to the student's visual impairment.

INDIRECT SERVICES

Services provided to individuals other than the child are considered indirect services. As mentioned previously, there are a number of variables determining the nature and extent of indirect services provided. The following discussion provides an overview of a variety of indirect services that might be provided by a resource/itinerant teacher.

Acquisition of materials

The acquisition of educational materials such as braille or enlarged-type texts, tapes, and tangible apparatus is one of the primary responsibilities of the resource/itinerant teacher. These materials must duplicate the content of the materials being used by the other students and must be obtained in the shortest possible time. There are several well-established procedures that will be used by the resource/itinerant teacher to obtain the needed material in the needed format without duplication of efforts. These procedures involve checking national and state agencies and volunteer groups prior to the actual transcription or production of the desired material.

Preparation of materials

If the needed educational material is not available from any agency in the desired format and all sources have been queried, it may be necessary to have a paid or volunteer transcriber-reproducer prepare the material. The resource/itinerant teacher would serve as the liaison between the classroom teacher and the transcriber-reproducer to ensure that the material is in the needed format and that it is completed in sufficient time.

Many day-to-day materials such as teacher-made tests, worksheets, and special projects obviously would not be available from outside agencies; therefore, it would be the responsibility of the resource/itinerant teacher to have these materials prepared or prepare them himself. The type of material needed would be quite varied, ranging from a teacher-made mathematics test to a geologic survey map of the county.

Often it is not practical or possible to have a text brailled on relatively short notice, or it may only be used once. In this event, the resource/itinerant teacher would assist in arranging for the material to be read aloud by another person. The use of "readers" is a technique used frequently by secondary school students, and if used properly, it can be a tremendous advantage to the visually impaired student.

Assist in adapting or modifying activities

The resource/itinerant teacher may assist the physical education, art, music, home economics, or industrial arts teacher in adapting or modifying a particular lesson or activity. If the resource/itinerant teacher has established a routine and ongoing communication system with all teachers, it is relatively easy to anticipate an activity that may need modification or adaptation. The resource/itinerant teacher may offer specific suggestions on how to change the activity in such a way that the visually impaired student can meet the objective of the lesson. Sometimes it is desirable for the resource/itinerant teacher to actually attend the activity to assist the student or his teacher.

Interpret medical information

Often the resource/itinerant teacher is expected to serve as a liaison between medical personnel and the regular classroom teachers. She may be asked to interpret medical reports and to explain the nature of the eye condition and the limitations imposed by it. In addition, she must share information concerning seating arrangements, lighting requirements, and levels of visual expectation for the partially seeing student. She may also be asked to evaluate the suitability of materials to be used, particularly in the areas of clarity of pictures, type size, spacing, and margins.

Conduct in-service education sessions

The resource/itinerant teacher may be responsible for the in-service education of regular teachers and administrators. She may be expected to acquaint a building staff with the rationale underlying integrated placement of the visually impaired student if the staff has not had previous experience with these students. The nature of the in-service education may be quite general and relate only to the philosophy of integrated education. In other instances it may be directed at a small group of teachers who will have the student in their classes and would specifically relate to techniques for modifying and adapting materials or teaching strategies.

The resource/itinerant teacher may conduct mini-in-service sessions with a group of students to acquaint them with the nature of impaired vision to ready them for a visually impaired classmate. At other times, student in-service sessions may relate to the special materials and techniques that will be used.

Another in-service role often assumed by the resource/itinerant teacher is to provide select journal articles, readings, or films for regular classroom teachers. These readings or materials would be directed at providing the needed competencies to more effectively work with the visually impaired student.

Assume responsibility for coordination of outside services

The resource/itinerant teacher often assumes responsibility for providing and coordinating many other services needed in addition to classroom activities. The resource/itinerant teacher may coordinate orientation and mobility services, or therapeutic recreation and leisure activities. She may also assist in planning and implementing work-study or vocational education programs. In general, her role is one of student advocacy—by providing all needed services and programs necessary for the student's complete educational and social development.

SUMMARY

Although children with severe visual impairments are usually easily identified prior to enrollment in school, there remains a significant number whose impaired vision goes undetected for many years. As a result it is imperative that regular classroom teachers be aware of common signs and behaviors that may indicate impaired vision and be familiar with the procedures necessary to ensure that the child will receive the needed further examination, corrective lenses, or professional services.

In this chapter we have provided specific suggestions that should be of assistance to regular classroom teachers and have reviewed the role and responsibility of special education resource/itinerant personnel. When considering the nature of educational programming for visually impaired children, it is quite obvious that the most significant changes relate to adapted educational materials and equipment.

Programming for these children does not require a special curriculum; however, materials and equipment must be modified and adapted so these children will be able to learn through channels other than vision. The acquisition, modification, and adaptation of these materials should be arranged by the resource/itinerant teacher. In addition, the resource/itinerant teacher will be able to suggest needed changes in the educational environment, specific suggestions in the area of orientation and mobility, and alternative teaching strategies that may facilitate the education of the visually impaired student.

The key to the successful integration of visually impaired students is communication between the regular classroom teacher and the resource/itinerant teacher. An open and ongoing communication system that will provide a sharing of information concerning the students' needs, interests, problems, and abilities must be established. Each professional must share unique expertise and competency with the other to provide the best possible program for these students.

Although many specific suggestions of assistance to the regular classroom teacher have been offered, some caution must be exercised so the child does not become so *special* that he becomes the "classroom pet." If this occurs because we have attempted to do too many special things for him, we have defeated the very purpose of an integrated program.

References and suggested readings

Alonso, L. "What the Teacher Can Do for the Child with Impaired Vision." *N. E. A. Journal,* November 1967, *56,* 42-43.

Barber, G. A. "Teaching the Blind: The Resource Room Approach." *Education,* February 1960, *80,* 333-336.

Barry, E. "Resource Program for the Visually Handicapped." *California Education,* May 1966, *3,* 6-8.

Bateman, B. "Sighted Children's Perceptions of Blind Children's Abilities." *Exceptional Children,* September 1962, *29,* 42-46.

Bruce, R. E. "Using the Overhead Projector with Visually Impaired Students." *Education of the Visually Handicapped,* May 1973, *5,* 43-46.

Buell, C. "Motor Performance of Visually Handicapped Children." Unpublished doctoral dissertation, 1950.

Buell, C. "Is Vigorous Physical Activity Feasible for Blind Children in Public Schools?" *Journal of Health, Physical Education, Recreation,* February 1969, *40,* 97-98.

Buell, C. "How to Include Blind and Partially Seeing Children in Public Secondary School Vigorous Physical Education." *Physical Education,* March 1972, *29,* 6-8.

Deahl, T., and Deahl, M. "Integrating Partially Sighted Children in the Classroom," *Instructor,* October 1973, *83,* 142-143.

Forman, E. "The Inclusion of Visually Limited and Blind Children in a Sighted Physical Education Program." *Education of the Visually Handicapped,* December 1969, 113-115.

Freund, C. "Teaching Art to the Blind Child Integrated with Sighted Children." *New Outlook for the Blind,* 1969, *63,* 205-210.

Haack, J. "The Visually Handicapped: In Your Classroom?" *Instructor,* March 1966, *75,* 62-64.

Hathaway, W. *Education and Health of the Partially Seeing Child,* New York: Columbia University Press, 1959.

Helping the Partially Seeing Child in the Regular Classroom. Pittsburgh, Pa.: Pittsburgh Branch of Pennsylvania Association for the Blind.

Hoffman, H. W. "Exceptional Child: 10 Ways to Help the Partially Sighted." *Teacher,* September 1972, *90,* 140-141.

Hulsey, S. "Blind Children Need Integration." *Times Educational Supplement,* November 9, 1973, 3050, 5.

Jacobson, I. "Getting Ready for Vision Screening." *Instructor,* October 1973, *83,* 143.

Johansen, G. "Integrating Visually Handicapped Children Into a Public Elementary School Physical Education Program." *Journal of Health, Physical Education, Recreation,* April 1971, *42,* 63-64.

Johnson, P. R. "Physical Education for Blind Children in Public Elementary Schools." *New Outlook for the Blind,* 1969, *63,* 264-271.

Johnson, Y. *A Blind Child Becomes a Member of Your Class.* New York: American Foundation for the Blind, 1961.

Jones, C. R. "Art for the Blind and Partially Seeing." *School Arts,* 1961, *60,* 21-22.

Jones, J. W., and Collins, A. P. "Trends in Program and Pupil Placement Practices in the Special Education of Visually Handicapped Children." *Education of the Blind,* 1965, *14,* 97-101.

Jose, R. T., and Rosenbloom, A. A., Jr. "The Role of the Low Vision Assistant In the Care of Visually Impaired Persons." *New Outlook for the Blind,* January 1975, *69,* 20-24.

Laufman, M. "Blind Children in Integrated Recreation." *New Outlook for the Blind,* 1962, *56,* 81-84.

Marsh, V., and Friedman, R. "Changing Public Attitudes Toward Blindness." *Exceptional Children,* January 1972, *38,* 426-428.

Moor, P. M. *A Blind Child, Too, Can Go to Nursery School.* New York: American Foundation for the Blind, 1952.

Morin, A. "Waukegan Finds Advantages in the Itinerant Teacher Plan." *Sight Saving Review,* Spring 1960, *30,* 33-35.

Napier, G., Kappan, D. L., Tuttle, D. W., Schrotberger, W. L., and Dennison, A. L. *Handbook for Teachers of the Visually Handicapped.* Louisville: American Printing House for the Blind, 1975.

National Society for the Prevention of Blindness. *Vocabulary of Terms Relating to the Eye,* Publication No. 172. New York: The Society, 1957.

Nezol, A. J. "Physical Education for Integrated Blind Students." *Education of the Visually Handicapped,* March 1972, *4,* 16-18.

Pelone, A. J. *Helping the Visually Handicapped Child in a Regular Class.* New York: Teachers College, Columbia University Press, 1957.

Poppelen, Van D. "Blind Triumph in a Seeing

School." *Arts and Activities,* April 1968, *63,* 21.

Randolph, L. G. "Don't Rearrange the Classroom! Why Not?" *Education of the Visually Handicapped,* October 1970, *2,* 83-86.

Scholl, G. *The Principal Works with the Visually Impaired.* Washington, D. C.: Council for Exceptional Children, 1968.

Skinner, D. "The Partially Sighted Child in the Regular Classroom." *Special Education— Canada,* March 1970, *44,* 26-28.

Stephens, T. M., and Birch, J. "Merits of Special Class, Resource, and Itinerant Plans for Teaching Partially Seeing Children." *Exceptional Children,* February 1969, *35,* 481-484.

Tait, P. E. "Believing Without Seeing: Teaching the Blind Child in a Regular Kindergarten."
Childhood Education, March 1974, *50,* 285-291.

Tonkovic, F. D. "An Approach to the Problem of Integrated Educaiton of Blind Children." *Education of the Blind,* May 1967, 115-119.

Trevena, T. M. "Integration of Sightless Children into Regular Physical Activities." *Journal of Health, Physical Education, Recreation,* June 1970, *41,* 42-43.

Winkley, W. M. "Public High School or Residential High School for Blind Students." *Education of the Visually Handicapped,* December 1972, *4,* 86-87.

"Workshop: Teaching Blind Children, First Take Them Out of Special Classes." *School Management,* September 1967, *2,* 15.

CHAPTER 5
Educational modifications and adaptations in education of the crippled and other health impaired

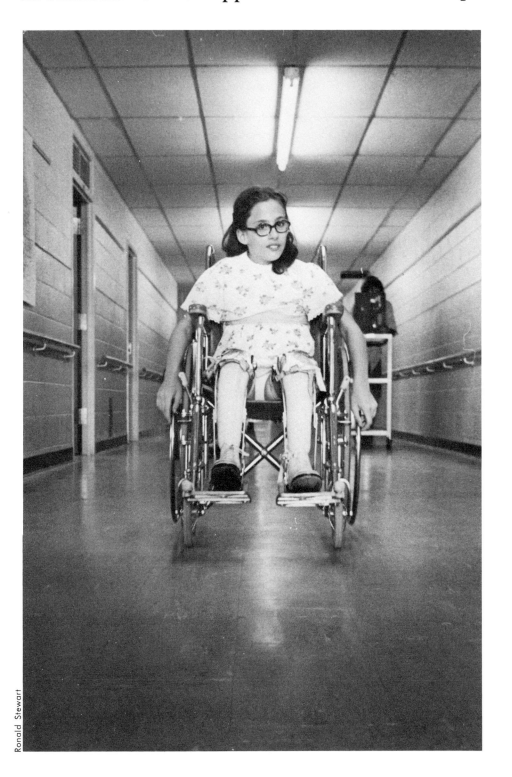

Ronald Stewart

Children with crippling conditions and other health impairments represent an extremely heterogeneous population. Children grouped under this broad category range from the cerebral palsied (a condition commonly associated with secondary or multiply-handicapping conditions) to the child with asthma and the child born without a limb. One child may have limited use of his arms but have good use of his legs, another may have use of all extremities but have considerable difficulty breathing, and another may be generally weak because of a progressive condition. One may be completely mobile in the classroom, another mobile with the use of crutches, or still another confined to a wheelchair.

MEDICAL AND TECHNOLOGICAL ADVANCES

Because of the diversity of problems presented by this population, a complete continuum of educational services must be offered ranging from full-time special-class placement, for the multihandicapped or severely physically disabled, to full-time regular-class placement for those able to function and achieve in that environment. Children who are temporarily disabled by infectious diseases or accidents may receive hospital or homebound instruction. The primary goal or direction of educational services should be the inclusion of these students in regular classrooms wherever possible. Today it is possible for more children to be educated in regular classes than in years past because of the reduction of architectural barriers. School buildings built around the turn of the century were typically multilevel buildings with many stairs and second story entrances whereas today's schools are generally one level and are much more accessible or adaptable for the child with limited mobility.

There are a number of other variables contributing to the increasing number of physically disabled students attending regular classes. One such factor is the changing nature of the population of children served. Because of advanced medical and techno-

logical procedures, many children are not as seriously disabled as children were thirty years ago with the same condition. For example, in the past, children born with a congenital heart defect were seriously disabled, generally for life, whereas today most of these defects are surgically corrected, and the child may live without serious restrictions. Changes in treatment procedures for conditions such as asthma, diabetes, and heart defects allow these children to participate in nearly all activities. Children are fitted with artificial limbs much earlier today than they were previously. Congenital defects such as club foot can generally be corrected early, and the child can participate fully in nearly all endeavors. Many of the children who might have attended special schools in years past are now attending regular public schools with minor modifications and adaptations.

The following information on disabilities and related adaptations is presented on the basis of medically derived or defined conditions. Although there are disadvantages to discussing a condition on the basis of medical diagnosis rather than educational implications, it is hoped that through this approach teachers will seek specific suggestions concerning educational procedures on the basis of a particular disability. For example, if a child has epilepsy, teachers are encouraged to seek information concerning the nature of the condition, the treatment procedures, educational implications, and the unique management techniques that must be employed.

As mentioned previously, this is an extremely heterogeneous population. There are more than two hundred possible conditions; however, we will discuss only the conditions most commonly found in regular classrooms. Discussion related to each condition will overview the nature of the condition, identification techniques (when appropriate), treatment procedures, and educational implications. This chapter is presented in a different format than other chapters in that educational implications are summarized after discussion of each condition rather than at the end of the chapter.

ALLERGIES

Nature of condition. An allergy is an adverse sensitivity or intolerance to a specific substance that may not be a problem to other individuals. When an allergic child comes in contact with the substance to which he is sensitive, he develops a reaction or an irritation. The reaction may take many forms, such as sneezing, watering eyes, runny nose, tiredness, itching, or a rash. The child may react to a number of different substances. Among the most common are inhalants (pollen, smoke, dust, and perfumes, for example), foods (eggs, chocolate, wheat, pork, strawberries, nuts, and citrus fruits, for example), infectious agents (bacteria and fungi, for example), substances which come in contact with the skin (poison ivy, poison sumac, fur, leather, animal hair, and dyes, for example), and drugs (vaccines, serums, and antibiotics, for example).

Treatment procedures. The first step is to determine the cause of the allergy. The medical doctor may prescribe medication for temporary relief; but generally, he will carefully study the child's medical history, home surroundings, eating habits, and so on to determine which allergens the child is sensitive to. He may conduct specific allergy tests such as skin tests on the arm or back to determine substances to which the child reacts. He may also suggest a series of shots to desensitize the child to a particular substance. The child with allergies can participate fully in nearly all educational programs. The teacher may, however, assist in identifying the specific sensitivity, particularly if the child seems to have more difficulty when at school. If an allergic reaction is suspected, this should be reported to the child's parents or school nurse, since treatment can do a great deal to ease the effects of the condition. In addition, there is a tendency for children with allergies to develop asthma, and this should be avoided if at all possible.

Educational implications. Although it is an entirely individual matter, some children with allergies may fatigue more easily while participating in physical activities. As a result, they may withdraw during recess or physical education while their classmates continue. This must be observed very carefully since withdrawal may have serious social and emotional resultants. Since physical fitness is an important component of treatment, the teacher may assist by modifying or adapting the activity so that the child is encouraged to participate as much as possible. The teacher should also carefully observe to see if there is any change in the child's condition as a result of activity and report this information to the parents or physician. The child must learn how to live with the limitations caused by allergies and develop a life-style that allows him a maximum amount of freedom.

ASTHMA

Nature of condition. Asthma, like allergies, usually results from an allergic state that causes an obstruction of the bronchial tubes or lungs, or both. When the suspected sensitivity flares into an attack, an excessive amount of mucus is produced, and there is a spasm of the bronchial musculature. As a result, breathing becomes unusually difficult during an attack, and the child may lose his color, wheeze, and perspire excessively. The attack may last for a few minutes, for hours, or for days.

An asthmatic attack can be a most frightening experience because of the labored breathing and other behaviors. The attack may be brought on by a specific sensitivity to an allergen, exposure to excessive physical activity, or possibly by an emotional reaction. The influence of emotional factors is not well established. Some authorities believe that the emotional environment plays an important role in asthma, whereas others believe there is little or no relationship.

Treatment procedures. Treatment procedures are similar to those employed in treating allergic individuals. Adrenalin administered by injection or by inhalation usually gives relief for brief periods; however, since asthma is a chronic condition, long-term treatment procedures must be employed.

Educational implications. An important consideration is the need to treat the child as normally as possible. Caution must be exercised to avoid overprotection from routine classroom activities. If care is not practiced, the child may become an asthmatic or emotional cripple. The teacher should be aware of the factors that precipitate an asthmatic attack and have information concerning the proper course of action should an attack occur. The teacher should also be aware of possible side effects or behavioral changes that may be related to prescribed drugs being used by the child. Teachers are in a unique position to observe the child during a variety of activities throughout the entire school day. Information provided by the teacher may be very helpful to the parents or the physician in determining subsequent treatment procedures.

There has been research recently concerning the extent to which asthmatic children should participate in physical activities. In years past, it was believed that these children should be excluded from physical education or physically exerting activities. The results of this research has clearly indicated that there are many beneficial effects of exercise and activity in relationship to long-term care and treatment (Seligman, Randel, and Stevens, 1970; Scherr and Charleston, 1958). Many of the limitations formerly placed on these children may have done more harm than good. Generally, the child will regulate himself—if he runs too long, he may start wheezing and naturally will then rest. Physical restrictions may have adverse psychological effects, which are as great a danger as the physical problem itself. A good general rule to follow with any of the health impairments, including asthma, is to check with the parents or physician to determine more specifically what the child can and cannot do.

ARTHRITIS

Nature of condition. Although arthritis is primarily a condition that occurs in adults, it can begin at any age. The most common form of arthritis in children is called *juvenile rheumatoid arthritis.* It may have a very sudden onset, or it may be a slow, gradual disease, with its effects and complications generally quite variable. In some instances it may only last a few weeks or months and not seriously limit the child. In other cases it may be a chronic condition that continues throughout the child's life, becoming worse as time goes on.

Osteoarthritis, or the wear-and-tear type of arthritis, generally is confined to one joint and does not affect the whole body. Rheumatoid arthritis also attacks the joints of the body, but in addition it may involve many organs, such as the heart, liver, and spleen. There may also be skin rash, inflammation of the eyes, possible retardation of growth, and swelling and pain in the fingers, wrists, elbows, knees, hips, and feet. As the disease progresses, the joints may stiffen, making movement very difficult and painful.

Treatment procedures. The major aim of treatment is to allow the child to live as normally as possible. Many times children with arthritis become "care-cripples." In other words, they are overprotected and not allowed to participate fully in the activities of home or school. Juvenile arthritis is self-limiting, and the child will ordinarily use good sense in determining whether he should participate in an activity.

Treatment procedures are generally highly individualized because no two cases are exactly alike. Because of the variance between patients and their individual response to drugs, the drugs prescribed by the doctor may be different in each case. Generally, aspirin is the single most effective drug used in the treatment of arthritis because it reduces pain and inflammation of the joints and is among the safest drugs on the market. Usually, large amounts are prescribed on a routine basis, and dosage must be continued even after the swelling and pain have subsided. Special exercises may be prescribed on a routine basis and will involve putting the joints through a full range of motion to prevent joint deformity and loss of strength in the muscles. Heat treatments may also be prescribed to enable joints to move more smoothly and with less pain. Heat treatments take a variety of forms and may be carried out at home or in a clinic. Surgical procedures are also used to prevent and correct deformity caused by this disease. For some children, splints, braces, or plaster casts are prescribed to subdue inflammation and protect the joint or joints from becoming frozen.

Educational implications. The educational modifications necessary for the child with juvenile arthritis will depend on his age, severity of condition, independent travel ability, and range of motion in the arms, hands, and fingers. This child probably will not need special curricular methods or materials in the academic areas. However, if the joints in his upper extremities are severely involved, he may need writing aids, adapted paper, or special pencils. It is more likely, however, that he will have the most difficulty in traveling since the knees, ankles, and hips may be more involved, and as he travels he may experience considerable pain. As a result, it may be well to consider somewhat limited movement. This, of course, depends on the individual child, since many children will not experience this difficulty to any great extent. Some children may need an individualized physical education program or a program carried out by a physical therapist, whereas others may need very little modification in their physical education program.

Teachers should watch for any changes in vision, since eye disease is commonly associated with rheumatoid arthritis. The child should be checked by a medical eye doctor at least every six to nine months.

Although it is not certain, there does seem to be some evidence that emotional stress is related to attacks of arthritis (Abruzze, 1971; Cobb and Stanislav, 1966; Decker, 1967). This does not imply that the teacher should modify academic and social standards but does dictate awareness of the general emotional climate and its possible effects on the child.

The teacher should be aware of other implications common to the arthritic child. For example, the child may miss a considerable amount of school when he has attacks. Faulty posture habits should be avoided, since good body alignment and posture are important in reducing the effects of arthritis. Activities such as extensive and prolonged writing may need to be avoided because it may be painful for the student. It may also be necessary to give the child extra time to get to and from classrooms and extra time for completing assignments.

The child must learn to live with arthritis and accept the limitations imposed by it. An understanding teacher can do a great deal to assist the child in living with this condition.

AMPUTATION

Nature of condition. An amputation may be congenital, acquired as a result of trauma, or elective as a result of disease or infection. In nearly all instances, the child will be fitted with an artificial arm or leg (prosthesis). Generally, the child with a congenital amputation will be fitted with the prosthesis very early and will have adapted to it by the time he begins school. The prosthesis may be made of wood, metal, or plastic. Plastic materials are being used with greater frequency today because they are light; this is a factor that may influence the child's functioning.

Educational implications. Children with a prosthesis are usually able to function at nearly normal capacity and will require very little educational modification. The extent of modifications, however, depends on the age of the child, the site of the amputation (the higher on the extremity, the more severe), and the child's adjustment to the disability.

There are a few factors of which the regular classroom teacher should be aware to ensure the best educational programming. The following suggestions should be considered:

1. Because of growth, a child's prosthesis will rarely fit for more than one year. As a result, the teacher must be certain the child is using the prosthesis effectively and that it fits properly. The child will visit the brace shop for routine adjustments and fitting.
2. The teacher should have general informa-

tion, particularly for a younger child, concerning the basic mechanics, proper fitting, and maintenance of the prosthesis. This information may be obtained from the child, the child's parents, the resource/itinerant teacher, or by visiting a brace shop. If the child feels comfortable in discussing his prosthesis, it would be of great social value for him to explain its function to the entire class. Of course, this depends on the age of the other children and the extent to which the child has adjusted to the amputation.

3. Proper exercise is very important for the child, particularly in the joints around the amputation. Physical education activities and games may be adapted or individualized for this child to ensure maximum fitness and exercise. It is not uncommon to read or hear about individuals with amputations who not only participate, but excel, in competitive athletic events. Many individuals with lower extremity amputations participate and compete successfully in activities such as bowling, snow and water skiing, golf, and even football.

4. Postural habits must be carefully observed to ensure that the child does not develop spinal curvatures such as scoliosis (lateral curvature of the spine resulting in a C-shaped curve). The child may develop unilateral habits such as using only one side of his body, causing postural problems. Postural problems can limit his body mechanics and general functioning. If the child has a lower extremity amputation, the teacher must observe to see that unusual gait or ambulation problems do not develop.

5. Proper hygienic principles must be exercised in the care of the stump. It should be kept clean and allowed to air for brief periods. Although these practices will typically be conducted at home, the teacher should be aware of this need.

6. Some children with amputations may use modified or adapted equipment such as pencil holders, page turners, or other reading and writing aids. Many of these ma-terials are available from commercial sources, others may be easily adapted or made by the teacher. The resource/itinerant teacher may be of assistance in modifying materials and equipment.

7. Curricular modifications may also be necessary. For example, typing may be taught using a one-handed method with very little modification. A book of instructions, which may be read by both the child and the typing instructor, is available from Southwestern Publishing Company in San Francisco entitled *Type With One Hand,* by Nina K. Richardson. The resource/itinerant teacher should have information concerning this type of material. The occupational therapist is a valuable resource person and should be consulted when questions arise. The occupational therapist can assist in modifying equipment and materials and can plan and initiate activities that will facilitate the child's maximum functioning. Amputations in children are generally not as severe as in adults because they are more tolerant and adaptable. They generally can participate in regular classrooms very successfully, with only minor modifications and adaptations.

DIABETES

Nature of the condition. Diabetes is a metabolic disorder wherein the individual's body is unable to utilize and properly store sugar. This condition is a result of the inability of the pancreas to produce a sufficient amount of the hormone *insulin.*

Although diabetes is most frequently seen in adults, it does occur in children and can become a serious problem if the proper treatment procedures are not adhered to. There are a number of symptoms classroom teachers should be aware of that may indicate diabetes. They are unusually frequent urination, abnormal thirst, extreme hunger, changes in weight (generally a rapid loss), drowsiness, general weakness, possible visual disturbances, and skin infections such as boils or itching. If a child indicates any of these symptoms, be certain to contact your school nurse and the child's parents as soon as possible. Prompt medical diagnosis and treatment are essential in the care of the diabetic child.

Treatment procedures. If diabetes is diagnosed, treatment procedures will probably involve daily injections of insulin, adherence to a rather strict diet to maintain the correct sugar level, and a balance between the right amounts of exercise and rest. The key to the treatment of diabetes is to maintain a regulation of medication, diet, and rest and activity. Generally, children with diabetes can have a happy childhood and adolescence, and can do almost everything their peers do except they may not fill up on sweets and must maintain a balance between the previously mentioned variables.

To most of us, the thought of daily injections seems like a serious proposition, but to the child with diabetes this will become a very routine matter. The injections are generally administered at home and become as routine as other hygienic practices such as bathing or brushing teeth. Often the child and his parents will attend a clinic that will teach them how to manage daily activities such as injections, diet, exercise, care of the feet (this can be a definite problem because of poor circulation), and necessary changes in life style to accommodate the condition. As a result of these clinics, the child will know a great deal about his condition and will know how to manage it.

Educational implications. There are several potential problems the classroom teacher should be aware of, such as an insulin reaction (hypoglycemia) and diabetic coma. The child may have an insulin reaction resulting from anything that may increase his metabolism rate, such as too much exercise, too much insulin, not enough food, or nervous tension. It may occur anytime during the day but most often occurs before meals or after strenuous exercise. The insulin reaction may follow a stereotyped pattern for each individual, so be certain to consult with the child or his parents to determine what these signs may be. Often, general irritability may be the first sign. One child may be despondent, cry readily, whereas another may be exuberant

or belligerent. The child may be hungry, perspire excessively, tremble, be unable to concentrate, and complain of being dizzy. These symptoms may vary in duration and will often disappear after providing the child with any of the following: sugar cube, pop, candy, raisins, fruit juice with sugar, or any other carbohydrate. Generally the symptoms will disappear after ten to fifteen minutes. If they do not, call the child's parents or physician.

The opposite of an insulin reaction is a diabetic coma. Although fairly rare, it does occur and can be serious if not treated immediately. A diabetic coma is the result of failure to take insulin, an illness, or neglect of proper diet. In this instance the child has too much sugar and must have an injection as soon as possible. Generally it is slow in onset, and the following symptoms may be observed: thirst, frequent urination, flushed face, labored breathing, nausea, and vomiting. Report to the parents, school nurse, or child's physician as soon as possible. Treatment will involve rest, injection of insulin, and possible hospitalization. The symptoms of diabetic coma and insulin reaction are indicated on the following chart:

	Insulin reaction	Diabetic coma
How it occurs	Rapidly	Slowly
Appearance of skin	Pale, moist	Flushed, dry
Breathing	Normal to rapid, shallow	Deep, labored
Vomiting	Absent	Present
Hunger	Present	Absent
Tongue	Moist	Dry
Thirst	Absent	Present
What teacher should do	Give carbohydrate (such as pop, sugar cube, candy, and raisins)	Keep child warm, resting; call parents, nurse, doctor
Nature of problem	Too much insulin	Too little insulin

There are several additional factors that should be considered:

1. Check with child's parents to see if he should have a midmorning snack. If so,

help him be as inconspicuous as possible about it. It may also be advisable to schedule the child for an early lunch period if it is possible.

2. Very active or strenuous physical activities might be avoided immediately before lunch.
3. Keep candy, raisins, or sugar handy in case the child needs them.
4. Be certain to inform special or substitute teachers that there is a child in the class with diabetes and indicate what they should do in case of insulin reaction or a coma.
5. Above all else, do not panic about having a child with diabetes; proceed calmly with the necessary steps if he has an insulin reaction or goes into a coma. For the vast majority of the time, he may be treated like any other child in the class.

The child must learn to live with his condition and to accept the limitations imposed by it. He must develop a life-style that will allow him the greatest possible freedom and still maintain a balance between diet, rest and activity, and medication.

EPILEPSY

Nature of condition. Epilepsy is not a disease in itself, but it is a sign or a symptom of some underlying disorder in the nervous system. Seizures may occur at any age, in any race, in both sexes, and in any individual. Approximately seventy-five percent of all epileptic seizures begin before the age of 25. Epilepsy occurs in one out of every fifty children.

Convulsions, or seizures, are the main symptoms in all types of epilepsy. The seizures occur when there are excessive electrical discharges released in some nerve cells of the brain. When this happens, the brain cannot function properly for a short time, and it loses control over muscles, consciousness, senses, and thoughts. The loss of these functions is only temporary, and the cells work properly between seizures. The most common types of seizures are (1) grand mal, (2) petit mal, and (3) psychomotor or temporal lobe.

Grand mal seizures are the most severe form. When a grand mal occurs the individual loses consciousness, falls, and has general convulsive movements. Breathing may be very labored, the child may produce a gurgling sound or may shout, and saliva may escape from the lips. The seizure may last for several minutes, and afterwards the individual may be confused or drowsy. He will not recall what happened or what was said to him during the seizure, and he may be very tired and want to sleep for a short time.

Petit mal seizures are generally short in duration, lasting from five to twenty seconds. They are most common in children and can occur as often as one hundred times a day. Often this child may be accused of being a daydreamer because he will lose contact with what is happening in the classroom during the seizure. The child may become pale, he may stare into space, his eyelids may twitch, or he may demonstrate slight jerky movements. After the seizure the child will continue with his activities almost as though nothing had happened, because he probably will not be aware that he had a seizure. Petit mal seizures have a tendency to disappear before or near puberty, but may be replaced by other types such as grand mal.

Psychomotor or *temporal lobe* seizures are the most complex because they not only affect the motor system but also affect the mental process as well. The seizure may last from a few minutes to several hours. During the seizure the individual may chew or smack his lips or appear to be confused. In some instances, the individual may carry out purposeless activities such as rubbing arms or legs, may walk, and may pick at or take off clothing. Some individuals may experience fear, anger, or rage. After the seizure they will probably not remember what happened and will want to sleep.

Identification. It is not difficult to identify the child who has grand mal seizures; however, teachers should be watchful for a number of other signs that may indicate petit mal or psychomotor epilepsy. Watch for repeated occurrences of two or more of the following signs: (1) head dropping, (2) daydreaming or lack of attentiveness, (3) slight jerky movements of arms or shoulders (ticlike movements), (4) eyes rolling upward or twitching, (5) chewing or swallowing movements, (6) rhythmic movements of the head, and (7) purposeless body movements or sounds. If any combination of these signs is observed, be certain that the school nurse and the child's parents are contacted to ensure that a proper medical examination is obtained. There is no cure for epilepsy, but seizures can be controlled through the use of anticonvulsant medication. Every effort should be made to seek the proper medical services for the child suspected of having epilepsy.

What to do if a child has a grand mal seizure. As mentioned previously, there are many misconceptions concerning epilepsy including the presumption of mental retardation, brain injury, or insanity. But there is a greater amount of misinformation about what should be done when an individual has a grand mal seizure. A grand mal seizure can be a frightening experience for the teacher unless she is well prepared and knows exactly what to do. The Epilepsy Foundation of America suggests that the following steps be taken in the event of a grand mal seizure:

1. Remain calm. Students will assume the same emotional reaction as their teacher. *The seizure itself is painless to the child.*
2. Do not try to restrain the child. Nothing can be done to stop a seizure once it has begun. It must run its course.
3. Clear the area around the student so that he does not injure himself on hard objects. Try not to interfere with his movements in any way.
4. Do not force anything between his teeth. If his mouth is already open, a soft object like a handkerchief may be placed between his side teeth.
5. It generally is not necessary to call a doctor unless the attack is immediately followed by another major seizure or if the seizure lasts more than ten minutes.
6. When the seizure is over, let the child rest if he needs to.
7. The child's parents and physician should be informed of the seizure.
8. Turn the incident into a learning experience for the entire class. Explain what a seizure is, that it is not contagious, and that it is nothing to be afraid of. Teach the class understanding toward the child —not pity, so that his classmates will continue to accept him as "one of the gang."

After the seizure and short rest, the child can generally carry on routinely. The way in which the teacher and the students react to the seizure is very important. If the teacher over-reacts, it can have a very negative effect on the child with epilepsy and on other children in the class. However, if the teacher has prepared and informed the students concerning what to do in the event of a seizure, a potentially traumatic and upsetting experience can be a routine matter.

Educational implications. Of the three most common types, it is difficult to establish which can cause the most severe educational problems. It is generally thought, however, that grand mal is probably the most serious because of possible bodily injury, and because it is so widely misunderstood. Petit mal seizures can seriously limit the child's achievement because he may miss a great deal of the material being covered during a seizure and the possibility of being labeled a behavior problem. Although psychomotor seizures are relatively uncommon in children, they too would impose serious limitations on school achievement and adjustment. It must be recognized that all three are serious, and minor modifications and adjustments may need to be made to accommodate the child with any of these conditions.

Special curricular modifications are not necessary for students with epilepsy. Their academic program and materials will be the same. However, there are several factors that should be taken into consideration by the teacher. The extent to which a student's seizures are controlled will determine the extent to which the following factors and suggestions should be considered. If the seizures have been controlled for several years, it will not be necessary to make many special provisions. However, if the seizures are not well controlled or if epilepsy has only recently been diagnosed, many of these factors will assume additional importance:

1. One of the most important considerations is to treat the student with epilepsy the same as the other students. The teacher's open mindedness and candor concerning the nature of the condition and the way she reacts during and after a seizure will determine how the other students react.
2. The teacher may want to discuss the condition with the student to obtain more complete information concerning how he feels about the condition, the extent of seizure control, and any individual aspects that need to be considered.
3. If the student takes medication for the control of seizures during the day, the teacher should participate by seeing that he gets it. The teacher may also be asked to carefully observe and record the child's behavior in regard to his reactions to the medication.
4. The teacher should not lower the level of expectation or set up protective devices that would single out the child with epilepsy. This must be avoided if the child is to develop a feeling of self-worth and a healthy personality.
5. School personnel, including other teachers, should be oriented to the nature of epilepsy and procedures employed in the event of a seizure.
6. In general, the student with epilepsy can participate in nearly all school activities. There are, however, some activities that probably should be avoided. Contact sports (boxing and football), which may result in head injury, and rope climbing or activities involving excessive fatigue should be avoided. It is also recommended that the student with epilepsy not swim alone because of the possibility of a seizure. It is difficult to generalize about activities in which a student should not participate because it is a very individual matter. The students' parents and physician should be consulted to determine which activities should be avoided.

7. Free information is available from the Epilepsy Foundation of America.* Their materials will assist all school personnel and students in becoming oriented to epilepsy.
8. Using materials from a national agency will familiarize the class with procedures that should be employed in the event of a seizure. Students can be assigned specific responsibilities so that care of the student with epilepsy is a routine matter. If the classroom is prepared for seizures, it may not be a disturbing experience.

CEREBRAL PALSY

Nature of condition. Cerebral palsy is not a progressive disease but a group of conditions that may seriously limit motor coordination. Of the serious crippling conditions cerebral palsy is the most common. Several years ago, polio was the number one crippling condition; today, cerebral palsy has replaced it. Cerebral palsy is most frequently present at birth, but it may be acquired anytime as the result of a head injury or an infectious disease, for example. It is characterized by varying degrees of disturbance of voluntary movements due to brain injury. Since there may be varying degrees of brain injury, the majority of these children will have multiple handicapping conditions, such as hearing impairments, visual difficulties, language disorders, and speech problems. By nature of the severity of this condition many cerebral palsied children will attend special schools or special classes, which provide the comprehensive educational and therapeutic services needed. There are, however, a number of children with mild or moderate cerebral palsy

---

*The Epilepsy Foundation of America has a program entitled "School Alert," which presents a basic educational program for classroom teachers, school nurses, and others in recognizing epilepsy and techniques of management in the school and classroom. The program provides educational materials, literature, posters, and other aids that can be adapted for a variety of age levels and situations. Write to: Epilepsy Foundation of America, 1828 L. St., N.W., Washington, D. C. 20036. A listing of agencies concerned with crippled and other health impaired appears in Appendix C.

who may attend regular classes for part or all of their school day.

The two most common types of cerebral palsy are *spastic* and *athetoid*. Spastic cerebral palsy is characterized by jerky or explosive motions when the child initiates a voluntary movement. For example, in a severe type, if the student was asked to draw a line from one point to another he may demonstrate erratic or jerky movements such as

The child with athetosis would also have difficulty with voluntary movements, but controlling the movement in the desired direction is an added problem. In other words, this child would demonstrate extra or purposeless movements. In drawing a line from one point to another, he may have considerable uncontrolled movement, such as

Educational implications. The degree of involvement and severity of the condition may vary considerably; therefore, a full continuum of educational services is needed. The severity will dictate where the child would best be served, but the emphasis should be placed on providing as "normal" an educational environment as possible. Wherever practicable, students with cerebral palsy should attend regular classes with their nondisabled peers. Classroom modifications will vary according to the individual needs of the child. Some will need no modifications, whereas others may need some minor adjustments.

Often an interdisciplinary approach is required in the care and treatment of the cerebral palsied. It may be necessary for some children to be served on a routine and continued basis by a physical, occupational, or speech therapist or a combination of these. If these therapies are initiated early, they may not be needed as frequently during the upper elementary and secondary school years. Therapy sessions may be attended during the school day or after school hours.

The physical therapist will probably direct attention to posture, movements, and the prevention of contractures (muscle shortening because of lack of neurostimulation and muscle use). It is necessary for the regular teacher to have a basic understanding of treatment procedures so that she may reinforce desirable movements and postural habits. The occupational therapist will primarily be concerned with activities such as buttoning, tying shoes, eating, or any of the routine activities required in our daily lives. Many of these routine activities may be seriously limited because of the lack of muscle coordination. It is important that the regular teacher have information concerning the skills being taught so that she may reinforce them in her classroom. Often the occupational therapist may assist in modifying and adapting educational materials to be used by the cerebral palsied student. The services offered by the speech therapist will also need to be reinforced by the teacher to ensure carry-over and maintenance of desired speech habits.

If the child with cerebral palsy is placed in the proper educational program, it should not be necessary to offer a curriculum different from his peers; however, it may be necessary to modify or adapt materials and equipment so that he may participate more fully in classroom activities. The extent of the modifications necessary will vary considerably. For example, some students may have limited use of their hands and arms but may have no difficulty getting around. As a result of the variance between individuals, it is difficult to offer specific suggestions. The following materials and equipment are provided as examples of ways that modifications may be made:

1. Pencil holders made of clay, Styrofoam balls, or plastic golf balls may be helpful for children with fine motor coordination difficulties.
2. Adapted typewriters may be useful for the child with fine motor coordination difficulties or the child with very weak muscles. A keyboard guard placed over the keys may be necessary for the child with uncontrolled or gross movements. A pencil, rather than the fingers, may be used to strike the keys if the involvement is very serious.

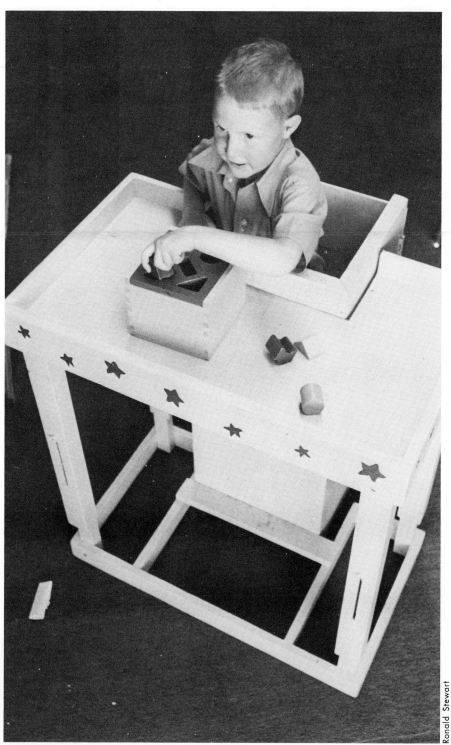

3. Page turners are useful for children with limited arm use. The turner may be attached to the head, elbow, or hand.
4. Weights (such as a small sandbag or bar bells) placed on the wrist or hand are used to eliminate random or uncontrolled movements.
5. Book holders that can be adjusted to any angle may be helpful for some children.
6. Paper holders may be necessary for children who have the use of only one arm or very limited use of both arms. A clipboard to hold the paper in position may be fastened to the desk, or a piece of unbleached muslin cloth may be attached to the desk and sprayed with a nonskid fluid.
7. Stand up tables are necessary for many children with cerebral palsy. Since a considerable amount of time is spent sitting, provisions should be made to allow them to stand for parts of the school day. This is needed to prevent muscle contractures, provide proper circulation, and maintain desired postural habits. Since standing unaided may be difficult, a stand-up table may be purchased or built inexpensively to provide the needed support while the student is standing. An individual standing table should be of a basic design with a tray for a work area approximately two feet square. A base of the same size should be used to avoid tipping over. The height of the table may be changed by raising or lowering the foot platform.

These are only a few of the modifications and adaptations that may be made. It is essential that the teacher remain open and flexible in trying a variety of aids to meet the unique needs of the child with cerebral palsy. The teacher will not have to modify and adapt materials and equipment alone since the therapists and resource/itinerant teacher will provide assistance when needed.

One of the most important factors to be considered by the regular teacher is that this child should be accepted as an individual. It is important to allow the child to carry out his own tasks. It may take him considerably longer than the other students to complete an assignment, because of the motor involvement, but he must be allowed to complete it independently.

SPINA BIFIDA

Nature of condition. Spina bifida is a serious birth defect in which the bones of the spine failed to close during the twelfth week of fetal development. As a result, a cyst or sack is present in the area of the lower back when the child is born. This protrusion is generally surgically treated during the child's first 24 to 48 hours of life. The extent of the disability resulting from this condition varies enormously. Some will have little or no disability, whereas others have varying degrees of paralysis of the legs and incontinence (lack of bowel and bladder control). In addition to the degrees of paralysis and incontinence, the child may have impaired autonomic nervous system functioning (absence of perspiration) and absence of sensation or feeling below the level of the spinal defect. In some respects this condition is similar to other crippling conditions that cause degrees of paralysis in the legs, but it is complicated by the lack of bowel and bladder control. Due to the deficiency of nerve fibers, the child may not be able to tell when his bladder is full. The bladder may overflow, and the child may not be aware of the situation until he sees the wetness through his outer clothing. There is a threat of infection from residual urine in the bladder, and the child may also have difficulty with bowel control.

There are surgical procedures that can assist in accommodating this condition, or artificial devices may be worn to collect the urine. The child may also regulate his fluid intake and adhere to a systematic voiding schedule. Generally, the child will be able to take care of his toileting needs, but younger children may need some assistance from a classroom aide, volunteer, parent, or resource/itinerant teacher.

Educational implications. It is important for the teacher to work in close harmony with medical personnel and especially the school nurse to ensure proper health care. The teacher must also maintain a close working relationship with physical and occupational therapists to meet the child's ambulation needs and activities of daily living. Last, but certainly not least, the teacher must implement and maintain an extremely close working relationship with the parents, especially concerning prescribed toilet-training programs. The teacher should be watchful for signs of urinary infection. Infections can generally be avoided with proper care, but in the event of infection the child may have to be hospitalized, necessitating absence from school. A flexible scheduling procedure providing specific times for toileting needs should be implemented.

Teachers should be alert for the presence of skin or pressure sores. Because of the lack of sensation in the legs, the sores often will not be noticed by the child. Problems imposed by wearing braces or using a wheelchair should also be considered. It may be necessary to reposition the child during the school day to prevent these problems and associated contractures.

If not handled properly, the psychosocial limitations imposed by this condition can be very serious. While this may seem to be a trivial matter, it is a very real concern expressed by many spina bifida children. The child may the brunt of other children's laughter or joking because of odor or an "accident." It is suggested that the teacher consider explaining, in a most factual manner, the limitations and problems associated with spina bifida to the other children.

The problems imposed by poor ambulation skills must be taken into consideration by therapists and teachers. However, this factor would not be any more significant for the child with spina bifida than for the child with cerebral palsy or any other major crippling condition.

Inasmuch as the child with spina bifida has good use of his upper body, arms, and hands, the educational modifications necessary are minimal. These children are capable of profiting from regular classroom attendance and instruction with only minor modifications and adaptations.

MUSCULAR DYSTROPHY

Nature of condition. This is a progressive condition in which the muscles are replaced by a fatty tissue. Although there are several types, the most common and most serious type, Duchenne, occurs in children. Duchenne, or childhood muscular dystrophy, is generally a fatal disease characterized by a slow deterioration of the voluntary muscles ending in a complete state of helplessness.

The age at onset is generally between the child's first and sixth year and rarely occurs after the child's first decade of life. Early signs of the condition include a tendency to fall easily, clumsiness in walking, difficulty in climbing stairs, and difficulty in rising from the floor. There is a steady progressive decline in the child's ability to walk. He falls more frequently and eventually will need crutches to move about. As he continues to lose his strength it will be necessary to move from crutches to a wheelchair. Later, nearly all large muscles will be involved and he will be bedridden. During the later stages, he may be unable to raise his arms, sit erect, or hold his head up. Fortunately, the small muscles of the hands and fingers maintain some strength even during the most advanced stages.

Educational implications. The regular classroom offers obvious educational advantages as compared to a school or special class for children with crippling or health impairments. In addition to the educational advantages, there are many recreational and social factors offered by regular school attendance. During the early stages, very few modifications and adaptations will be necessary, but as the condition progresses there will be need for some modifications. Eventually, the student may not be able to attend any educational program and will have to receive homebound instruction; however, every effort should be made to maintain the student with muscular dystrophy in regular classrooms as long as possible.

Muscular dystrophy imposes a set of contradictions. On one hand, it is known that it is generally fatal, and on the other, we ask the student, his parents, teachers, and others to carry on as though he were going to live a rich and full life. This apparent contradiction must be dealt with, and guidance and counseling services can do a great deal to accommodate the acceptance of this conflict. There is little question that if the child and parents are to accept this contradiction, ongoing counseling must be offered. Counseling programs should be conducted in cooperation with the child's parents, brothers and sisters, therapists, teachers, and physicians.

It is important that the student attend adapted physical education classes and maintain a balance between diet, activity, and rest since there is a tendency for the child to become overweight. He should be encouraged to participate as fully as possible in recreational and physical activities. Although the effects of the condition cannot be stopped by physical activity, there is some indication that it may assist in delaying some of the debilitative effects. Some caution must be exercised, however, as the child may become very easily fatigued. He should be allowed intermittent periods of rest as needed.

Several studies have been conducted to determine if mental retardation is associated with muscular dystrophy. There have been no indications that there is a greater incidence of mental retardation in children with muscular dystrophy than in the population as a whole. A large number of research studies have also attempted to identify particular personality characteristics that might be associated with muscular dystrophy. Though some researchers have found personality patterns unique to these students, others have not been able to do so; therefore, it is reasonable to assume that differences in personality may be attributed to something other than the muscular dystrophy. If there is no mental retardation or particular personality configuration that may be associated with muscular dystrophy, then achievement and adjustment in school should be similar to that of other students. Perhaps the most important role of the teacher is to stimulate these students

academically, recreationally, and socially as much as possible without making exceptions and by expecting the same of these students as others.

PURPOSE, CARE, AND MAINTENANCE OF BRACES, CRUTCHES, AND WHEELCHAIRS

Many children with cerebral palsy, spina bifida, muscular dystrophy, and other crippling conditions will need braces, crutches, or wheelchairs; therefore, the regular teacher should be acquainted with the purpose, care, and maintenance of this equipment. Generally, braces are classified into three general types: (1) corrective, (2) control, and (3) supportive. Corrective braces are used for prevention and correction of deformity during the child's rapid growth period. Often during this period the tendons (cords that attach muscles to bones) do not keep pace with the growth of the long bones. When this happens the heel cords may tighten, and surgery may be required to lengthen them to keep up with the long bone growth. Corrective braces may prevent or delay this surgery. Control braces are used to prevent or eliminate much of the purposeless movement, particularly in the child with athetoid cerebral palsy, or to allow movement in only one or two desired directions. Support braces are used to provide the needed support for the child who needs assistance in standing. Some children will wear braces for only a short time, whereas others will need them for many years and perhaps their entire lives.

It will not be the primary responsibility of the regular classroom teacher to take care of or maintain this equipment. She will be assisted by the therapists, resource/itinerant teacher, and the child's parents; however, she may have more contact with the child than the others and may be able to spot-check it periodically. For example, the teacher should be watchful for torn or worn leather pieces and should check to see that the brace is not rubbing against the body causing pressure sores to develop. She may also want to check periodically for loose or missing screws

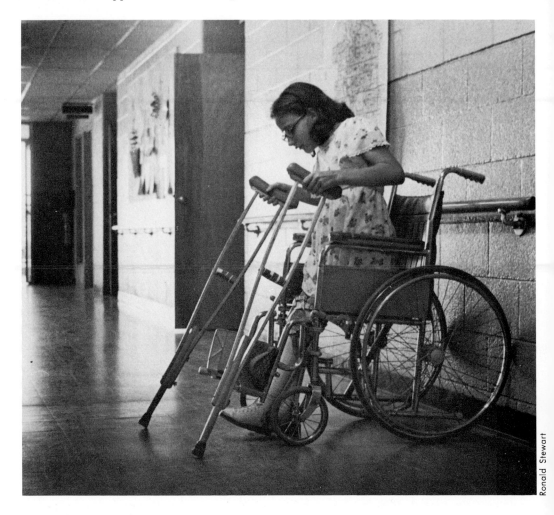

Ronald Stewart

and the general condition of buckles, locks, and joints.

Crutches are used to stabilize the trunk and to provide needed support while standing and walking. Generally, crutches do not call for a great deal of care or maintenance but should be checked periodically for loose screws, worn rubber tips, and proper height adjustments.

Wheelchairs are most frequently used by children with severe crippling conditions, but it is possible that some children who attend regular classes may need a wheelchair for part or all of their school day. This may be necessary because of slowness, fatigue, or lack of independent travel skills. Wheelchairs must also be checked periodically for worn or broken parts, and the teacher should be aware of posture, fit, and comfort of the child. If the teacher notices any equipment in need of repair, she should immediately report it to the child's therapist, resource/ itinerant teacher, or parents.

In the preceding pages we have discussed the most common crippling and other health impairments that may be found in regular classrooms and that may require modifications and adaptations of curriculum or materials. We have not discussed all of the possible conditions because many will require no modifications. The following are some of the most common not requiring extensive modifications:

Congenital dislocation of the hip
Cystic fibrosis
Club foot
Heart defects
Hemophilia

Hip disorders
Multiple sclerosis
Nephrosis
Osteomyelitis
Poliomyelitis
Tuberculosis

ROLE AND RESPONSIBILITY OF RESOURCE/ITINERANT PERSONNEL

The role and responsibility of resource/ itinerant personnel is extremely varied depending on the age of the students, number of students served, number of schools, distance between schools, and the type and severity of crippling and other health impairments. The resource/itinerant teacher must have a very good understanding of the nature of the condition, the limitations imposed by the condition, the medical and therapeutic treatment procedures employed, the influence of psychosocial limitations, and a knowledge of equipment and materials used by or modified for the child with a crippling condition or health impairment.

The following roles and responsibilities are typical of resource/itinerant teachers:

1. Assume responsibility for coordination of referrals from teachers, administrators, and school health personnel. Coordinate initial information on the child's readiness to attend an integrated program. Assist in program planning and staffing. If the staffing team suggests regular classroom placement, the resource/itinerant teacher will begin specific planning to determine the best possible school and teacher or teachers, transportation, and availability of therapies.

2. Coordinate information between medical agencies, therapeutic services, parents, and teachers. Often the resource/itinerant teacher serves as the liaison between the agencies serving the child and regular teachers and parents. For example, medical services may make specific suggestions concerning the care of a child with a health impairment, and it may be necessary for the resource/itinerant teacher to interpret these recommendations to either the parents or the child's regular classroom teacher.

3. Interpret occupational, physical, or speech therapy to the child's teacher or teachers. The therapist may make recommendations concerning activities, methods of ambulation, or ways to modify materials to be carried out in the regular classroom. It would be the responsibility of the resource/itinerant teacher to interpret these recommendations and to assist in carrying them out. It would also be necessary for the resource/itinerant teacher to obtain up-to-date evaluations, recommendations, and changes in treatment procedures.

4. Assist therapist in actual therapy sessions to more fully understand the treatment priority and the methods used to correct or prevent an undesirable behavior or ambulation pattern.

5. Observe child in classroom, playground, or school community to ensure that desired ambulation patterns are being transferred and maintained outside of therapeutic settings.

6. Assist regular classroom teacher in spot-checking braces, crutches, and wheelchairs and observe to see if the equipment is functioning properly.

7. Observe specific children in classrooms and offer suggestions on ways to modify and adapt equipment and materials so that the child may participate fully in all activities.

8. Assist in modifying architectural barriers or physical restrictions, such as removing desk bottoms for wheelchairs and providing adjustable chairs and stand-up tables if needed. The resource/itinerant teacher may also arrange for construction of special equipment or assist in modifying barriers, such as putting short ramps or ground barriers or installing handrails in toilet stalls.

9. As mentioned previously, the resource/ itinerant teacher may have primary responsibility for arranging special transportation to and from school and to any special activities.

10. Keep abreast of current technological advances and new materials and equipment that may facilitate the integration of these students.
11. Supplement or reinforce instruction of the regular classroom teacher or the physical education teacher in selected areas. It may be necessary, for example, to tutor a child in an academic area in which he cannot complete assignments as rapidly as the other children. Some resource/itinerant teachers have also had considerable success in working with small groups of children in the regular classroom.
12. Provide guidance and counseling to regular teachers through in-service meetings with an entire school staff or individually. In some instances the resource/itinerant teacher may conduct mini-in-service sessions or small group discussions with children concerning a particular disability.
13. Coordinate volunteer services or classroom aides used in the regular classroom. This role may involve the selection, training, placement, and scheduling of aides for activities such as assisting in physical education, physical therapy, toileting, or adapting materials.
14. Assist in planning recreational activities and leisure skills during school hours and possibly after school hours and weekends.
15. Assist in planning and implementing work-study, vocational education, and vocational rehabilitation services for secondary students. The resource/itinerant teacher may have to serve as the catalyst to ensure that these services are offered and that there is continuity of services.

In general, the role of the resource/itinerant teacher is a helping and assisting role in working with the child, teachers, administrators, parents, therapists, and all others involved. The role is a combination of child advocacy and facilitation to provide the needed individualized services.

SUMMARY

Children with crippling conditions and health impairments represent an extremely heterogenous group, ranging from the cerebral palsied, who are commonly multiply handicapped, to children with minor health impairments. A limited number of these children will be most effectively served in special classes on a full- or part-time basis, whereas the majority can attend regular classrooms with only minimal modifications and adaptions. Many (particularly those with crippling conditions) will need the paraeducational services of physical, occupational, and speech therapy. The need for these therapies will be greater during the child's early school years and will decrease as the child becomes older, thereby allowing increased regular classroom attendance. During the child's secondary school years, he may only attend therapy sessions on a weekly or biweekly basis.

If the child with a crippling condition or health impairment is attending a regular classroom, the modifications and adaptations may be very minimal. There may, however, be a need for environmental modifications, such as provision of ramps instead of stairs, provision of wide aisles, installation of handrails, and modification of restrooms. Classroom modifications will be minimal, but if necessary, the special education resource/itinerant teacher would provide the needed assistance in this area.

The format of this chapter is somewhat different than that of other chapters because the discussion was presented on the basis of a particular type of disability or condition. This is not intended to mean that the suggestions offered are related only to that particular condition; in fact, many of the suggestions are equally appropriate to other conditions. For example, the need for an adapted physical education program is not unique to children with allergies or asthma, but may be equally appropriate for children with arthritis or epilepsy. As a result, teachers are encouraged to consider all of the suggestions, regardless of their immediate interest.

Many of these children may have experienced repeated absences from school because of medical treatment procedures to correct or alleviate their conditions. These absences may have a profound influence on the child's educational achievement and on his feelings about his condition and himself. Teachers must carefully weigh the influence of these absences, not only in relationship to academic achievement but also in relation to their impact on the child's feelings about his condition and how he sees himself as a person. Regular classroom teachers must work very closely with the child's parents and the resource/itinerant teacher to better understand the influence of the condition on the child.

Perhaps the most important factor for the regular classroom teacher to understand is the influence of her attitude on the attitude of the nondisabled children and on the attitude of the child with a crippling condition or health impairment (this attitudinal influence applies equally to *all* children). The following adage indicates the need for an objective attitude:

> What you think of *me*,
> I will think of *me*,
> What I think of *me*,
> WILL BE *ME*

If the child's teachers, parents, siblings, and friends perceive him in a negative way, he may assume that attitude about himself! If, on the other hand, others important in his environment see him positively, he probably will also see himself in this way. He may come to see himself not as a disabled individual but first and foremost as *an individual* who has *many abilities* and who, incidentally and lastly, is disabled.

References and suggested readings

Abruzze, J. L. "Rheumatoid Arthritis: Reflection on Etiology and Pathogensis." *American Academy of Physical Medicine and Rehabilitation,* January 1971, 30-39.

American Academy of Pediatrics Committee on Children with Handicaps. "The Epileptic Child and Competitive School Athletics," *Pediatrics,* October 1968, *42,* 700-702.

Blakeslee, B. *The Limb-Deficient Child.* Berkeley: University of California Press, 1963.

Buchanan, R., and Mullins, J. "Integration of a Spina Bifida Child in a Kindergarten for Normal Children." *Young Children,* September 1968, 339-343.

Cobb, S., and Stanislav, K. "The Epidemiology of Rheumatoid Arthritis." *American Journal of Public Health,* October 1966, *56,* 1657-1663.

Collier, R. N., Jr. "The Adolescent with Diabetes and the Public Schools—A Misunderstanding." *Personnel and Guidance Journal,* April 1969, *47,* 753-757.

Conine, T., and Brennan, W. T. "Orthopedically Handicapped Children in Regular Classrooms." *Journal of School Health,* January 1969, *39,* 59-63.

Deahl, T., and Deahl, M. "The Orthopedically Handicapped." *Instructor,* 1971, *80,* 34.

Decker, J. L. "Closing in on Rheumatoid Arthritis: The Number One Crippler." *Today's Health,* June 1967, *45,* 44-47, 71.

Drash, A. "Diabetes Mellitus in Childhood." *Journal of Pediatrics,* June 1971, *78,* 919-937.

Ducas, D. "Winning the Battle Against Asthma." *Today's Health,* August 1967, *45,* 28-32.

Dunn, L. M. "Education for Children With Epilepsy." *Rehabilitation Record,* January-February 1967, 4-7.

England, G. O. "Treating 'C.P's' as Persons." *Cerebral Palsy Review,* July-August 1964, *25,* 10-11.

Finnell, C. "Despite Cerebral Palsy—I Have the Chance to Try." *Today's Education,* November 1970, *59,* 74-75.

Forsythe, W. I., and Kinley, J. G. "Bowel Control of Children with Spina Bifida." *Developmental Medicine and Child Neurology,* February 1970, *12,* 27-31.

Gault, P. L. "Care of the Child with Meningitis." *RN,* October 1969, *32,* 44.

Harlin, V. K. "Experiences with Epileptic Children in a Public School Program." *Journal of School Health,* January 1965, *35,* 20-24.

Haskell, S. H., and Anderson, E. M. "The Education of Physically Handicapped Children in Ordinary Schools." *Irish Journal of Education,* Summer 1969, *3,* 41-54.

Haskell, S. H. "Physically Handicapped Children: Special or Normal Schooling." *Slow Learning Child,* November 1969, *16,* 150-161.

Hill, M. L., Shurtleff, D. B., Chapman, W. H., and Ansell, J. S. "The Myelodysplastic Child—Bowel and Bladder Control." *American Journal of Nursing,* March 1969, *69,* 545-550.

Holley, L. "The Physical Therapist: Who, What, and How." *American Journal of Nursing.* July 1970, *70,* 1521-1524.

Klein, R. A., and Hummel, L. "The Hemophiliac: An Exceptional Child." *Journal of School Health,* June 1967, *37,* 303-306.

Livingston, S. "What the Teacher Can Do For the Student With Epilepsy." *N. E. A. Journal,* November 1966, *65,* 24-26.

Lord, D. W., and Root, H. F. "Brighter Future for Children With Diabetes." *Parents Magazine.* November 1966, *41,* 70-71 and 156-158.

Martin, J. W. "Attitudes Toward Epileptic Students in a City High School System." *The Journal of School Health.* 1974, *28,* 144-146.

Merley, F. "Toward a Normal Life." *Science News,* August 1968, *94,* 163.

Mitchell, M. M. "Occupational Therapy and Special Education." *Children,* September-October 1971, *18,* 183-186.

Moore, M. L. "Diabetes in Children." *American Journal of Nursing,* January 1967, *67,* 104-107.

Noon, E. F. "Don't Be Afraid of the Child with Epilepsy." *Instructor,* 1968, *78,* 57.

Patthoff, C. J. "Insulin Reaction." *Today's Health,* October 1969, *47,* 74.

Puthoff, M. "New Dimensions in Physical Activity for Children with Asthma and Other Respiratory Conditions." *Journal of Health, Physical Education, Recreation,* September 1972, *43,* 75-77.

Robins, H., and Schaltner, R. "Obstacles in the Social Integration of Orthopedically Handicapped Children." *Journal of Jewish Community Services,* Winter 1968, *45,* 190.

Russo, J. R. "Mainstreaming Handicapped Students: Are Your Facilities Suitable?" *American School and University,* October 1974, *47,* 25-32.

Sauer, L. W. "Heart Diseases in Children." *PTA Magazine,* November 1967, *66,* 29-30.

Scherr, M. S., and Charleston, L. F. "A Physical Conditioning Program for Asthmatic Children." *Journal of the American Medical Association,* 1958, *168*(15), 1196-2000.

Schwartz, A., and Lieberman, M. "Integrating the Orthopedically Handicapped Child into the Center." *Jewish Community Center Program Aids,* Summer 1963.

Seligman, T., Randel, H. O., and Stevens, J. J. "Conditioning Program for Children with Asthma." *Physical Therapy Journal,* May 1970, *50,* 641-647.

Semans, S. "Principles of Treatment in Cerebral Palsy." *Journal of the American Physical Therapy Association,* July 1966, *46,* 318-325.

Soldwedel, B., and Terrill, I. "Sociometric Aspects of Physically Handicapped and Nonhandicapped Children in the Same Elementary School." *Exceptional Children,* May 1957, *23,* 371-383.

Solow, R. A. "Psychological Aspects of Muscular Dystrophy." *Exceptional Children,* October 1965, *32,* 99-103.

Stratch, E. H. "Rehabilitation of Young Spina Bifida Children." *Rehabilitation,* April-June 1969, *69,* 17-20.

Sugar, M., and Ames, M.D. "The Child with Spina Bifida Cystica: His Medical Problems and Habilitation." *Rehabilitation Literature,* December 1965, *26,* 362-366.

Swack, M. J. "Training Special Education Teachers in Physical Therapy Techniques by Means of Programmed Demonstrations." *Exceptional Children,* April 1967, *33,* 529-534.

Waleski, D. "The Physically Handicapped in the Regular Classroom." *Today's Education,* December 1964, *52,* 12-16.

West, W. L. "Occupational Therapy: Philosophy and Perspective." *American Journal of Nursing,* August 1968, *68,* 1708-1711.

Winnick, J. P. "Planning Physical Activity for the Diabetic." *Physical Educator,* March 1970, *27,* 18-20.

CHAPTER 6
Speech problems

Ronald Stewart

It is likely that more classroom teachers have had contact with the speech clinician than with any other specialist who works with handicapped children. Speech clinicians (or therapists or pathologists) have been a visible part of the public school scene, particularly at the elementary school level, for many years. Until recently, there was no question but that more speech handicapped children were served by the public schools than children with any other handicapping condition. This may be true today; however, the rapid growth of programs for children with learning disabilities has caused this program to surpass the speech program in number of children served in at least some school districts. Despite this acceptance of, and at least limited familarity with the speech therapy program, classroom teachers have typically played relatively inactive roles in the remediation of speech deficits in children in their classrooms. One exception relates to speech improvement programs implemented in kindergarten classrooms on an on-again, off-again basis for the past fifteen to twenty years.

Perhaps the major reason for this lack of involvement has been that the speech therapist has been relatively self-sufficient and has too seldom asked for assistance. Although teacher-therapist conferences in which the teacher is given suggestions for use with a specific child are often scheduled, the teacher has been asked to do very little, and so, in most cases, very little has been done. With increased emphasis on the role of the regular classroom teacher in working with other handicapped children, it is only natural that we take another look at his role with children with speech problems.

In this chapter we will consider (1) how speech and language normally develop, (2) major types of speech problems, (3) the classroom teacher's role, and (4) the role of the speech clinician. In the process of discussing these four topics, we will present a variety of ideas for assisting the child with speech problems and additional sources of ideas and information.

DEVELOPMENT OF NORMAL SPEECH AND LANGUAGE

According to Schreiber (1973), "Speech is the most complex behavior in the animal kingdom." Through speech, humans are able to transform thoughts, including very abstract concepts, into auditory signals (spoken words) and thus communicate with other humans. Once speech and language are learned, this process takes place almost instantaneously. Though this process has been studied extensively, much about it remains unknown. One major fact is self-evident; most humans develop speech and language with apparent ease, and thus it is taken for granted. For the minority who do not, we become concerned, uncertain how to proceed, and often feel uncomfortable and ill at ease.

Egland (1970) notes that we know little of how language originated in the human race and that we also know little about how a child first learns to vocalize his needs and desires to communicate with others around him. We do know that speech and language are learned behaviors and that they seem to follow the laws of learning that apply in lower animals and in humans in relation to other types of learned behavior. We know that although similarities exist between the more than one thousand languages spoken by man, there are highly significant differences; there is little apparent logic as to why each race or culture has its specific language patterns. We also know, by observation, that languages are perpetuated as children learn the language spoken around them to communicate their needs and desires.

For a child to learn to speak normally, and thus to develop language, certain abilities must be present. He must have the ability to hear, have normal or near normal speech mechanisms, and have adequate (normal or near normal) brain and central nervous system functioning. If he cannot hear or has impaired hearing, he does not receive accurate auditory input to imitate; this results in slow speech development or faulty articulation, or both. (For a review of this problem, see pp. 41-42, relating to the hearing impaired.) If he does not have normal or near normal speech organs, he may be unable to articulate in a manner that is acceptably imitative of others. (This *may* be correctable through surgery; see p. 103.) If his central nervous system is to some degree dysfunctional, he may not be able to receive the proper sensory input, make the necessary associations, or coordinate the muscles of articulation. If he is mentally retarded, his speech and language development may not follow normal patterns of development. The type of neural dysfunction and the degree of mental retardation will have significant effects on the type and degree of speech and language problem. If all of these abilities are normal and if the child has normal environmental stimulation and opportunity to learn, the development of speech will follow a predictable developmental pattern.

For most children the first sounds uttered following birth are those accompanying the first exhalation. The newborn child exhales, coughs out accumulated amniotic fluid, and in so doing produces the so-called birth cry. Very soon, however, real crying begins, and this develops into the characteristic crying that parents learn to interpret in terms of specific wants and needs. This may be considered as primary communication, but it is not speech. At least three distinctive types of crying seem to be common to all very young babies: a cry that says, "I'm not comfortable!" (wet or too warm, for example), a cry that says, "I'm in pain!" and a cry that says, "I'm hungry—feed me."

These first primitive attempts at communication may appear to be primarily one-way (from the child to anyone who may hear), but in fact they are preliminary to other meaningful sounds to which most parents respond, thus triggering more sounds from the child. This is the start of meaningful, two-way communication and provides the base for later speech and communication.

Babbling begins at the age of 6 to 8 weeks in most children and consists of a great variety of combinations of syllables in an apparently random order. It is a highly impor-

tant step in prespeech vocalization, and it is important that the parent babble or talk back to the child. In addition to the reinforcement the child receives from the parents' returned babbling, there is an obvious element of pleasure that all children seem to derive from hearing their own babbling. If the child cannot hear his own babbling because of severe hearing impairment, he is not reinforced to continue babbling and thus begins a series of events that may result in severe retardation in speech and language development.

Following babbling, which is pure vocal exercise, the child enters an imitative stage that Schreiber (1973) calls "lallation." During this stage the child begins to deliberately imitate sounds, either his own or those of others. When a child begins this lalling stage, we can be certain he hears. This stage has other imitative aspects, such as gestural and facial expression imitation.

A jargon stage, in which the child begins to exhibit noticeable patterns of emphasis and rhythm, usually follows the lalling stage, but some children move from lalling immediately into speaking, that is, vocalizing an identifiable word. It is likely that if an objective, independent jury of speech specialists were to monitor a child's early vocalizations, they might identify a somewhat different time of occurrence of the first spoken word than that claimed by parents, for parents tend to be highly tuned for this occurrence and may not be the most objective audience. Nevertheless, it is likely that many children will actually say their first word by the time they are 1 year old, though some may not speak a distinguishable word until many months later. A few months' difference at this point is not critical. The exact time at which the first word is spoken is less important than giving the child every opportunity to proceed through the requisite developmental steps with the necessary environmental support and surroundings. This includes, but is not limited to, (1) a maximum of personal interaction with the child—not "smothering" but including the child in a maximum of activities and settings consistent with his other physical needs and limitations, (2) a careful evaluation of the adult speech surrounding the child to make certain it provides a good model, and (3) a concerted effort to *talk* to the child, using a variety of words, facial expressions, and voice inflections at a level at which the child may be maximally stimulated. (This also includes a deliberate inclusion of the child in conversations when small groups of individuals are together in the presence of the child.) If these steps are followed and the child receives a maximum of love and care, he has been given the best possible chance to develop normal speech in later childhood.

During the ensuing preschool years, the preceding suggestions will be of continuing value if adjusted to the level of the child as he progresses through the production of simple sentences, through the stage of almost ceaseless questions (when it would be nice to be able to "shut him off" rather than encourage his speaking), and through a continuing, almost dizzying, process of vocabulary acquisition.

It must be recognized that during these preschool years, children almost invariably exhibit many speech characteristics that will be viewed as speech problems requiring corrective efforts if they are in existence several years later. Articulation problems abound with almost all children. These are simply the reflection of partially developed speech production and a partially trained "ear" for sounds and words. Nonfluencies will undoubtedly develop, some of which might be called stuttering, but most will vanish if parents accept them for what they are—a part of the developmental process of most children. The existence of certain normal nonfluencies is emphasized by many authors because the efforts some parents, and later some teachers, make to correct nonfluencies appear to be an important causal factor for stuttering. Too much reaction to normal nonfluencies, by parents and well-intentioned but uninformed teachers, may promote rather than reduce stuttering (see pp. 102-103 for further discussion of stuttering).

The preceding discussion of how speech and language develop is purposefully brief but perhaps sufficient to provide a basis for further consideration of speech problems of school age children. The reader who desires further information about this interesting topic will find excellent discussions in most of the general speech texts listed at the close of this chapter. We do suggest one very simple, inexpensive, and technically accurate paperback for those who want the basic facts in a painless, non-college-textbook form— *Your Child's Speech* (Flora Schreiber, 1973).

MAJOR TYPES OF SPEECH PROBLEMS WITH SOME SUGGESTIONS FOR REMEDIATION

Speech problems may be divided or categorized in a variety of ways; for purposes of discussion we will consider the following categories: (1) articulation problems, (2) language problems, (3) voice problems, (4) stuttering or other nonfluency problems, and (5) other types of speech problems. Speech problems might also be considered in relation to the likelihood of occurrence in the general population of school age children, and amenability to assistance from the classroom teacher. These two considerations will be given priority in our discussion of speech problems.

A question that must be considered before reviewing the major types of speech problems is—"When is a *difference* in speech sufficiently different or significant to consider it a *handicap?*" The various authorities appear to agree that a speech problem may be called a handicap if (1) it interferes with communication, (2) it causes the speaker to be maladjusted, or (3) it calls undue attention to the speech (as opposed to what the speaker is saying). Stated another way, if the speech causes communication problems (for example, unintelligibility) or if it causes negative reactions on the part of the speaker or the audience, it is a speech problem. Note that the preceding relates to the effects of the speech, not to the physiology of speech production. The speech clinician is concerned with assisting the child to produce speech in the most normal manner possible, to use speech effectively in normal communication, in a manner permitting the speaker to concentrate on what he is saying, not how he is saying it. The preceding generalizations about speech should be kept in mind as we review the categories of speech problems.

Articulation problems

Articulation problems will be mentioned first because they are, by a wide margin, the most common type of speech problem encountered. Articulation problems at the preschool level are common and may often be ignored, but even here there may be reason to refer children for speech therapy. Hendrick notes that although many distortions, substitutions, and omissions are the rule in nursery school, referral is warranted if the child has generally unintelligible speech after the age of 3 or 3½ years (Hendrick, 1975, p. 209). If the teacher is conscientious and refers when in doubt and the speech clinician indicates that no special help is needed, it can be (as Hendrick puts it) "mildly embarrassing." This can be a *more* embarrassing problem if the parent was resistive from the beginning, but this is one of the risks that must be taken in attempting to help children with articulation problems. *The risk must be taken* if the teacher is truly concerned about the future of the child. Better to be mildly embarrassed, several times if necessary, than to allow children to grow into adulthood with uncorrected speech problems.

Articulation errors are those involving omissions, substitutions, distortions, or additions when pronouncing (or articulating) words. If there is an organic base for the problem, remediation measures may differ considerably from those articulation difficulties present when there appear to be no known causal factors. A major category of articulation problems includes those labeled "functional" when no causal factors may be discerned.

The following are examples of articulation errors:

Substitution: "dat" for that, "wabbit" for rabbit, "thum" for some
Omission: "pay" for play, "cool" for school, "ift" for lift
Distortion: "shled" for sled
Additions: "buhrown" for brown, "cuhow" for cow, "puhlease" for please

Certain generalizations applicable in nearly all cases of articulation error therapy may be made. These may be used as guidelines for remedial efforts. First, *the child must hear the error*. In most cases the letter or letters are pointed out to him in writing or in print, so that there is no question just what letter or letters are under consideration; then, he must learn to hear the sound—as properly articulated by the teacher or therapist. Often he must learn to listen for the sound in initial, medial, and final positions; then, he must learn to differentiate between the sound properly articulated and the sound as he articulates it. One way this may be done is through the use of a tape recorder. The teacher may deliberately mispronounce the sound, and on the playback the child may learn to discriminate the error sound from the correctly produced sound in varying phonetic contexts. After this stage, recordings of both the child and the teacher may be made to assist in recognizing the varying productions. Other methods or materials may be used to enable the child to recognize differences between accurate and inaccurate pronunciations (articulation) of speech sounds. Learning to *hear* errors is an absolute prerequisite to any further work with articulation problems and is sometimes called *ear training* or *auditory training*.

Second, *reduction or elimination of known causal factors should be attempted*. This is not possible in all cases, but the provision of a good model and the expectation of good articulation can be encouraged in the classroom and in the home. Parent conferences are required to explain the speech goals, and parents may sometimes be quite sensitive to the idea that they may have helped cause the problem, even if it is not stated this way. Perhaps the best way to approach parents is to indicate that we cannot always determine the cause but that we do know good speech models are essential as part of the remedial scheme.

After being absolutely certain that the child can hear the difference between correct articulation and misarticulation of the sounds in question, *it is necessary that the child learn to produce the correct sound.* This may be accomplished through games, exercises, behavior shaping (using approximations of the right sound production and slowly approaching the correct articulation), or any method that seems appropriate to the age and interests of the child. Many young children see little reason to change their speech patterns; this applies to all speech correction but perhaps most often to articulation problems. They seem to get by, and unless they are embarrassed by the reactions of others, they may not care. In some instances we must *make them care enough to hear articulatory differences,* and then motivate them to learn to make the correct sound.

A fourth step is to *have the child incorporate the newly learned, accurately articulated sound in familiar words.* Even though the child learns to hear the difference between accurate and inaccurate articulation and to produce the required sound, until it is regularly used in language, he has not overcome the problem. The child has had months or years of practice in saying the sound incorrectly; it takes a fair amount of repetition to develop new speech habits and patterns. Here again, motivation is highly important; with young children, games are often valuable. Reward systems, extrinsic and intrinsic, have been used to good advantage in the remediation of articulation problems.

In addition to the preceding general rules for remediation, it may be generally stated for *all* speech problem remediation that *if the child is being seen by a speech clinician, the teacher should consult with the specialist to be certain that any special efforts in the classroom are complementary, not contradictory, to efforts of the speech clinician.*

In addition to the activities previously mentioned, certain other tools or materials that may be used effectively by both the speech clinician and the classroom teacher include the following: (1) reading stories in which accurate articulation is modeled is a good technique, particulary with younger children; (2) word rhyming is an effective approach with some children; and (3) puppetry is an excellent way to overcome self-consciousness, which may be a serious deterrent to successful speech therapy for some children.

Teachers, as well as parents, must remember that children develop language as an imitative function. Teachers, as professionals whose primary responsibility is the welfare of the child, have a very special reason to provide a good model of correct articulation and broad language usage. The *teacher's articulation* and the *teacher's language patterns* have a dramatic effect on the children for whom she is responsible; the teacher should be constantly aware of this effect.

Regular efforts to promote speech improvement for all children in the class and individualized efforts to assist specific children with known articulation problems are the two ways in which regular classroom teachers are most likely to become involved with speech and speech problems. These are the areas in which the teacher is most likely to be able to achieve significant success. The preceding discussion of articulation problems should provide sufficient information for the teacher to get started. It should also make it difficult for the conscientious teacher to ever again say, "I just don't know enough about speech correction to even make a start at helping Jimmy." If a speech clinician is available, *try to obtain help from her* and *work with her if she is seeing the child in question.* If there is no specialized help, start from the base of the preceding information and do additional reading in some of the suggested readings at the close of this chapter; the positive results may be surprising.

Language problems

Language problems may be classified in a variety of ways; according to Egland (1970), this area of speech correction may have more loosely classified and poorly defined terms than any other area. Some authorities would include such disorders as dyslexia, dysgraphia, and aphasia under this general category. These disorders are believed to relate to specific causation, and many believe they indicate central nervous system dysfunction or brain disorders. We consider these disorders in a general way when we consider learning disabilities (Chapter 7), but in this discussion we will focus primarily on the more general, nonspecific language problems and on delayed speech. It is well to remember that in many cases the problems first recognized in relation to poor language development are multifaceted and deserve the attention of a competent, interdisciplinary diagnostic team. Therefore, when the teacher is considering language problems, particularly if there seem to be many pieces of the "puzzle" missing as the observations are recorded and assessed, it is best to refer to a source having good interdisciplinary potential.

Language problems are undoubtedly the most difficult of the varying speech problems to assess, if for no other reason than their degree of interrelatedness with all facets of the child's life. We earlier emphasized the importance of articulation as it relates to the child's effective communication. Spoken language is the major means whereby young children communicate; it provides the basis for reading and writing. It is a societal invention used for social, and to some degree, technical purposes; spoken language has value and meaning only as society gives it value and meaning. But for the human species, it is valued above almost all else.

Language abnormalities have been the topic of much debate in recent years, as we have recognized, for example, that some ghetto language, though abnormal by middle-class standards, is quite normal in its home setting. At this point in history, no one can safely predict what direction this particular issue will take. If we go back to the definition of a speech problem, we see that language problems should be considered significant if they interfere with communication, if they cause the speaker to be malad-

justed, or if they cause problems for the listener. In settings that are far removed from the ghetto, the extremes in ghetto language might well cause problems for the listener—who simply would not understand much of what the speaker is saying. This problem and that of teaching bilingual (for example, Spanish speaking) children to communicate in English create problems other than "how-to-do-it." There are questions of preservation of culture, individual rights, and school district policy. We cannot make pronouncements that will apply in all settings but must comment that these are real problems and that teachers should use all of their available influence (such as teacher organizations and legislative influence) to encourage local schools to take an official position and to make some provision for the specialized programs and curriculum adjustments required by this type of youngster.

Before considering delayed speech and various ways in which the teacher may work to prevent or to correct language problems in the classroom, we should be reminded that some language problems are related to other causal factors and may be taken care of, at least in part, in programming directed at these more basic factors. One prime example is that of the hearing impaired. If the hearing impaired child does *not* have problems with language, it is considered highly unusual. This topic is treated in Chapter 3 and will not be further pursued here. However, we must remember that children with mild hearing impairment may have been overlooked somehow in screening procedures and that language problems may be the clue to identification. Therefore, *if a child has a language problem, the teacher should immediately check to make certain he has had a recent audiological examination.* If he has not, this should be the first order of business, and the teacher should pursue this with vigor. Two other conditions often leading to language problems are mental retardation and learning disabilities. Some mildly mentally handicapped show only a small degree of language development problems, but in general, they will tend to have language development below expectations for their chronological age. The lower the intellectual level, the lower the language level is likely to be. With the learning disabled, the picture is not so clear-cut. If the learning disability is the type that is closely related to spoken language, there will be definite language problems. If the learning disability is related almost totally to reading ability and visual channel problems, the child may have average or above average spoken language. In fact, the large discrepancy between spoken language level, and ability to decode written language is one of the indicators of learning disability in many cases.

Delayed speech, considered here as a type of language problem, is mentioned as a separate category in some texts in the field of speech pathology. Schreiber (1973), in a guide intended mainly for parents, indicated that one of the more common causes of delayed speech may be lack of need for the child to talk; others may be a bilingual home or the fact of being a twin (thus able to communicate more without speech). If parents attempt to anticipate the child's every need, so that he need not ask for much, it may delay his speech. Or, if parents literally believe that children should be seen and not heard, this may delay speech. Fortunately, children with such parents usually play with other children in the neighborhood; here they have the opportunity and the need to speak to be a successful part of the group. The term "delayed speech" is often used to refer to the speech patterns of hearing impaired and mentally handicapped chidren, but it does not mean the same thing as delayed speech in children who have adequate hearing and normal or above normal mental ability. For parents who become overly concerned with the fact that their 2½-year-old child does not speak and thus wonder if something is basically wrong, it is well to cite the case of Albert Einstein, who did not speak until after his third birthday. It is a somewhat different situation if the child comes to school at age 5 and still has seriously delayed speech. This may require special attention, and planning

should start with a complete physical check-up to eliminate the possibility of structural defects. If there are no such disabilities and the intellectual level appears to be at least normal, then environmental background should be reviewed. In all cases the teacher should supply every possible opportunity for use of language but should not use undue pressure tactics. Sometimes we find children with speech patterns that are two to three years behind that which would be predicted from chronological age, intellectual level, opportunity to learn, and other such factors. After complete examination by a team of specialists from all disciplines, the only answer may be *delayed speech—unknown etiology,* which simply means we do not always know. After seeing such a case, it may be tempting to conclude that we should just deal with the delayed speech in all cases, rather than go through the cost and effort of various evaluations. This is a questionable decision, for in many cases the examination results in the discovery of causes that may be treated directly, and in some cases the problem may be remedied relatively quickly.

If causes are known, they should be carefully considered when planning remediation of delayed speech. If the child has not had sufficient language experience, then we should provide it for him. This may include games in which language development plays an important role. If the child likes to listen to tapes, it may mean listening to stories that will broaden his vocabulary and widen his language experience. Rhymes may be of value, or sentence-building exercises may be appropriate, depending on the particular case. The parents help may be enlisted when it seems likely that they can and will cooperate. Parents may be given specific types of exercises or activities, or it may be well to review such things as the role they should play in monitoring television programs to broaden language experience, taking time to really talk to children, even if time is limited, taking children to surroundings that will bring about the need for broadened vocabulary and more communication, and other similar activities.

Encouraging more oral reading, to other students, to parents, or in whatever way is effective in a given setting, may help a great deal. The key words in planning such activities are exposure, encouragement, involvement, interest, variety, opportunity, and innovation. The goal can be accomplished if sufficient effort is made.

The question, "How much delay in speech is too much?" brings us to the final, and prehaps the most important, consideration. Many children have not developed their speech and language as well as they might have if they had been in a different setting in their early years. Most of these are not sufficiently retarded in speech development to require separate special programming (such as with the speech clinician). If the teacher plans many of the daily activities to maximize speech and language usage, these children can be helped to catch up to the correct speech level. Situations should be structured for all children to broaden vocabulary and maximize language experience. Children should be encouraged to answer in complete sentences rather than one word. They should have an opportunity to play word games and dictionary games that accomplish this goal. We suggest *Speech and Language Problems: A Guide for the Classroom Teacher* (Egland, 1970) as one such source of specific suggestions for classroom use in relation to all types of speech programs. Many larger schools or state departments of education have good handbooks that provide specific suggestions, but busy teachers often become so involved in the details of teaching that they lose sight of the larger goals. Speech and language development must be included as one of the major goals, and with careful attention, many speech and language problems may be greatly reduced or eliminated.

Voice problems

Voice problems or voice disorders may require somewhat different consideration than other speech problems reviewed here. Schreiber, in advising parents about various speech problems, states: "The minute you think you notice something wrong with your child's voice, start counting. If whatever it is hasn't gone away by the third day, take him to the doctor" (Schreiber, 1973, pp. 127-128). This is not to indicate that every child with a voice disorder needs an immediate medical examination, but rather that if a significant change is noted (other than the voice changes usually experienced at puberty), there is the possibility of medical problems, some of which may require immediate treatment to prevent serious complications. This is not likely in the majority of voice problems but should be viewed as a distinct possibility. The role of the teacher, if this type of problem is suspected, is immediate referral to the speech clinician (if available). If a speech clinician is not available, the school nurse and the parents should be notified, suggesting the possibility of medical referral.

Voice disorders generally fall into one of four categories, pitch, intensity, quality, or flexibility. These problems do not have the same kind of direct carryover to the learning of basic skills as, for example, serious articulation problems may have. In fact, unless they are very different from the norm, they are often accepted as part of the uniqueness of the individual. The following generalizations regarding these four types of voice disorders are presented so the classroom teacher may have an overall view of voice disorders and a base from which to consider the possible need for referral, either to the speech clinician, or through the parents, to the physician.

Pitch problems seldom cause any serious difficulty to the speaker, with the exception of the high falsetto voice in the upper-teenage or adult male. For girls and women a variety of pitch is accepted, with some women considered to have "sexy" voices if the pitch is low and others considered to have feminine voices if the pitch is high. For men, the problem may be different. Despite a number of recent societal changes in concepts of masculinity and femininity, there is a stubborn persistence of the belief that men should have a voice that is of low or medium pitch. Therefore, a boy with a high-pitched voice that apparently is carrying over into his upper-teenage years may benefit from therapy to attempt to assist him to lower the pitch. Sometimes pitch can be lowered, and sometimes it cannot; the matter is often a sensitive one, but if assistance can be provided, it may help greatly in the social arena.

Voice intensity, too loud or too soft, is not often a problem in and of itself. One fact to remember here is that unusually loud speech may mean that the individual does not hear his own voice distinctly, and thus this serves as a cue to recheck the possibility of a hearing problem. The teacher should also note that if a child speaks indistinctly (as opposed to too softly) and is asked to *speak up,* the result may be even more unsatisfactory than before. In speaking up, many children with indistinct speech will give voice to very loud vowel sounds, which will even further drown out the weaker consonant sounds. Therefore the teacher (or speech clinician) must work on more preciseness in consonant production.

Voice quality is the most often observed voice disorder of the four major types. The three most common types of voice quality problems are breathiness, harshness, and nasality. Harshness or breathiness may be caused by vocal abuse (such as occurs at a hard-fought football game) or may be the result of infection or inflammation of the vocal cords. These temporary problems usually go away after a few days of vocal rest. A more serious problem is that which occurs as a result of continued vocal abuse, causing growths to develop on the vocal cords. Such benign growths are fairly common among singers and, to some extent, among those who do a great deal of public speaking. These too may go away with vocal rest or if the individual receives therapy to assist in more normal voice production. It is also possible that such growths are malignant; thus the advice to parents mentioned at the start of this discussion also may be considered applicable to older children and of course to adults. Malignant growths cause the same type of quality problem as benign growths; the only way to check out this possibility is through referral to a qualified specialist. The

classroom teacher should be alert for voice disorders and should be particularly alert for rapid changes in voice quality, especially hoarseness or breathiness. If the teacher is in doubt, an immediate referral to the speech clinician or the physician is in order.

The fourth type of voice problem is a *flexibility disorder.* The most common type of flexibility problem is exhibited by the monotone speaker. This may be due to many different causes, such as physical tiredness, emotional difficulties, voice pitch too near the top or the bottom of the vocal range, or a hearing problem. If the voice is very unpleasant due to a flexibility disorder and the problem persists, referral to the speech clinician is the proper course of action. Seldom is the classroom teacher in a position (of technical knowledge and skill) to assess and attempt to remediate this type problem on her own.

In summary, voice problems may be of such minor nature that they may be properly overlooked. An exception is the case of unusual voice changes, particularly those which might be typified as hoarseness, harshness, or breathiness. If these persist, even for a few weeks, referral to a speech clinician or physician is recommended. Most voice disorders are of such nature that if the classroom teacher is to be involved in remedial efforts, it should be under the direction of the speech clinician.

Stuttering and other nonfluency problems

Stuttering is an area of speech production that, although it does not involve a high percentage of the total number of speech problems, does represent a major target of speech therapy efforts and research. Perhaps the reason stuttering receives so much attention is that it is such a debilitating disorder in so many instances. There is no general agreement as to the cause of stuttering, but theories fall into two major categorical groups, organic and behavioral. Van Riper (1972) believes that stuttering has many origins. Organic theories indicate a variety of neurological causations for stuttering, ranging from older theories relating to lack of cerebral dominance to those that liken stuttering to epileptic seizures. In many of these theories the fact that stutterers do not always stutter is accounted for by postulating a constitutional weakness (of one of the types just mentioned) that tends to "give" under pressure.

According to Lundeen (1972), there are four current nonorganic theories. (1) The *diagnosogenic theory* places the blame for stuttering on individuals in the child's early environment who labeled normal disfluencies as stuttering. The child then responds by attempting to eliminate his disfluencies; he overreacts and becomes overanxious; a vicious circle results. Fear, tension, and anxiety maintain the reaction. (2) The *frustration theory* is based on the idea that a child may have an unusual need to be listened to and in the drive to keep the listener's attention, normal disfluencies cause him (the speaker) to become more and more frustrated. As he struggles to be more fluent (due to his own drive—not to an outside influence) his tension leads to more disfluency. (3) The *pressure theory* places emphasis on developmental pressures, which in turn promote disfluency. Then, as the child or others in his environment react negatively, more pressure is felt and continued stuttering results. (4) A variety of theories based on *neurotic tendencies* of the child view stuttering as the outcome of needs, such as a need to satisfy anal or oral desires, infantile tendencies, or high levels of hostility. These in turn are the result of inadequate or unsatisfactory relationships with parents and may be related to various Freudian child-parent conflict hypotheses.

Though stuttering therapy, even long-term therapy by highly competent therapists, has not been notably successful, those who espouse the preceding theories tend to agree on certain guidelines for all who work with the stuttering child. The following suggestions indicate an attitude that must be adopted by the teacher and others who deal with children who stutter.

1. Do not mention the stuttering; try to reduce the child's awareness of this problem.
2. Minimize those settings and situations that appear to cause increased stuttering.
3. Minimize conflict of all types when possible.
4. Encourage speaking when all is going well, and immediately minimize demands to communicate when stuttering becomes more pronounced.

Primary, or beginning, stutterers may likely overcome the problem if those around them play their role properly. For secondary, or confirmed, stutterers, major goals may be acceptance of stuttering as a part of the language pattern and learning to stutter more easily or "gracefully." It is interesting to observe that most stutterers can sing without stuttering and that many can talk to animals without stuttering. For young children, singing and choral reading may be activities in which fluency may be achieved.

More recently, various applications of behavior modification techniques have been unusually successful with *some* stutterers, but no one approach works with any real degree of success with all stutterers.

Other types of speech problems

Other types of speech problems often mentioned in basic speech pathology texts include those related to *cleft lip or cleft palate, cerebral palsy, and hearing loss.* Cleft lip and cleft palate problems vary in effect on speech, depending on the depth of the cleft and the success of surgical procedures. Since midcentury, most children born with a facial cleft of any severity have been treated surgically during the first 2 or 3 months of life. Cleft lip, after surgical treatment, seldom causes any serious speech problem, but cleft palate is not often completely corrected surgically. The effects of cleft palate commonly include articulation errors and problems with nasality. Correction of these physiologically based speech problems is usually best left to the speech clinician. As a result of all of the related problems, children with cleft palate may tend to avoid speaking and may become retarded in vocabulary and overall language development.

Speech problems relating to cerebral palsy may cause speech that is quite difficult for the listener to understand, although a small percentage of cerebral palsied children (perhaps twenty-five to thirty percent) do not have significant speech problems. Speech problems among the cerebral palsied vary for a number of reasons, but primarily in relation to the type of cerebral palsy and degree of involvement. For the most part, the teacher should try to give the cerebral palsied child with speech problems sufficient time to try to communicate as needed for class purposes. Speech therapy for the cerebral palsied is best left to the speech clinician.

Speech problems relating to hearing loss are discussed in Chapter 3 and are not mentioned here except to note that speech and language problems are to be expected with the child with a hearing loss. In a similar manner, children who are mentally retarded will likely have problems with delayed speech, vocabulary development, and grammatical usage.

There are a number of physiological causes of speech problems, such as faulty dentition and abnormal laryngeal structure. Under the direction of a speech clinician, the classroom teacher may be of great assistance in nearly all such cases.

THE CLASSROOM TEACHER'S ROLE

With all of the differences that may be a part of developmental variations and with cautions about overreaction to nonfluencies, the classroom teacher may well wonder, "So how am I supposed to know if a child has a speech problem?" A partial answer is, "You can't always know," but this is obviously not satisfactory. Therefore, we will consider some alternatives that influence how the question may be best answered.

In cases in which the services of a qualified speech clinician are readily available, the child should be referred to the specialist if the teacher has any doubt concerning a speech problem. Then, if the problem is one requiring specific assistance, the speech clinician will do his part and will assist the teacher to play her role. The teacher's role will depend on the type and extent of the problem. Activities that will support the clinician's therapy will be suggested, and some "don'ts" along with positive suggestions will help de-termine the teacher's role. Even in an ideal setting there may be problems if the teacher is uninformed regarding speech problems, for experience indicates that some teachers, like some parents, may adjust to speech problems to the point that they no longer hear them. Therefore, each teacher must be aware of certain more obvious identifying characteristics of each disorder. In other words, a child with an articulation disorder will either be omitting, substituting, distorting, or adding certain speech sounds to his speech. The other major speech disorders also have certain unique characteristics, as enumerated in the preceding discussion.

When the teacher does recognize a problem, or a possible problem, she will be faced with the question of the importance or degree of severity of the problem. Careful observation of the problem as it presently exists should be coupled with information concerning potential problems in later life that each speech problem may generate. In settings in which the speech clinician is overloaded with cases (a common situation), the teacher may be of much help if he can describe the type and extent of the problem accurately. It is not enough to say the child lisps. There are many other factors, such as how consistently does it occur, does it occur mainly under pressure or when the child is tired, is it noticed by other children, is it a true lisp, and so on. In each of the speech problem categories, there are specific points to note that will help the teacher, or the teacher and the clinician in conference, to decide what to do next.

As indicated earlier, speech therapy services are provided in all corners of the nation; thus we have sometimes tended to think, "Let's leave it up to the specialist." That might be a satisfactory answer if there were sufficient speech therapists to serve all children who need help. Unfortunately, this is not the case, and as a result, in some school districts, there is little or no service for certain grade levels, unless the problem is very serious. This leaves the classroom teacher in the position of trying to decide whether or not to refer a given child to an already overloaded speech clinician; this decision must be made on the basis of degree of seriousness of the child's speech disorder. This is a major reason why the teacher must be familiar with identifying characteristics of speech problems if she is to be able to fulfill her role in planning and implementing speech remediation for children in her classroom.

In summary, the role of the teacher may have several different aspects, and the degree to which the teacher is involved depends on the grade level at which she teaches and the availability of adequate services from a speech specialist. In most settings the teacher must be deliberately aware of speech problems, must refer serious cases to the speech clinicians, must assist—at the direction of the speech clinician—in the classroom program of children with whom the speech clinician is working, and must be alert for every opportunity to promote better speech production by all children in her classroom. The teacher must also be aware of the effect of her own speech and language patterns on the children she teaches, with this influence being especially important at the lower grade levels. To fulfill the preceding responsibilities, the teacher must know how to listen to be able to refer accurately and how each type of speech problem may handicap the child, in the educational-academic setting and in the social setting. She should also know what remedial measures may be effective, whether the clinician is or is not available.

ROLE OF THE SPEECH CLINICIAN

Speech clinicians have been a part of the public schools in the United States since shortly after the beginning of the twentieth century but have been widely accepted as a necessary part of the public schools since only about midcentury. Unfortunately, there are still a few school systems who view the speech clinician as a "luxury"; thus we may not assume that all schools have speech therapy service available. The large majority of public schools today have speech clinicians; they usually serve on an itinerant basis, visiting four to six schools, twice each week.

Children are generally seen for thirty to forty minutes in groups of three to five children, twice each week. More severe cases may be seen more often or on a one-to-one basis. In addition to speech therapy, the speech clinician may provide audiological services, do special work with the hearing impaired, and work as part of a team effort with the learning disabled. Some speech clinicians do certain types of specialized testing in relation to total school district diagnostic and evaluative efforts, but this varies greatly and is dependent on the administrative policies and regulations of local and state agencies. Speech clinicians who have more recently completed their academic programs have been trained in the administration and interpretation of a wide variety of diagnostic tools in addition to those related to a specific speech disability.

Training programs for speech clinicians are moving more and more in the direction of language development and communication disorders training, and speech clinicians may be expected to do more along these lines in the future. In some school districts the speech clinician is part of a continuing program in which classroom teachers, particularly those who teach kindergarten and first grade, are trained and assisted in the provision of regular speech improvement in their classes. This movement has waxed and waned over the years, and it is difficult to predict which way it is moving now.

Speech clinicians may be used in special schools or in clinic centers in large school districts in special programs for the physically handicapped, the cerebral palsied, or the multihandicapped. In this case, a clinician may be assigned to a single school on a full-time basis. More often the clinician serves a caseload of sixty to one hundred children at any one time; however, the effectiveness of her service is reduced if her caseload is more than sixty to sixty-five.

Though many of the preceding comments would seem to indicate considerable variability in what speech clinicians are doing, the number of children they serve and where their major area of emphasis may be, one statement may be made with much confidence. If the speech clinician has the assistance of knowledgeable, interested classroom teachers and if she will help these teachers know what to do and how to do it, her services will be much more effective, and children will be better served.

SUMMARY

Some classroom teachers have worked cooperatively with speech clinicians over the years, and have provided valuable assistance to speech handicapped children. Unfortunately, speech clinicians have not always asked for assistance, and in some school districts there is little or no specialized speech therapy program; therefore, it is necessary for regular classroom teachers to become better informed about the types of speech problems that may be found in their classes, and what they may be able to do to assist children who have such problems.

Though professional speech clinicians would likely classify speech handicaps into more specific categories than we have done here, for the classroom teacher, articulation, language, voice, and stuttering problems are the major considerations. Of these problems, articulation disorders compose the large majority and provide the most fruitful area for assistance within the classroom. Articulation problems have a variety of types of causation, but most can be approached by (1) making certain the child hears the error, (2) reducing causal or contributive factors, (3) assisting and encouraging the child to learn to make the correct sound, and (4) planning so that the newly learned, accurately articulated sound is incorporated into familiar words and used regularly. A highly important rule applies in the correction of articulation problems and with all other correction carried out by the classroom teacher: if the child is being seen by a speech clinician, either one employed by the school or a clinician from a private or university clinic, the teacher should consult with the clinician to make certain that classroom efforts are *consistent with and complementary to the specialized efforts provided in therapy*. The speech clinician should contact the teacher,

but if she does not, the teacher should contact the clinician.

Language problems come in a variety of sizes and shapes and have various causations. Mentally handicapped or hearing impaired children will likely have less well-developed language than children of normal intelligence or normal hearing ability. Language development efforts with the mentally handicapped or the hearing impaired should be coordinated with other special programming. Children from culturally different settings will often have more language problems than children from major ethnic and cultural groups and should receive assistance in developing better English language usage; however, this may be best accomplished through special curriculum offerings that are planned to assist with standard English while at the same time protect the child's right to maintain another culture or language. In remedying most language problems, careful planning of enriched language experiences, with all possible motivational techniques employed, is an effective way to start. With language problems, the teacher should remember to double check to make certain that the child has had a recent audiological evaluation, for hearing impairments are sometimes overlooked for years.

Voice problems, for the most part, are of such nature that if they require therapy, it should be provided by the speech clinician. The one role the regular classroom teacher should assume is that of referral to the speech clinician, and in the case of a child who undergoes a very rapid voice change (such as unusual harshness or breathiness), referral to the clinician or the physician, or both.

Stuttering therapy is best left to the speech clinician, but the teacher should consider the following guidelines unless specifically told not to by the speech clinician: (1) do not mention the stuttering—try to overlook it, (2) minimize settings that appear to cause increased stuttering, (3) minimize all types of conflict, (4) encourage speaking when the child is speaking fluently, and (5) reduce or minimize demands (as unobtrusively as possible) when stuttering becomes worse.

Speech is the most complex of human behaviors, and accurate, fluent speech, appropriate to the experience and age of the child, is critical to educational success. Some variations in speech and language development exist between different children, and delayed development is not always indicative of problems, but provision of adequate opportunity to develop speech and language is the best available insurance. All teachers should do their utmost to provide a setting in which children exercise their language skills and develop new skills consistent with normal speech and language development.

References and suggested readings

Allen, E. "The Child with Speech Defects." *N. E. A. Journal,* November 1967, *56,* 35-36.

Black, M. *School Speech Therapy: A Source Book.* Pittsburgh, Pa.: Stanwix House, Inc., 1970.

Broman, B., and Shipley, S. "Language Development." *Instructor,* October 1969, *79,* 132.

Cazden, D. *Child Language and Education.* New York: Holt, Rinehart and Winston, Inc., 1972.

Crews, R. "Linguistics in the Elementary Classroom." *N. E. A. Journal,* February 1968, *57,* 26-28.

Dixon, C. "Speech Problems—How and When to Step In." *Grade Teacher,* February 1968, 51-52.

Egland, G. *Speech and Language Problems: A Guide for the Classroom Teacher.* Englewood Cliffs, N. J.: Prentice-Hall, Inc., 1970.

Fundula, J. "Applied Awareness: Speech Improvement in an Elementary Classroom." *Teaching Exceptional Children,* Summer 1973, *5,* 190-194.

Hendrick, J. *The Whole Child: New Trends in Early Education.* St. Louis: The C. V. Mosby Co., 1975.

Karnes, M. *Helping Young Children Develop Language Skills: A Book of Activities.* Washington, D. C.: Council for Exceptional Children, 1968.

Lundeen, D. "Speech Disorders." In Gearheart, B. R. (ed.). *Education of the Exceptional Child: History, Present Practices and Trends.* Scranton, Pa.: Intext Educational Publishers, 1972.

Sacco, P. "How do You Help the Stutterer?" *Instructor,* June-July 1974, *83,* 35.

Schreiber, F. *Your Child's Speech.* New York: Ballantyne Books, Inc., 1973.

Travis, L. *Handbook of Speech Pathology and Audiology.* New York: Appleton-Century-Crofts, 1971.

Van Riper, C. *Speech Correction: Principles and Methods* (5th ed.). Englewood Cliffs, N. J.: Prentice-Hall, Inc., 1972.

CHAPTER 7

The learning disabled
and mildly mentally handicapped

From Chinn, P. C., Drew, C. J., and Logan, D. R.: Mental retardation: a life cycle approach,
St. Louis, 1975, The C. V. Mosby Co.

In preceding chapters we indicated that the teacher should have a basic understanding about the nature of the handicapping condition under consideration. We then described the handicap and its relationship to learning. With the learning disabled and the mildly mentally handicapped, we will attempt to follow a similar procedure, but there are certain factors that will make this a more difficult task. These factors, which might be called definitional variables, could also be called "factors of confusion" because this is their net effect on discussions of the learning disabled and the mildly mentally handicapped. We do not intend to belabor this point, and confusion is exactly what we wish to avoid, but to ignore the significant debates, definitional variations, and issues surrounding these two areas of handicap would be a disservice to the teacher, who may find much confusion in what is presently being said by various authorities in these fields. These are not clear-cut areas of handicap, and their existence cannot be demonstrated in the same manner as a visual or hearing impairment. They relate to how the brain and total neurosystem is functioning, an area of study containing many unknowns.

One further point before we enter this discussion: we believe that both mental handicap (or mental retardation) and learning disabilities are real, significant handicapping conditions. We feel that they are different and, in some cases, relatively easy to identify. However, in other instances, particularly with younger children, they are extremely difficult to differentiate. We will discuss mental handicap and learning disabilities in this one chapter and will attempt to indicate how they are alike and how they are different. In addition, we will indicate methods and procedures that may be of value with both types of handicap plus methods and procedures that may be more appropriate for only one of these handicapping conditions.

MILDLY MENTALLY HANDICAPPED (OR RETARDED)

The mildly mentally handicapped, often called the educable mentally handicapped or educable mentally retarded, were the subject of many of the court suits outlined in Chapter 1. The reason, in many instances, was the fact that it was established to the satisfaction of the court that a number of children who were labeled as educable mentally handicapped and placed in classes for the mentally handicapped were not properly diagnosed. This leaves a number of important questions to be answered. These include the following: (1) How do we know who is mentally handicapped? (2) How was this error in diagnosis and placement made with so many children? (3) If there are all these questions and uncertainties, can we be certain that any given child is mentally handicapped? (4) Is there really such a thing as a mildly mentally handicapped child? (5) If there are some children who are really mildly mentally handicapped, what is the best educational program for them? All of these questions have been asked over and over again, and there remains considerable debate about many of them. We will attempt to answer these questions, or at least pose tentative answers that we believe represent the most acceptable answers in the light of present evidence.

The educable mentally handicapped (EMH), or educable mentally retarded (EMR), was a recognized category of handicap, as the visually impaired and the hearing impaired, in all but one or two states in the United States during the 1960s. In nearly all of these states, children were placed into programs for the EMR or EMH based on referral by a teacher or principal indicating that the child was having educational difficulties and on the results of an individual test of intelligence (usually the Wechsler Intelligence Scale for Children or the Stanford-Binet). In most states, parents were consulted; at least this was written into the regulations. Upper IQ limits for such placement varied from state to state, but the most common upper limits for inclusion in such programs were IQ's of 70, 75, or 80. In most cases, state officials had the responsibility of monitoring these programs to be certain that children with IQ's above this upper limit were not included. In a few states, there was some mention of adaptive behavior, that is, the way the child functions in various societal settings other than the academic, as another criteria for classification as EMH, but this was seldom followed. In summary, then, to be identified as educable mentally handicapped required an IQ of 50 to 70 (or 75 or 80), and that was essentially all that was required.

This overdependence on IQ test results led to a wide variety of abuses and inappropriate placements (Dunn, 1968). Many children from cultural backgrounds that were significantly different from middle-class whites could not perform adequately on such tests, and when they had difficulties in the regular class they were tested and placed in special programs for the EMH. Many bilingual children who had initially learned another language received depressed scores on English language IQ tests. Therefore, many minority children who had more potential intellectual ability than indicated by the IQ were labeled EMH.

Another factor had serious implications for the effectiveness of such programming in some areas of the nation. This has not been as carefully researched and documented as the biased IQ test effect but has been repeatedly observed by many professional special educators. Unfortunately, it has been common for children who were known to have normal mental ability but who were disruptive or for some other reason could not be easily managed in the regular class to be placed in special classes for the EMH. This often was the only "special class" available, and since it was limited to twelve to fifteen children, such placements were justified on the basis of an, "It's the best place we have for him!" philosophy. This was not in keeping with state regulations for special reimbursement for EMH programs, but this happened so regularly it was accepted practice in many school districts. Thus, such children became "mildly mentally handicapped," even though they in no way fit any definition or concept of mental handicap. The presence of these children in special programs for the

EMH child often reduced the effectiveness of the program for the children who were truly mentally handicapped, in addition to being inappropriate for the nonmentally handicapped child (Coonley, 1974).

Another very significant influence for change must be recognized. Whereas the mentally handicapped have been, for the most part, considered as permanently mentally handicapped, recent efforts have indicated that IQ as measured by the best available tests can be increased. This often relates to minority children but also includes the white, middle-class child who, for some reason, has not developed to his full intellectual potential. Intelligence, as measured by tests of intelligence, is *not* a static fact of life but in some cases (not necessarily all) can be changed. Thus some, perhaps many, children called mildly mentally handicapped may have underdeveloped, normal-range intelligence.

The effect of the preceding factors, plus the fact that studies of classes for the mildly mentally handicapped leave some doubt as to their value, has led to questions in the minds of some as to whether the existence of the mildly mentally handicapped should even be recognized. The following statements reflect our beliefs in this controversial matter.

1. Many children who have been identified as mentally handicapped have been mislabeled due to inappropriate or biased tests or insufficient data or both.

2. Many children who might be viewed as mildly mentally handicapped can be assisted to develop intellectually/cognitively to approach the level of normal mental ability.

3. There are "true" mildly mentally handicapped children (just as there are more severely mentally retarded children—a fact few will deny), and they may occur in all races, ethnic groups, and socioeconomic levels.

4. The mildly mentally handicapped should be identified by multiple criteria, including (a) level of functioning in social situations, (b) level of language development, (c) functioning on an individual test of intelligence (full-scale or global

IQ, plus consideration of patterns of sub-test scores), (d) emotional maturity, and (e) academic achievement. Ethnic, cultural, social, and economic background must also be considered.

5. Many mildly mentally handicapped children can be effectively educated in the regular class for the major part of the day if the teacher receives assistance with materials and specific methods.

6. Children who score at the lower end of the range often ascribed to the mildly mentally handicapped (those who have a measured IQ of 50 to 60; other indicators supporting this measure) may require a special class program for a major part of the school day.

7. Most mildly mentally handicapped children are likely to benefit from a special, work-experience type program at the secondary level. To this extent, they can greatly benefit from a special program at this academic level.

Although the preceding seven points cannot properly be called a definition, they represent the most precise and succinct way we can express our conceptualization of the mildly mentally handicapped.

CHILDREN WITH LEARNING DISABILITIES

The term learning disabilities is much more recent than the terms mental retardation or mental handicap, but in many school districts this has become the largest single program for handicapped children. Learning disabilities programs were essentially non-existent until the late 1960s and did not reach full recognition in some parts of the nation until the mid 1970s. Some debate continues as to whether learning disabilities really exist, with much of the concern focussed on the lack of definitional explicitness. We will consider what might be called a middle-of-the-road definition and will discuss some of the reasons for the confusion before attempting to consider what the classroom teacher can do to help such children. We *do* believe that learning disabilities are "real" or we would not discuss them.

Children with learning disabilities exhibit a disorder in learning, which may be manifested as a problem in reading, writing, spelling, arithmetic, talking, thinking, or listening. Usually this involves processes relating to language usage (either spoken or written). To be considered a learning disability, there must be a significant discrepancy between the individual's achievement/performance and his apparent ability to achieve or perform. Learning disabilities is an umbrella term and is meant to include disorders that have previously been called dyslexia, dyscalculia, agnosia, minimal brain dysfunction, and others in which the preceding condition of significant discrepancy is met. The category of learning disabilities is *not* meant to include learning problems in which the *primary* or basic cause is mental retardation, visual or hearing impairment, emotional disturbance, or environmental disadvantage.

This definition is a composite of various definitions of learning disabilities that have been in use over the past few years, and like the definition of mental retardation or mental handicap, it should be expanded and discussed before proceeding.

There are a multitude of problems posed by this or most any other definition of learning disabilities. One of the major problems is due to the fact that it is most difficult to determine what degree of learning problem is sufficient to lead to the decision that a learning disability exists. Some writers have suggested that as many as twenty, thirty, or even forty percent of all school age children have a learning disability. We believe that these percentage estimates are *much* too high for the concept of learning disabilities that was intended by those who initiated the term and are so high that specialized educational assistance for learning disabled children who are in great need of help (the more severe cases) is endangered by such thinking. The reason is simple; if so many children have this need, it is no longer "special," but is "usual" or "normal." In addition, from a practical point of view, legislators cannot be expected to provide special funds for this high percentage of children. We would therefore suggest that those children who seem to meet the other criteria and who represent perhaps two to four percent or in some unusual situations even six percent of the school age population might be considered learning disabled.

A second problem with this definition is that it excludes those children who have other primary handicapping conditions. For example, a child with a moderate hearing impairment, if we interpret this definition literally, cannot be thought of as learning disabled. We believe that the two should not be confused (which was the intent of the definition) but that it is quite possible for the hearing impaired child to have an additional problem that *is* a learning disability and is in no way related to the hearing impairment. This child needs the help that may be provided through *both* kinds of programs.

The environmentally disadvantaged were excluded from most original definitions of learning disabilities because learning problems that originate because a child has not been *exposed* to educational opportunity are quite different from, for example, learning process difficulties in those who have had a chance to learn. We agree that this is a valid point but are concerned that some have interpreted this to mean that the culturally disadvantaged or the culturally different *cannot* have learning disabilities. We believe that the child raised in a substandard learning environment in the ghetto or the bilingual child may just as likely have a learning disability as a middle-class, white child and deserves the benefit of special programming if he needs it. These two issues and the needs they generate should not be confused, but the fact that *one* exists should not automatically exclude the possibility of the other.

A number of additional points could be made regarding this problem of an acceptable definition of learning disabilities, but the preceding discussion should provide at least a minimum level of understanding of the problem (for a more detailed consideration of this problem, see Gearheart, 1976).

As was the case with the mentally handicapped, we do not propose that we can formulate a totally acceptable definition for learning disabilities. However, we can enumerate our beliefs in the form of generalized statements that will indicate the basis for the remainder of our discussion of the learning disabled in this chapter.

1. Many children with very mild problems, which give every indication that they will likely be temporary in nature, have been improperly called learning disabled.

2. In too many instances, the term learning disabilities has been used as a convenient and more socially acceptable way to relabel some of the mildly mentally retarded.

3. Although many have broadened the definition of learning disabilities to include too many children, it would be just as unacceptable to narrow the definition (as some have proposed) to include only those for whom we can find definite signs of neurological impairment.

4. Although many learning disabled children do have perceptual problems, attempts to make "perceptually handicapped" synonomous with learning disabilities have led some educators to believe that all learning disabilities are perceptual handicaps. Thus they have ignored the existence of disabilities in such areas as memory (or imagery) and conceptual abilities.

5. There are certain guidelines for assisting the learning disabled that can provide the framework for educational planning by either the learning disability specialist or the regular classroom teacher (outlined on pp. 122-128).

These five points, the discussion of the definition of learning disabilities preceding them, and the ten principles for learning disabilities planning and programming (pp. 122-128) should, in total, provide a practical conceptualization of learning disabilities, if not a highly specific definition.

IDENTIFICATION OF THE LEARNING DISABLED AND THE MILDLY MENTALLY HANDICAPPED

The mildly learning disabled and the mildly mentally handicapped may be difficult to identify at an early age. If there is no outward effect of their disability, there is no reason to identify them—unless it relates to a disability that is likely to become much worse or relates to a problem that might be prevented through direct intervention. Examples of the preceding include such factors as severe malnourishment or malnutrition that is just beginning to cause observable difficulties in school performance. If this is not discovered until school age, much of the damage is already done, but additional effects may be reduced if quick action is taken. There is a considerable body of medical evidence on the effect of malnutrition on the developing brain, and much of this data has been provided in popular form by Elie Schneour, a highly regarded neurochemist.* The essence of such evidence is that the mind can be permanently damaged (or underdeveloped) as a result of inadequate nutrition. Too many children may have enough quantity but are sadly lacking in the right dietary components. Such children may then become "learning disabled" or "mildly mentally handicapped" and carry the disadvantage of a handicapping condition for the rest of their lives.

In a somewhat similar manner, even if the brain and neurosystem are fully developed and have been functioning adequately, children may develop problems such as hypoglycemia (a condition in which the brain does not receive an adequate amount of glucose owing to a fluctuating and inadequate supply of circulating glucose in the body). A child with hypoglycemia will perform as though he were either mentally handicapped or learning disabled. In fact, it might be said that he is temporarily learning disabled and that continuance of this condition over a long period of time may result in more permanent effects. Severe allergy problems may also lead to this type situation. Though

---

*We recommend *The Malnourished Mind* (Schneour, 1974). This book is highly commended by renowned scientists, medical doctors, individuals such as Senators George McGovern and Edward Kennedy, and a host of other well-known public figures. It may well be to the field of nutrition (and malnutrition in children) what Rachel Carson's *Silent Spring* was to environmental protection.

malnourishment, hypoglycemic, and allergy-related causes for learning problems do not affect a majority of learning problem cases (or we do not believe they do), they are significant enough to warrant concern.

For children (other than those for whom medical referral may be in order) who have only very mild problems, *identification* as learning disabled or mentally handicapped may have few advantages and more than a few disadvantages. *Identification can be justified only if it leads to some educational provision and assistance that would not be provided without such identification.* If the regular classroom teacher is sensitive to the unique educational needs of children with mild learning problems and has the knowledge, materials and techniques to effectively assist them, in many cases it may be best to forget all about what "type" of child he is. However, the more severe the learning problem, the more likely that help from outside the classroom may be needed, but as in all problems in educational planning and programming, a host of variables may come into play.

In school districts that have viable programs of itinerant or resource room assistance for children with learning problems (either learning disabilities or mild mental handicap), it is necessary to identify the child to make such assistance available. Some districts call such programs their "learning assistance program," and children may be served without specific identification other than that they require learning assistance owing to some type of academic difficulty. The manner in which children come to the attention of or are temporarily assigned to such centers (usually it is one or two hours per day) varies greatly from area to area, but usually it is a matter of teacher referral through the principal or perhaps through the counselor in the secondary school.

Characteristics of the learning disabled and the mildly mentally handicapped

As indicated in the discussion of a definition of learning disabilities, one characteristic must be present or a child may not be called

| Don | Mike |

Age: 10

Grade: 4

Years in school: 5½

Reading achievement: 2.1 (grade equivalent)

Group IQ score: 77

Age: 10

Grade: 4

Years in school: 5½

Reading achievement: 2.1 (grade equivalent)

Group IQ score: 77

The preceding description of Don and Mike is obviously identical until the IQ as indicated by an *individual* test of intelligence is considered. Then it is found that

Full-scale WISC IQ: 74

Full-scale WISC IQ: 105

Through the individual test of intelligence it is found that Don is very likely a borderline slow learner/mildly mentally handicapped youngster, whereas Mike is probably a learning disabled child. Additional information is then assembled.

Mathematics—fundamental addition, subtraction, multiplication, and division: 2.3 (grade equivalent)

Mathematics—fundamental addition, subtraction, multiplication, and division: 3.7 (grade equivalent)

Generally, the mildly mentally handicapped child will have basic skills in mathematics that are about the same level as his reading skills, though sometimes they will be higher if they involve mainly rote memory. In contrast, many learning disabled children who have severe problems in reading may do grade level work in mathematics, as long as reading is not required. The reverse may also be true of the learning disabled child; he may do satisfactory work in reading and have significant problems in mathematics. It is the inconsistency in performance between various academic areas and various types of activities that characterizes the learning disabled child. Additional information about the two boys' abilities in classroom interaction, apparent ability to learn from peers, and ability to conceptualize follows:

In classroom interaction regarding relationship of planets and the Sun in the solar system, Don had real difficulty in following the idea of relative movement. Don does a little better when things are explained verbally but has trouble in integrating information. Don can follow class discussion as long as concepts are simple but has difficulty in making generalizations. Class members know they can fool him verbally, and some do, just to "make fun" of him. Don's speaking vocabulary is better than his reading vocabulary, but it is still far below the class average.

In classroom interaction regarding relationship of planets and the Sun, Mike was one of the first in the class to really understand. In fact, in most topics related to science, if no classroom reading is involved, Mike does very well. He learns exceptionally well from films or narrated filmstrips. Mike can follow class discussions at least as well as the average of the class. In some respects, he is superior to the class average. On a verbal level, he conceptualizes and generalizes well. Mike's reading vocabulary (words he can recognize in print) is no better than Don's; however, his spoken vocabulary is up to the average of the class in all respects and in science areas is far above average.

Almost always the learning disabled child has a performance profile (in such areas as reading achievement, arithmetic achievement, vocabulary, ability to generalize, and ability to conceptualize) that is characterized by many "ups" and "downs." He sometimes (or in some academic areas) seems quite average, or perhaps above average, but in some areas (perhaps recognition of visually presented symbols) he may be even less able than the mentally handicapped. It is possible for a learning disabled child to be low in *all* areas of achievement and class interaction, but it is unusual. In contrast, the performance profile of the mentally handicapped is usually relatively "flat."

learning disabled. This one characteristic is that the child must be achieving significantly less than other indicators, particularly intellectual ability, would predict he should achieve. In contrast, the mildly mentally handicapped child is achieving less than his age peers, but there are indications that this is due, at least in part, to lower than average intellectual ability. To illustrate this point, let us consider two boys, Don and Mike, described on the opposite page.

The illustration concerning Don and Mike provides an example of how a 10-year-old learning disabled boy and a 10-year-old mentally handicapped boy might be alike and how they might be different. There are many possible variations in this alike-different contrast—perhaps as many as there are children who may be called learning disabled or mentally handicapped, but usually a general pattern of slowness in most all areas of achievement and performance will be seen with the mentally handicapped, whereas some considerable inconsistencies, some high and some low performances, will be seen with the learning disabled. *By definition,* we must have normal range (or above) intelligence with the learning disabled and below normal intelligence with the mentally handicapped. The contrast between such children becomes more evident after a few years in school. At the preschool or kindergarten level it might have been very difficult to tell Don and Mike apart, but as the years pass, the differences become more evident.

Characteristics associated mainly with the learning disabled

Certain characteristics seem to occur with the learning disabled child much more frequently than with the normal child or with the mentally handicapped. No one child would demonstrate all of these characteristics, and it is possible, though not likely, that a learning disabled child who did not exhibit any of the following characteristics might be found.

Hyperactivity. Many learning disability children are hyperactive. This is particularly true among those with actual brain insult. It is not always that any one action is so much a problem, but rather that the child is moving in triple time nearly all of the time and is a problem to others. With so much movement, it is difficult for him to attend to anything long enough to achieve much academically.

Hypoactivity. Hypoactivity is just the opposite of hyperactivity. Although not found as often among the learning disabled as hyperactivity, it is found often enough to be worthy of mention.

Lack of motivation. Although lack of motivation may be a *result* of the individual's difficulty in learning, it is recorded as a characteristic on the referral report of many children who are later placed in a learning disabilities program.

Lack of coordination. Although highly coordinated children may have learning problems, lack of coordination is often observed in children with learning disabilities. The child with learning disabilities is often slower to develop the ability to throw or catch a ball, to skip, or to run. He is also likely to have difficulty in writing and other fine motor skills. He may be generally clumsy; he may stumble or fall frequently. Some coordination problems are related to an inability to properly assess position in space or to balance problems, or both.

Perseveration. A child may perseverate, or repeat persistently, in almost any behavioral area, but this is more often seen in writing or copying. A child may copy a word over and over again involuntarily. He may also perseverate in oral response.

Inattention. Inattention may or may not be related to the hyperactivity or lack of motivation. It can simply be a matter of inability to focus on any particular activity for any length of time.

Overattention. A child with overattention, which might also be called attention fixation, will focus on one particular object and seem unable to break the focus.

Perceptual disorders. Perceptual disorders might include disorders of visual, auditory, tactual, or kinesthetic perception. The child with visual-perceptual problems may not be able to copy letters correctly or to perceive the difference between a hexagon and an octagon. He may reverse letters or produce mirror writing. The child with auditory perception problems may not perceive the difference between various consonant blends or be able to differentiate between the front doorbell and the first ring of the telephone. All these perceptual problems may at first make the child seem to be lacking in sensory acuity (that is, seem to have a visual loss or be hard of hearing), but when acuity checks out as normal, the possibility of perceptual disorder must be considered.

Memory disorders. Memory disorders may include either auditory or visual memory. Memory is a highly complicated process and is not fully understood, although various individuals have established theories that seem to explain the various observable facets of memory. In case study reports we hear of individuals who cannot remember where the window is or on which side of the room their bed is placed, even though it has been there for months. In others we hear of children who cannot repeat a simple sequence of three words immediately after hearing them. These types of memory deficit seriously affect the learning process.

Some of the preceding characteristics are exact opposites (for example, hypoactivity and hyperactivity), and some are overlapping (for example, overattention and perseveration). In combination, problems such as these lead to difficulties in symbolic processes. Some of these characteristics go almost unnoticed until the child is asked to complete school tasks; thus we see why it is difficult to identify mild learning disabilities until age 5 or 6.

Care must be taken not to overpredict on the basis of this type of characteristic alone. Many children have problems at some time early in life with copying or writing letters backwards. In most cases this is *not* a sign that the child will have a learning disability. However, if the difficulty persists and there are a number of other problems, it may well be time to look at the child more carefully. In a similar manner, because children differ in energy levels, some children are much

more active than others. The term *hyperactive* has been used too much and too loosely, and it is easy to make inaccurate assumptions based on activity level. (When you see a *really* hyperactive child—often called a "wall climber"—you then know what hyperactivity is.) A great deal of caution must be used with the concept of hyperactivity, but it is, in fact, a symptom or characteristic of many learning disabled children.

Only one characteristic may be ascribed to *all* learning disabled children. That is the existence of a significant educational lag or discrepancy between expected and actual achievement. Various definitions supported by a wide range of authorities will tend to further limit the application or determination of this one characteristic, but all have this component either implicitly or explicitly included.

Characteristics associated mainly with the mildly mentally handicapped

The concept of mild or educable level mental handicap (or retardation) implies that the child can be educated and that with proper educational opportunity he can be a self-supporting, participating member of society. It is likely that the reader knows of mildly mentally handicapped individuals who appear to contradict this statement. They apparently cannot support themselves and certainly do not seem to be capable of contributory participation in society. In nearly every case of this type that we have seen over the years, the reasons for the inability to be self-supporting and participating members of society were either (1) the existence of other handicapping conditions (in addition to the mild mental handicap) or (2) inappropriate or insufficient educational opportunity. Very often it was a combination of these factors. Those in whom intellectual deficit alone is the cause for failure are almost always below the range of mild mental retardation.

The concept of mild mental handicap indicates a measurable deficit in intellectual functioning. Such deficits are almost always measured through use of an individual test of intelligence such as the Wechsler Intelligence Scales or the Stanford-Binet. As indicated earlier in this chapter, such tests may be suspect in use with minority or bilingual children, but if the test is given by a well-trained and experienced diagnostician, the fact that the test is not measuring adequately is usually evident. Such tests should then be considered invalid. Even if valid test results can be obtained, a second characteristic should be investigated. Most authorities would require both the lower-than-average IQ score plus significantly lower-than-average adaptive behavior. Adaptive behavior is also sometimes called "street behavior," indicating the manner in which the child is able to perform or function in the everyday requirements of living. This would include but not be restricted to such things as getting to and from school (walking or using the school bus, for example), functioning as a member of a peer group, following simple instructions, and ability to discuss, with peers and with adults, common day-to-day topics of interest. Some might characterize adequate behavior as ability to function with peers without "standing out" as different. Of course, many nonmentally handicapped youngsters may have subaverage adaptive behavior, but mentally handicapped will be used here to mean that youngster who is performing considerably below average in the academic areas, who has a measurable deficit in intellectual functioning (as reflected by an individual test of intelligence), and who has subaverage adaptive behavior. If these conditions are met, then we will tentatively consider the child to be mildly mentally handicapped.

The following characteristics, and certain subcharacteristics that relate to and grow out of these, will more often be found in the mildly mentally handicapped than in age peers of normal mental ability. It is not likely that all of these characteristics will be found in all mildly mentally handicapped, but some combination of these characteristics are found in most mildly mentally handicapped. These characteristics are highly interrelated (for example, below average language ability and academic retardation), and all are related to the below normal level of mental functioning of the mildly mentally handicapped.

Sensory and motor coordination handicaps. Though many mildly mentally handicapped children have no visual or hearing impairments, there tend to be more such impairments among the mentally handicapped population than among the total population of children of the same age. In a similar manner, there is more likelihood that mildly mentally handicapped children will have less well-developed motor skills, though many will have average motor ability and some will have above average motor ability.

Low tolerance for frustration. Low tolerance for frustration is regularly mentioned in relation to the mildly mentally handicapped, in an academic setting established for age-peers of normal or above normal intellectual ability. It is altogether possible that it is the result of academic expectations beyond their capability, and content and concepts for which they are not ready, rather than some sort of "built-in" characteristic.

Poor self-concept. The cumulative effect of failure in academic and social situations may contribute to a low self-concept. The mildly mentally handicapped may lack confidence because of previous experiences and may not be willing to attempt new tasks because of failure. Their past experiences and the effect of lower expectations may contribute significantly to their lower self-esteem.

Short attention span. These students may demonstrate a relatively short attention span. This may be due to their failure in past academic efforts, the inappropriateness of present academic expectations, or to auditory or visual distractions in the classroom. Each of these factors can limit a student's ability to attend, and in combination, the effect may be quite serious.

Below average language ability. Although language ability that is below average might indicate hearing impairment, learning disability, lack of opportunity to develop language, or other causal factors, the mildly mentally handicapped will almost always have below average (for age) language ability.

The only exception that we have seen to this generalization has been with upper borderline mildly mentally handicapped in situations in which well-informed, highly motivated parents have invested unusual efforts at the preschool level. In such cases, these children may enter school with normal language ability. Usually it will slowly become lower than that of the normal peer group, as other children have opportunity to grow in this area.

Below average ability to generalize and conceptualize. Below average ability to generalize and conceptualize are at least partially measured by most individual tests of intelligence and thus are to be expected in most mildly mentally handicapped, since intelligence test results are a significant part of the base for determining mild mental handicap. It is useful for the classroom teacher to think in terms of the child's abilities in these areas, but care should be taken to avoid confusion between ability to generalize or conceptualize relating to what is read, and ability to generalize or conceptualize in other settings. (A learning disabled child with a serious reading problem may appear to be unable to conceptualize if initial information on which to base conceptualizations must be read. However, he may be able to conceptualize quite well if initial information is given verbally. In contrast, the mentally handicapped child will have a tendency to have difficulty with generalization and conceptualization in a variety of settings.)

General academic retardation. The mildly mentally handicapped child will usually be academically retarded in such areas as reading, arithmetic, and spelling. If he is retarded academically in, for example, only reading but is normal or above normal in academic ability in arithmetic, he probably is not mentally handicapped.

Play interests below those of age peers. A play interest below those of age peers is not always observed but is apparent in enough cases to deserve mention. Many types of play are related to an ability to understand rules and to integrate cause-effect factors and relationships. Whereas a particular activity may "stretch" the mental ability of most other children of a given age, the mildly mentally handicapped child will likely not understand. He may therefore turn to more simple play activities or to younger children.

REFERRING THE CHILD WITH SUSPECTED LEARNING DISABILITIES OR MILD MENTAL HANDICAP FOR SPECIAL EDUCATIONAL ASSISTANCE

Referral procedures vary from district to district, but if specialized assistance is available for either of these conditions, there will usually be a special referral form to be completed by the classroom teacher. In addition to name, age, grade, and sex, most referral forms will ask such questions as (1) grade level in academic areas (usually means grade equivalent on a standardized achievement test), (2) data on behavior (interpersonal relations with other children and with teachers, for example), (3) specific reading strengths and deficits (for example, word attack skills, memory for words, and ability t read orally), (4) ability (related to others i class) in class discussion and interaction, (5) strengths and weaknesses in nonacademic areas, (6) any unusual family data that might be pertinent, and (7) a summary of any methods or approaches that may have been unusually successful in the classroom. A variety of screening devices may be used to assist in identifying the mentally handicapped or learning disabled child. One such device is shown in Appendix F. This type of screening instrument is useful as a guide to assist the classroom teacher in objectifying his observations and in enumerating factors that should be considered in deciding whether to further pursue the referral procedure. We have seen teachers who were about to refer a child for consideration for special education assistance, but after completing a data form similar to that shown in Appendix F they realized that the child was really quite normal, except for perhaps one personality component, which was the real reason they were making the referral. Therefore, in addition to being of value as the starting point for possible specialized assistance, at times referral forms, screening forms, or scales may be of value to the teacher as a structure through which the child's strengths and weaknesses may be systematically summarized and analyzed.

There are a variety of ways in which the learning disabled or mentally handicapped child may receive additional assistance in the public schools. In mild cases of learning disabilities and mental handicap, the regular classroom teacher may be able to provide meaningful and stimulating opportunities for learning with suggestions from a resource or itinerant teacher. In other cases, some time may be needed in a specialized setting. In this chapter we will reverse the usual order of presentation of information and will review what the special education specialist may do to assist in programming. We will then discuss suggestions for the regular classroom teacher.

ROLE AND RESPONSIBILITIES OF SPECIAL EDUCATION PERSONNEL IN LEARNING DISABILITIES PROGRAMMING

If a child is referred and found to be in need of assistance owing to a learning disability, the most often utilized service delivery method is the resource room (see p. 25). The following description of an actual learning disabilities resource room is perhaps the most effective way to indicate what a resource room teacher may do. Note that these children spend the *major* part of their school day in the regular class and that full-time return to the regular class is the goal for all children who receive assistance through such a program.

A DIAGNOSTIC-PRESCRIPTIVE CENTER FOR CHILDREN WITH LEARNING DISABILITIES*

The following outline is intended to include sufficient description to permit understanding of

*Robinson Primary School, Pitt County Schools; Winterville, North Carolina. Our appreciation to Jean Averette, Blanie Moye, Betty Quinn, and Alan Sheinker, who assisted in providing this summary.

general program operation. As with any such program, the materials, structure, and outward appearance of effectiveness would be of little value without the support of the principal and building staff and without acceptance by the parents. Robinson Primary School has all of these. Any such specialized program must have a good, knowledgeable teacher who can provide special assistance to boys and girls and work harmoniously with building staff. Robinson School has such a teacher and, in addition, a highly competent aide.

Teacher referral

At the beginning of the school year, classroom teachers are given a brief overview of the learning disability program, a list of characteristics of learning disabled children, and referral forms. They are instructed to complete a referral form for each child with average or above average intelligence who seems to possess those characteristics displayed by children with learning disabilities. These forms are turned in to the school principal, who may add comments as appropriate. The principal then gives them to the learning disabilities resource teacher.

Screening/assessment

The following instruments are administered by resource personnel and are used in the screening/ assessment process in Pitt County:
1. Peabody Picture Vocabulary Test
2. Slosson Intelligence Test
3. Slosson Drawing Coordination Test
4. Wide Range Achievement Test
5. Peabody Individual Achievement Test
6. Wepman Auditory Discrimination Test
7. Slosson Oral Reading Test
8. Draw-A-Man Test

Informal assessment is another vital part of the screening process. The following activities are used:
1. Write complete name
2. Write alphabet (small letters)
3. Write numbers (1 to 10)
4. Distinguish between *b, d, p, g,* and *q*
5. Distinguish between "saw" and "was"
6. Visual discrimination activity
7. Write a sentence
8. Eye dominance test
9. Informal reading inventory

The following questions are considered in identifying children with learning disabilities:
1. Is the child average or above average in intelligence?

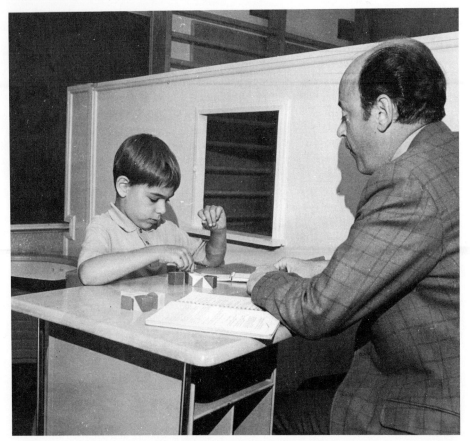

From Gearheart, B. R.: Learning disabilities: educational strategies, St. Louis, 1973, The C. V. Mosby Co.

2. Is his achievement two years or more behind his current grade placement?
3. Does he appear to have visual-motor problems that could affect reading, writing, or spelling?
4. Does he have a distorted conception of the human figure and interrelationship of its parts?

The parents of those children whose test results indicate learning disabilities are sent a letter requesting their permission for psychological testing. When permission is received, the children are given the Wechsler Intelligence Scale for Children and other tests as required to determine their level of intelligence.

Parent conferences

Individual parent conferences are held with the parents of the children identified as having learning disabilities. The learning disabilities program is explained and permission is obtained to place the child in a resource room to work on areas in which deficits have been indicated if the placement committee so recommends.

Placement committee

Test results and the information obtained on each child is presented to a placement committee for consideration for placement in the resource room. The committee may consist of the learning disabilities teacher, the principal, the medical-social counselor, the special education supervisor, the classroom teacher, and others as may be necessary in an individual case. The committee must reach substantial agreement on the need for placement before such placement is made.

Diagnosis and prescription

The following diagnostic instruments are commonly used to prescribe for the individual needs of each child:
1. Illinois Test of Psycholinguistic Abilities

2. Basic Education Skills Inventory—Math and Reading
3. Frostig Test of Visual Perception
4. KeyMath
5. Slingerland Screening Test
6. Goldman-Fristoe-Woodcock Test of Auditory Discrimination
7. Woodcock Reading Mastery Test
8. Sucher-Allred Reading Placement Inventory

Others are used as may be required.

Learning lab

The learning lab is a diagnostic/prescriptive center designed to meet the individual needs of each child. Assets, deficits, and long-range prescriptions are recorded in individual folders for each child.

Each day as the child enters the learning lab, he picks up his "tote" tray containing his *daily task folder* and other materials he keeps in his tray. The prescription centers (reading and language, writing, math, auditory perception, visual perception, and kinesthetic-tactile) are identified by Walt Disney characters. The child goes to the centers in the order of arrangement of the Walt Disney picture cards in the pockets of his task folder. Once the child is in the center to which he has been assigned, the teacher or aide assists him in getting the appropriate materials, understanding the instructions, and beginning the assigned task. The teacher then leaves the child to work independently and goes to other children in much the same manner. "Help, Please" signs are available at each center as a means of letting the teacher know that the child requires help in completing a task or is ready to have his work checked.

The children may work in two or three centers each day in the learning lab. Constant monitoring and individual assistance are paramount in the individualized approach. Incomplete tasks or unfinished center activities are ordinarily assigned for the next class period in an orderly, sequential manner throughout the week. At the close of each day, individual daily prescriptions are written for the following day.

The center activities and tasks consist of commercial programmed materials, teacher-made games, laminated task cards, record players, cassette tape players, books, puppets, and assorted activity folders. Although most of the tasks are individually oriented, there is planned opportunity for social development through games, peer teaching, puppetry, and group activities.

Approximately twenty children are served in the learning lab on a daily basis under the supervision of the resource teacher. The resource teacher also serves as a consulting teacher for a limited number of children who do not come to the resource room. The maximum number of children the teacher can serve is twenty-five, as specified by regulations of the state of North Carolina.

Ages of the children served in the learning lab range from 7 to 10. The majority of the children are second and third graders, and intelligence quotients range from 90 to 130. The most significant academic discrepancy is in the area of reading. The perceptual area causing the greatest difficulty is in the area of auditory learning.

Five or six children at a time are served in the learning lab for a period of 1 to 1½ hours each day (Monday through Thursday). Friday is designated as a day for individual evaluations and testing, teacher and parent conferences, classroom observations, and follow-up activities in the regular classroom.

Summary

The learning disabled child is provided an opportunity through success-oriented tasks to improve his self-concept. Since each child works at his own level, at his own rate, and with materials designed to remediate his specific problems, the program is truly individualized. Teaching the child to work independently in the resource room and to continue to do so in his regular classroom is of prime concern. The ultimate goal is to enable the child to function well within his regular classroom, thereby phasing him out of the resource room as soon as the necessary remediation has been completed.

Although individual pupil growth and progress are observable to the resource teacher, specific test data must be recorded as a means of verifying pupil progress. Examples of individual pupil progress in academic areas are determined from pretest and posttest scores on the Peabody Individual Achievement Tests. One second grade repeater gained, during the period from October to May; in math (1.9 to 3.5), in reading word recognition (2.2 to 3.3), in reading comprehension (too low for grade equivalent to 2.9), and in spelling (1.1 to 2.7). Another second grade pupil showed significant gains in reading word recognition (1.6 to 2.6), reading comprehension (too low for grade equivalent to 3.4), and spelling (1.5 to 3.4).

Other school districts may choose to pursue slightly different emphases in the learning lab (prescriptive centers other than the six used in Robinson School), but the manner in which children are selected for the program, evaluated, and placed provides a good model. The use of long-range prescription, based on assets and deficits, and daily prescriptions, replanned for the following day at the close of each day, provides an excellent model. The use of the simple but highly effective and unusually motivating daily prescriptive folder with "library-card-type" pockets directing the child to appropriate learning centers through use of Walt Disney characters is frosting on an already unusually good cake.

The resource room is presently very popular, but many learning disabled children are provided assistance through the efforts of an itinerant teacher, who may provide many similar types of activities and efforts to those indicated in the Robinson Primary School description.

Though an exception to the general rule, when children have *very severe* learning problems, particularly if they are extremely hyperactive or have other disabilities, a self-contained room may be the best type of service provision. Even in this extreme and exceptional setting, the purpose of the class is to prepare for eventual return to the regular class. The regular classroom teacher is the main armament in the school's arsenal to attack the problem of learning disabilities. Specialized personnel must be viewed as providing temporary, supplementary assistance.

HOW THE TEACHER CAN ASSIST THE LEARNING DISABLED CHILD IN THE REGULAR CLASS

In this discussion we will review guidelines and principles for providing assistance to the learning disabled child, wherever he may be in the educational system. Following the guidelines, we will outline specific methods that *may* work with the child with learn-

ing disabilities, depending on his unique needs and the other variables present.* We must keep in mind the "umbrella" nature of the learning disabilities definition, which leads to the inclusion of children with a wide variety of causal factors and remedial needs. Some of these same methods may be effective with the mildly mentally handicapped for a different set of reasons. The following principles are not *specific techniques* but are general guidelines that may assist the classroom teacher in working with learning disabled or mildly mentally handicapped children. Many of these principles are followed by special education resource personnel, and we believe they will be of value to classroom teachers.

PRINCIPLE 1
There is no single "right" method to use with learning disability children

Children are referred for assistance in learning disability programs because they are *not* learning effectively through the approach used in the classroom with the general population of boys and girls. Before further discussion, we should review the manner in which it is decided which approach, or approaches, will be used in education. The area of reading will be used as an example. Although educators tend to pass through cycles of emphasis on phonic or sight recognition approaches in reading and individual teachers may vary their application of written local district philosophy, the major determinant in most cases is the variety of basal readers published and the variety, or lack of variety, provided through this source of basic materials.

We do not question the effectiveness of basal readers for the seventy-five to eighty-five percent of the children who find success

---

*Please note the use of the word "may." Though we have made the point in numerous ways, our experience leads us to believe that it would be difficult to overemphasize it. We cannot, with professional honesty, recommend a method that *will* work with all learning disabled children. Those children included under this categorical label are too heterogeneous in nature and too diverse in needs for any single method to be universally effective.

through their use. If one looks into the research evidence indicating that "method A" or "method B" should be used, one would typically find that method A was most effective for perhaps seventy-eight percent of the children who were taught in this manner, while method B was most effective for eighty-three percent. (There may have been a method C, D, and E, which we will presume in this hypothetical example were less effective.) Obviously, the most effective method should be used, which was method B. The only remaining problem is that even the best method, method B, was relatively ineffective for seventeen percent of the children.

What about teacher-initiated variations in approach? In too many cases these are little more than the use of another basal reader; in others it is simply a matter of placing a child in a lower reading group with the hope that more of the same, at a lower level, will work. In rare cases, the teacher will actually use a fundamentally different teaching approach, based on careful observations of the child and how he learns most effectively. When this is done, it is often quite effective, but the factor saving public education from an even higher rate of failure is the fact that the human organism (the child) is highly resilient and learns in spite of our inadequate efforts. Educators must remain thankful for this fact but can take little credit for it.

It is doubtful that a teacher who knew he was working with a deaf child would attempt to use an approach that was primarily auditory in teaching word attack skills, but many teachers continue to use a method that relies heavily on hearing sounds accurately with students who do not have the required ability to discriminate between the very sounds the teacher is using. A student may *hear sound* as well as other children but be unable to discriminate between certain phonemes that are different yet somewhat similar. A similar situation may exist in relation to a child who has good visual acuity but who cannot accurately discriminate between certain letters and thus does not do well with an approach based primarily on sight recognition.

If the two children described in the preceding paragraph were referred to the same learning disability resource room, it is unlikely that they would have the same educational program, either of remediation or with respect to attempts to build reading skills through utilization of existing abilities. Both may be fifth grade boys, 11 years of age, of average intelligence, and at a beginning second grade reading level, but this does not dictate the same program or the same methodological approach (see Major Principles for Remediation, pp. 134-135).

To at least a limited extent, both might have learned to read effectively if the school had recognized their learning strengths and weaknesses and approached them appropriately at the first or second grade level. However, they were taught through a "most acceptable for the average" approach and are now in trouble academically. Very likely, in response to their obvious lack of success, they are also in trouble in terms of unacceptable acting-out behavior.

It would be the height of absurdity to move from one "right" approach, which was not right for them, to another "right" approach, which may be equally inappropriate.

The idea of one right method in learning disabilities violates common sense and is the outgrowth of lack of understanding. We cannot always tell, through present assessment techniques, exactly how to approach each child with learning disabilities, but we can avoid the error of belief in a single approach and can know that we may need to try a number of approaches and methods in certain difficult cases.

PRINCIPLE 2
All other factors being equal, the "newest" possible method should be used

When gathering data relative to educational history and background, the teacher should make every attempt to determine which approaches and materials have been used with each child. This may not be significant data in all cases but will be in many. Analysis of this information can have several

---

*"Newest" means new to the child.

applications. If certain approaches have been used with little or no success, this may indicate the inappropriateness of such approaches. This will not always be true, for such approaches may have been poorly implemented or the child may not have had certain requisite abilities at an earlier date and may possess them now; however, this does provide a starting point for further investigation.

An equally important point, and one too often overlooked, is that many children tend to develop a failure syndrome after trying to accomplish a task only to be met by repeated failure. In the case of learning to read, the teacher will likely feel it necessary to continue to attempt to assist the child to learn to read, or to read more effectively, but *the teacher should make a deliberate attempt to use a method that "looks" and "feels" different to the child*. The more severe the learning problem and the longer it has been recognized and felt by the child, the greater the need for this procedure. This principle dictates that when a variety of approach paths appear possible, all other factors being approximately equal, the most different approach (different from earlier methods used) is likely to be the most effective. It also dictates that we gather information as to which methods have been previously used in the regular classroom and in any earlier remedial attempts. The importance of checking on previous remedial attempts may be seen in cases in which earlier, poorly implemented remedial efforts have tended to cancel out the effectiveness of a particular approach, even though all other clues and evaluative results indicate the probable effectiveness of such an approach. Sometimes the effect of such unsuccessful efforts can be overcome, but knowledge of their existence is essential.

PRINCIPLE 3
Some type of positive reconditioning should be implemented

Pioneers in the learning disabilities field such as Fernald and Gillingham (see Gearheart, 1973, pp. 76-77, 104-105) recognized the value of this principle, a value that remains today. The "newest possible method" (principle 2) is a part of this positive reconditioning effort, but additional attempts should be directed toward convincing the child that his inability to develop adequate reading (or arithmetic or language) skills is not his fault. Rather, it is caused by the failure of the school and teachers to recognize that he needed to learn by methods different than those used for other children. The obvious point of this effort is to convince the child that *he* is "O.K.," to boost his self-concept to the point that he will approach the learning task with increased confidence, and thus to maximize his chances of success. A considerable amount has been written about the "self-fulfilling prophecy" effect on teachers when they are told that a given child is mentally handicapped and therefore will not likely learn as well as or as much as a normal child (see pp. 181-183). Think how much more devastating this effect must be when *you* as an individual become convinced, through painful experience, that you cannot learn. Unfortunately, most schools are organized in such a way that children with learning difficulties are reminded daily, sometimes hourly, that they are failures. There is a scarcity of research on this topic (the effects of planned positive reconditioning), but the experience of a number of learning disability teachers with whom we have worked, the historical testimony of Fernald and Gillingham, and simple logic indicate that *success must be planned*.

PRINCIPLE 4
High motivation is a prerequisite to success; deliberate consideration of the affective domain is essential

Because this is such an obvious principle, there may be a lack of proper emphasis, and attempts to maximize motivation are difficult to measure or monitor and may seem unglamorous, except as related to some unusual type of behavior modification system. Principles 2 and 3 are a part of the overall attempt to maximize motivation, but deliberate efforts beyond these two must be planned.

In the case of older children who may have developed the basic learning abilities necessary for academic success, but developed them several years late, a program to promote higher motivation may be about the only workable procedure. The fact that various behavior modification techniques are in common use, many with apparent success, attests to the validity of this principle.

This principle also dictates some sort of planned investigation of the affective domain—a look at how the child feels about himself, both in general (in the world outside the academic boundaries) and with respect to his specific feelings as he attempts to achieve within the school setting. Some learning disabled children have such obvious emotional problems that they can scarcely be overlooked. With these children, the best approach is to plan and initiate attempts to counteract, remediate, or in some manner attend to these problems. Many of the other principles have the effect of attending to the problems of low self-esteem, and if academic aehievement improves, this has an "automatic" positive effect. But beyond these positive vectors, it is imperative that the affective components be deliberately considered to maximize the potential of other remedial efforts and to prevent the growth of negative emotional components, even if they are minimal in nature and extent. This investigation of the affective domain, even when there is no outer indication of such problems, must be a part of the program of evaluation and planning for the learning disabled.

PRINCIPLE 5
The existence of nonspecific or difficult-to-define disabilities, particularly with older children, must be recognized

A serious educational problem in reading or arithmetic can be defined, but if an older child has experienced, for example, significant visual perceptual problems at an early age, did not have the visual perceptual skills necessary for success in reading at ages 6, 7, and 8, but developed them later, it may be almost impossible to pinpoint the specific disability. What may exist is significant edu-

cational retardation and, in many cases, a negative attitude toward school. The need may be to develop second or third grade reading skills in a 15-year-old student who has learned many ways to circumvent his reading problem. Some authorities, who want to describe learning disabilities only in terms of specific disabilities that may be carefully defined, might say that this is not a learning disability. Our point of view is that this is a learning disability and that it requires very careful consideration and planning.

One caution regarding this principle. In recognizing the possibility of such nonspecific disabilities, we must be careful to not use this possibility as an "out," a convenient reason to not fully investigate each individual case to attempt to determine specific guidelines for remediation and skill development programming based on careful evaluation.

PRINCIPLE 6
Complete, accurate information about the learning strengths and weaknesses is essential

Educational planning for the child with learning disabilities must be based on recent, complete, accurate information that can be used to provide the basis for determining which areas require maximum remedial efforts and which solid abilities are present that may be used as approach avenues in attacking disabilities. Accurate assessment of strengths also indicates intact abilities that may be utilized in the continuing attempt to teach content and concepts during the major part of the day during which remedial efforts will not be the major point of focus.

This principle dictates that we must not use a single assessment tool to attempt to determine strengths or weaknesses and that even if several assessment tools and techniques are used, every effort should be made to use at least two different measures to verify the existence of each specific area of dysfunction or low-level functioning. It also dictates that *when one problem area is discovered, it should not be automatically assumed that this is the major cause of the academic retardation, which was the basic reason for referral.* For example, we have seen situations in which those conducting a learning disability program were so involved with the idea of visual perceptual problems and so geared to provide programming in this one area of remediation, that this was essentially the only type of disability they looked for. In many cases, even if they could document this type of problem, it was a less significant problem than others that were fairly evident on the basis of observational assessment. Complete accurate information requires a comprehensive investigation of all possible causal factors, the compilation of accurate historical information, and the existence of an objective attitude on the part of those interpreting such data. It means not accepting the first evidence of problem areas as the final answer, and also means a structured system whereby continual assessment and scheduled reevaluation are accomplished.

PRINCIPLE 7

Symptoms often associated with learning disabilities do not necessarily indicate the presence of learning disabilities or predict future learning disabilities

One of the common learning problem labels that has existed for many years is dyslexia. There are a variety of definitions for dyslexia, but usually dyslexia indicates a severe reading disability accompanied by visual perceptual problems, problems in writing, such as reversals and mirror writing. Reversals, mirror writing, and a variety of visual perceptual problems also appear quite regularly in children who are medically diagnosed as brain injured and who are served in learning disability programs in relation to severe learning problems. Reversals and mirror writing have, therefore, come to be associated with learning disabilities and there is a tendency to become concerned about the likelihood of future learning problems when a child consistently exhibits this type of writing. This concern may be well founded but is often overdone and may be totally inaccurate as may be illustrated by the following abbreviated case study.

John S. was 4 years, 11 months old and was just about to start kindergarten. His parents had some questions about appropriate educational programming for John and were concerned that he might not enjoy school. (It should be noted that we are deliberately leaving out a number of details so that the reader may better appreciate the conclusion to this study. It is one that we personally conducted.) It was decided that a minimal initial study of John would be made and that further study and investigation would be initiated as the initial study indicated necessary.

An individual test of intelligence and a variety of additional measures to attempt to predict future educational success were given to John. Two results follow:

1. John tended to exhibit reversals when writing his name.
2. John had poorly developed motor skills.

If we were to "guess" about John's educational future based only on this information, we might be inclined to wonder about the reversals and whether he would have future problems in reading. If we were to base educational planning on such skimpy information, we might suggest that the kindergarten teacher should look into a variety of types of readiness material and training to help ensure John's readiness for entrance into first grade reading after a year of kindergarten.

Now for the additional information revealed in this study:

3. John was reading, with good understanding, at midfifth grade level.
4. John's IQ was approximately 155.
5. Though John could not do very well in spelling if he were asked to write out spelling words (due to poor motor ability), he could spell aloud at the mid–third grade level.
6. Arithmetic ability, again determined verbally, was upper second grade level, but he had some fourth grade arithmetic skills.

It should be noted that John was referred because of concern about future educational programming. The concern, however, was that school personnel might not know how to handle this remarkable boy. He was somewhat shy; was slightly retarded in motor skill development, and did provide some beautiful examples of reversals. He also provided an excellent, if somewhat exaggerated, example of why we should not confuse the presence of certain symptoms often associated with learning disabilities with the existence of learning disabilities.

PRINCIPLE 8

Educational time and effort must be carefully maximized for the child with learning disabilities

The learning disability child is already educationally retarded in terms of what his intelligence would indicate he should be learning, so time is of the essence. A number of major variables must be considered in educational planning for each child; placement in a learning disability program is an insufficient solution. The following variables must be considered:

1. What is the learning disability (or disabilities) to be overcome? Be as specific as possible for this leads to determination of abilities to be developed.

2. In addition to the learning ability to be developed (perhaps, auditory discrimination appropriate to age and general developmental level), academic skill areas to be considered must be emphasized, due to the effect of the disability on these areas. This may be in a broad area such as reading or may be more narrowly defined such as ability to hear specific phonemes with sufficient accuracy to permit effective use of phonetic approaches to reading.

3. What content, either factual or conceptual, is of prime importance at this point in educational planning for the child?

The most effective way to balance these three major variables for each child depends in turn on such things as how and where the learning disabled child is served by the educational system. If the child is in a resource room for ninety minutes each day, the major task must be approached in the preceding order with most of the third task to be accomplished by the regular classroom teacher. The longer the daily session in the specialized setting, the more the specialist will likely become involved in this task, the teaching of content.

To maximize educational time and effort, it is suggested that these three tasks be combined as much as possible; that is, after initial determination of disabilities and of academic areas that should receive major attention, remedial efforts should be directed first toward developing specific learning abilities and second toward developing them within the framework of the academic area that needs the most attention; then, content or conceptual development goals should be considered when possible. The arbitrary manner in which some school systems have indicated that learning disability personnel should "remediate disabilities," but not "teach or remediate reading," is unacceptable, unprofessional, and wasteful of precious educational time for the child and expensive professional efforts on the part of educators.

PRINCIPLE 9

Learning disability planning should be based on a learning theory, or theories, to be most effective

If the idea of a learning *disability* is to be accepted, then we are indicating that there are certain definable learning abilities that children must have to be able to learn normally. Although it is possible to pinpoint the fact that a given child has significant problems in auditory discrimination and to assist him to improve his auditory discrimination, it is also necessary to help him build reading and language skills that have been retarded due to the existence of the discrimination problem. It is therefore necessary to know how children develop adequate reading and language skills so that the manner in which his earlier problem retarded development in these areas may be postulated. It is our point of view that there are a number of different types of learning and that it is logical and advantageous in learning disability planning to assume the existence of different learning processes for these different types of learning. For a discussion of learning theories and their application in learning disabilities, see Gearheart (1976).

PRINCIPLE 10

It is critically important to be concerned and involved with both process and task oriented assistance and remediation

It is of the utmost importance that this principle be followed to make possible the accomplishment of principle 8, effective use of time and effort. Many of the earliest efforts to assist learning disabled boys and girls centered on remediation of process skills, with little or no attention to assisting the child to carry over these skills into the task of learning to read or to understand arithmetic. Experience has indicated that most children require help in applying newly developed process abilities in the academic setting. The regular classroom teacher must play an important part in this matter, whether it be in a planned, coordinated effort with the learning disabilities specialist or in a situation in which the regular class teacher must provide the total program for the child. If a child cannot discriminate (visually) between *ab* and *ad,* he must learn to do so, but he also needs planned practice in using this newly developed ability in a variety of settings. In a similar manner, if a child cannot tell the difference (auditorially) between the *b* sound and the *d* sound, he must learn to do so and must exercise this newly developed auditory discrimination. If the teacher is aware of this need and alert for opportunities to provide this practice or exercise, it is of great value. Many specific activities may be suggested by resource personnel.

· · ·

These ten principles provide the general guidelines within which planning for the learning disabled child should take place. If the child is also being taught by a learning disabilities teacher, efforts should be jointly planned to ensure a coordinated program with fully complementary activities and efforts. It the regular classroom teacher must plan for the child without outside help, these principles will provide a starting point from which to consider various alternative methods and approaches. A number of methods books from which the teacher may obtain specific, detailed suggestions are listed at the close of this chapter.

On the following pages we will review, in some detail, specific approaches that we believe may be of considerable value to regular classroom teachers. Although the suggestions offered by these approaches are more often used by special education personnel, we feel that they should be seriously considered by regular classroom teachers. These approaches need not be used in total, but include potentially effective components that may be of significant value. Another source that may be useful for many other methods, suggestions, and ideas is *Teaching the Learning Disabled: A Combined Task-process Approach* (Gearheart, 1976).

Tactile and kinesthetic approaches to learning

Children learn through all of the sensory modalities, but for most students, a majority of school-based learning is through the visual and auditory learning channels. This has proved to be the most effective general procedure, and the questions that relate to sensory modalities in planning the teaching of reading usually concern the balance between the use of auditory and visual channels. Most educators agree that children *must* be able to discriminate between visual symbols (letters) to be able to learn to read. In a similar manner, the role of adequate auditory abilities in the development of effective language is well known to educators and is thought to be essential to the normal development of reading skills. The role of tactile, kinesthetic, gustatory, and olfactory modalities are for the most part ignored.

An exception may be seen in the education of the blind and visually impaired. For students who cannot see, the sense of touch, the ability to feel shapes and forms and configurations, provides an effective substitute for sight, as applied to developing the ability to read. Certainly braille is different from the letters of the Roman alphabet, but the process is similar, except that the incoming signals are through the fingers rather than through the eyes.

This strength of the tactile and kinesthetic learning channels can be utilized to assist some learning disability students to learn to read. It may be used in a number of different ways.

Activities in which the young child learns

to differentiate between two similar, but different, solid objects without looking at them appear to assist in the development of better visual discrimination. This may be accomplished in a variety of ways, many of which are outlined in the wide range of learning activity books presently on the market (see References and Suggested Readings at the end of this chapter). Simple examples include the use of solid objects in a cloth bag, or the use of a blindfold so that objects placed in front of the child cannot be seen. Sandpaper letters or geometric configurations provide another variety of this same principle. With 5 and 6 year olds these activities can be accomplished in a game format.

In each of the preceding examples, the major purpose is to provide tactile and kinesthetic support for the visual modality, either to assist in developing skills that have been slow in developing or to attempt to "straighten out" previously scrambled reception and interpretation of visual signals. In some cases it may be well to have children "feel" a letter or word while also looking at it, thus providing simultaneous signal reception through the visual and tactile senses. In other cases it may prove to be more effective to cut off the visual signal to be certain that the student is one hundred percent accurate in tactile sensing alone before adding the visual. In all of the preceding activities, *the important thing to understand is the principle of utilization of additional sensory modalities to assist in the development of other modalities.* The most common use of this principle is in the use of the tactile sense to support or assist the visual sense.

A somewhat different application of this same principle involves the teacher or a helping student tracing out letters, or sometimes words, on the arm or back of the student who needs help. This is significantly different in that the student receives no kinesthetic input, only the tactile. He may be looking at letter cards on his desk, attempting to find one matching the letter he feels traced out on his back, or he may have his eyes closed, concentrating on feeling the let-

ter or word accurately. In any event, a whole variety of games or activities may be developed using this type of assistance *when the evidence indicates that this is in fact a need of the child.* This type activity can be misused or overdone if not carefully monitored.

The preceding activities and approaches are most appropriate with primary age children who give evidence of developmental or remedial needs in the visual-perceptual abilities required for reading.

A simultaneous visual-auditory-kinesthetic-tactile approach

During the early 1920s, Grace Fernald began the development of a simultaneous Visual-Auditory-Kinesthetic-Tactile (VAKT) approach designed to assist children with severe reading disabilities. The account of her methodology (1943) is detailed in a full-length text, which has been used—with various adaptations—to this day. Reports of her work indicate a high degree of effectiveness, particularly with children of normal or above mental ability who have been in school at least two or three years.

Her approach has variously been called multisensory, a tracing approach, or a kinesthetic method. The terms tracing and kinesthetic have been applied because those are unique features of the approach, but the most accurately descriptive title is that of "simultaneous VAKT," which indicates the manner in which her methods are different from most others that have been called multisensory or VAKT.

Prior to actually starting a remedial program, the Fernald procedure requires "positive reconditioning." This is based on the assumption that almost all children who have experienced school failure have developed a low self-concept, particularly in relation to anything connected with school or formal education. Four conditions are viewed as ones to be carefully avoided in initiating and carrying through the remedial program:

1. *Avoid calling attention to emotionally loaded situations.* Attempts, either by teachers or parents, to urge the child to do better generally have negative effects.

Reminding the child of the future importance of academic success or telling him how important it is to his family should be avoided. If the child is already a failure and knows it, these admonitions or urgings are at best useless and sometimes result in a nearly complete emotional block.

2. *Avoid using methods that previous experience suggests are likely to be ineffective.* This is important during remediation and during the time of reentry to the regular class. If the child is experiencing success in a temporary, out-of-class remedial setting (after school or for a set time period each day) and then must return to class and to methods by which he was earlier unable to learn, the remedial program may be negated. Or, if after a period in which he has been out of class on a full-day basis and has found success in a new method, he must make an immediate return to the former methods with no planned transition, he may return to his old inability to learn.

3. *Avoid conditions that may cause embarrassment.* Sometimes a new method used in the new setting is effective and satisfactory, whereas in the old setting, unless some special provisions are made, it may seem childish or silly. For example, the tracing involved in the Fernald approach may seem so unusual as to be absurd in the regular classroom. The reward, that is, the learning, may not be worth the feelings of conspicuousness and embarrassment.

4. *Avoid directing attention to what the child cannot do.* This is just a special kind of problem that might be included as a part of the first condition.

Regardless of what is required, attempting to bring about positive reconditioning and avoiding emotional reversal after the reconditioning has taken place are of prime importance.

Fernald VAKT approach. The first step in each remedial case in the actual classroom or clinic procedure is to explain to the child that there is a new way of learning words that really works. The child is told that others have had the same problem he is having and have learned easily through this new method.

The second step is to ask the child to select any word he wants to learn, regardless of length, and then to teach him to write and recognize (read) it, using the following method:

1. The word chosen by the child is written for him, usually with a crayon in plain, blackboard-size cursive writing. In most cases, regardless of age, cursive writing is used rather than manuscript. This is because the child will then tend to see and "feel" the word as a single entity, rather than a group of separate letters.

2. The child traces the word with his fingers in contact with the paper, saying the word as he traces it. This is repeated as many times as necessary until he can write the word without looking at the copy.

3. He writes the word on scrap paper, demonstrating to himself that it is now "his" word. Several words are taught in this manner, and as much time as necessary is taken to completely master them.

4. When the child has internalized the fact that he can write and recognize words, he is encouraged to start writing stories. His stories are whatever he wishes them to be at first, and the instructor gives him any words (in addition to those he has mastered) he needs to complete the story.

5. After the story is written, it is typed for him, and he is to read it in typed form while it is still fresh in his mind. It is important that this be done immediately.

6. After the story is completed and the new word has been used in a meaningful way, the new word is written by the child on a card that he files alphabetically in his own individual word file. This word file is used as a meaningful way to teach the alphabet without undue emphasis on rote memory.

This procedure is often called the Fernald tracing method because the tracing is an added feature in contrast to the usual methods of teaching reading or word recognition.

However, it should be noted that the child is simultaneously *feeling, seeing, saying,* and *hearing* the word. Thus this is truly a multisensory approach.

There are several points to be carefully observed and followed for maximum success:

1. *The word should be selected by the student.* If it is, motivation is maximized, and the likelihood of interest in using the word in a story is greater than with a teacher-selected word. In Fernald's case studies and in cases that we have known personally, children are able to master long, complicated words and in fact may be able to do so with more ease than with short ones in some instances.

2. *Finger contact is essential,* using either one or two fingers.

3. *The child should write the word, after tracing it several times, without looking at the copy.* Looking back and forth tends to break the word into small and sometimes meaningless units. He must learn to see, think, and feel the word as a total unit.

4. Because the word must be seen as a unit, *in case of error or interruption in writing, the word should be crossed out and a new start made.* If necessary, the child should go back to the tracing stage, but correcting the word through erasures is not permitted.

5. *Words should be used in context.* If the word the child wants to use is unfamiliar, a different one should be encouraged, or at least he should learn the meaning of the word before going through this procedure. He must learn that the group of alphabetic symbols called a word really means something.

6. *The child must always say the word aloud or to himself as he traces it and as he writes it.*

Although many additional details could be given, the preceding outlines the essence of the Fernald approach. Addition of the tactile and kinesthetic avenues, or channels, to the visual and auditory ones deserves the major credit for any success this method has over more traditional approaches. After a period of tracing, stage one, which may vary in time from a few weeks to a few months, the child will be able to enter what Fernald calls stage two. In stage two, tracing is no longer required. The child simply looks at the new word in cursive writing, says it to himself as he looks at it, and then writes it without looking at the copy. He proceeds in the same manner as in stage one, except that he does not trace. In theory, the child is now "tracing" the word mentally.

If, during stage two, the child encounters difficulty with any particular word, he should go back to actual tracing until he masters that word. As soon as tracing is no longer necessary (except rarely), the large box used as a word file for the large, cursive words is exchanged for a smaller one for typed words.

In stage three, the child is able to study new words directly from a book or other printed copy. He should now be able to pronounce words to himself and write them from memory. Books consistent with his developing ability and interests are provided. He is told words which he cannot decode by himself, and these are recorded, reviewed, and written from memory after he finishes each section of the book. He no longer keeps a file on each new word.

Stage four involves decoding new words from their resemblance to words previously learned. He is not now "told" words but is helped to learn to figure them out through a sequence of structural analysis skills. If he is about to read difficult material, particularly that including technical terms (such as in science), he is encouraged to look over each paragraph in advance to find new words. These are to be mastered ahead of time to permit reading with comprehension.

This approach has been used with various children having a variety of problems, including those with problems in the auditory channel. However, it is likely most beneficial for children with visual channel problems, particularly those of visual sequential memory or visual imagery.

There are a number of methods and materials on the commercial market advertised as multisensory. Technically speaking, they may be multisensory, but few are of the total, balanced, simultaneously multisensory nature of the Fernald approach. Some approaches are initially visual then become multisensory. Others are initially phonetic and later evolve into multisensory. These may be more or less effective than the Fernald VAKT approach, but the alert practitioner will do well to look carefully into what takes place in a given method, and the order in which it takes place, when analyzing it for possible use.

Summary. The simultaneous VAKT approach is likely to be most effective with children who have spent at least two years in school and thus have been rather thoroughly exposed to reading. It is one of a few approaches that, in our experience, has been effective with secondary school students. Because much of its effectiveness depends on the ability to receive kinesthetic and tactile signals accurately, it will obviously have greatly reduced effectiveness with students in whom these channels are poorly developed. One other caution: *it is believed by some that certain types of neurological dysfunction may lead to a tendency for the receptive mechanisms of the brain to "short-circuit" if there are too many signals arriving simultaneously.* This is not an established fact, but the possibility of this type reaction to multiple stimuli should be kept in mind, particularly when dealing with hyperactive children.

Language development approaches

A number of different learning disability approaches relate specifically to language development. The following description of one of the more highly recognized language development approaches contains a number of elements or components that may be implemented in the regular classroom.

Language development systems. Johnson and Myklebust (1967) believe that remediation of learning disabilities should circumvent the major deficit but must include simultaneous work on areas of weakness. For example, children with a visual deficit usually have difficulty in learning to read

through a sight-word approach, since they cannot hold a sequence of letters in mind. However, many of these children can learn sounds and sound blending. In contrast, youngsters with auditory deficits may have difficulty in learning to read through phonics, but may be able to learn by the sight-word approach.

Johnson and Myklebust believe that, with training, both auditory and visual learners can acquire a sight vocabulary and phonetic skills. Consequently, the focus of initial training is on the acquisition of a systematic approach for decoding words.

Auditory learners. Remedial procedures for auditory learners involve teaching isolated sounds and then blending them into meaningful words. Before initiating this approach, the teacher must evaluate the student's ability to blend sounds. If the child cannot blend sounds, the sight-word method with emphasis on tactile and kinesthetic support should be used. Briefly, the guidelines are as follow:

1. Letter sounds are taught, beginning with consonants that are different in appearance as well as sound.
2. The child is asked to think of words beginning with each sound.
3. The child is taught to associate the sound with the letter having that sound. At first, the youngster should be taught only one sound with each letter or letter combination.
4. One or two vowel sounds are presented after three or four consonants have been learned.
5. The child is taught to blend sounds into meaningful words. Then he must tell what each word means and use it in a sentence.
6. Word families are taught, such as it, hit, sit, and mit. The pupil learns how to change the initial and final consonants to form new words.
7. Two-letter consonant blends are introduced.
8. Long vowel combinations and consonant groupings representing a single sound are taught.

9. The teacher writes simple sentences, paragraphs, and stories containing the child's reading vocabulary. Sentence structure should be similar to the pupil's spoken vocabulary.

Visual learners. Children who are visual learners are taught to read by the sight-word approach, since they generally have difficulty learning by phonetic methods. Therefore, a student is taught to make a direct association between the printed symbol and experience; each new word is said for him. The auditory learner is taught from the part to the whole, whereas the visual learner works from the whole to the part. The procedures for visual learners are as follows:

1. The auditory-visual correspondence is taught by demonstrating to the student that spoken words can also be written.
2. Nouns in the child's spoken vocabulary and different in auditory and visual configuration are selected. The pupil matches the printed word with the corresponding object.
3. The printed word is matched with experience through labeling objects in the room, such as flag, chalk, and pencil. Action verbs also are associated with experience. The child is asked to hop, walk, or run and then is shown the printed symbol representing each action verb.
4. The child is introduced to simple phrases and sentences within his reading vocabulary. At the same time, prepositions and adjectives are presented. Pictures are used to illustrate the reading material.
5. As the child progresses, experience stories are integrated into the reading activities. Frequently, a picture representing a new word is drawn below that word to aid the reading process.

Deficits in both major learning modalities (auditory and visual). Johnson and Myklebust recommend a version of the Fernald approach for use with children who have deficits in both the auditory and the visual modality. Modifications should be made according to the child's pattern of strengths and weaknesses. Modifications include the following:

1. Selection of a controlled vocabulary, emphasizing meaningful nouns and verbs that are relatively phonetic.
2. Maintenance of a balance of sensory stimulation, depending on the child's needs. For instance, some children profit from looking, saying, and tracing, whereas others learn better by only looking and tracing.

Johnson and Myklebust are definite in their approach to educational planning and believe that the most important single factor is the completion of an intensive diagnostic study. This diagnosis should lead to an evaluation of the disability with five multidimensional considerations:

1. Is the disability within a single modality, does it extend to more than one modality, and does it include intersensory functions? This assists in planning remediational processes (for the defective functions) and in planning which sensory channels to use to provide content input (the intact modalities).
2. What is the level of the involvement within the hierarchy of experience? Is it experienced first at the perceptual, imagery, symbolic, or conceptual level?
3. Is the deficiency one in which the sensations reaching the brain are meaningful or nonmeaningful? Is the problem basically verbal or nonverbal? For example, is the basic problem in auditory reception or visual imagery? Is it one of abstracting-conceptualizing, that is, of gaining meaning?
4. Which of the subject matter areas does this disability affect most? Is it primarily a reading or an arithmetic problem, or does it also show up in art and physical education? This is important in remediation planning and in guidance regarding such areas as course work and life planning.
5. What are the effects, present and potential, of the disability on the development of social maturity? If the goal of education includes development of independent, responsible, self-supporting citizens, this dimension is of prime importance.

An educational/remedial plan that does

not take all the foregoing considerations into account and does not coordinate the efforts of all who deal with the child cannot be maximally effective.

A second important part of the educational plan is a determination of the child's state of readiness, in terms of various sub-aspects of total readiness. For example, a child may be ready in terms of auditory, visual, and integrative functions but may be unable or unready to learn in the normal class setting due to social unreadiness or hyperactivity problems, or both. He may be ready and able to function in class discussions at his chronological age level but be three years retarded in readiness for reading. The child must be approached and taught not at his *level* of readiness, but at his *levels* of readiness. Teaching that follows and takes into consideration obtaining complete knowledge of the child—information regarding his various levels of functioning and understanding of the material to be taught—is what Johnson and Myklebust call *clinical teaching*. This, they believe, is the only acceptable procedure with the learning disability child.

In addition to the five multidimensional considerations for teaching the learning disability child, Johnson and Myklebust provide thirteen principles for remediation (Johnson and Myklebust, 1967, pp. 58-63). These principles are derived from the five multidimensional considerations, plus their long experience with deaf and aphasic children. Although developed for a language-approach system and more auditorily than visually oriented, these principles are applicable to the methodology of many of the other systems.

Major principles for remediation

1. *Individualize the problem.* The teacher must formulate an educational plan for *each specific child.* She should be aware of his deficits, his integrities, and his levels of language function, including reading, spoken, and written language. She should know him—his intelligence, his emotional status, his educational history. The program must be *the child's* program, not *a* program.

2. *Teach to the level of involvement.* Teaching must be aimed at the lowest level of involvement—perception, imagery, symbolization, or conceptualization.

3. *Teach to the type of involvement.* Does the disability involve intrasensory or intersensory learning? Does it involve verbal or nonverbal factors? Does it primarily relate to integrative functions? Whatever the case, teach appropriately for that type of involvement.

4. *Teach according to readiness.* Follow the principle of multiple readiness levels as presented in the preceding discussion.

5. *Remember that input precedes output.* Consider the fact that either, or both, input and output disabilities could be involved in the problem. Remember that output difficulties may actually reflect input problems.

6. *Consider tolerance levels.* Overloading is always a possibility. Certain types of stimulation may be distracting, either by themselves or by interfering with other modalities. The possibility that psychological and neurological tolerance levels may be grossly abnormal in a learning disability child must be carefully considered.

7. *Consider the multisensory approach.* The multisensory approach—teaching through several or perhaps all sensory channels—is always a possible alternative but must be approached with tolerance level and overloading potential in mind.

8. *Teaching to deficits alone is limited.* Teaching only to and through the deficient areas is a restricted, unitary approach and is unacceptable in the light of available evidence.

9. *Teaching only to and through integrities is limited.* This approach is insufficient when used alone. It presumes interneurosensory learning, which is not an acceptable assumption in many instances.

10. *Do not assume the need for perceptual training.* Perceptual training alone may be most inadequate. To stress perceptual training, except as diagnostic informa-

tion so dictates, can be a waste of time or in some cases detrimental.

11. *Control important variables.* This principle calls for teacher control of variables such as attention (control elements that lead to distractions), proximity (to the teacher or to other children), rate (as in rate of presentation of materials), and size (of writing, objects, for example).

12. *Emphasize verbal and nonverbal learning.* Deliberately attend to the verbal and nonverbal components of the learning problem with planned efforts to interrelate the two. Myklebust recommends interweaving verbal and nonverbal components.

13. *Keep psychoneurological considerations in mind.* The educator must attend to remediational needs in view of the behavioral components of the problem but should also consider the physical findings that indicate the status of the neurological system. The two must be incorporated into a single plan of educational remediation.

A major strength of the Johnson and Myklebust approach is that it contains provisions for different types of learning disabilities. These provisions take into account the strong and weak modalities, building on one and attempting to strengthen the other.

Tactile, Kinesthetic, or VAKT approaches have been found to be valuable with a number of learning disabled children. If properly approached, the simultaneous VAKT approach is one of just a few that have had considerable applicability with secondary level students. At this level, the VAKT approach can be of value if the student can be sufficiently motivated to try the unusual tracing activity. Great care must be taken to keep it from appearing "childish." One suggestion is to indicate that it has been used in the past with adults in the Army who were near nonreaders. This sometimes gives it respectability for use with older children and youth.

Language development approaches, like the one by Johnson and Myklebust, provide a basis for planning programs in terms of specific strengths and weaknesses. We would suggest more detailed reading of Johnson and Myklebust's text (1967) for teachers who must plan the program for a learning disabled child without the assistance of a learning disability specialist. Like the VAKT method, it is far from a "cure-all," but these two approaches have more general applicability than many others.

Much less work has been done with learning disabilities that relate to the area of mathematics, but we would suggest the discussion and suggestions provided by Marsh (1976).

ROLE AND RESPONSIBILITIES OF SPECIAL EDUCATION PERSONNEL IN PROGRAMMING FOR THE MILDLY MENTALLY HANDICAPPED

When a child is referred and found to be in need of special assistance owing to mild mental handicap, a variety of types of service may be considered. All of these may not be available in every community, but if the total continuum of services concept is followed, they should be. At the lower grade levels (first and second grades), suggestions and the provision of some special materials may permit the child to remain full time in the regular classroom. If the handicap is greater in degree (lower level of intelligence, other handicapping conditions, or very inadequate experiential background), a part-time placement in a resource room may be of value. In this setting the child will receive much more individual help in developing basic reading and numbers skills, and the resource room teacher will attempt to determine those approaches that will provide maximum growth when the child is back in the regular class. Many of these children will later be able to come back to the regular class on a full-time basis; however, some will need to move into a part-time, special class program if the resource room setting proves to be insufficient to provide for unique educational needs. A few children may continue in a part-time special program throughout their school years, but every effort should be made to achieve maximum integration in the regular class.

For mildly handicapped children who continue to have significant academic difficulties, more years in school mean a growing discrepancy between their level of achievement and that of their age peers. The use of high-interest, low-vocabulary materials will permit the teaching of many of the essential concepts and understandings, but some curriculum modification becomes inevitable if education is to remain meaningful. If a child receives the benefit of several years of special programming that helps others to return to the regular class but is of much less help to him, by age 12 or 13 a more special program must be considered. Such a program should focus on learning the social skills required of adults and habits, attitudes, skills, and understandings that will maximize his ability to obtain and retain employment. In conjunction with this emphasis on employability, special efforts to assist him to become a knowledgeable consumer and a responsible parent and citizen must be initiated. Such programs are often called prevocational at the junior high level and vocational, work-study, or work-experience at the senior high level. Involvement with sections of the regular class program remains, with emphasis on classes such as driver education, typing, metalwork, body and fender work, and various semiskilled trades as deemed individually appropriate. The vocational rehabilitation counselor from the state rehabilitation services agency can assist in a number of ways, including arrangements for special vocational school training, payment of employers for training functions, and others as seem advisable. At the high school level, a work-study coordinator should be employed to assist in arranging and supervising off-campus work activities.

For the mildly mentally handicapped for whom initial special programming does not lead to nearly complete reintegration into the regular class, the amount of special programming required will likely increase as the student progresses through school. This will happen for some mildly mentally handi-

capped, but for others there will be a type of remedial effect that permits functioning within the regular classroom. The major emphasis of the special educator who works with the mildly mentally handicapped student for whom the remedial effect is not significant is that of a modified curriculum promoting the learning of essential, age-level concepts within the framework of a learning vehicle appropriate for the student's academic skill level.

HOW THE TEACHER CAN ASSIST THE MILDLY MENTALLY HANDICAPPED CHILD IN THE REGULAR CLASS

Much of what the regular classroom teacher can do with or for the mildly mentally handicapped child relates to understandings and attitudes. Once the teacher realizes that all children thought to be mildly mentally handicapped are not lost causes as far as successful functioning in the regular class is concerned, he has made a good start toward success. He must then realize that all mildly mentally handicapped cannot necessarily be expected to function on a full-time basis in the regular class—some *do* require special help in varying degrees. This must be realized, or in some cases valuable time is wasted for children who have little academic time to waste. A concept of mild mental retardation indicating that all retardation is pseudoretardation is just as unrealistic as one suggesting that all mildly mentally handicapped are permanently mentally handicapped with no hope of change.

As mentioned previously, many of the principles offered as suggestions in working with the learning disabled are equally applicable to the mildly mentally handicapped. In this discussion we will briefly review techniques that may be used with mildly mentally handicapped students. These suggestions are based on the characteristics most commonly associated with limited intellectual ability outlined on pp. 116-118.

We must again emphasize that "characteristics" do not *identify* the mildly mentally handicapped. They are descriptive of many of the mildly mentally handicapped, but similar characteristics may be found in children of average or above average intellectual ability.

Sensory and motor coordination handicaps

The mildly mentally handicapped who have visual or hearing impairments may be assisted with these sensory impairments in the manner outlined in Chapters 3 and 4. Certain modifications may be needed, but these will vary with individual differences.

Motor coordination problems often take the form of general, delayed development, that is, motor ability characteristics of children of somewhat younger chronological age (Johnson, 1975). There is also some tendency to have more difficulty with complex motor skills that require the integration of more than one motor skill component, but the generalized lower level of ability is seen more often. Since certain motor skills may be prerequisites for academic tasks (such as writing), it is important that the teacher do everything possible to provide special opportunities for development of such skills. It is equally important that the teacher not attempt to require any child to perform tasks for which the child does not have the prerequisite skills.

Simplified programs of games and specific motor exercise in areas of deficiency have proved to be worthwhile in various research studies (Cratty, 1971). Unlike some other skill areas, motor development tends to be amenable to direct remediation through practice (exercise), though too much emphasis on one specific area of difficulty will reduce the child's enthusiasm for the task. Games such as bean-bag throw and hopscotch, jumping games, games that promote eye-hand coordination, and other games as consistent with individual needs are of value. The major requirement is that teachers focus on this need and plan an attempt to remediate it. Special education resource teachers and physical educators are often of great assistance.

In addition to the need to develop specific motor skills as prerequisites to academically related tasks, there is evidence that improved physical performance may contribute to a success syndrome and have carry-over effects as the child's self-concept is improved through successful competition in physical activities. This appears to be particularly true of boys (Cratty, 1969). The important point to remember is that motor skill development is amenable to improvement through practice; planned physical activities with the mildly mentally handicapped have been successful. The special education resource teacher should provide the main source of more specific assistance in determining deficits and in planning remediation.

Low tolerance for frustration

Every classroom teacher has observed that some children are more easily discouraged and give up more quickly than others. This characteristic is not in itself an indication of the presence of a mild mental handicap but is often observed in the mentally handicapped. The teacher should make every effort to understand the cause of the child's inability to handle frustration. In doing this, the teacher might confer with parents, with other teachers, or simply ask the child what is bothering him. In other words, the teacher should look beyond the immediate incident to understand the cause of a child's behavior. What is observed in the classroom may be directly related to what happens in the home or on the playground. For example, the child may have been scolded for being late for breakfast that morning; the mother may have asked the child why he could not dress himself as quickly as his little sister; he may have been the last to be chosen or he may have been teased or ridiculed by his peers on the playground. What the teacher observes in the classroom may be one event in a long sequence of events accounting for the child's striking out at the teacher or giving up on a lesson.

If the teacher understands the child's environmental influences outside the classroom, the nature of the handicap and its manifestation in easy frustration, he can make better decisions in eliminating frustrating situations in the classroom. Although there are no magic formulas or easy answers to dictate these decisions or judgments, there are certain suggestions that may be of value.

Work within the level of ability of the student should be assigned. Activities should be shifted more frequently, always ending before fatigue. The school setting should provide for group experiences so the mildly mentally handicapped student may share in group success, but the teacher should not assume that a skill has been learned until the child can use it independently.

These students will experience frustrating situations in their lives; this is consistent with the realities of life. An awareness of their relative low tolerance for frustration and careful planning may reduce the number of potentially frustrating situations of no obvious benefit for them at a particular time. At other times, it may be necessary for the child to experience difficulty and frustration, since these are essential to the growth of any individual.

Poor self-concept

Long before they enter school, children perceive that there are times when they cannot perform at the level that others expect. When that difference becomes marked and persistent, the child may acquire a poor self-concept. When a child is told repeatedly that he is a slow learner, he behaves as a slow learner. Since a mildly mentally handicapped student is continually confronted with a disparity between expectation and performance, he almost invariably develops a feeling of low self-esteem and may set up defenses against further failures. For example, such a child may be reluctant to attempt new tasks or repeat those he has already failed. The teacher must seek new ways to develop in the child a basis for self-appraisal that leads to some feeling of success. This development is crucial not only for the academic success but for the overall quality of the child's adjustment to society.

Obviously, it would be desirable to reverse the process by which a poor self-concept is formed. For example, responsible behavior is more apt to occur if the teacher treats the child as if he were responsible. But, caution must be exercised here. A mildly mentally handicapped child will not behave normally simply because he is treated as if he were not handicapped. Moreover, children are remarkably sensitive to a teacher's insincere or patronizing attitude.

Recognition should be given whenever possible, but only when actually earned. The student should be praised for small accomplishments and always for work well done. Persistence, even in a task not satisfactorily completed, should also be recognized. As the student begins to demonstrate increasing signs of self-confidence, the realities of failure should be allowed to enter the plan. Occasional failure plus an understanding of why failure occurred is important for everyone. The student should be taught to recognize his own ability to make judgments and to participate in vicarious experiences. For example, the student can read part of a story and guess what logical ending it might have. The characters can be evaluated. The events in the story or an experience like a field trip can be listed, and the student can be asked what is more important and why.

A routine can be established and followed to help give the student a sense of security and confidence. The improvement of the student's self-concept can be accomplished not by removing failure from experience, but by controlling it. The student can then learn to cope with failure and understand why it occurs, thus reducing the possibility of repeated failure in the future.

Short attention span

The mildly mentally handicapped student may find it easier to sustain attention and later to recall those things that are concrete rather than abstract, familiar rather than remote, and simple rather than complex. Teachers should seek to make their language and ideas as concrete, familiar, and simple as possible. Any teacher can, with conscious effort, tie new experiences to the familiar. Use real objects instead of numbers alone to give directions that are clear, precise, and logical. Give shorter assignments and more frequent review over a longer period of time.

The extent to which the student is able to attend to an assigned task may be directly related to whether he comprehends or is interested in the task. If he does not understand the task or is not interested, he may leave the scene in some way—by doodling, daydreaming, talking to a classmate, or putting his head down. At other times the student may demonstrate his lack of understanding or interest in an unacceptable manner such as teasing, fighting, or throwing something. Whenever possible, attempt to give assignments that are geared to a realistic level of understanding. In addition, shift activities before the child becomes fatigued, and attempt to give only one set of directions at a time.

Each of us can understand the difference suggested by the proposition that two plus two equals four and by the question, "If I had two apples and two oranges, how much food would I have all together?" The former is an abstract mathematical statement; the latter is a concrete application dramatizing the principle of addition.

The mildly mentally handicapped student may have more difficulty in understanding the relationship between (to continue our mathematical illustration) mechanical computation and the principle of addition. He may learn how to add, subtract, multiply, and divide, but have difficulty understanding the principles of these functions. He may not know when to perform one rather than the other.

This student may also be distracted by conflicting auditory or visual information. A classroom that is cluttered with highly distracting visual material (bulletin boards and pictures, for example) may negatively influence the student's attention span. A classroom that is "noisy" may also decrease the student's ability to attend. These factors should be seriously considered by classroom teachers, since many students, not only those with limited ability, may be distracted by excessive visual or auditory "clutter."

Teachers should be cautious in interpreting lack of interest (often due to inappropriate level of materials) as short attention span. Sometimes the attention span could be dramatically increased by providing more interesting materials.

Below average language ability

The mildly mentally handicapped student may have difficulty in language development. Most of us will have a common recognition of the word "framly." The vocalization of "framly" will be similar for most of us, but its definition is a different matter. A child may learn to read by relying on recognition and pronunciation rather than comprehension. He may have learned a substantial portion of his reading vocabulary as you have just learned the word "framly." Teachers must create opportunity for verbal expression; they must use high frequency words again and again. When introducing new ideas, they should be related to the concrete rather than the abstract. And, to repeat an earlier generalization, students must tie new experiences to the familiar ones.

Language development requires *experience,* and the mildly mentally handicapped require *more* experience with language (to develop a given level of language ability) than children with average or above average intellectual ability. One final complicating factor is that if earlier school experiences and provisions have been inconsistent with the child's level of readiness, he may be even more retarded in language development than his intellectual level would predict. A further complication is the effect of bilingual or bicultural components or influences.

The provision of wide, concretely oriented language experience, appropriate to the child's present level of language development and consistent with his interest, is the one technique that may always be employed.

Below average ability to generalize and conceptualize

These students may have difficulty in seeing the commonality between two separate situations; they may be unable to generalize one set of conditions or rules to another similar situation. A young student may quickly recognize the plus sign in a mathematical equation but have difficulty understanding that the word "and" (as in 6 and 7 are 13) means the same as plus. He may learn the rules governing behavior in the cafeteria line but have difficulty relating the same rules to another situation, such as the recess line.

The teacher should attempt to integrate mechanical and conceptual skills into the lessons whenever possible and point out to the student how one principle may apply to other academic or social situations. By actual practice in generalization and conceptual skills, the student will acquire a repertoire of experiences that will provide for maximum development of these abilities.

Play interests below those of age peers

It is important that the regular classroom teacher be aware of this characteristic so that he may be able to assist the student in overcoming problems in this area. This difficulty may be directly related to the student's poor motor coordination or difficulty in following the rules of games played by his age mates. Teachers may provide assistance by interpreting or modifying game rules and activities to enable the student to participate fully.

It should be reemphasized that an awareness by the teacher of this potential problem is perhaps the most important consideration. By recognizing that a problem may occur, teachers may do a great deal to facilitate more normal play activities with age peers. This characteristic should not necessarily be interpreted as a problem except as interaction with younger children inhibits growth in other areas (language development and social skills appropriate to age, for example).

The preceding suggestions have been "keyed" to characteristics because many classroom teachers have indicated a preference for this approach. They do not constitute "an approach," but rather ideas to be considered when utilizing the usual classroom approach.

We suggest one specific approach, the si-

multaneous VAKT approach (pp. 129-132), as having been of value in programs we have observed. Possibly, this approach works because the child has all four learning channels working for him at one time, or perhaps it works because the child is able to build stories that are real and meaningful to him. In any event, it is worth trying as one possible alternative approach.

SUMMARY

Learning disabled and mildly mentally handicapped children make up the largest special group with which the regular class teacher will work. Except for the disruptive, acting out child, they may also pose the most significant set of problems. At the kindergarten and first and second grade levels, it may be difficult to differentiate between these two handicapping conditions, but as the child grows older, differences tend to become more obvious.

With the mildly mentally handicapped, particularly those very near the borderline of average mental ability, it may be possible to provide the total educational program within the regular class. The normal range of course and program offerings can provide an opportunity for success *if* school personnel are student oriented, as opposed to course oriented. (Sixth grade social studies, for example, can be made to be meaningful and within the reach of most of these children *with modifications*. However, if the attitude is, "They must all be able to read in the sixth grade social studies text or I'll fail them," then there is little chance for success.) As the mildly mentally handicapped enter the secondary school level, additional modifications of curriculum should be made, with emphasis on preparation for the world of work, responsibilities as citizens, as parents, and so forth. This means additional special program provisions, but this is consistent with other special program provisions for students who take more work in business, in math and science, and other areas of interest.

Some children who appear to be mildly mentally handicapped at the lower grade levels may gradually improve in their academic functioning and not require this specialized programming at the secondary level. Every effort should be made to maximize the number of students in this category.

Learning disabled children are more likely to exhibit "spotty" performance, with more academic success in some areas than others or apparent normal success when learning through class discussions, audiovisual presentations, or other approaches that are not primarily dependent on reading. A smaller percentage of the learning disabled may do grade-level work in reading, with disabilities appearing in the area of mathematics, but reading is the usual focal point of learning disability remedial efforts.

Learning disabilities may be defined in a variety of ways, but in general, we think of the child who has average or above average mental ability but is not achieving academically in proportion to this ability. Causes for learning disabilities are often associated with perceptual dysfunctioning, but this is only one type of possible causation. The idea of minimal brain dysfunction is also commonly associated with learning disabilities, but this concept has little practical application for the classroom teacher. A number of guidelines for learning disabilities programming were presented in this chapter, but there is no one acceptable method or approach for all children with learning disabilities. Learning disabilities indicates, by definition, the potential for remediation and near-normal functioning; this is the goal of all learning disabilities programming.

Learning disabled and mildly mentally handicapped children may be served by specialized personnel through the resource room or through itinerant teacher service. It is more likely that the mildly mentally handicapped may need separate, special programming, with such help more often required at the secondary school level. Inaccurate diagnosis and inappropriate labeling of children as mentally handicapped has led to a situation in which any such diagnosis is held suspect. We believe there are mentally handicapped children and learning disabled children, but care must be taken in making any sort of final determination or categorization, particularly with regard to the mentally handicapped. Retention in the regular classroom, with perhaps some specialized assistance, without the application of hard and fast labels is one type of safeguard against errors that may have serious consequences.

References and suggested readings

Bloomer, C. "The L. D. Tightrope." *Teacher,* 1975, *92,* 54-58.

Bruininks, R., Gross, H., and Rynders, J. "Social Acceptance of Mildly Retarded Pupils in Resource Room and Regular Classes." *American Journal of Mental Deficiency,* January 1974, *78,* 377-383.

Cratty, B. *Perceptual-Motor Behavior and Educational Processes.* Springfield, Ill.: Charles C Thomas, Publisher, 1969.

Cratty, B. *Active Learning.* Englewood Cliffs, N. J.: Prentice-Hall, Inc., 1971.

Coonley, P. Personal communication regarding observations in classes for the mentally retarded. 1974.

Dunn, L. "Special Education for the Mildly Retarded: Is much of it justifiable?" *Exceptional Children,* 1968, *35,* 5-22.

Fernald, G. *Remedial Techniques in Basic School Subjects.* New York: McGraw-Hill Book Company, 1943.

Fisher, K. "Effects of Perceptual-Motor Training on the Educable Mentally Retarded." *Exceptional Children,* November 1971, *38,* 264-266.

Gearheart, B. *Learning Disabilities: Educational Strategies.* St. Louis: The C. V. Mosby Co., 1973.

Gearheart, B. *Teaching the Learning Disabled: A Combined Task-process Approach.* St. Louis: The C. V. Mosby Co., 1976.

Guerin, G., and Szatlocky, K. "Integration Programs for the Mildly Retarded." *Exceptional Children,* November 1974, *41,* 173-179.

Haring, N., Krug, D. "Placement in Regular Programs: Procedures and Results." *Exceptional Children,* 1975, *41,* 413-417.

Iano, R., Ayers, D., Heller, H., McGettigan, J., and Walker, V. "Sociometric Status of Retarded Children in an Integrative Setting." *Exceptional Children,* January 1974, *40,* 267-272.

Johnson, D., and Myklebust, H. *Learning Disabilities: Educational Principles and Practices.* New York: Grune & Stratton, Inc., 1967.

Johnson, G. "The Education of Mentally Retarded Children." In Cruickshank, W., and Johnson, G. (Eds.). *Education of Exceptional Children and Youth* (3rd ed.). Englewood Cliffs, N. J.: Prentice-Hall, Inc., 1975.

Marsh, G. "Teaching Mathematics to the Learning Disabled." In Gearheart, B. *Teaching the Learning Disabled: A Combined Task-process Approach.* St. Louis: The C. V. Mosby Co., 1976.

Neer, W., Foster, D., Jones, J., and Reynolds, D. "Socioeconomic Bias in the Diagnosis of Mental Retardation." *Exceptional Children,* September 1973, *40,* 5-13.

Sheare, J. "Social Acceptance of EMR Adolescents in Integrated Programs." *American Journal of Mental Deficiency,* May 1974, *78,* 678-682.

Shneour, E. *The Mal-Nourished Mind.* New York: Doubleday & Company, Inc., 1975.

Tonn, M. "The Case for Keeping Mentally Retarded Children in Your Regular Classroom." *American School Board Journal,* August 1974, *161,* p. 45.

Vogel, A. "Integration of Nine Severe Learning-Disabled Children in a Junior High School Core Program." *Academic Therapy,* Fall 1973, *9*(50), 99-104.

CHAPTER 8

Strategies for working with troubled students

Barbara Coloroso

Eric W. Blackhurst

Dear Teacher,

"What do I do with the troubled, disturbed, or acting out child?" is one of the questions we are asked most frequently by teachers. The reason is fairly obvious; in addition to being a problem to themselves, such children tend to interfere with class proceedings to such an extent that many other children are also negatively affected. We have asked a teacher-educator who formerly taught such children to share some of the insights that we have heard her share with teachers in many workshops and in-service meetings. Barbara Coloroso has been an inspiration to other teachers, and her ideas have been of practical help in many settings, as evidenced by comments we have received from various places she has been. These suggestions and ideas are by no means the final answer. The problem is much too complex to be subject to any such pat answer or standard formula. These strategies are, in our opinion, a starting place for the classroom teacher who has a troubled child (or troubled children) in her classroom.

We have asked Barbara to speak directly to you, the teacher, much as she does in in-service efforts. Therefore, the personal pronoun "you" will be found quite often in this chapter. We trust that this deviation from a more formal form of writing will be acceptable and perhaps more effective in conveying meaning in this critically important consideration of the troubled child.

BILL GEARHEART and MEL WEISHAHN

Troubled students—we know them; have them in class; hear them in the halls; see them on the playground, in parking lots, and on street corners. Of all the students who walk through the school doors, the troubled ones offer the most frustrating problems and the most potentially rewarding challenge to teachers.

Their behaviors range from extreme withdrawal to intense hostile aggression. They may cry easily or often or may refuse to cry at all. They may consistently fold under emotional stress and become depressed, hostile, or withdrawn, or they may resort to daydreaming to combat the stress. They may be battered and abused sexually, emotionally, or physically. Most of these troubled youth are in the regular classroom. They are often labeled emotionally disturbed, socially maladjusted, or delinquent, labels that do little to help the regular classroom teacher work effectively with these children. The term *troubled* will be used throughout this chapter to describe the youth who exhibits behaviors that are deviant or have a damaging effect on his positive self-development and his relationship with others. Troubled does not connote an illness or disease as does "emotional disturbance," nor does it connote a severe character disorder. It does not assume that the problem is only within the child; it implies that the difficulty may be the result of the youth's interaction with his environment or significant others in his life. Troubled defies static definition and is not a damning or lasting label.

This chapter will briefly overview (1) the nature of deviant behavior, (2) common behaviors of troubled children, (3) identification of the troubled child, (4) referral procedures, (5) overview of major approaches, (6) the responsibility-oriented classroom, (7) the role and responsibility of special education resource personnel, and (8) supportive services in the community.

NATURE OF DEVIANT BEHAVIOR

A child's deviant behavior can result from forces within the child or within the child's environment, including his interaction with "significant others" in his life.

Forces from within the child may be viewed as (1) physiological factors and (2) psychological factors. Physiological factors include brain injury and physiological anomalies. An example of a physiological factor follows:

A student who was seemingly daydreaming, losing his place during reading, and accused of not listening was in fact experiencing petit mal seizures. He would "black out" for a few seconds, just long enough to miss important instruction for class. Once aware of the seizures, the teacher would repeat instructions for the class enabling the student to reorient himself in the learning setting.

Although this example is relatively uncommon and less commonly diagnosed, it does occur and should be given consideration as a possible cause.

Irritability caused by glandular disturbances may appear as anger or hostility. Close observation by the regular classroom teacher, however, might disclose that these episodes occur everyday just before lunch when the child's body is reacting to a basically physiological disorder. Teachers must be aware of the possible physiological reasons for deviant behavior and should make every effort to have them controlled or corrected through medical procedures.

Psychological factors may be the result of a discrepancy between the troubled child's capacity to relate realistically and the requirements of his environment. He may suffer from a marked lack of "coping skills." If a child is forced to attempt an assignment that he feels he cannot perform he may run from the task either physically or mentally. He may become excited or tense and may respond in anger to his textbook, the other students, or the teacher. He may resort to hostile behavior or withdraw when teased.

Environmental factors include variables such as extreme poverty, racial discrimination, school pressures, and deteriorating family units. The following are examples of environmental factors:

A poor child with large holes in his dirty socks reacted violently to being told to take off his shoes in P.E. and chose to be removed from class rather than be humiliated by classmates.

A teenager ditched school rather than face his classmates and teachers after the local paper carried a front-page story on an accident involving his drunk father.

A child who has experienced considerable failure in oral reading may demonstrate extremes of behavior when asked to read orally before his class.

A child who is identified as troubled because of his persistent withdrawal into fantasy or his frightful striking out at those around him may be a normal child defending himself against damaging environmental pressures. Fritz Redl (1959*a*) indicates the following three causes of such behavior:

1. Inconsistent and sometimes borderline psychopathic behaviors by adults in the child's life—a battering parent or a sadistic teacher.
2. An environmental setting other than the normal home and school life every child needs.
3. Conflicts or challenges beyond those with which the child is able to cope, for example, a move from a stable rural setting into a large industrial city.

School can play a big part in pushing children into deviant behaviors. Exaggerated emphasis on grades or rate of progress contribute to acting-out or withdrawn behaviors. Rigid rules encourage rebellion. A teacher's comments can seriously damage a child's self-concept: "Why can't you be like your older brother? He was such a good student." "You are the slowest in the class, always the last to get anything done." "Your papers are so sloppy; can't you do anything right?"

Teacher conversations in the lounge or on final grade reports may leave little hope for a troubled child to rise above his past behaviors. "Oh, you have Johnny—he's a little thief. Watch out or he'll steal you blind." "Jill is such a cry baby." "Joey is so slow—he'll never learn to read."

Academic requirements may be unrealistic for the student in relation to his present level of readiness or to his abilities. A child may hit his peers or make loud noises during oral reading to draw attention away from the fact that he cannot read. In such a situation he may also be trying to get some kind of acknowledgement that he exists; he cannot get the acknowledgement by reading, so he will try a less appropriate form of behavior to get attention. Everyone needs to be acknowledged by significant others. We usually try appropriate behaviors first. If we are unsuccessful in this attempt, we may resort to more deviant forms of behavior to reach the same or similar ends. Children try to succeed and to be the best at something, but many recognize that they cannot be the best in reading or math or the best runner so they become the "best-worst." These children become the "best-worst" trouble makers. We cannot deny, however, that they are "the best" even though their behavior is socially unacceptable. A child may try to please his parents by cleaning his room. If he doesn't receive praise or acknowledgement from his parents or if they yell at him for not making the bed perfectly, he will cease trying to gain recognition through appropriate behaviors and attempt to gain their acknowledgement through deviant behaviors.

COMMON BEHAVIORS OF TROUBLED CHILDREN

The following behaviors or characteristics are commonly seen in troubled children. These same behaviors may be seen in all children during stressful situations in their lives. It is the frequency, persistence, and intensity of these behaviors that would indicate a need for real concern by the regular classroom teacher. Reinert (1976) has described troubled youth as being "too precise, too worried, too angry, too happy; too easily disappointed and manipulate others too much." Common behaviors include the following:

Hostile aggressiveness. Perhaps the most obvious sign or indication of a troubled child is his hostile aggression toward teachers, peers, and parents. Kicking, hitting, biting, and fighting are means of expressing fears and anxieties.

Withdrawal into fantasy. The isolate in the class, the one who shuns involvement with peers or teachers, is sometimes far more troubled and in greater need of assistance than the aggressive child. However, the shy or withdrawn child is often overlooked by teachers. This child does not express antagonism toward authority and therefore may be ignored as the teacher exerts every effort toward finding help for the aggressive child.

Perfectionism. Fearing failure and criticism, this child is likely to destroy his assignment or art work or "quit and take his ball home" if he makes a mistake or if things do not go his way.

Regression. A child may regress to forms of behavior that worked in previous situations (whining, thumbsucking, and infantile speech, for example).

Depression. The child is generally unhappy or depressed, even in situations that nearly all other children enjoy.

Unrealistic fears and phobias. This child attempts to avoid his real anxieties by developing unrealistic fears.

Bellyaches and headaches. This child complains of pains at the most opportune times, before math exams or during physical education, for example. He is constantly worrying about his health; a few drops of blood means bleeding to death and a rash must be an exotic disease with no known cure.

Accident proneness. This child falls out of chairs, trips down or up stairs, and collapses on level ground. He seems to thrive on the attention given to his wounds.

Overly dependent. This child is overly dependent on peers and teachers. He does not attempt a new task until he has received assurance from his peers or the teacher.

The "smelly" kid. Although this child may not be a troubled child because of his body odor or obesity, the resultant peer interaction (or lack of it) may cause the child to become a loner or isolate.

Although some of the preceding behaviors or characteristics are at opposite ends of the continuum, others are of such nature that they overlap and appear in combination. Examples might include a combination of some form of withdrawal and regression and infantile behavior or perfectionism and some degree of hostile aggressiveness. As indicated at the outset, some degree of these behaviors may be expected in nearly all children; it is, however, the unusual frequency or intensity that is a signal that the child needs help. These behaviors are exhibited "in the wrong places, at the wrong time, in the presence of the wrong people, and to an inappropriate degree" (Reinert, 1976).

IDENTIFICATION OF THE TROUBLED CHILD

The regular classroom teacher is often the first to identify troubled or troublesome children. She may be unable to clinically label the problem, but she knows one exists. She can be instrumental in screening or referring students who require a more careful diagnosis by special education personnel and possible mental health intervention beyond the school setting. A teacher can gather enough pertinent information about a troubled child during daily contacts with the child to make fairly accurate professional predictions about that child's future success or failure in school.

Checklists and rating scales for classroom teachers are not intended for clinical diagnosis. Knowing the clinical description for a child's deviant behavior, for example, psychotic, neurotic, sadistic, does not tell a teacher how a child learns and how he may respond to the many pressures and problems in the classroom. Therefore, screening instruments used by a regular classroom teacher should focus on behaviors relevant to the educational process, not to clinical diagnosis. The scales should be easy to administer and should help the teacher objectify behavioral judgments about pupils.

Care must be taken to select a screening device that meets the needs of a specific situation. Bower (1969) listed a number of specific criteria for evaluating screening tests. These include the following:

1. The screening procedure should include only that information a teacher can obtain without professional assistance.
2. The instrument should be easy to administer and score.
3. The results should be tentative—identifying troubled students who could benefit most from a more thorough diagnosis.
4. The procedure should actively discourage the teacher from diagnosing emotional problems, drawing conclusions about causes, or labeling the child being tested.
5. Privacy of the individual child should not be invaded, nor should the questions be in poor taste.
6. The procedure should not be a threat to the child.
7. The screening test should be inexpensive.

The following list is indicative of the type and variety of screening instruments in use from kindergarten through twelfth grade. Reference texts on assessment and evaluation will provide the names of additional checklists that would be appropriate for regular classroom teachers.

DEVEREUX ELEMENTARY SCHOOL BEHAVIOR RATING SCALE (GRADES K–6)

The Devereux Elementary School Behavior Rating Scale (DESB) measures behaviors that indicate the child's overall adaptation to the classroom setting and his subsequent academic achievement in the classroom. The scale consists of forty-seven items that define the following eleven behavioral factors:

1. Classroom disturbance
2. Impatience
3. Disrespect/defiance
4. External blame
5. Achievement anxiety
6. External reliance
7. Comprehension
8. Inattentive and withdrawn
9. Irrelevant/responsiveness
10. Creative/initiative
11. Closeness to teachers

The Devereux Scale is based on the teacher's subjective norm of how the average child of the same sex and age behaves in the classroom. This instrument is easy to administer, taking about eight minutes to complete, and provides a profile of behaviors that interfere with classroom performance.

BY: Spivack and Swift
PUBLISHER: Devereux Foundation Press

HAHNEMANN HIGH SCHOOL BEHAVIOR RATING SCALE (GRADES 7–12)

The Hahnemann High School Behavior Rating Scale (HHSB), a forty-five-item rating scale, measures overt classroom behaviors related to a student's adjustment to the demands of a regular classroom at the junior and senior high school level. There are thirteen factors in the scale. Five of the factors relate positively to academic success:

1. Reasoning ability
2. Verbal interaction
3. Originality
4. Rapport with the teacher
5. Anxious producer (inner pressure to master a task)

The remaining factors relate negatively to academic success. These factors, in respect to an entire behavior profile, suggest negative feelings and behaviors:

1. General anxiety
2. Quiet/withdrawn
3. Poor work habits
4. Lack of intellectual independence
5. Dogmatic/inflexible
6. Verbal negativism
7. Disturbance/restless
8. Expressed inability

The HHSB provides norms and a method of charting the behavior profile. It is a valid instrument and is easy to use. The forty-five items are similar to those found in the DESB, with rating and scoring methods essentially the same.

BY: Swift and Spivack
PUBLISHER: Hahnemann Medical College

PUPIL BEHAVIOR INVENTORY (GRADES 7–12)

The Pupil Behavior Inventory measures "behavioral and attitudinal factors which affect the degree of success a pupil will have in accomplishing his educational objectives" (Vinter et al., 1966, p. 1). This one-page inventory lists behavioral items a teacher can readily observe. The items are rated on a five-point scale from "very frequently" to "very infrequently." The dimensions covered include the following:

1. Classroom conduct
2. Academic motivation and performance
3. Socioemotional state
4. Teacher dependence
5. Personal behavior

It is a very usable scale with explicit, easy-to-follow directions and is easy to score. Norms are available for junior and senior high.

BY: Vinter, Sarri, Vorwaller, and Schafer
PUBLISHER: Campus Publishers, Ann Arbor, Michigan

WALKER PROBLEM BEHAVIOR IDENTIFICATION CHECKLIST
(GRADES 4–6)

The Walker Problem Behavior Identification Checklist (WPBIC) is a tool "the elementary teacher can rely upon in the difficult task of selecting children with behavior problems who should be referred for further psychological evaluation, referral and treatment" (Walker, 1967, p. 1). The checklist consists of fifty observable symptomatic behaviors that might limit a child's adjustment in school. The following are sample items from this checklist:

"Will destroy or take apart something he has made rather than show it or ask to have it displayed

"Disturbs other children: teasing, provoking fights, and interrupting others

"Refers to himself as dumb, stupid, or incapable

"Openly strikes back with angry behavior to teasing of other children

"Easily distracted away from the task at hand by ordinary classroom stimuli, minor movements of others and noises, for example."*

The factors scored include the following:

1. Acting out (disruptive and aggressive behavior)
2. Withdrawing (socially passive and avoidant behaviors)
3. Distractibility (poor attentiveness and restlessness)
4. Disturbed peer relations
5. Immaturity

This is an initial screening device, not intended as an educational planning tool. It is easy to use and takes eight to ten minutes to complete.

BY: Hill M. Walker
PUBLISHER: Western Psychological Services

---

*Reprinted with permission. © 1970 by Western Psychological Services.

BEHAVIOR PROBLEM CHECKLIST
(GRADES K–8)

The Behavior Problem Checklist consists of sixty-nine items that are limited to the most frequently occurring behaviors of children referred to a psychiatric clinic. The items are rated on a three-point scale: does not constitute a problem, is a mild problem, and is a severe problem. In the factoring process, the following four personality types are identified:

1. Conduct problem
2. Personality—neurotic
3. Inadequacy, immaturity
4. Socialized delinquency

The following are sample items from this checklist:

"1. Does not know how to have fun; behaves like a little adult
"2. Fighting
"3. Anxiety, chronic general fearfulness
"4. Depression, chronic sadness
"5. Often has physical complaints, e.g. headaches, stomach aches."

It is easily administered and scored. A unique aspect of this checklist is that Quay has developed educational programs that he feels are appropriate for the different personality types identified.

BY: Quay and Peterson
PUBLISHER: Children's Research Center, Champaign, Ill.

BOWER-LAMBERT SCALES FOR IN-SCHOOL SCREENING OF EMOTIONALLY HANDICAPPED CHILDREN

The screening procedure developed by Bower and Lambert consists of three rating scales used in combination with each other for one total evaluation of each pupil:

Teacher-rating scale
Peer-rating scale
Self-rating scale

It is the most extensive of the screening devices described in this chapter.

Teacher rating of pupils (all grades)

The teacher, using a normal distribution, indicates the relative position of each student on eight scales.

Peer rating

Class pictures (grades K–3)
Class play (grades 3–7)
Student survey (grades 7–12)

These three activities are designed for use at the different grade levels to analyze how children are perceived by their peers.

Self rating

    Picture game (grades K–3). This activity is designed to give a measure of a child's perception of himself.

    Thinking about yourself (grades 3–7). This activity is designed to show the degree of discrepancy between a child's perception of himself as he is and as he would like to be.

    A self test (grades 7–12). This test is designed to obtain a measure of the difference between self and ideal self.

Information from the three sources—teacher, peer, and self—are collated and weighted to arrive at behavioral evaluation of the child.

    BY: Bower and Lambert

    PUBLISHER: Education Testing Service

Many behavioral checklists are part of a total pupil rating scale that attempts to give a total educational profile of the student. One such checklist is part IV of the Pupil Behavior Rating Scale, a scale used for diagnosis in learning disabilities (see Appendix E).

It would be impractical to attempt to list all of the checklists or screening instruments used in the screening of behavioral deviances across the United States. Published checklists are continually being revised, adapted, and combined with other instruments by various school districts to fit the needs of the district and available services.

They do have the potential, however, to assist regular classroom teachers in identifying more objectively the students in their classrooms who may be in need of further assistance from special education personnel or from professionals outside of the school district.

REFERRAL PROCEDURES

Screening checklists and rating scales should not be substituted for concrete assistance or intervention. Once a teacher has identified a troubled child as being in need of assistance beyond what she can provide in a regular class setting, she should refer the child to the resource person or school psychologist for an in-depth evaluation.

When making the referral, the classroom teacher should be ready to describe the *specific behaviors* the child is exhibiting that

lead her to believe the child needs special assistance. This is the situation in which screening checklists and rating scales help. Also helpful are brief anecdotal notes a teacher might keep, similar to an abbreviated diary, noting events of each day. This requires very little time if completed at the close of every day. It can become a regular part of the daily routine, and it must be done *daily* if notes are to be of maximum accuracy and objectivity.

In many school systems the child is staffed by a team composed of the principal, the regular classroom teacher, the resource teacher, the school psychologist, the school social worker, the director of special education, and a member of the medical profession. The child's parents are often included, although they may not always participate in the total staffing.

The staffing team reviews and discusses all pertinent information and makes recommendations concerning educational placement and programming. The educational recommendations often include professional help and a modified educational program. The professional help can range from support to the regular classroom teacher by a resource person to psychiatric therapy in a mental health setting. The modified educational program can be as simple as establishing a behavior contract with the child or as involved as moving the child into a therapeutic detention home or residential facility.

One critical question is whether the child can function in the regular class with certain behavioral and educational adaptations. Should he be placed in a special class, or is his behavior so deviant that even special classes will be ineffective? The regular classroom teacher's input is invaluable at this time. Because of her interactions with the child, her perception of his behavior may be closer to the true operational reality of the child's difficulty than the information obtained from a complete diagnostic study, test results, or clinical interviews. She is the one who has experienced the child responding in anger or frustration in the educational setting.

There are many advantages in keeping the troubled student in the regular classroom, provided the classroom is responsibility and reality oriented. The following are just a few advantages offered by regular classroom placement:

1. The student has an opportunity to observe appropriate behavior of his peers, interact with peers, and receive support from peers.
2. The student has the opportunity to "dispel the delusion of uniqueness," to reinforce the feeling that he is more like other children than different from them.
3. The student has the opportunity to function responsibly and realistically in a safe milieu in which creative abilities can be channeled into academic pursuits.
4. The student can see and experience appropriate responsible expressions of emotions.

There are several steps a regular classroom teacher can take before and during the referral process to make the classroom situation more tolerable and, perhaps, creative and constructive for the teacher and the troubled student. These steps are also applicable if the troubled student, after screening, is to remain in the regular class with supportive services from a resource person or mental health personnel.

Step 1: What is it that the student is doing or not doing that upsets you. Write it down! How often does he do it, and when does he do it? If there is more than one behavior, and there usually is, list them according to the priority of your concern. What do you do when he exhibits the behaviors you recorded. If he is still throwing books, your approach is not affecting his behavior positively.

Step 2: Share your notes with the student—level with him. Determine what he is doing and what you are doing that is not working; then ask for his help in coming up with new "cue cards"! Alschuler and Shea (1974) have developed this step into a technique called "social literacy training," in which discipline problems are recognized as games with rules that can be renegotiated to change negative discipline cycles into the discipline of learning. You are not threatening or punishing the student—just acknowledging your awareness of the problem and your desire to work constructively with the student. Too often, everyone in the teacher's lounge knows about your awareness of Johnny's problem, but Johnny isn't aware that you know. Confronting the troubled student in a nonthreatening way and exploring with him alternatives to his deviant behavior is sometimes enough of a catalyst for a positive change. *It is important that your meeting with the student be nonthreatening and as positive as possible.*

Step 3: Greet the troubled student at the front door if necessary. Give him a positive stroke everday—a compliment, a smile, or a touch on the shoulder *before* he has a chance to behave irresponsibly. Look for things he does well and share your observations with him. Often, when a student is experiencing difficulty, all the teacher thinks about are the negative things. It is generally an easy task to establish an extensive listing of things the student does not do well; why not attend to what he does well? *Every student has many desirable behaviors and characteristics;* you may have to observe carefully for a short period of time, but the desirable behaviors are present. Watch for them, and let the student know that you are aware of them. It may be a beautiful smile or a great laugh. Sometimes we can reverse the pattern of undesirable behavior simply by attending to the positive aspects and by letting the student know that he is seen as a positive, worthwhile, and valued individual. Acknowledge his presence in a positive way before he forces you to acknowledge him in a negative way. Then, when he has behaved in a positive, responsible way, acknowledge his behavior in writing.

Glad notes and glad phone calls

Glad notes, note cards with positive comments about a student, can be used to encourage and compliment the troubled student. They are effective positive reinforcers. Have a drawer full of different types of glad notes. When the student has worked extra hard to overcome some social or academic difficulty, fill out a glad note with a positive, personal message and give it to the student. You will find younger students taking these notes home to share with their parents; older students may stick the notes in their book to reread on a "down day." Glad notes may also be mailed home to the student's parents.

After the troubled student has had a good day in school, a *glad phone call* to his parents to share the good news can help establish positive communication and cooperation between parents, student, and school. Too often, most of the correspondence between the parents of a troubled student and the school is on a negative note: "What did he do wrong this time?" Parents need to hear about the beautiful side of their children. Parent cooperation can be increased through your recognition and acknowledgement of their child's assets. They are already well aware of his liabilities. The use of glad notes or glad phone calls is effective with all students, not just those who are troubled. The following are examples of glad notes that have been used with young students. Consider making your own, appropriate for the age and interests of the students with whom you work.

For staying
in your seat

SIGNATURE_____

DATE_____

For being on time!!
(AND PREPARED)

SIGNATURE_____

DATE_____

We all
have our
ups and
downs

SIGNATURE_____ DATE_____

For being
so friendly

SIGNATURE_____ DATE_____

MAJOR APPROACHES USED IN WORKING WITH TROUBLED STUDENTS

There is no one "correct" way of working with troubled students. A teacher must be aware of various approaches that may be used realistically and effectively in the classroom. The following reference to authorities and contributors in this field is for the purpose of acquainting the reader with various approaches that may be investigated further.

Psychoanalytic approach

Bruno Bettelheim (1949), who was among the first to develop a specific school program for troubled students, used an orthodox psychoanalytic approach. The role of the teacher using this approach is to provide ways in which students can bring into consciousness their unconscious repressions.

The program is extremely permissive, with all program cueing coming from the child. The program developed by Bettelheim is carried out in a residential school, the Sonia Shankman Orthogenic School, and is not adaptable to a public school setting.

Fritz Redl (1959) and Ruth Newman (1967) have also taken a psychoanalytic approach in dealing with troubled youth. They stress the importance of bringing unconscious repressions into consciousness and developing the ego. They differ philosophically from Bettleheim in that their approaches involve much more external structure.

Fritz Redl is known for his work with delinquent boys in residential treatment programs. He believes in a structure that allows for a wide range of choice in behavioral responses. Life space interviewing, a technique developed by Redl, exploits a life event at the time of the event or soon after. It is a way of offering "ego support on the spot" to achieve a developmental gain. This technique has been used successfully by classroom teachers and is suited to a teacher's responsibility in group management, social learning, and social adjustment.

Ruth Newman suggests that an essential part of the educational programming for the troubled child is allowing the child to act out. Her techniques initially involve the acceptance of unacceptable symptoms, followed by tolerance but not acceptance, and finally setting a limit to the behavior.

Other psychoanalytically inclined authors include Pearson (1954), Slavson (1954), and Hirshberg (1953).

Humanistic approach

The humanistic approach in working with troubled children involves the acceptance of a child's behavior and the reflection of the behavior back to the child. It is through this reflection process that the child grows in his capacity to develop insight and modify his own behavior. This approach, with its direct and uncomplicated framework, encourages the child to learn, to express, and to better understand his feelings in a caring, reflective environment.

Clark Moustakas (1953) considers the regular classroom teacher as having the potential to be a genuinely effective therapist by establishing an atmosphere of acceptance and warmth in the classroom.

Another humanistic psychologist, Carl Rogers (1951), advocates a permissive relationship, within defined limits, for a child's self-expression. Rogers feels that schools are too punitive for nondirective therapy and has made suggestions for adjusting teaching techniques to work in conjunction with treatment agencies.

Thomas Gordon (1974), utilizing Rogers' philosophy and basic attitudes about persons, elaborates on active listening, an integral part of the humanistic approach, in his book, *T.E.T. Teacher Effectiveness Training.* Also part of Gordon's approach to helping troubled children is group-centered problem solving, in which the students and teacher work cooperatively to make the educational experience a responsible and profitable one.

Virginia Axline (1947) is known for her work in play therapy. She feels that by providing understanding, acceptance, and recognition and clarification of feelings, a teacher can help a child grow in his understanding and acceptance of himself.

The humanistic system is a viable approach in dealing with troubled students in the public school setting if the attitudes of acceptance, trust, and empathic understanding are present.

Behavior modification

Behavior modification techniques offer the tools and systematic procedures that teachers may implement to change or modify behavior that is unacceptable or deviant and to encourage more acceptable and appropriate behaviors. The fundamental concept of behavior modification is that behavior, abnormal as well as normal, is learned. Environmental consequences may accelerate-increase the behavioral response or decelerate-decrease the frequency or rate of behavior.

The application of behavior modification principles with children in the regular classroom is a systematic and complex process. The dispensing of M & M's or gold stars cannot be properly called behavior modification. Behavior modification requires systematic and planned effort to be used effectively.

Behavior modification theorists are not primarily concerned with the causes of deviant behavior. Rather, they are concerned with exhibited, overt behavior. The behavior is observed, measured, and analyzed quantitatively. Appropriate behavior modification techniques are applied in relation to the observable measurements.

Some of the individuals who have systematically applied behavior modification techniques in the classroom or have developed behavior modification techniques that can be used in the classroom include Homme (1970), Hewett (1968), Walker (1970), Lindsley (1971), Haring and Phillips (1962), and Patterson and Gullion (1968).

Other conceptual frameworks

Two other persons who have developed specific techniques for use in the regular classroom are Rudolph Dreikurs and William Glasser.

Rudolph Dreikurs, his philosophy rooted in Adlerian theory, suggests that schools must become truly democratic, with students playing an active role in the process of their education. Advocating the "art of encouragement" as a crucial tool in improving the adjustment a troubled child must make, he recommends that teachers give up punitive retaliation and begin sharing responsibility with the students, encouraging them to participate in decision making. Dreikurs believes that a teacher must understand the roles and the importance of the peer group as it relates to classroom conduct (Dreikurs, Grunwald, and Pepper, 1971).

William Glasser (1969) suggests that teachers, grading, and imposed curricula contribute to students' failure. According to Glasser (1969):

The schools assume built-in motivation, but when it does not occur, they attempt to motivate children with methods analogous to using a gun. Although guns have never worked, the schools, struggling to solve their problems, resort to using bigger and bigger guns—more restrictions and rules, more threats and punishments.

He has developed techniques for classroom meetings that give students more freedom to talk and think, to be responsible for their own behavior and academic success.

Other individuals could be mentioned, but such a review is not the purpose of this text. Those who wish to read further may find additional material provided in the references and suggested readings at the end of this chapter.

RESPONSIBILITY-ORIENTED CLASSROOM

In this discussion I will review techniques that reflect a combination of approaches that have been effectively used by teachers working with troubled students in the regular classroom.* This approach takes into consideration the *beauty of each student, provides an opportunity for each student to take an active part in his academic planning, and*

---

*I have worked with troubled students as a teacher in self-contained classrooms, as a resource teacher, and as a teacher educator in preservice and inservice programs. This discussion reflects a composite of ideas, concepts, and methods that I have found to be of value.

does not involve elaborate techniques. It also allows for an exercise of the unique skills and competencies of each teacher.

You, as a regular class teacher, have the opportunity to provide a "safe" place for the troubled student and alternatives and choices to help the student change his attitudes and behaviors. Whether it be for the whole day, half day, or one period, your class can be a place where the student can feel O.K.— needed, valued, and responsible.

In such a classroom, the student is responsible for his own behavior, academic success, and failures. He *owns* his actions. He cannot blame his environment, parents, or peers for his own behavior. He has the ability to choose.

You, as the teacher, have the responsibility to be yourself, establish structure that is realistic, program academic materials to fit the needs and abilities of your students, and encourage academic and social responsibility.

You cannot *make* a student behave responsibly or realistically. You can coerce, threaten, or physically restrain a student, but then both you and the student lose. You and a student may set up destructive game rules in which neither of you can be a winner.

A responsibility-oriented classroom involves the use of natural and realistic consequences, a simple structure, reasonable rules, the labeling and acceptance of feelings, group meetings, and the use of contracts.

Consequences

Rather than threaten, you can establish realistic and natural consequences and make it (hopefully) more comfortable for the student to choose the more responsible activity. The choice is still the student's to make. The idea is to make him aware of the negative and positive consequences of his choice. If the student does not know what to expect if he completes his assignment or what to expect if he does not get his assignment done, he does not really make a choice. The goal is to help a student see himself as responsible for and in control of what happens to him.

There is no one positive consequence or negative consequence that will work with all students. For example, staying in from recesss may be positively reinforcing for one student, whereas another may feel that it is punitive. The consequences need to fit the situation and be such that the teacher and the student can follow through with them. If you say to a student, "I'll break your arm if I catch you stealing again!" what are your choices if he does steal again?

One way to find realistic and meaningful consequences is to ask your students to help you decide on the consequences. What the students consider positive or negative consequences may not have even occurred to you as being reinforcing.

The following are positive consequences that can be used in the regular classroom setting.

Positive consequences for elementary age children

Go to the free corner
Help a slower classmate
Be a teacher-helper
Stay after school
Have free time with the teacher
Plan a media project
Present a project to the class
Be first in line
Draw
Paint
Work with clay
Take a five-minute break to play a game with a friend in the quiet corner
Listen to a record or radio with earphones
Use the overhead projector or tape recorder
Go to the classroom or school store
Operate the filmstrip projector for the class
Help the secretary, janitor, or principal
Be class messenger for the day
Use class camera and film
Use a typewriter
Read a motorcycle magazine

Positive consequences for secondary age students

Work as a tutor for elementary students
Work with the janitor, secretary, or principal

Work in the guidance office

Plan own assignment schedule for the week

Read magazines of their choice

Plant a garden

Create a film or slide presentation

Take apart and assemble electrical or mechanical equipment

Use a calculator or typewriter

Extra time in the class to work on homework assignments

Snack break

Free day

Card games

Plan, film, and show a videotape sequence

Listen to records or radio with earphones

Design and build playground equipment for young children

Refinish desks

Time off to volunteer at social service and other community agencies

Shoot baskets

Build a terrarium

Macrame

Leatherwork

Swim break

These are not the only positive consequences available to teachers. Be creative and encourage students to assist in determining positive consequences.

Structure and rules

You probably know which rules are most appropriate for your class to maintain some semblance of sanity, keep the room intact, and see that valuable learning takes place.

Rather than post rules and dictate them, ask your students to help you come up with realistic guidelines for the class. Your role becomes that of guiding the discussion and offering suggestions. It is important that the rules help create a structure that serves as a backbone for learning, not as a brick wall. The rules should be simple and consistently administered. Too little structure can result in chaos; too much structure, in defiance and rebellion. The structure should provide opportunity for the child to grow, and time to think. The environment should be positive, acceptable, and nonthreatening. *A responsibility-oriented classroom is neither a teacher-dominated nor student-controlled room.*

Rather, it is a joint effort to learn, relate, and experience.

Labeling and accepting feelings

The following was presented by Freed (1974):

> Remember, feelings are just as real
> as noses and toeses.
> So, let your feelings come out.
> You'll feel better, be happier and
> so will everybody else.

There are only two things to remember: (1) find someone who cares to listen to your feelings; and (2) don't dump your feelings on little people.

Another way to get rid of your angry feelings is to hit pillows. You can have neat temper tantrums in your room and not hurt anyone. You could pound clay, hammer your peg board, throw bean bags . . . or if you can find a safe place, throw clods of mud that won't hurt anybody. You can throw them at a tree, makes a nice thud.

Students need to know that it is all right to be angry, to be unhappy, and to be afraid and that there are responsible ways to express these feelings. A child who, in anger or frustration, throws a math book across the room may not be aware of other ways to express his anger. He may have witnessed his parents in anger throwing plates across the room. The child who beats up his peers may himself be brutally beaten by his parents for making a mistake or for just being in the way. The child who throws himself on the floor kicking and screaming when he doesn't get his own way has learned that this technique hooks his parents and teachers. In all three of these situations the actions of the students are learned behaviors. Students, therefore, can learn to replace these irresponsible actions with more appropriate expressions of their feelings.

You as a teacher will not have to contrive situations to express feelings of anger or hurt in the classroom. The situations are there. Labeling your feelings and encouraging a student to label his are the two essential components of the first step toward helping a troubled child accept and deal with his frustrations and anger.

The second step, discussing appropriate and realistic ways to express feelings, can be accomplished through the discussion of incidents in the class, group meetings (refer to an explanation of the Magic Circle on pp. 158-159), and role playing.

The third step is to actively encourage the appropriate expression of feelings in the classroom. When students express their feelings irresponsibly, you can talk through their anger, hurt, or fright and help them arrive at alternative behaviors with which they can feel comfortable.

More than structure, rules, and academia, you must convey to your students your trust and belief in them—all of them. They each have something unique and beautiful to bring to your class. You must believe in the troubled student to help him believe in himself. In developing a positive relationship it is important that you recognize and accept small efforts by the troubled student and freely express your real appreciation for that student's good behavior. The student needs to find that joy, delight, and enthusiasm can be a part of his learning experience.

Group meetings

An integral part of a responsibility-oriented classroom is the group meeting. It fosters student involvement and initiative in learning. Teachers are teaching students to teach themselves.

Formats for these meetings have been described in detail by Glasser (1969); Dreikurs, Grunwald, and Pepper (1971); and others in the field of education. Group meetings are like kids—they come in all shapes and sizes. They can be five minutes or fifty minutes long and can involve two or thirty people.

There are three types of meetings, with many different labels, that seem to fit most of the situations arising in most classes. These are:
1. Academic planning meetings
2. Problem-solving meetings
3. Crisis meetings

Academic planning meetings. In this type of meeting, the teacher and the students plan the academic program. This includes a discussion of the students' present academic status, where they are going, and the steps they will need to accomplish to reach their

goal. Students, then, assume a responsible role in their own educational planning.

Students usually have a good idea of their level of progress in reading—especially if they are behind their classmates. Try as we might to disguise levels of reading groups, the "Buzzards" know that they are the bottom level if they are the poorest readers. Being straight with a student helps him to accept his level. What you are saying is that you know he is behind, he is okay, his present level is okay for now, you know he can learn more, and you have a plan to help him get ahead. The slow or underachieving student will then no longer feel hopelessly behind. He now has a goal and a realistic means to achieve that goal. You and the student become coplanners in the learning experience.

Openly discussing different levels of achievement takes the bite out of classmates' malicious or hurtful talk that can destroy a child's self-esteem, "John's so dumb, he can't even read yet" or "Ha Ha, look at all the math problems Jill missed." Because you accept each one of them, you can help students accept themselves and one another for what they are, where they are, and where they are going.

At the beginning of each quarter you should discuss the learning objectives so the students can get an idea of the total learning picture for the next nine weeks. Each week you should present the objectives for the individual week in relation to the whole term. At this time, students can discuss what they have already mastered and how they are going to accomplish their goals for the week. Keeping the learning experience on a positive note and in perspective with larger goals will not only help students learn to organize their time, but will enable them to see themselves progress. You will find that your teaching is more organized and realistic.

The time spent in this type of meeting does take away from the reading or math periods, but you will find the time well worth while as students go about the business of learning with a feeling that they are in control.

Problem-solving meetings. The problem-solving meeting is perhaps the most fun and challenging of the three. Students learn to examine situations, propose solutions, and evaluate the results. The problem is stated simply and clearly; then the problem is clarified. The students select options and discuss the feasibility of their choices. Solutions are proposed and a plan of action is agreed on and carried out if possible. Students present their own ideas, listen to one another's reasoning, and work cooperatively to arrive at a solution.

The students begin to see, through these interactions, that there is not always a definite right and a definite wrong. Group choices involve give and take and much cooperation on the part of all concerned.

From this exercise, you and the students can move on to problem situations in the classroom, for example, where to go on a field trip when there is a gas shortage and a fifty-mile radius limit, how to get more equipment for the playground, or how to rearrange schedules.

Crisis meeting. This meeting differs from the other two in that it is rarely planned; it is conducted whenever necessary. It can be held by two individuals, three individuals, or a group on the playground, in the classroom, or in the lunchroom. The rules for this meeting include the following:

1. All parties concerned must speak in soft tones—no shouting is permitted. A cooling-off time may be necessary before the parties can begin discussing the situation. Lowering your voice helps to quiet the students.
2. The first child expresses his feelings and states the problem situation *as he sees it*.
3. The other child (or children) is asked to repeat what he heard the first child say. This is an important step. Repeating what the other child said helps to take the edge off of any remaining anger.
4. Child number two then gives his side of the story and the first child repeats what he heard.
5. Now the situation is discussed at length. Could this situation have been avoided? How? What alternative behaviors might the students use in the future to avoid a similar situation? What should the consequences be for the students' irresponsible

behavior? It is often quite effective to have the students determine the consequences. They are most fair (and sometimes very hard on themselves).

These instant meetings can help a child come to grips with his emotions and help him see alternatives to the irresponsible ways in which he may have expressed his anger or hurt.

Magic Circle. Complete systems have been devised to help students develop self-esteem and the skills necessary for living a creative, responsible life.

One such system is the *Magic Circle,* developed by the Human Development Training Institute in La Mesa, California. It is a preventative program that can be used to help troubled students dispel the delusion of uniqueness—the delusion that they are so different from those around them. By talking and listening, children learn from one another that they have much in common. The program consists of specifically and developmentally programmed *topics* introduced by the teacher in daily twenty-minute sessions. During these sessions, students deal with negative and positive feelings and practice resolutions of conflict in an atmosphere of trust and acceptance. In planned stages, children learn how to express themselves meaningfully, to become confident in their abilities and to interact creatively and constructively with one another.

Through the Magic Circle you can foster an atmosphere of warmth and honesty in which each child contributes a part of himself, and listens respectfully to his peers.

The program is based on the following three areas of human experience:

awareness knowing who he is, his own thoughts, feelings and actions. To own his own behavior, and his hurt and happy feelings.

mastery knowing his abilities and liabilities and how to utilize his abilities constructively and creatively.

social interaction knowing other people, how to be a friend, how to care for others.

The three work together to decrease a child's fear of facing everyday frustrations and give him confidence in dealing creatively with everyday situations. The program is developed through the ninth grade, complete with manuals and suggested supplementary activities that relate to the affective domain.

One note of caution with group meetings that deal with feelings and self-expression: keep the discussion from becoming a "show and tell all about family secrets" meeting.

If a student blurts out in the group that his parents had a big fight last night or his dad came home drunk and beat up his mom, quietly express your concern and let him know you will talk about it with him at break or free time, as soon as possible. Care about the hurt the child is feeling and be supportive, not probing. Be certain to provide time that day for the child to talk with you alone.

THE USE OF CONTRACTS AND CONTRACTING

Contracts are a joint agreement between a student and teacher to accomplish a specific objective. The student and teacher may contract for a specific academic task or a desired behavior. Contracts may be drawn up to include most phases of school (and home) life. They involve a student and a teacher in a commitment to one another to relate realistically and responsibly. Contracts can be directed at a specific behavior or be more general in nature, that is, directed at improving a total relationship between a student and all school personnel in contact with the student. Most importantly, the student must state that the behavior established in the contract is one *he* feels the need to change and that the goal is one *he* wants to achieve. One important factor to make a contract most effective is to be certain that the student is involved in deciding how it is going to work, that he feels it is fair, and that he makes a commitment to change his behavior.

Guidelines

Time. Contracts may be short periods of time (fifteen-minute segments), a class period, a school day, or an entire week. For the student who has difficulty disciplining himself, organizing his time and structuring his own activities, it would not be realistic or profitable to agree to a contract that was for an entire quarter. Smaller segments work best because the students may see success in a relatively short time.

Responsibility. The student is responsible for his contract, his behavior, and his acceptance of the consequences of that behavior. He cannot blame anyone else for his irresponsibility or accuse anyone of punishing him. He can take credit for his own positive behavior. The student is making the choice to complete or not complete an assignment, to behave responsibily or irresponsibly, and to accept the consequences of his choices, be they positive or negative.

Consequences. Consequences should be realistic and relevant to the situation. A student needs to know what to expect if he completes a task and what to expect if he chooses not to complete a task.

Types of contracts. The types of contracts to be considered here include the minicontract, the academic contract, and systematic suspension contract. The minicontract is a short-term agreement directed at a specific behavior. The academic contract is a daily or weekly agreement for completion of specific academic assignments. The systematic suspension contract is an agreement between a student, his parents, and all school personnel directly involved with the student. It is aimed at changing a total relationship pattern.

Minicontract

The minicontract is a short-term agreement drawn up by a student and teacher for the purpose of changing a specific behavior that both parties agree should be changed. Examples of such behaviors might include swearing, tardiness, incomplete assignments, kicking, or day dreaming. This type of contract is most effective if the student himself records his appropriate behaviors. You let him know you believe he is a responsible person capable of managing this contract with your support.

Weekly academic contract

The weekly academic contract may be drawn up for an individual student or an entire class. If it is done for an individual student, the student and teacher should dis-

MINICONTRACT

SHOP

_____FIND SEAT QUICKLY—NO RUNNING AROUND

_____LISTEN AND FOLLOW DIRECTIONS

_____HANDS OFF MATERIALS THAT ARE NOT FOR YOUR USE

_____STAY THE WHOLE PERIOD

STUDENT: _____

INSTRUCTOR: _____

MINICONTRACT

P. E.

_____LISTEN AND FOLLOW DIRECTIONS

_____PARTICIPATE IN ACTIVITIES

_____STAY THE WHOLE PERIOD

STUDENT: _____

INSTRUCTOR: _____

cuss the student's academic level in a specific academic area, his goal for the quarter (or semester), his goal for the week, and his daily goal.

Weekly, the student and teacher should review what the student has accomplished that week in relation to his goal for the quarter.

The purpose of determining goals for all three time intervals is to permit the student to see realistically where he is in a given subject area, where he is going, and how he can, step-by-step, reach his goal. For a student who is behind in school, this is most important. If he is three years behind in math at the beginning of the semester and 2½ years behind at the end of the semester, without the step-by-step goals he might not be able to see any improvement. Without the short-term goals, he is just "still behind." With the goals, he is moving ahead.

Directions for use. The teacher and student plan the activities in math (or any other subject) for the week. The specific assignments are written in the assignment column. There are several variations that could be used in this column.

1. *Green circles.* Write down the number of the problems a student is expected to complete. If a student chooses to do more

NO SWEARING CARD						
8:45-9:00	☺	☺	☺	☺	☺	
9:00-9:15		☺		☺	☺	
9:15-9:30	☺		☺	☺	☺	
9:30-9:45	☺	☺	☺		☺	
9:45-10:00	☺		☺	☺		
10:00-10:15		☺			☺	
10:15-10:30	☺	☺	☺	☺		
10:30-10:45				☺	☺	
10:45-11:00			☺	☺	☺	
11:00-11:15	☺	☺			☺	
	M	T	W	TH	F	

problems, write the additional numbers down and circle these number in green. A student will often try to do more than what is expected of him, especially if the type of material is geared to his abilities. The problems circled in green serve as a message to the student's parents that the student did more than was assigned.

2. *Free day.* Write free day in one square. The student may use any math materials (or reading or language arts) that are available in the room or that he can bring from home. The only rule is that the student spend the entire period on the assignment of his choice.

3. *Listening day.* Some class activities do not require a written assignment. The student needs to learn to listen in an active, responsible manner. Discuss with the student the general rules for acceptable listening behavior during the class session. Write listening day in the appropriate assignment column.

The comments column is perhaps the most important and profitable part of the contract. It is a space for *positive* evaluation of a student's work habits and attitude, *not* his grades. At the end of each class, you should assess with the student his performance for that class period. Place a *smile face* or positive comment in this column.

If a student did not do well that day, *no* comment is placed in the column. If a negative comment is written, a student may become frustrated, tear the contract up, or refuse to continue with the plan. Accent the positive, put it in writing. Remember, this is not a grade report. It reflects work habits and attitudes. The slow learner and the underachieving student have a chance to be successful. Inform parents that they too can accent the positive and assume that a blank space indicates the student had a problem that day and that the problem was handled adequately at school. It need not be further elaborated at home.

The contract also contains space for writing consequences. These consequences should be stated positively if at all possible. This should be a joint effort by the student and teacher, in determining relevant consequences.

The student and teacher sign the contract on the indicated lines. The signing respects the integrity of the student and teacher and establishes a written commitment on the part of both parties.

Once the contract is signed, the two parties agree to be responsible for it. This can often be more difficult for the teacher than the student. For example:

Johnny draws during math period. You remind him of the contract (do not nag—just remind and offer him your help). You and he agreed to the consequences beforehand. Math class is over and his math is not completed. It is a beautiful day, and his friends are getting up a basketball game.

He comes up to you with crocodile tears and begs, "Please let me go out today, I promise to do my math tomorrow." If you let him go out, you are doing the student an injustice. An appropriate response would be, "We agreed to the contract, and I want to help you be responsible. Today you chose not to complete your math during the class period, and the consequence of your choice is to stay in and complete your math during break." Then, walk away; do not argue with him. It was his choice. You are not punishing him. You offered your help; you reminded him of the contract; and now you must let him accept the consequences of his own behavior.

If you really care and the student knows this, he will respect you for your resistance

WEEKLY ACADEMIC CONTRACT
Contract

	DATE	ASSIGNMENT	COMMENTS
MATH	MONDAY		
	TUESDAY		
	WEDNESDAY		
	THURSDAY		
	FRIDAY		

CONSEQUENCES:_____

_____

_____

_____

STUDENT: _____

TEACHER: _____

DATES: _____

ADDITIONAL COMMENTS:

to his pleading or arguments. He will also move one step toward being a more responsible individual.

If you give in to the tears today, the student may indeed get his work done tomorrow. However, the next time he feels like not working, he will again pull his tear game hoping you will give in to him, allowing him to be irresponsible. He does not grow. At best, he refines his game, enabling him to more easily manipulate and control you.

You can also "dress up" the contract with cartoons or write legal terms in it. The following are other examples of contracts:

Contract

Subject	MONDAY	TUESDAY	WEDNESDAY	THURSDAY	FRIDAY
MATH					
READING					
SPELLING					
P. E.					

IF ALL ASSIGNMENTS ARE COMPLETED EACH DAY I MAY

_____

IF ALL ASSIGNMENTS FOR THE WEEK ARE COMPLETED I MAY

_____

IF I DO NOT COMPLETE AN ASSIGNMENT DURING THE ALLOTTED TIME I WILL

_____

STUDENT: _____

TEACHER: _____

DATE: _____

COMPLETED ASSIGNMENTS:

Reading baseball

SCORE BY COMPLETING THE FOLLOWING TASKS:

2nd
base _____

3rd
base _____

1st
base _____

Home
run! _____

AS A VICTORY CELEBRATION I WILL _____

_____

_____

_____

_____

_____

BATTER: _____   PITCHER: _____

DATE: _____

Math football

TO REACH YOUR GOAL COMPLETE THE FOLLOWING TASKS:

50 Yd. _____ 50 Yd.

40 Yd. _____ 40 Yd.

30 Yd. _____ 30 Yd.

20 Yd. _____ 20 Yd.

10 Yd. _____ 10 Yd.

GOAL _____ GOAL

TOUCHDOWN!

AFTER EACH 10 YARD GAIN I WILL _____

_____

AS A VICTORY CELEBRATION I WILL _____

_____

DATE: _____ PLAYER: _____

COACH: _____

Responsibility contract

The undersigned _____ **hereby** agrees to undertake the following *responsibility:*

_____

_____

_____

_____

for which he shall receive upon successful completion of his responsibility certain *privileges,* stated below:

1. _____

_____

_____

_____

2. _____

_____

_____

_____

3. _____

_____

_____

_____

This contract shall be binding for the **week** of _____

DATE SIGNED: _____ STUDENT: _____

RENEGOTIATION DATE: _____ TEACHER: _____

SYSTEMATIC SUSPENSION

The systematic suspension contract is a plan to send home a troubled student on any day that he is not able to conform to a set of standards previously agreed on by the teacher, pupil, and parents (Chapman, 1962). The student is suspended immediately on violation of any term of the contract but may return to class the next day and remain as long as he controls his behavior. It requires full cooperation by parents, teachers, principal, and counselor to be an effective behavior management tool. If the parents are reluctant, systematic suspension is presented to them as a possible solution along with permanent exclusion and residential placement.

Systematic suspension is used as a last resort, after the usual methods of behavior management have failed. It is not a substitute for these methods but is used when the usual approach has not been successful. It is a therapeutic tool to help with discipline and control.

Chapman (1962) has provided specific procedures to be used in systematic suspension.

The following contract illustrates the intent and essential procedures that should be followed:

Systematic suspension contract

PARTICIPANTS

1. _____ (student)
2. _____ (principal)
3. _____ (counselor)
4. _____ (teacher)
5. _____ (parent)
6. _____ (parent)
7. _____ (teacher)
8. _____ (teacher)

GENERAL RULE

On violation of any stated limit STUDENT will be sent from the classroom to the counseling office. His parents will be called and STUDENT will be sent home for the remainder of the day.

LIMITS

1. Not being in attendance at every class to which STUDENT is assigned is a violation.
2. Kicking, hitting, biting, pinching, poking, shoving, jabbing, or tripping any other person is a violation.
3. Add additional limits as needed: _____

_____

RESPONSIBILITIES

1. Student: STUDENT agrees that he is fully responsible for himself and that everything he does or does not do is done or not done by his own choice. He agrees to take credit for his failure, as well as his success, regardless of how people treat him.
2. Teacher: On detection of a violation the teacher will send STUDENT to the counseling

Continued.

SYSTEMATIC SUSPENSION CONTRACT—cont'd

RESPONSIBILITIES—cont'd

office. The teacher will on no occasion try to influence him to do or not do anything (no urging, reminding, coaxing, encouraging, or scolding). The teacher agrees to respect the pupil's right to fail or succeed on his own and to acknowledge that he is not responsible for the success or failure of this pupil.

3. Counselor: On notification of any violation, the counseling office will receive STUDENT and call his parents. The counselor agrees not to discuss with STUDENT in any way his behavior (there will be no persuasion, encouragement, reminders, or scolding).
4. Parents: On being called by the counseling office, Mr. and Mrs. PARENT agree to pick up STUDENT and remove him from the school for the remainder of the day. The parents agree not to discuss with STUDENT in any way his behavior (there will be no scolding, persuasion, encouragement, reminders, or urging). The parents agree to keep the counseling office informed as to where they can be reached at all times during the school day. STUDENT must stay at home during the time school is in session but after school is over, can do whatever he usually does after school.
5. Principal: The principal agrees to the content of this contract and will enforce it in all regards.

PROMISE OF THE SCHOOL

1. To allow STUDENT freedom to choose to be a responsible student.
2. To issue to STUDENT a weekly pass that allows him to come to the counseling office on request by him.
3. To allow STUDENT to choose which activity he will pursue during his daily independent-study period.
4. To encourage the other students to facilitate STUDENT in fulfilling the requirements of this contract by supporting his responsible actions.

In witness whereof, this agreement is signed and sealed by the following:

STUDENT: _____ PARENT: _____

PRINCIPAL: _____ PARENT: _____

COUNSELOR: _____ TEACHER: _____

TEACHER: _____ TEACHER: _____

DATE: _____

GENERAL GUIDELINES AND SUGGESTIONS

When working with a troubled child in the classroom, it is your attitude that counts most; whatever you do for or with the child reflects your attitude. Do not let an opportunity to care and to show your concern for him go by. If you do not do it, it may never be done.

Be friendly, smile, notice him in a positive way

Point out his successes

Point out his good points to him and to his peers

Encourage him

Call on him

Teach him a skill he can be proud to share with others

Plan activities in which he can succeed

The following are some basic techniques that can help in managing misbehavior in the regular class. This is not meant to imply that they will be the "answer" to your problem. They are techniques I have found to be helpful in the classroom.

1. Stop misbehavior in time. Do not wait until the situation is totally out of hand before stopping it. Stop the act before you become angry and lose control or before the whole class gets into the act.

2. Program for a variety of changes. Activities with a great deal of manual emphasis are more likely to succeed than heavy doses of desk work.

3. Make tasks clear and orderly and give the child time to complete one task before beginning another. A troubled child needs to know what is expected of him in an activity. He needs closure on one activity before he can freely and without frustration move onto a new task. Insist that the student complete an activity. Be sure that the task is on the student's ability level and that he understands the directions.

4. Comment positively when the student is attending appropriately to a task. Let him know you know he is working constructively. Praise him. Smile.

5. Establish limits and maintain consistent, clear ground rules. This structure gives the student the necessary backbone to function successfully in the class. He needs to know what is appropriate or inappropriate. He needs to know what the consequences of his behavior will be. Be consistent in following through with legitimate consequences. Threats and bribes will not work.

6. Manage transitional times with quieting down periods between two activities. Take the time to allow a child to slow down from one activity, such as physical education, to be ready for another activity, such as reading.

7. Set up filler corners, activity centers a child can go to when he has completed required activities. These can be media corners or game corners.

8. Set up a quiet corner where a child can go to be alone, to cry, or to calm down. The corner should not be used for punishment; rather it should be a place to gain control. If a child needs to be sent to the quiet corner, send him calmly and quickly. He is to stay in the corner until *he* feels able to return and behave responsibly. Do not set a time limit. Let the student decide when *he* is in control of feelings and behavior.

9. Plan for anger breaks; give a distraught, anxious, or angry student a chance to swim laps in a pool, run laps around a track, beat pillows, hit a punching bag, throw bean bags at a wall, pedal an exercise bike, jump rope, or pound clay. Follow this anger break by providing activities that trigger a heavy dose of laughter; then, arrange for a quiet period.

10. Provide success; be sure the material is relevant, interesting, and appropriate for the child.

Steps that are *inappropriate* for helping a troubled student include the following:

1. Using brute force: "You hit me, I'll hit you back!"

2. Accusing the student of misbehaving. You are, in a sense, forcing the child to lie to save face.

3. Comparing the student's behavior with that of his peers.

4. Arguing—you cannot win an argument with a student. Usually, you both lose.

5. Embarrassing the student in front of his peers.

6. Removing the student from activities he does well and enjoys doing.

7. Ridiculing the student for his mistakes or misbehavior.

Most of the preceding suggestions and guidelines are simple, "applied common sense." All teachers might do better in dealing with troubled children if it were not for the fact that teachers are human too and that they too can become angry and lose their perspective. With thirty plus children in a class, with emphasis on academic standards, and with societal pressure to "remain in control of the schools," it is easy and natural to say and do what is precisely the wrong thing. Thinking through problems and alternatives in advance, as suggested here, may help to save the day for the teacher and for the troubled child.

As you consider and implement various plans or systems, you must recognize that students can continue to say no to being responsible—the choice is theirs. The teacher can not *make* them behave responsibly. If all of the resources of a school or school district have been tried and none of them have been effective or adequate, you must recognize that certain troubled students need help beyond that which can be provided in a public school setting.

In a responsibility-oriented classroom the structure and rules are simple, reasonable, and defined; consequences for appropriate and inappropriate behaviors are realistic and natural. Students learn to label, accept, and express feelings appropriately. The students themselves also play an important role in their own educational programming.

A responsibility-oriented classroom is neither a teacher-dominated nor student-controlled room. Rather, it is a joint effort to learn, relate, and experience.

ROLE OF THE SPECIAL EDUCATION/RESOURCE PERSONNEL

Owing to the scarcity of treatment facilities and adequate programs, most of the seriously troubled students in the United States remain in regular classrooms. School administrators and resource personnel are becoming more aware that to help this growing number of students effectively, they must, for the most part, change their emphasis from helping individual students to helping regular classroom teachers work with these students in their classrooms. The role and responsibility of the resource personnel will vary greatly, depending on the age or grade level of the troubled children served, number of teachers or buildings served by the resource person, and the local school district policy concerning specific responsibilities.

The most common type of resource position used in school districts is the *crisis* or *helping teacher* (Morse, 1962). The crisis or helping teacher provides temporary support and control to troubled students when the students are unable or unwilling to cope with the demands of the regular classroom. The type of service the crisis teacher provides requires that she be available at the time of the crisis. Working closely with the regular classroom teachers, she provides support, reassurance, and behavioral management strategies. Troubled students come and go either on a regular or an episodic basis, depending on the needs of the individual student. When the resource teacher is not dealing with a crisis, she can be helping less troubled students academically and behaviorally. She can make referrals to supportive services, provide the needed intensive assistance for the more severely troubled students, and follow up on specific recommendations. She becomes an active partner with the teacher, mental health personnel, and parents in helping this student.

Cooperation

The key to a successful learning program for the troubled student is the cooperative working arrangement between the regular classroom teachers, resource persons, and support services. The regular classroom teacher should feel free to ask for help and not feel that she has failed because she has been unable to deal effectively with a troubled student. Often, the resource person can observe situations in the classroom objectively and help the classroom teacher see games or unhealthy transactions occurring between the teacher and student. The resource person and the teacher can jointly plan behavioral strategies and modify educational materials to fit the unique needs and abilities of the student.

Orientation/in-service

Resource teachers play an important role in the in-service education (formal and informal) of regular classroom teachers. In-service education can range from an overview of child growth and motivation to more specific behavior management techniques. Resource teachers may offer workshops on contracting, group meetings, behavior management, and parent education.

It is important that the resource person make herself visible to the teachers with whom she works and readily available to help and support them.

Demonstration teaching

The resource teacher can help set up group meetings in a classroom, leading the initial meeting and helping the regular classroom teacher plan follow-up meetings. She can also take small groups of students in the class and work with them on self-concept development through the use of games, dialogues, and role playing. Working in the regular classroom, she can organize her groups to include children with various behavioral abilities and liabilities. By nature of her training, the resource teacher may demonstrate new materials and materials that are unfamiliar to the regular teacher.

Modify, adapt, and procure materials

The resource teacher can help the regular classroom teacher develop contracts, glad notes, and relevant consequences for the troubled child. She can also work closely with several teachers who may be teaching the same child to ensure that the contracts and consequences will be consistent throughout the day.

Assignments often need to be restructured and defined clearly for the student. The resource teacher can present academic materials to the student in a nonthreatening way, offering him a successful learning experience that can be carried over into the regular class. A child needs to learn that he can learn—school can be a positive experience.

Serve as a liaison between mental health personnel, parents, administrators, community agencies, and the regular teacher

The resource person generally has a good understanding of behavioral deviance, delinquency, and therapeutic techniques for the troubled child. She can serve as a communication link between the psychologist or mental health therapist, the regular teacher, and the parents. In addition, she could serve as a liaison between social services agencies, juvenile authorities, and the public school. She can translate the recommendations from these agencies into workable educational strategies. She will be responsible for following up and evaluating the implementation of these strategies.

Counseling

The resource person may assist the regular teachers in counseling the troubled child and his family. She can also attempt to help parents and the troubled student to relate more effectively with one another.

SUPPORTIVE SERVICES

A wide continuum of services must be provided to meet the needs of the troubled child, ranging from a protective institutional setting for troubled children who are unable to respond to intensive treatment, to assistance to the regular classroom teacher through consultation and program modification. An adequate program will require the total range of coordinated services, diagnostic and treatment centers, special classes, and mental health units for children too disturbed for school programs. Typical local services include such agencies as the mental health center, department of social services, and juvenile authorities.

The management of troubled children does not reside completely within the regular classroom. Since it is the regular classroom teacher that is often the first person to refer a troubled student for special services, it is important that she be aware of the various agencies and services available for troubled youth in her own community. Coordinated services make it possible to give the child the help he needs. (Teachers should consult with resource/itinerant specialists regarding agencies that may provide assistance.)

SUMMARY

Troubled students offer perhaps the most frustrating and rewarding challenge to teachers. Their behaviors are in extremes; they cry too easily, are too worried, and are too angry. It is the unusual frequency or intensity of these behaviors that signal the need for help. A troubled child's deviant behavior can result from forces from within himself or from forces in his environment, including his interaction with "significant others" in his life. Forces within the child can be either physiological or psychological. Environmental factors include extreme poverty, racial discrimination, deteriorating family units, and school pressures, such as unrealistic academic requirements, rigid rules, unreasonable teacher expectations, and exaggerated emphasis on grades. A child who is identified as troubled because of his deviant behaviors may be a normal child defending himself against damaging environmental pressures.

Once a child is identified as being in need of assistance beyond that which can be provided in the regular classroom, he is referred to the resource person or school psychologist for an in-depth evaluation. Following the evaluation, a staffing team should review the pertinent information available on the child and make recommendations concerning educational programming and placement. There are a number of positive steps the teacher can take to make the situation creative and constructive for both the troubled student and teacher. Many of these can be effectively implemented within a responsibility-oriented classroom.

A responsibility-oriented classroom is a setting in which students and teacher work cooperatively, sharing educational responsibilities. The student is responsible for his own behavior, academic success, and failures. Realistic consequences are established and carried out. Feelings are labeled, appropriate ways of expressing them are explored and actively encouraged. More than structure, rules, and academia must be conveyed by the classroom teacher; she must convey trust and belief in each student. An integral part of the responsibility-oriented class is the group meeting. It fosters student involvement and initiative in learning. Three types of meetings, the academic planning meeting, the problem-solving meeting, and the crisis meeting, have demonstrated merit in practice.

The use of contracts is also an important part of the responsibility-oriented classroom. They involve the student and the teacher in a commitment to one another to relate realistically and responsibly.

Owing to the scarcity of treatment facilities and adequate programs, most troubled students remain in the regular classroom. It is the role of the resource person to provide support, reassurance, and behavioral management strategies to help the regular classroom teacher effectively work with the troubled student.

The troubled student needs a safe place where he can be himself, learn to know himself, and take important, frightening steps toward an *okay* life position. A *safe* classroom atmosphere in which, with peer and teacher support, the troubled student can relate more realistically, responsibly, and constructively with his environment should be the goal of education.

References and suggested readings

Alschuler, A., and Shea, J. "The Discipline Game: Playing Without Losers." *Learning,* 1974, *3*(1), 80-90.

Axline, V. *Play Therapy.* Boston: Houghton Mifflin Company, 1947.

Axline, V. *Dibs: In Search of Self.* Boston: Houghton Mifflin Company, 1964.

Bettleheim, B. *Love Is Not Enough.* New York: The Free Press, 1949.

Blanco, R. *Prescriptions for Children with Learning and Adjustive Problems.* Springfield, Ill.: Charles C Thomas, Publisher, 1972.

Bower, E. M. "The Emotionally Handicapped Child and the School: An Analysis of Programs and Trends." *Exceptional Children,* 1959, *26,* 182-188.

Bower, E. M. *Early Identification of Emotionally Handicapped Children in School.* Springfield, Ill.: Charles C Thomas, Publisher, 1969.

Bower, E. M., and Lambert, N. M. *Teachers Manual for In-school Screening of Emotionally Handicapped Children.* Princeton, N. J.: Educational Testing Service, 1961.

Chapman, A. H. *The Games Children Play.* New York: Berkley Medallion Books, 1971.

Chapman, R. W. "School Suspension as Therapy," *Personnel and Guidance Journal,* 1962, *40,* 731-732.

Clark, D., and Lesser, G. *Emotional Disturbance and School Learning: A Book of Readings.*

Chicago: Science Research Associates, Inc., 1965.

Cleaver, E. *Soul on Ice.* New York: McGraw-Hill Book Company, 1968.

Dee, V. "Contingency Management in a Crisis Class." *Exceptional Children,* 1972, *38,* 631-634.

Dispert, L. *The Emotionally Disturbed Child: An Inquiry into Family Patterns.* Garden City, N. Y.: Anchor Books, 1965.

Dreikurs, R., Grunwald, B., and Pepper, F. *Maintaining Sanity in the Classroom: Illustrated Teaching Techniques.* New York: Harper & Row, Publishers, 1971.

Ellis, D., and Miller, L. "Teachers' Attitudes and Child Behavior Problems." *Journal of Educational Psychology,* 1936, *27,* 501-511.

Farber, J. *The Student as Nigger* (2nd ed.). New York: Pocket Books, 1970.

Fargo, G., Behrns, C., and Nolen, R. *Behavior Modification in the Classroom.* Belmont, Calif.: Wadsworth Publishing Co., Inc., 1970.

Feder, B. "Resolving Classroom Tensions: A Group Approach." *Psychology in the School,* 1967, *4,* 36-39.

Freed, A. *T.A. for Tots.* Los Angeles, Calif.: Price/Stern/Sloan Publishers, Inc., 1974.

Gearheart, B. *Learning Disabilities: Educational Strategies.* St. Louis: The C. V. Mosby Co., 1973.

Glasser, W. *Reality Therapy.* New York: Harper & Row, Publishers, 1965.

Glasser, W. *Schools Without Failure.* New York: Harper & Row, Publishers, 1969.

Glavin, J., Quay, H., Annesley, F., and Werry, J. "An Experimental Resource Room for Behavior Problem Children." *Exceptional Children,* 1971, *38,* 131-137.

Glidewell, J. *Parental Attitudes and Child Behavior.* Springfield, Ill.: Charles C Thomas, Publisher, 1961.

Gordon, T. *T.E.T. Teacher Effectiveness Training.* New York: Peter H. Wyden/Publisher, 1974.

Gullotta, T. "Teacher Attitudes Toward the Moderately Disturbed Child." *Exceptional Children,* 1974, *41,* 49-50.

Haring, N., and Phillips, E. *Educating Emotionally Disturbed Children.* New York: McGraw-Hill Book Company, 1962.

Harshman, H. (Ed.). *Educating the Emotionally Disturbed: A Book of Readings.* New York: Thomas Y. Crowell Company, Inc., 1969.

Hentoff, N. *Our Children Are Dying.* New York: The Viking Press, Inc., 1966.

Hewett, F. *The Emotionally Disturbed Child in the Classroom.* Boston: Allyn & Bacon, Inc., 1968.

Hirshberg, J. C. "The Role of Education in the Treatment of Emotionally Disturbed Children Through Planned Ego Development." *American Journal of Orthopsychiatry,* 1953, *23,* 684-690.

Homme, L. *How To Use Contingency Contracting in the Classroom.* Champaign, Ill.: Research Press, 1970.

Johnson, O. G. "The Teacher and the Withdrawn Child." *Mental Hygiene,* 1956, *40,* 529-534.

Kirk, S., and Weiner, B. (Eds.). *Behavioral Research on Exceptional Children.* Washington, D. C.: Council For Exceptional Children, 1963.

Kounin, J., Friesen, W., and Norton, A. "Managing Emotionally Disturbed Children in Regular Classrooms." *Journal of Educational Psychology,* 1966, *57*(1), 1-13.

Krasner, L., and Ullman, L. P. *Research in Behavior Modification.* New York: Holt, Rinehart and Winston, Inc., 1965.

Lindsley, O. "Precision Teaching in Perspective: An Interview with Ogdan R. Lindsley." *Teaching Exceptional Children,* Spring, *3*(3), 1971.

Long, N., Morse, W., and Newman, R. (Eds.). *Conflict in the Classroom.* Belmont, Calif.: Wadsworth Publishing Co., Inc., 1971.

Lovin, G., and Simmons, J. "Response to Praise by Emotionally Disturbed Boys." *Psychological Reports,* 1962, *11,* 10.

MacMillan, D. *Behavior Modification in Education.* New York: Macmillan, Inc., 1973.

Madsen, C., Becker, W., and Thomas, D. "Rules, Praise and Ignoring: Elements of Elementary School Control." *Journal of Applied Behavior Analysis,* 1968, *1,* 139-150.

Maes, W. "The Identification of Emotionally Disturbed Children." *Exceptional Children,* 1966, *32,* 607-613.

Morse, W. C. "The Crisis Teacher: Public School Provisions for the Disturbed Pupil." University of Michigan, *School of Education Bulletin,* 1962, *37,* 101-104.

Moustakas, C. E. *Children in Play Therapy.* New York: McGraw-Hill Book Company, 1953.

Moustakas, C. E. *The Teacher and the Child.* New York: McGraw-Hill Book Company, 1956.

Nelson, C. "Techniques for Screening Conduct

Disturbed Children." *Exceptional Children,* 1971, *37,* 501-507.

Newman, R. G., and Keith, M. M. *The School-Centered Life Space Interview.* Washington, D. C.: School Research Program, Washington School of Psychiatry, 1967.

Patterson, G. R., and Gullion, M. *Living with Children: New Methods for Parents and Teachers.* Champaign, Ill.: Research Press, 1968.

Pearson, G. H. J. *Emotional Disorders of Children.* New York: W. W. Norton & Company, Inc., 1954.

Peter L. *Prescriptive Teaching.* New York: McGraw-Hill Book Company, 1965.

Powers, H. "Dietary Measures To Improve Behavior and Achievement." *Academic Therapy,* 1973-1974, *9,* 203-214.

Quay, H. C., and Peterson, D. R. *Manual for the Behavior Problem Checklist.* Champaign, Ill.: Children's Research Center, University of Illinois, 1967.

Redl, F. The Concept of a Therapeutic Milieu. *American Journal of Orthopsychiatry,* 1959a, *29,* 721-734.

Redl, F. "The Life Space Interview." *American Journal of Orthopsychiatry,* January 1959b, *29,* 1-18.

Reinert, H. R. *Children in Conflict: Educational Strategies.* St. Louis: The C. V. Mosby Co., 1976.

Rogers, C. R. *Client-Centered Therapy.* Boston: Houghton Mifflin Company, 1951.

Slavson, S. *Re-Educating the Delinquent Through Group and Community Participation.* New York: Harper & Row, Publishers, 1954.

Spivack, G., and Swift, M. Devereux Elementary School Behavior Rating Scale Manual. Devon, Pa.: Devereux Foundation, 1967.

Spivack, G., and Swift, M. "The Classroom Behavior of Children: A Critical Review of Teacher-Administered Rating Scales." *Journal of Special Education,* 1973, *7,* 55-89.

Swift, M., and Spivack, G. Hahnemann High School Behavior Rating Manual, Philadelphia: Departmental Health Sciences, Hahnemann Medical College and Hospital, 1972.

Szasz, T. *The Myth of Mental Illness: Foundation of a Theory of Personal Conduct.* New York: Harper & Row, Publishers, 1961.

Tallman, I., and Leving, S. "The Emotionally Disturbed Child in the Classroom Situation." *Exceptional Children,* 1960, *27,* 114-126.

Vinter, R., Saari, R., Vorwaller, D., and Schafer, W. *Pupil Behavior Inventory.* Ann Arbor, Mich.: Campus Publishers, 1966.

Walker, H. *Walker Problem Behavior Checklist Manual.* Los Angeles: Western Psychological Services, 1970.

Walker, H., and Buckley, N. *Modifying Classroom Behavior: a Manual of Procedures for Classroom Teachers.* Champaign, Ill.: Research Press, 1970.

Whelan, R., and Haring, N. "Modification and Maintenance of Behavior Through Systematic Application of Consequences." *Exceptional Children,* 1966, *32,* 281-289.

Woody, R. *Behavior Problem Children in the Schools.* New York: Appleton-Century-Crofts, 1969.

Zax, M., and Cowen, E. "Early Identification and Prevention of Emotional Disturbance in a Public School." In Cowen, E., Gardner, E., and Zax, M. (Eds.). *Emergent Approaches to Mental Health Problems.* New York: Appleton-Century-Crofts, 1967.

CHAPTER 9

The importance of good personal interaction (or what it's really all about)

From Reinert, H. R.: Children in conflict: educational strategies, St. Louis, 1975, The C. V. Mosby Co.

September, 19 (whatever)
Public Schoolsville, U.S.A.

Dear Teacher,

We want to tell you about several teachers in your school who have come to our attention. We would like to ask your help in changing some of these professionals who work just down the hall from you. We know you are busy, but the actions of these teachers have such devastating effects on children, we are sure you will want to help. Please read through the following vignettes and anecdotes and see if you recognize members of your professional staff. If you do, please help them, for their own sake and for the sake of the children in your school.

Our sincere appreciation,
BILL GEARHEART and MEL WEISHAHN

PAIN IN SCHOOL IS having an indifferent teacher*

My unhappy experience was when I was—well—just last year. I worked on a project for about two weeks 'cause my parents didn't think I was doing enough extra projects for school. So, they wanted me to do one. So I did it. Then, when I brought it to school (these were the last few days) my teacher told me that—well—she didn't really tell me—but she didn't pay very much attention to my project. I made a map. And it just sat in the back of the room for a few days and I finally brought it home. I never got a grade on it, or anything.

PAIN IN SCHOOL IS learning to feel embarrassed*

While in the second grade a question was asked and I raised my hand with much anticipation because I knew the answer and I was the only one who had any idea of the correct answer.

I was wrong and the teacher proceeded to tell me how dumb I was to think that I could do better than her more well-versed students. This tirade went on for about ten minutes while she told me to go to the head of the class and talk about why I had made such a "stupid" answer. At the end of this she told me my zipper was down which gave me much more embarrassment.

PAIN IN SCHOOL IS traveling a lonely road with a hurt that takes many years to heal*

"I am sure you will be better off in the service. The service can teach you a trade. Maybe you can finish high school while in the service."

Seventeen years old and my world had just completely collapsed around me. I had just been told by my counselor that I would be better off in the service than in school.

He was polite, very sympathetic but he was still saying "Sorry, boy, you are too dumb for school!" Even today I would like to tell him to stick his advice in his ear! My work in school had not been good, but I felt much of that was due to the fact that I did more playing than studying.

When I left school that day I wondered what I would tell my parents. What could I tell myself? How could I fight a gnawing, cancerous emotion of worthlessness? I wondered how I could face my buddies. I remember having an overwhelming urge to run, to hide, to get away. But, where does a seventeen-year-old boy hide? The only hiding place I could find was the service. That day, I enlisted in the Navy before I went home. There was only one paper to be signed before I left for the service, that was a parental permission paper for men under eighteen years of age—they signed!

The hurt I felt that day almost twelve years ago has actually helped me today. When I am working with a boy who is called stupid, can't read, maybe he feels like he isn't worth much. I can go a little further than just sympathizing with him, I can feel what he feels. . .

Some refer to such feeling as sensitivity. Call it what you will, but I can simply tell my students to "move over, brother, you have company. I've been down this road before once by myself. It's a lonely road, let me travel with you."

I TAUGHT THEM ALL*
Naomi J. White

I have taught in high school for ten years. During that time I have given assignments, among others, to a murderer, an evangelist, a pugilist, a thief, and an imbecile.

The murderer was a quiet little boy who sat on the front seat and regarded me with pale blue eyes; the evangelist, easily the most popular boy in school, had the lead in the junior play; the pugilist lounged by the window and let loose at intervals a raucous laugh that startled even the geraniums; the thief was a gay-hearted Lothario with a song on his lips; and the imbecile, a soft-eyed little animal seeking the shadows.

The murderer awaits death in the state penitentiary; the evangelist has lain a year now in the village churchyard; the pugilist lost an eye in a brawl in Hong Kong; the thief, by standing on tiptoe, can see the windows of my room from the county jail; and the once gentle-eyed little moron beats his head against a padded wall in the state asylum.

All of these pupils once sat in my room, sat and looked at me gravely across worn brown desks. I must have been a great help to these pupils—I taught them the rhyming scheme of the Elizabethan sonnet and how to diagram a complex sentence.

*From Schultz, E., Heuchert, C., and Stampf, S. *Pain & Joy in School.* Champaign, Ill.: Research Press, 1973. Used with permission.

*From *The Clearing House,* November 1937. Used with permission.

ABOUT SCHOOL

This poem was handed to a high school English teacher the day before the writer committed suicide. Original source unknown.

He always wanted to explain things,
but no one cared.
So he drew.

Sometimes he would just draw
and it wasn't anything.
He wanted to carve it in stone
or write it in the sky
and the things inside him that needed saying.

And it was after that that he drew the picture.
It was a beautiful picture.
He kept it under his pillow
and would let no one see it.
And he would look at it every night
and think about it.
And it was all of him and he loved it.

When he started school he brought it with him.
Not to show anyone, but just to have it with him
like a friend.

It was funny about school.
He sat in a square brown desk
like all the other square brown desks
and he thought it would be red.
And his room was a square brown room
like all the other rooms.
And it was tight and close. And stiff.

He hated to hold the pencil and chalk,
with his arm stiff and his feet flat on the floor,
stiff,
with the teacher watching and watching.

The teacher came and spoke to him.
She told him to wear a tie like all the other boys.
He said he didn't like them
and she said it didn't matter.
After that he drew. And he drew all yellow
and it was the way he felt about morning.
And it was beautiful.

The teacher came and smiled at him.
"What's this?" she said.
"Why don't you draw something
like Ken's drawing?
Isn't it beautiful?"
After that his mother bought him a tie
and he always drew airplanes and rockets
like everyone else.

And he threw the old picture away.

And when he lay out alone looking at the sky,
it was big and blue, and all of everything,
but he wasn't anymore.
He was square and brown inside
and his hands were stiff.
And he was like everyone else.
All the things inside him that needed saying
didn't need it anymore.

It had stopped pushing. It was crushed.
Stiff.
Like everything else.

THE POOR SCHOLAR'S SOLILOQUY*

No, I'm not very good in school. This is my second year in the seventh grade and I'm bigger and taller than the other kids. They like me alright though even if I don't say much in the classroom because outside I can tell them how to do a lot of things. They tag me around and that sort of makes up for what goes on in school.

I don't know why the teachers don't like me. They never have very much. Seems like they don't think you know anything unless you can name the book it comes out of. I've got a lot of books in my room at home—books like *Popular Science Mechanical Encyclopedia,* and the Sears' and Ward's catalogues—but I don't very often just sit down and read them through like they make us do in school. I use my books when I want to find something out, like whenever Mom buys anything secondhand I look it up in Sears' or Ward's first and tell her if she's getting stung or not. I can use the index in a hurry.

In school though we've got to learn whatever is in the book and I just can't memorize the stuff. Last year I stayed after school every night for two weeks trying to learn the names of the Presidents. Of course, I knew some of them like Washington and Jefferson and Lincoln, but there must have been thirty altogether, and I never did get them straight.

I'm not too sorry though because the kids who learned the Presidents had to turn right around and learn all the Vice Presidents. I am taking the seventh grade over but our teacher this year isn't so interested in the names of the Presidents. She has us trying to learn the names of all the great American inventors.

I guess I just can't remember names in history. Anyway, this year I've been trying to learn about trucks because my uncle owns three and

---

*From *Childhood Education,* January 1944. Used with permission.

he says I can drive one when I'm sixteen. I already know the horsepower and number of forward and backward speeds of 26 American trucks, some of them Diesels and I can spot each make a long way off. It's funny how that Diesel works. I started to tell my teacher all about it last Wednesday in science class when the pump we were using to make a vacuum in a bell jar got hot but she said she didn't see what a Diesel engine had to do with our experiment on air pressure so I just kept still. The kids seemed interested though. I took four of them around to my uncle's garage after school and we saw the mechanic, Gus, tear a big truck Diesel down. Boy, does he know his stuff!

I'm not very good in geography either. They call it economic geography this year. We've been studying the imports and exports of Chile all week, but I couldn't tell you what they are. Maybe the reason is I had to miss school yesterday because my uncle took me and his big trailer truck down state about 200 miles, and we brought almost 10 tons of stock to the Chicago market.

He had told me where we were going, and I had to figure out the highways to take and also the mileage. He didn't do anything but drive and turn where I told him to. Was that fun! I sat with a map in my lap and told him to turn south, or south-east or some other direction. We made 7 stops, and drove over 500 miles round trip. I'm figuring now what his oil cost and also the wear and tear on the truck—he calls it depreciation—so we'll know how much we made.

I even write out all the bills and send letters to the farmers about what their pigs and beef cattle brought at the stockyards. I only made three mistakes in 17 letters last time, my aunt said, all commas. She's been through high school and reads them over. I wish I could write school themes that way. The last one I had to write was on "What a Daffodil Thinks of Spring," and I just couldn't get going.

I don't do very well in school arithmetic either. Seems I just can't keep my mind on the problems. We had one the other day like this:

"If a 57 ft. telephone pole falls across a cement highway so that 17 3/5 feet extend from one side and 14 9/17 feet from the other, how wide is the highway?"

That seemed to me like an awfully silly way to get the width of a highway. I didn't even try to answer it because it didn't say whether the pole had fallen straight across or not.

Even in shop I don't get very good grades. All of us kids made a broom holder and a bookend this term and mine were sloppy. I just couldn't get interested. Mom doesn't use a broom anymore with her new vacuum cleaner, and all our books are in a bookcase with glass doors in the parlor. Anyway I wanted to make an end gate for my uncle's trailer, but the shop teacher said that meant using metal and wood both, and I'd have to learn how to work with wood first. I didn't see why, but I kept still, and made a tie rack at school and the tail gate after school at my uncle's garage. He said I saved him ten dollars.

Civics is hard for me, too. I've been staying after school trying to learn the "Articles of Confederation" for almost a week, because the teacher said we couldn't be good citizens unless we did. I really tried because I want to be a good citizen. I did hate to stay after school, because a bunch of us boys from the south end of town have been cleaning up the old lot across from Taylor's Machine Shop to make a playground out of it for the little kids from the Methodist home. I made the jungle gym from old pipe, and the guys made me Grand Mogul to keep the playground going. We raised enough money collecting scrap this month to build a wire fence clear around the lot.

Dad says I can quit school when I am fifteen and I am sort of anxious to because there are a lot of things I want to learn how to do, and as my uncle says, I'm not getting any younger.

The following excerpts reflect children's thoughts about their teachers:

THE GERANIUM ON THE WINDOW SILL JUST DIED BUT TEACHER YOU WENT RIGHT ON*
Albert Cullum

You're so proud of your shiny new car.
You're so proud of you new color hair,
your vacation tan,
and your nice clean blackboards.
I sit in the third row, last seat.
Teacher, are you ever proud of me?

• • •

I'm so quiet sitting in the first row,
first seat.
I feel you like me.
I mind, and I am never late.
Do you like me?
I always do all of my homework,

---

*From the Harlin Quist Book by Albert Cullum.

and I gave you the biggest valentine
of all.
Do you like me?
Sometimes I'm scared of you though.
The way you look, the way you smile.
But that's when you like me best of all—
when I'm scared.

. . .

I want you to come to my house,
and yet I don't.
You're so important,
but our screen door has a hole in it.
And my mother has no fancy cake to serve.
I want you to come to my house, teacher,
and yet I don't.
My brother chews with his mouth wide open
and sometimes my dad burps.
I wish I could trust you enough, teacher,
to invite you to my house.

. . .

You talk funny when you talk to the
principal.
Or when the teacher next door borrows
some paper.
And when my mother comes to see you,
you talk funny.
Why don't you talk to them like you
talk to us?

CIPHER IN THE SNOW*
Jean E. Mitzer

It started with tragedy on a biting cold
February morning. I was driving behind the
Milford Corners bus as I did most snowy mornings on my way to school. It veered and stopped
short at the hotel, which it had no business doing,
and I was annoyed as I had to come to an un-
expected stop. A boy lurched out of the bus,
reeled, stumbled, and collapsed on the snowbank
at the curb. The bus driver and I reached him at
the same moment. His thin, hollow face was
white even against the snow.

"He's dead," the driver whispered.

It didn't register for a minute. I glanced
quickly at the scared young faces staring down
at us from the school bus. "A doctor! Quick! I'll
phone from the hotel . . ."

"No use. I tell you he's dead." The driver
looked down at the boy's still form. "He never

*From the *N.E.A. Journal*, November 1964. Used
with permission.

even said he felt bad," he muttered, "just tapped
me on the shoulder and said, real quiet, 'I'm
sorry. I have to get off at the hotel.' That's all.
Polite and apologizing like."

At school, the giggling, shuffling morning noise
quieted as the news went down the halls. I passed
a huddle of girls. "Who was it? Who dropped
dead on the way to school?" I heard one of them
half-whisper.

"Don't know his name; some kid from Milford
Corners," was the reply.

It was like that in the faculty room and the
principal's office. "I'd appreciate your going to
tell the parents," the principal told me. "They
haven't a phone and, anyway, somebody from
school should go there in person. I'll cover your
classes."

"Why me?" I asked. "Wouldn't it be better if
you did it?"

"I didn't know the boy," the principal admitted levelly. "And in last year's sophomore
personalities column I note that you were listed
as his favorite teacher."

I drove through the snow and cold down the
bad canyon road to the Evans place and thought
about the boy, Cliff Evans. His favorite teacher!
I thought. He hasn't spoken two words to me in
two years! I could see him in my mind's eye
all right, sitting back there in the last seat in
my afternoon literature class. "Cliff Evans," I
muttered to myself, "a boy who never talked."
I thought a minute. "A boy who never smiled. I
never saw him smile once."

The big ranch kitchen was clean and warm. I
blurted out my news somehow. Mrs. Evans
reached blindly toward a chair. "He never said
anything about bein' ailing."

His stepfather snorted. "He ain't said nothing
about anything since I moved in here."

Mrs. Evans pushed a pan back off the stove
and began to untie her apron. "Now hold on,"
her husband snapped. "I got to have breakfast
before I go to town. Nothin' we can do now
anyway. If Cliff hadn't been so dumb, he'd have
told us he didn't feel good."

After school I sat in the office and stared
bleakly at the records spread out before me. I
was to close the file and write the obituary for
the school paper. The almost bare sheets mocked
the effort. Cliff Evans, white, never legally
adopted by stepfather, five young half-brothers
and sisters. These meager strands of information
and the list of D grades were all the records had
to offer.

Cliff Evans had silently come in the school door in the mornings and gone out of the school door in the evenings, and that was all. He had never belonged to a club. He had never played on a team. He had never held an office. As far as I could tell, he had never done one happy, noisy kid thing. He had never been anybody at all.

How do you go about making a boy into a zero? The grade-school records showed me. The first and second grade teachers' annotations read "sweet, shy child"; "timid but eager." Then the third grade note had opened the attack. Some teacher had written in a good, firm hand, "Cliff won't talk. Uncooperative, Slow learner." The other academic sheep had followed with :dull", "slow-witted"; "low (I.Q.)." They became correct. The boy's IQ score in the ninth grade had been listed at 83. But his IQ in the third grade had been 106. The score didn't go under 100 until the seventh grade. Even shy, timid, sweet children have resilience. It takes time to break them.

I stomped to the typewriter and wrote a savage report, pointing out what education had done to Cliff Evans. I slapped a copy on the principal's desk and another in the sad, dog-eared file. I banged the typewriter and slammed the file and crashed the door shut, but I didn't feel much better. A little boy kept walking after me, a little boy with a peaked, pale face; a skinny body in faded jeans, and big eyes that had looked and searched for a long time and then had become veiled.

I could guess how many times he'd been chosen last to play sides in a game, how many whispered child conversations had excluded him, how many times he hadn't been asked. I could see and hear the faces and voices that said over and over, "You're a nothing, Cliff Evans."

A child is a believing creature. Cliff undoubtedly believed them. Suddenly it seemed clear to me: when finally there was nothing left at all for Cliff Evans, he collapsed on a snowbank and went away. The doctor might list "heart failure" as the cause of death, but that wouldn't change my mind.

We couldn't find ten students in the school who had known Cliff well enough to attend the funeral as his friends. So the student body officers and a committee from the junior class went as a group to the church, being politely sad. I attended the services with them, and sat through it with a lump of cold lead in my chest and a big resolve growing through me.

I've never forgotten Cliff Evans nor that resolve. He has been my challenge year after year, class after class. I look up and down for veiled eyes and bodies slumped into a seat in an alien world. "Look, kids," I say silently, "I may not do anything else for you this year, but not one of you is going to come out of here a nobody. I'll work or fight to the bitter end doing battle with society and the school board, but I don't want to have one of you coming out of here thinking himself a zero."

Most of the time—not always, but most of the time—I've succeeded.

• • •

These illustrations, although somewhat extreme, are representative of teacher-student interactions. Throughout this book it has been emphasized that the teacher is the single most important factor in the successful integration of handicapped students. There is little question that teachers have a *profound influence* on student behavior and achievement. We want to encourage every teacher to be aware of this influence and to make certain that it is *positive* in nature.

In this chapter we will consider the interaction between teachers and students by reviewing several studies that have demonstrated the influence of teacher expectation on student behavior and achievement and by reviewing ways in which these interactions may be assessed through formal and informal instruments. Student interactions will be reviewed and techniques and materials will be described that may enhance positive interactions. At the conclusion of this chapter, vignettes and anecdotes reflecting the importance of positive interactions will be presented. We will admit in advance that we are deliberately attempting a "hard sell" of the importance of positive interactions between teachers and students. We believe that in this one instance this is the only tenable position to take. We further believe that those who "buy" this idea will be better teachers and happier persons for having made this decision.

THE BASIS OF A HANDICAP

It has been clearly established that many students with handicapping conditions have limitations imposed as a result of their handicap. By the very nature of the condition, certain limitations must be accounted for educationally by modifying or adapting curriculum, materials, or teaching strategies, or a combination of these factors. A student with impaired vision, for example, must have modified materials to participate fully in regular classrooms. Hearing impaired students need adapted approaches and the specialized services of support personnel, and students with crippling or other health impairments may need to have architectural barriers removed and some special equipment provided if they are to be educated in regular classrooms. When considering the limitations imposed by these handicapping conditions, it is quite clear that the condition itself necessitates modifications or adaptations. There are, however, a relatively large number of students for whom we cannot clearly establish the reason for school difficulties. For these students it may not be educationally sound to assume that there is some internal factor contributing to their failure. In these instances, there may be external factors (something operating *outside* of the student) contributing to his failure, or the student's failure may be the result of the interaction of a number of factors.

If a student is having difficulty in reading or math, for example, or is withdrawn or acting out in class, we must consider a number of variables that may have an influence on his poor achievement or unusual behavior. Among the variables that should be considered are (1) the student, (2) the teacher or teachers, (3) the materials being used, and (4) the environment. The influence of these variables is depicted in the following diagram:

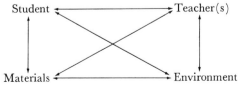

It is possible that the primary nature of the student's problem may rest with any one of these variables, but more commonly it is the *interaction* of one or more of these factors that influence the student's achievement and behavior. To assess the difficulty, we must analyze the interaction between these factors.

Student—environment

We have all observed poor student-environment interactions in which a student was being reinforced by his classmates (environment) for being the classroom clown. In other situations, we have seen the influence of a poor student-environment interaction demonstrated by a student who was highly distracted by a noisy classroom (environment) or a classroom that was visually distracting. As a result, this student was not able to attend to the task or assignment. In these situations, is it safe to assume that the problem is necessarily *within* the student? In all likelihood it is not; the difficulty may relate to the interaction between the student and environmental factors.

Student—materials

The appropriateness of the educational materials may also influence a student's achievement or behavior. This may seem to be a very obvious statement, but we believe that not enough time and effort are directed toward observation, planning, and evaluation of materials. There is some evidence that students have preferred learning styles (auditory, visual, tactual, and kinesthetic), and if an assessment is made of the preferred learning style or channel and if materials are matched to this preferred channel, we can increase the learning rate and improve achievement. Also related to the interaction of student and materials is the concept of using highly motivating and possibly new materials with students who are having difficulty (see pp. 123-125).

This four-point interaction matrix should be given serious consideration when efforts are initiated to determine the nature of an educational problem. It may not be safe to assume that the failure of a student is primarily the fault of the student. Rather, it may relate to inadequacies in the environment, educational materials, instructional techniques, or interactional patterns utilized in the classroom. This may be particularly true when applied to a student who is exhibiting only mild problems and for whom there is no known reason for the difficulty.

The preceding discussion has related to the interaction between student-environment and student-materials, which has been very briefly reviewed because both of these areas have been discussed in earlier chapters. Teacher-student and student-student interaction will be the central focus of the remainder of this chapter.

INFLUENCE OF TEACHER-STUDENT INTERACTION

As mentioned in the preceding discussion, the teacher has a profound influence on student behavior and achievement, and the role of the teacher can either impede or facilitate a student's success in school. This interaction is an important factor to consider with all children but has even more implications for the student who is not achieving, is apathetic, nonconforming, acting out in the classroom, or identified as "handicapped."

The nature of the interaction between teacher and student may be strongly influenced by the teacher's expectations. These are essentially an influence or perception of what may (or should) be expected of a particular student or group of students. The expectation may be low, that is, expecting only minimal achievement or little acceptable behavior. At the opposite extreme, the expectation may be high, which may cause the teacher to pressure the student to achieve beyond his capabilities, resulting in discouragement, behavior problems, or failure. Expectations are not in and of themselves bad if teachers are willing to modify an initial expectation as a result of additional information and experience. It must be emphasized that we all form expectations to some extent on the basis of preconceived information or as a result of initial interactions, but we must maintain a *flexible attitude* concerning these expectations and be willing to change them.

It is possible that the teacher's expectation of a particular student may become a self-fulfilling prophecy for the teacher. If she expects a particular type of behavior from a student, she may only observe and relate to those behaviors that were initially expected. The following may serve as an example:

A discussion among teachers in the teachers' lounge centered around the antisocial and disruptive behavior of a number of children from the same family. Teachers who had previously worked with members of this family indicated that they *all* were troublemakers and, in general, were the most disruptive members of their classes. As a result of this discussion, Mr. Carlson, the sixth grade teacher, had a preconceived notion about the expected behavior of Jimmy Jones, a new arrival in his sixth grade classroom. Mr. Carlson was ready and waiting for disruptive behavior from Jimmy. Whenever Jimmy was the least bit disruptive (even though his behavior was not serious compared to other class members), Mr. Carlson was able to fulfill his prophecy, "I knew Jimmy was a problem, and I'm going to make certain he knows about it." In this instance, Mr. Carlson was so certain that he would observe disruptive behavior, he interpreted only minor problems as disruptive.

It must be noted here that not all teacher expectations will become self-fulfilling if the teacher is willing to modify and adjust expectations on the basis of new information or interactions.

Expectations, student behavior, and achievement

In this discussion we will briefly review research studies that have demonstrated a relationship between teacher expectations, student behavior, and achievement and discuss the implications of these studies.

The most commonly quoted research study related to this topic was conducted by Rosenthal and Jacobsen (1968). Although this study has been seriously questioned because of reported methodical weaknesses, it served as the catalyst for many studies that have reported essentially the same findings.

The main purpose of this study was to determine if teachers' favorable expectations could be responsible for significant IQ gains of students. A group-administered test (with which the teachers were unfamiliar) was given to all students who would be returning to one elementary school the next fall. The test, the Harvard Test of Inflected Acquisition, was interpreted as being a test that would predict with near absolute certainty the students who would show "academic spurt"—to designate "late blooming." The test in actuality was Flannigan's Test of General Ability (1960) and yielded scores in verbal ability, reasoning, and a total IQ score. Upon completion of the testing, twenty percent of the students were selected to participate in the study, were randomly assigned to an experimental group, and labeled as "bloomers." Teachers were given a list of the children in their classrooms who might exhibit marked intellectual growth. From this information the teachers erroneously assumed that the other children (those who were not identified) did not have the potential for the marked intellectual growth.

The findings of this study indicated a significant expectancy advantage in favor of the students who were identified as "late bloomers." In other words, the students who were identified as most likely to show "academic spurt" did spurt as evidenced by mean gains in total IQ.

As mentioned previously, this study was the subject of considerable debate and is not unanimously accepted by professionals. There have been, however, numerous other studies that have examined the influence of teacher-student interaction, and they have established that teacher expectation does have the potential to seriously impede or facilitate student achievement and behavior (Beez, 1972; Rubin and Balow, 1971; Keogh and Becker, 1973; Adelman, 1970; Rothbart, Dalfen, and Barnett, 1971).

To this point our discussion has related to the general nature of the effect of teacher expectation on student behavior and achievement. Among the specific factors and student characteristics demonstrated to be strong determinants of negative teacher interaction are tracking based on ability grouping, identification of certain students as "handicapped," achievement test results, and membership in racial and ethnic minority groups.

Tracking

Students who are grouped on the basis of ability (tracking) may be seriously limited by such grouping. Although this practice has been challenged in the courts, it is still widely practiced in many schools. Although it is seen as an advantage for some students to be in a group of the same ability if they are in a high track, it may impose serious limitations on the student who is placed in a low track. In a study by Hargreaves (1972), it was found that seventy-three percent of the students in the low track felt that their relationships with teachers were poor, whereas only ten percent of the students in the upper track felt this way. Hargreaves also found that upper track students are much more oriented to their teachers' values than were lower track students. The frustration felt by students in lower tracks is demonstrated in the following quotation: "I don't like the work here. In the first year we was doing addition and all that and we're still doing that now. . . . It's not worth it, is it? We should have learnt more in third year, but we didn't" (Hargreaves, 1972). Tracking may maximize the achievement of students placed in higher tracks but is likely to minimize the achievement of students in lower tracks.

"Handicapped" students

Students identified and labeled "handicapped" may be stereotyped on the basis of some preconceived attitude or experience with handicapped individuals. Although the sterotype may reflect either positive or negative behavior and expectations, it generally reflects a negative attitude about a population as a whole. Once the student has been labeled, there seems to be a generalized influence on the teacher's views of the student. The label "mentally handicapped," for ex-

ample, often carries a very negative conno-
tation and may result in a significantly lower
level of expectation. The results of the label
may not only lower the level of expectation
but may also reinforce the regular classroom
teacher's feeling that "I (the teacher) don't
know enough about teaching mentally handicapped children; the student should be in a
special classroom."

Achievement test results

There is considerable evidence that
achievement test scores may negatively influence teacher expectations. In a study conducted by Beez (1972), it was found that
teachers who expected high performance
from students tried to teach more, and
teachers expecting low performance tended
to teach less. He demonstrated this by randomly assigning a group of students to high
and low achievement groups by using falsi-
fied achievement scores. At the end of the
term teachers were asked to rate the students
using a five-point scale, with five being high
and one being low in the following areas:
social competency, achievement, and intellectual ability. Table 5 reflects the teacher
ratings.

Good (1970) indicated that teachers interact more often with high achieving than
with low achieving students and that their
interactions with high achievers are more
facilitative and positive than with low
achievers. Other studies have indicated that
students of different achievement levels are
exposed to different verbal interactions. Students in lower groups receive less praise and
more negative comments or criticisms than
their classmates in higher groups (Beez, 1968;
Morrison and McIntyre, 1969).

Table 5. Teacher ratings

	Social com- petency	Achieve- ment	Intel- lectual ability
Students identified as high achieving	3.33	3.50	3.43
Students identified as low achieving	2.57	1.90	1.93

Membership in racial or minority groups

Membership in racial and ethnic minority
groups also appears to contribute to lowered
teacher expectations and different patterns
of interaction when compared with those for
other students. For example, there is an indication that white students are held in
higher esteem than black students by white
teachers (Leacock, 1969). The quantity and
quality of verbal interaction also seems to be
influenced by minority group membership—
in a negative direction (Jackson and Cosca,
1974).

Other student characteristics

There are a number of other student characteristics that lead to negative attitudes,
lower expectations, and less desirable interactions. Among the more common are sex
(Palardy, 1969; Arnold, 1968), speech and
language characteristics (Williams, Whitehead, and Miller, 1972), physical attractive-
ness (Dion, Berscheid, and Walster, 1972;
Fleming and Anttonen, 1971), and personality (Schmuck, 1963; Feshback, 1969).

There is one other type of interaction between teachers and students that must be
considered—the interaction between teachers
and physically impaired students (visually
impaired, hearing impaired, and crippled and
other health impaired) who are being educated in regular classrooms. The interaction
with these students may be the opposite of
what we have reviewed in the preceding paragraphs. Rather than negative or demeaning
interactions, the teachers may demonstrate a
very sympathetic, pitying, or oversolicitous attitude toward the child. This type of attitude
may also be demonstrated by comments such
as, "Isn't it wonderful that a blind student
can do so well!" or "I think, because she is
in a wheelchair, that she deserves a letter
grade of B." Although it may be difficult to
criticize this type of comment, teachers must
be made aware of the inherent dangers of
such an attitude. This type of attitude and
interaction may defeat the very purpose of
an integrated educational program. To set
the student up as someone so special that
he becomes the "classroom pet" may do a

serious disservice to that student. Teachers must be aware of the influence of their attitudes, be they negative, sympathetic, pitying, or positive.

We have only briefly reviewed the nature of teacher expectations and the specific student characteristics that appear to influence the interaction between teachers and students. This topic is certainly more complicated than the cursory treatment we have given it, but we feel that it is an important factor for teachers to consider. It is imperative that teachers recognize the *profound influence* they have on student behavior and achievement and that they also recognize the factors that may contribute to negative interactions. Brophy and Good (1974) identified several variables that may communicate low expectations. They are as follows:

1. Waiting less time for lows (low achieving students) to answer
2. Staying with lows in failure situations (persisting in such a manner as to call attention to failure)
3. Rewarding inappropriate behavior of lows (praising marginal or inaccurate responses)
4. Criticizing lows more frequently than highs
5. Praising lows less frequently than highs
6. Not giving feedback to public responses of lows
7. Paying less attention to lows
8. Calling on lows less often
9. Differing interaction patterns to highs and lows
10. Seating lows farther from the teacher
11. Demanding less from lows

By recognizing these variables, teachers may begin to understand the basis of their perceptions and consider modifying their interactions (if such modification is needed) by maintaining a flexible and open attitude about all students.

MONITORING/EVALUATION TECHNIQUES

Since students depend so heavily on their interaction with teachers for clues to their success, it is crucial that teachers attempt to analyze their interactions with their students. There are a number of ways that teachers may assess their interactions; some are informal and do not require specific instruments or a great deal of training in their use, whereas others are the product of research studies and provide very specific information concerning interactions.

Informal techniques*

The number and variety of available informal techniques is limited only by individual ingenuity, but certain types of approaches appear to be in fairly common use. We will relate to these techniques, but teachers should feel free and in fact be encouraged to modify these approaches to fit individual need. This modification is not possible with standardized or formal techniques.

Time analysis. The time analysis technique may provide information concerning the teacher's interaction with students. Fill out the following checklist:

I	II	III
Students: most time	How is time spent?	Pleasurable or nonpleasurable
1. 2. 3. 4. 5.		
Students: least time		
1. 2. 3. 4. 5.		

Column I. List the five students in the class with whom the most time is spent. List five with whom the least time is spent.

Column II. Identify what is done with the child during that time—how is the time spent?

Sample key

XH = Extra help, academic

BM = Behavior management

*Our thanks to Clifford Baker, who provided a number of informal techniques presented in this discussion.

L = Listening to the student
T = Talking to the student
PL = Playing with the student

Column III. Write a "P" if the time spent is pleasurable and "NP" if it was nonpleasurable.

Analyze the results. The following questions should be answered:

1. At what kinds of activities do you spend most of your time?
2. Is most of your time spent with these ten students pleasurable?
3. What is different about the students with whom you spend the most time?
4. Do the children with whom you spend more time need you more?
5. What is the difference between the students with whom the time spent is pleasurable and the students with whom the time spent is nonpleasurable?

The teacher may add any number of questions to analyze the findings—dependent on the specific purpose.

This time analysis technique is simple to administer and interpret. It may, however, provide considerable information concerning how the teacher spends her time and the nature of her interactions.

Videotape. The teacher should arrange to have her teaching videotaped. She should view the videotape alone, noticing how she interacts with different children. Next, if desired, the teacher could view and discuss the videotape with a colleague. It may be necessary to tape several sessions so that typical patterns of behavior and interaction will be recorded and not just "showmanship" on the teacher's or students' behalf. It may be helpful to arrange for a series of taping sessions, for example, once every two or three months. Nearly every school district has videotaping equipment. A course in media may be taught in a local high school, and personnel there may be willing to do the taping. Consult with the local instructional media center; they may be able to assist with the taping.

Role playing. Another useful way to determine interaction is to have students role play typical classroom situations. To be most effective, it is advisable for the regular teacher to switch classes with another teacher so the students are not inhibited by their own teacher's presence. The students may be asked to act out the role of a good teacher and a poor teacher, for example. Other roles might be

1. How does your teacher act when he is happy or sad?
2. How does your teacher look and what does he say when you interrupt him?
3. How does your teacher look and what does he say when you ask him to repeat the directions for an assignment?
4. How does your teacher look and what does he say when you make a mistake?
5. How does your teacher look and what does he say when you misbehave?
6. How does your teacher look and what does he say when you do something well?

Teachers may add other situations about which they are most interested in obtaining feedback. The role playing may be taped on a video or audio recorder so that a firsthand evaluation is received. Again, it may be helpful for the regular classroom teacher to exchange classes with a colleague so the students will not be inhibited by their own teacher's presence. This technique is particularly appropriate with elementary level students.

Peer (teacher)—observer. A trusted colleague could come in and observe the teacher in action. The colleague should keep a series of running notes during a period of several days on the teacher's interactions. The colleague should observe specific situations or record general impressions of teacher behavior.

Teacher-made checklists. The teacher may make a checklist that fits the unique situation. The items on the checklist can relate to the teacher's interaction through verbal or nonverbal behavior or general classroom procedures. Devise a system to weigh the statements, such as 1 through 3 or smiling faces (see opposite page for example).

The teacher may add questions of interest. This procedure could also be used to assess such factors as the classroom environment, grading procedures, and teacher friendliness by modifying the nature of the questions. The students should not be asked to sign their

	Al-ways 3	Sel-dom 2	Never 1
1. I can get extra help from the teacher when I need it.	—	—	—
2. The teacher praises me when I do well.	—	—	—
3. The teacher smiles when I do something well.	—	—	—
4. The teacher listens attentively.	—	—	—
5. The teacher accepts me as an individual.	—	—	—
6. The teacher encourages me to try something new.	—	—	—
7. The teacher respects the feelings of others.	—	—	—
8. My work is usually good enough.	—	—	—
9. I am called on when I raise my hand.	—	—	—
10. The same students always get praised by the teacher.	—	—	—

names since this may inhibit their openness and sincerity. Analyze the results by averaging the responses and plotting the averages so that it is possible to get a picture of teacher interactions.

There are many other informal assessment techniques that may be used. Teachers may devise their own procedure, unique to their situations and interest, or may consider using formal inventories that have been developed by researchers (for additional discussion of the use of pupil-reaction inventories, see Medley and Klein, 1957).

Formal techniques

The more formal techniques offer concrete indications of a teacher's instructional strategies and various interactions with students. By design, these techniques for measuring teacher-student interaction may facilitate the decision-making process concerning teaching style and interactions with students. These interaction analysis systems are generally quite reliable, offer a descriptive picture rather than a subjective judgmental impression, and emphasize the interaction process rather than the end product. Some are quite time consuming and require considerable training to obtain reliable results, whereas others do not require a great deal of intensive preparation. Some instruments analyze interactions by examining verbal behavior of teachers and students, some are concerned primarily with the verbal behavior of teachers, whereas other instruments measure nonverbal behavior (teacher moves or acts). Although each has its unique emphasis, all have the potential of providing teachers with a record of instructional strategies and interactions that may serve as a basis for change.

On the following pages we will review a few of the more commonly used interaction analysis instruments. To effectively use any of these systems, it would be necessary to initiate a more detailed study of that specific system.

Flanders' classroom interaction analysis. The Flanders procedure is one of the most widely used systems. In fact, the name Flanders has become synonymous with interaction analysis, and these terms often are used interchangeably in describing this procedure (Flanders, 1965). This procedure takes into consideration the verbal behavior of the teacher and the student. Interaction is analyzed on the basis of ten categories. Seven are used when the teacher is talking; two are used when the student is talking; and the last category is used to indicate silence, noise, or confusion. These categories are believed to exhaust all possibilities and would include all communication (see p. 188).

The Flanders is concerned with two kinds of events, response and initiation. To initiate means to make the first move (to lead, to introduce an idea or concept for the first time). To respond means to take action after an initiation (to expand, to counter, to react to ideas already expressed). The ten major categories take into account these two factors.

An observer in the classroom records the communication patterns by placing a tally in the category that is best represented. Obser-

Teacher talk	Response	1. Accepts feelings 2. Praises or encourages 3. Accepts or uses ideas of pupils
	Initiation	4. Asks questions
		5. Lectures 6. Gives directions 7. Criticizes or justifies authority
Pupil talk		8. Response
		9. Initiation
No communication		10. Silence, noise, or confusion

vation continues at a rate of twenty to twenty-five tallies per minute—approximately one tally every three seconds. Tape recording and later video recording may be used to assist with this task.

Specific systems are described that assist in determining if there is an imbalance between initiation and response. These specific systems also assist in determining ways to decode, procedures for displaying data, and more complicated or flexible category systems. As mentioned previously, this is a precise system requiring considerable study, understanding, and practice to be used effectively. It has the potential to assist in making decisions and desired changes in teacher-student interaction.

Galloway's nonverbal system. Galloway (1968) developed a system to measure the nonverbal behavior of the teacher. It is based on the premise that teacher nonverbal behavior is either encouraging or restricting to communication/interaction. This system contains a procedure for recording nonverbal cues associated with six of the seven teacher behaviors of the Flanders ten-category system.

Galloway notes four teacher activities that are more likely to set the tone in the classroom than verbal interaction.
1. Use of space—such as the physical setup of desks, chairs, and the teacher's desk

2. Teacher travel—such as movement of the teacher to the blackboard, remaining at desk, and away from or near students
3. Use of time—the amount of time the teacher spends on a topic or topics
4. Control maneuvers—nonverbal cues, such as hands on hips, smiling, and fingers at lips

He suggests that these acts may play a more significant role than many of the verbal cues.

This system places teacher nonverbal communication into a model with six dimensions, each on a continuum ranging from encouraging to restricting.

The coding/analysis system used is the same as the Flanders, or it may be used as an extension of the Flanders by using a double coding: a verbal code for the Flanders and a nonverbal code for the Galloway.

Hughes' system. A system to measure interaction developed by Hughes (1959) relates only to the verbal behavior of the teacher. Teacher functions are divided into thirty-three categories. These thirty-three categories are grouped into seven general teacher functions. This system provides a very detailed analysis of teacher verbal behavior and is not directed toward student talk or teacher-student talk. The observer uses either shorthand or a tape recorder to record the entire teacher verbalization, which later is coded by classifying each teacher function into one of the thirty-three categories. When the results have been coded, the record of the interaction is interpreted by someone who is trained in the use of this system.

Teacher-move analysis. *Teacher Move Analysis* (Arnold, Glaser, and Ernst, 1971) goes beyond verbal interaction between teacher and student by placing teaching behavior into eight categories, called teacher moves (see opposite page).

The eight teacher moves are classified on the basis of the following three general areas: (1) noninstructional, (2) input moves (moves that cause student passivity), and (3) output moves (moves that call for student activity).

The classroom observer records teacher moves on an 8½ × 11-inch grid (cells one-half

1. Class management move	Noninstructional move
2. Exposition move 3. Illustration move 4. Demonstration move	Input moves
5. Discussion—closed move 6. Discussion—open move 7. Exploration—regulate move 8. Exploration—free move	Output moves

inch square) approximately every five seconds or whenever there is a change from one type of move to another by using the preceding numerical values. Upon completion of a particular observation, it is necessary to obtain percentages for respective move categories. The analysis may relate to the relative amount of input/output moves or to any of the eight specific moves. In addition, a framework is provided enabling the individual to record and analyze teacher moves in light of the stated purposes of a lesson. Teacher-move analysis is described in a well-written, but brief, programmed instructional manual. The procedure requires very little time on the part of the teacher to complete, is easy to use, and allows teachers to quickly get "on with" measurement of their interactions.

Other formal observational systems that also may be of interest have been reported by Medley and Mitzel (1958), Perkins (1964), Medley (1963), Fink and Semmel (1971), and Soar, Soar, and Ragosta (1971).

Summary of interaction analysis

We have reviewed only a few of the formal teacher-student observational systems available. Individuals interested in obtaining information or competency in the use of these instruments should check the references and suggested readings at the end of this chapter to obtain more information about a specific system.

A prerequisite to the use of any of these systems is an interest and desire to change or enhance interactions with students. This requires time, but teachers who are sincerely motivated to change their interactive style

will find these systems to be a valuable aid. Self-examination is one of the most effective ways to grow, personally and professionally.

STUDENT INTERACTIONS

The extent to which a handicapped child (or any child) may be accepted as a contributing and valuable member of a classroom is dependent on the following three factors: (1) the extent to which the teacher accepts the student as an individual, (2) the interactions between students, and (3) the attitudes and the value systems of the nonhandicapped students.

A positive teacher attitude is valuable

We have emphasized repeatedly that the teacher has a profound influence on each student's behavior and achievement, but in addition, the teacher also has a tremendous influence on how students perceive each other. The way in which the teacher interacts with a particular student may determine how other students interact with that student. If the teacher either overtly or covertly rejects a particular student (regardless of whether this student is labeled "handicapped"), it is very likely that other students will model this attitude and type of interaction. Conversely, if the teacher accepts each student as a unique and valued individual, this positive attitude may be modeled by nearly all students. A specific attitude is often observed when a physically disabled student (hearing impaired, visually impaired, or crippled) is being educated in a regular classroom situation. Although this attitude may be acceptable to the inexperienced, it is potentially very harmful to the physically disabled child. It has been observed by the authors on a number of occasions that the handicapped child has been treated very differently from the other students (by the teacher), and as a direct result of this teacher-student interaction, the nonhandicapped students have modeled this attitude.

These interactions between the students may be a reflection of the teacher's attitudes, or they may relate to their own attitudes and values based on limited previous experience or the attitudes and values held by their parents. Although it may not be possible or desirable to attempt to change the attitudes of their parents, it is possible to assist the students in clarifying their own attitudes and values in relation to individuals who are different.

Assuming that the interaction is not positive, there are a number of ways teachers may examine the interaction of students in their classroom. One such technique is to administer a sociometric scale to determine the degree of acceptance or rejection. There are many ways in which sociometric data may be obtained, but we would suggest the teacher develop a preference form similar to the following:

Name: _____

Work With:

1. _____

2. _____

3. _____

Play With:

1. _____

2. _____

3. _____

Sit Near:

1. _____

2. _____

3. _____

The directions for administration would be:

1. "Today I am going to ask you to indicate on your paper the name of a classmate with whom you would like to share certain activities. We all work better when we have the opportunity to work with someone we get along with well. I am gathering this information to find out who in this class would work well together. I hope you will be completely honest. No other student will know whom you have chosen."
2. Hand out preference forms with three questions (similar to those we have indicated).
3. "At the top of this form, write the names

of three classmates you would like to work with in school if you had a free choice."
4. "Write in the middle of your paper the names of three classmates that you would like to play with outside of school. You may write down any or all of the three names used previously."
5. "At the bottom of this form write the names of three classmates you would like to sit near in school if you had a free choice. You may write any or all of the names previously used."

After the students have made their choices, the teacher can tabulate the results.

Any reasonable status categories may be used to determine the sociometric status of any specific student, for example:

Star: One who was chosen fourteen or more times by his classmates.
Above average: One who received from nine to thirteen choices.
Below average: One who was chosen between three and eight times.
Neglected: One who was chosen less than three times.
(These numbers are based on an average classroom enrollment of between twenty-eight and thirty-five and may be changed depending on the size of the class.)

The use of sociometric information should not stop with the tabulation of choices and an assignment of sociometric status. Several meaningful extensions can be made. For example, it may be helpful to determine the number of mutual choices (two children who chose each other). It may also be of interest to determine whether the handicapped student was chosen in academic or social areas. The teacher should devise her own method of analysis that is unique to her situation. The use of sociometric data may provide considerable insight into a student's status academically or socially. It may provide direction for procedures to facilitate interaction.

What if the handicapped child's status is low? What can be done to improve his status?

Buddy system. One technique that has been found to be quite successful is the buddy system. The most important factor to consider when selecting a buddy is the compatibility of the two students. This situation must be handled very carefully and the teacher must observe closely to be certain the handicapped child is gaining independence. Time must be taken to carefully select the buddy and inform him of his responsibilities. The buddy's responsibilities will usually depend on the particular type of handicap—auditory, visual, crippling, intellectual, or emotional. The buddy or helper may be rotated every few weeks so that one child is not burdened with the responsibility.

An example may be a "seeing" helper for the child who is visually impaired. His role may consist of orienting the visually impaired student to his school so that he can travel more independently. The helper may explain tasks that are largely visual, such as quietly interpreting what is being presented in a film being shown to the entire class.

Rap session. Rap sessions may be held to bring students together to discuss such things as the nature of the handicap, the degree of the handicap, how the handicap affects learning, levels of realistic expectation, prognosis, and cause of the handicap. The type of handicap and how comfortable the teacher and handicapped student feel about the topic should be considered when determining who is included in the rap session. For some reason, society (people and students, for example) usually associate more negative connotations with intellectual handicaps as compared to physical handicaps. Generally, it is a good idea to include the student with a physical impairment (hearing, vision, or crippling condition) in the rap session, but occasionally it may be best to discuss the problems in an open manner without the handicapped student present. These sessions may be handled by the special education resource teacher or the regular class teacher, or both. If the rap session is handled properly, it can do a great deal to increase the nonhandicapped students' understanding of the handicapped and often greatly enhances the interaction between students.

Mini-in-service sessions. Mini-in-service sessions are most appropriate for students with physical disabilities. If the handicapped student uses special equipment (braille typewriter, hearing aid, or wheel chair, for example), the other students may not understand its use and purpose. In a mini-in-service session the student can explain the use of and actually demonstrate how the various equipment operates. Often the other children's curiosity and lack of understanding about the special equipment may distract them from their own work. Once the special equipment is demonstrated and its use explained, the distraction usually is alleviated.

An example may be the visually impaired student demonstrating magnification devices and explaining their value and use. He may also explain the rationale for using a regular typewriter in elementary school or the use of braille or large-type materials. There may be other types of aids and appliances, such as tape recorders, tape players, talking book machines, arithmetic aids, and embossed or enlarged maps, that may be demonstrated.

Units of study on the eye or ear may be presented by the regular classroom teacher or special education resource teacher in cooperation with the visually or hearing impaired child.

The age of the handicapped child and his willingness to participate are factors the teacher should consider when planning the mini-in-service session. If the child is unwilling, perhaps the special education teacher (vision specialist or hearing specialist) may conduct the in-service session. Regardless of who participates, the session must be handled very carefully so the child is not made too "special." If the presentation implies that the handicapped child is someone "super" or someone to feel sorry for, the very purpose of the session may be defeated.

Reading books about handicapped persons. There are many films and trade books available that relate to handicapped persons (see Appendix F for an annotated listing of books). They are appropriate for various grade levels and relate to a variety of topics. Some are stories about animals that are handicapped, whereas others relate to the adjustment of handicapped children and adults. The films may be shown in class, and the reading materials may be placed on a reading shelf or in the library; students may be encouraged to read these materials. Generally, these materials provide a great deal of insight into the problems of the disabled and the feelings handicapped persons have about themselves. The viewing of a film or a report on one of the books could serve as a starting point for the previously mentioned rap sessions or mini-in-service sessions.

Another suggestion that is worthy of consideration is the use of values clarification materials. Values clarification activities and materials have been used with increasing frequency and may be of considerable assistance in facilitating the positive interaction between handicapped and nonhandicapped students.

Although these materials (books, journal articles, and commercially developed materials) are to assist individuals to reexamine and clarify their beliefs, feelings, attitudes, and values, it appears that they may also be appropriate in facilitating a more positive interaction between students. By design these activities relate to values such as cooperation, trust, acceptance, respect for individual differences, and understanding. These values are an important prerequisite to positive interactions, and through the use of these activities and materials, it is likely that the individual may direct his attention to self-actualization. An assumption underlying the use of value clarification activities and materials is that if an individual is concerned with self-actualization and is provided the opportunity to reexamine his values, he will, as a result, become more self-actualizing. He thus may be more accepting of differences in other individuals—differences that are found in every classroom.

These activities and materials have three major goals/components:

1. To encourage the individuals to think about his values and to share his thoughts with others through group discussion, role playing, games, and simulation activities

2. To learn to discuss the thoughts, beliefs, ideas, and feelings of others in a nonjudgmental way and to encourage each individual to accept, without criticism, the other person's feelings

3. To stimulate additional thinking, so an individual can become more accepting, and to move toward a more comprehensive way of valuing

The following materials are representative of those available from commercial sources. We believe that by reading these brief descriptions the teacher may better understand the nature of values education materials, how they might be used, and their potential for use in the classroom.

THE ABLED DISABLED PICTURE KIT

This innovative picture kit was developed for use as a tool in helping nonhandicapped children to perceive the person with a mobility impairment in a more realistic way. The nine pictures deal with people with "orthopedic handicaps" and spinal cord injury. The pictures depict children and adults in everyday roles, such as going to school, teaching, mothering, and participating in adapted sports.

SOURCE: Shirley Saville, Treasurer
Upstate Spina Bifida Association
Bradley Street
Argle, New York 12809

DEVELOPING UNDERSTANDING OF SELF AND OTHERS (GRADES K–LOWER PRIMARY AND 4–8)

There are two Developing Understanding of Self and Others (DUSO) kits, level I (K–lower primary) and level II (grades 4–8). Each kit contains materials and suggested activities designed to help students better understand social and emotional behavior. They are designed to help the student become more aware of interpersonal and intrapersonal relationships—relationships between himself and others and relationships within/between his own needs and goals.

The program is structured for use on a daily basis; however, selected activities may be used to fit specific needs. The eight units are interrelated and provide a variety of activities, for example, role playing, group discussion, and puppetry.

Includes: story books, records, cassettes, posters, discussion cards, puppetry and role playing cards, puppets, and teacher's manual.

BY: Dinkmeyer

PUBLISHER: American Guidance Service, Inc.
Circle Pines, Minnesota 55014

SEARCH FOR VALUES (GRADES 9–12)

A tool kit of strategies and techniques designed to help students direct their actions and sort out their feelings about the world within and around them. This can help the students see more clearly the directions their day-to-day choices are taking and can help the student come to grips with their personal value system.

Includes: teacher's guide and spirit masters.

BY: Curwin, Curwin, Kramer, Simmons, and Walsh

PUBLISHER: Pflaum Publishing
2285 Arbor Blvd.
Dayton, Ohio 45439

ANALYSIS OF PUBLIC ISSUES PROGRAM (GRADES 9–12)

This program consists of a set of concepts necessary for analyzing public issues plus the materials and strategies for teaching them. It relates to issues such as biases, stereotypes, value conflicts, and differing frames of reference.

Includes: multimedia materials, including cassettes, filmstrips, overhead visuals, student text, duplicating masters, instructor's manual, and problem books.

BY: Shaver and Larkins

PUBLISHER: Houghton Mifflin Company
One Beacon Street
Boston, Massachusetts 02107

THE ADVENTURES OF THE LOLLIPOP DRAGON (PRESCHOOL, KINDERGARTEN, AND LOWER PRIMARY)

This multimedia kit is illustrated in cartoon style. The stories use the Lollipop Dragon and the children of Tum-Tum to demonstrate the positive values and conduct stated in the following areas: sharing, working together, and taking turns, for example.

Includes: filmstrips, cassettes, script/guides, coloring book, and teacher's materials.

BY: Singer Society for Visual Education, Inc. in cooperation with Lollipop Dragon Productions, Inc. Copyright LPD, Inc.
1345 Diversey Parkway
Chicago, Illinois 60614

DEVELOPING BASIC VALUES (GRADES 2–6)

This kit presents stories and samples of class discussions that illustrate the following basic values: consideration for others, acceptance of differences, and recognition of responsibilities.

Includes: filmstrips, cassettes, script/guides, and teacher's materials.

BY: Singer Society for Visual Education, Inc.
1345 Diversey Parkway
Chicago, Illinois 60614

FIRST THINGS: VALUES (GRADES 2–5)

This series consists of six sound filmstrips designed to help elementary students reason about moral issues. The kits are entitled, The Trouble with Truth; That's No Fair!; You Promised!; But It Isn't Your . . .; What Do You Do About Rules?; and A Strategy for Teaching Values.

Includes: six audiovisual kits, each containing color filmstrips, record or cassette tape, and teacher's guide. Five kits are classroom materials; one is a teacher training kit.

BY: Kohlberg and Selman

PUBLISHER: Guidance Associates, Inc.
Pleasantville, New York 10570

FIRST THINGS: SOCIAL REASONING (GRADES 2–5)

This series is based on research findings indicating that social reasoning is based largely on the ability to understand other people's perspectives. This perspective-taking ability develops through a logical sequence of levels. Development of perspective-taking skills helps children solve social problems, enrich personal relationships, communicate effectively, and make reasoned ethical or "fairness" judgments. First Things: Social Reasoning can help the teacher facilitate perspective-taking development in several ways.

Includes: filmstrips, cassettes, discussion guide.

BY: Kohlberg, Byrne, Selman, and Low

PUBLISHER: Guidance Associates, Inc.
Pleasantville, New York 10570

MAKING VALUE JUDGMENTS: DECISIONS FOR TODAY (GRADES 7–12)

This book uses an inquiry-oriented approach to help students clarify their values to find their own identity and give purposeful direction to their lives. After exposing students to the nature of values and the steps in the decision-making process, it presents available facts and various viewpoints on vital problem areas. Students are then encouraged to make choices from alternatives, to consider the consequences, and to use the values they choose for themselves as a basis for action.

Each chapter involves students through special features and activities designed to promote analysis and decision making. Profile—brief biographies of people who have made important decisions based on their own value judgments; Put Yourself in His/Her Place—case studies that involve students in open-ended, problem-solving situations; What Do You Think?—thought-provoking, open-ended discussion questions; How Can You Get Involved?—suggested activities; Value Response Statements—statements of commonly held value judgments for students to analyze.

BY: Elder
PUBLISHER: Charles E. Merrill
1300 Alum Creek Drive
Columbus, Ohio 43216

DECISION: A VALUES APPROACH TO DECISION MAKING (GRADES 7–12)

This multimedia program provides a semester course in which students can clarify values and analyze processes of decision making. Emphasis is on inductive thinking, primarily in group discussion format, with the teacher acting as a facilitator of activities. The student-oriented nature of the program encourages self-analysis of problems and values and personal response to hypothetical values–challenging situations.

Includes: activity cards, student data sheets, sound filmstrips, cassettes, and teacher's manual.

BY: Miguel, Elder, Raths, Harmin, and Simon
PUBLISHER: Charles E. Merrill
1300 Alum Creek Drive
Columbus, Ohio 43216

SEARCHING FOR VALUES: A FILM ANTHOLOGY (GRADES 9–12)

A series of fifteen edited and adapted popular motion pictures (averaging sixteen minutes showing time) that may be used in the classroom are included in this package. The films depict conflicts and problem situations by the characters. After a showing, the students are asked to discuss the values, conflicts, and decisions of the characters, as well as broaden the themes and issues. Some motion pictures used are *Bridge on the River Kwai*, *Bless the Beasts and the Children*, *On the Waterfront*, and *To Sir, With Love*.

Includes: films and teacher's materials.
BY: Hanley and Thompson
PUBLISHER: Learning Corporation of America
711 Fifth Avenue
New York, New York 10022

PREJUDICE: THE INVISIBLE WALL (GRADES 7–12)

This kit consists of stories, articles, plays, letters, cartoons, and pictures that relate to the theme of prejudice and to the interests of today's teenagers.

Includes: Student booklets, teacher's materials, posters, a logbook, and a record.

BY: GoodyKoontz
PUBLISHER: Scholastic Book Services
904 Sylvan Avenue
Englewood Cliffs, New Jersey
07632

THE HUMAN VALUES SERIES (GRADES K–6)

This is a supplementary reading program for K–6. Primary level materials include a set of ten mounted pictures and a comprehensive teacher's edition providing read-aloud stories correlated with the pictures and lesson plans for introducing value concepts to kindergarten and primary children. The prime objectives of the series are to provide opportunities for children (1) to formulate concepts about what human values are, (2) to communicate about human value relationships, (3) to develop strategies for self-concept enhancement and for contributing to the development of the self-concepts of others, and (4) to provide motivation for reading comprehension through having a different reason for reading.

BY: Arnspiger, Blanchette, Brill, and Rucker
PUBLISHER: Steck-Vaughn Company
807 Brazos, Box 2028
Austin, Texas 78767

UNDERSTANDING VALUES (GRADES 5–12)

Understanding Values is a filmstrip series that presents open-ended situations. The situations deal with difficult areas of values, such as Other's Values/Your Values, Who Cares/Staying Involved, Cheating, and Lies.

Includes: filmstrips, cassettes, and teacher's materials.

PUBLISHER: Eyegate
146 Archer Avenue
Jamaica, New York 11435

FOCUS ON SELF DEVELOPMENT
(GRADES K–6)

This program is available in three different stages. Each stage contains materials that can be used throughout one school year. The materials have been compiled into separate units that can be used sequentially, in different topical arrangements, or whenever a classroom situation seems to point to use of a specific unit.

Stage One (K–2): Child's awareness of self, others, and environment

Stage Two (2–4): Encourages child's response to personal, social, emotional, and intellectual life

Stage Three (4–6): Encourages child to examine his involvement with self, others, and environment.

Includes: filmstrips, story records, photoboards, activity books, and teacher's materials.

PUBLISHER: Science Research Associates
259 East Erie Street
Chicago, Illinois 60611

INSIDE/OUT (GRADES 3–6)

This thirty-lesson series engages the minds and feelings of 8- to 10-year-old students through the presentation of situations common to their own lives. The programs deal compellingly with social, emotional, and physical problems that have traditionally been the concerns of health educators. However, the series takes an affective approach to the problems, showing that an open-minded understanding of human feelings is needed to balance knowledge of a more factual or cognitive kind.

Includes: teacher's materials and thirty, fifteen-minute color programs that serve as the stimulus for discussion.

SOURCE: Agency for Instructional Television
(formally National Instructional Television)
Box A
Bloomington, Indiana 47401

OPEN-ENDED STORIES
(PRIMARY–LOWER INTERMEDIATE)

As each story unfolds, a realistic conflict situation arises, presenting serious consequences to the children involved. The stories end unresolved but with several alternatives apparent. The viewers are asked to discuss the possible solutions.

This set can be used to involve children in examining and strengthening positive values. It does not preach. Instead, by presenting true-life adventures, it allows children to talk about their own feelings and examine what they feel is right and good and important. Thus the set aims at an affective level of learning. The values involved are integrity, responsibility, courage, friendship, and respect for the property of others.

Includes: filmstrips, records or cassettes, study guide, and teacher's materials

PUBLISHER: Learning Resources Company
P. O. Drawer 3709
202 Lake Miriam Drive
Lakeland, Florida 33803

THEY NEED ME (PRIMARY–INTERMEDIATE)

This set was designed to make children aware of emotional and social interdependence between themselves and their family, friends, and community.

The format of this set is somewhat unusual. A need situation is shown by a filmstrip with a question that calls for a solution. The following frame offers a resolution pictorially but with no caption. This structure is repeated throughout the set as each filmstrip presents a number of situations, requiring the class to discuss the responsible part that children can play in everyday relationships.

A child can emerge from these experiences with a greater feeling of worth and a clearer picture of the role he plays in his community. Although designed for use at the primary level, this set also can be used effectively with older children in special education classes.

Includes: captioned filmstrips and teacher's materials.

PUBLISHER: Learning Resources Company
P. O. Drawer 3709
202 Lake Miriam Drive
Lakeland, Florida 33803

HOW DO YOU FEEL?
(PRIMARY–INTERMEDIATE)

The recurring theme of these filmstrips is that everyone is different and has different feelings about other people and about daily events.

Children of various ages and backgrounds, from urban and rural environments, are seen reacting to everyday experiences. No value judgments are made, but by identifying with the positive and negative feelings presented in each filmstrip, children are led to realize that their own feelings are neither unique nor inherently "bad." Many questions are used to provoke thought and discussion, thereby helping children to achieve a better understanding of their own values and of themselves in relation to others.

Includes: captioned filmstrips and teacher's materials.

PUBLISHER: Learning Resources Company
P. O. Drawer 3709
202 Lake Miriam Drive
Lakeland, Florida 33803

WHAT DO YOU THINK?
(PRIMARY–INTERMEDIATE)

The universal childhood conflicts enacted in these filmstrips encourage children to think critically about their own values and behaviors. The open-ended questions the filmstrips pose cannot be answered by an easy yes or no. Instead, they stimulate children to express their feelings about the people portrayed and to discuss why these people act as they do.

This set of filmstrips can be used across a wide range of grade levels because the students' responses will vary according to their maturity and personal experiences.

Includes: captioned filmstrips and teacher's materials.

PUBLISHER: Learning Resources Company
P. O. Drawer 3709
202 Lake Miriam Drive
Lakeland, Florida 33803

TWO SIDES TO EVERY STORY
(PRIMARY–INTERMEDIATE)

The purpose of this set is to present different points of view from which children can see themselves in relation to other people. Familiar problems and conflicts are examined candidly—misunderstanding, hurt feelings, a child's role in family relationships, and individual needs.

Each filmstrip motivates students to consider the origin and possible resolution of these problems. By encouraging self-awareness, this set enables children to appreciate the feelings of other people. It also prepares them to discuss values and standards of behavior within the family, peer groups, and the community at large.

Includes: captioned filmstrips and teacher's materials.

PUBLISHER: Learning Resources Company
P. O. Drawer 3709
202 Lake Miriam Drive
Lakeland, Florida 33803

In addition to the preceding commercial materials there are many activities that have been described by teachers and reported in professional journals. For a listing of journal articles and published books, consult the references and suggested readings at the end of this chapter.

We believe that through the use of values, education, materials, and activities, *students may come to better appreciate and respect themselves and differences between themselves and their classmates.* It is apparent that we must provide the conditions that will enable students to work toward satisfying these basic needs so they may grow to become more self-actualized and more accepting and appreciative of all types of differences—differences found in all students.

SUMMARY

There are a number of factors that appear to have a very direct influence on student behavior and achievement. Traditionally, we have believed that a student's difficulty was caused by something *within* the student. There are some instances in which this may be the case, but there is growing recognition that there are many outside influences that have a profound influence on student behavior and achievement. Among the more common are the teacher or teachers, the educational materials being used by the student, and the student's environment (classroom and peers, for example). Of these, the teacher appears to have the most profound educational influence.

A teacher's interaction with a student can serve as a valuable source of information about himself and his work. The student may use his teacher as a mirror. If he sees a positive reflection, he may become what he sees, his achievement may increase, and more positive behavior may result. However, when the reflection is negative, the student may assume a negative attitude about himself. Since students depend so heavily on the teacher's behavior for clues to their success, it is crucial that the teacher analyze his interaction with students. When the teacher has analyzed the interaction (using informal and formal observation techniques), he may begin to modify the interactions if such modifications are needed.

In addition to teacher-student interactions,

interactions between students have a significant influence on all students. Interactions between students may be a reflection of the teacher's attitudes toward a particular student or may relate to their own attitudes and values based on limited previous experience. Teachers should assess the interaction between students in their classrooms and, if they are poor, should attempt to improve them through sociometric study, buddy systems, rap sessions, mini-in-service sessions, and values clarification materials.

The regular classroom teacher must play the major role in education of *all* children, including the handicapped. This requires a variety of skills and understandings, general and specialized, plus positive feelings and attitudes toward all girls and boys.

We sincerely hope this volume has stimulated your thinking and added to your fund of knowledge in this important area of concern.

May, 19 (whatever)
Public Schoolsville, U.S.A.

Dear Teacher,

We really appreciate your help in assisting other teachers to develop more sensitivity in their relationships with children. Their change in attitude has improved the emotional climate of your school and has resulted in increased academic performance on the part of many children. We would hope it has made it a more pleasant place for you to work, in addition to the positive benefits to children.

We have decided we should share some additional anecdotes with you. These are about really *good* teachers. They, too, are in your building. Are you one of them?

Thanks again for your assistance,
BILL GEARHEART and MEL WEISHAHN

JOY IN SCHOOL IS having a contagious teacher*

My first taste of geography came in the fourth grade, and I didn't think much of it. I approached fifth grade geography with a fairly negative attitude, but the first few classes brought with them a pleasant surprise.

My teacher was really interested in the subject material. She knew what she was talking about and she was enthusiastic about introducing us to the subject.

I think it was as much my teacher as her methods of instruction that made fifth grade geography so enjoyable. She had a genuine concern for us as individuals as well as an interest in our academic growth, and she let us know it.

JOY IN SCHOOL IS mutual respect*

My senior homeroom teacher and I had very different, if not opposite, approaches to almost everything. I respected and feared her to a degree and yet I challenged some of her opinions. Throughout the year, she had always given the impression of being angered by my statements and I used to wonder whether I should just shut up and leave her alone. Graduation night, she made a special effort to find me and she said, "I enjoyed having you in my class. I think we've both learned a lot from each other."

JOY IN SCHOOL IS having a sensitive teacher*

The happiest thing that ever happened to me was when I was first coming into school. All the

---

*From Schultz, E., Heuchert, C., and Stampt, S. *Pain & Joy in School*. Champaign, Ill.: Research Press, 1973. Used with permission.

kids made fun of me and the teacher took me in and was kind to me.

TEACHERS WHO BELIEVE PEOPLE ARE DEPENDABLE*
Arthur Combs

Let me use this example also to show you why you cannot tell the difference between the good ones and the poor ones on the basis of the methods which they use. Take two teachers, each of whom believes children are "able." Now one of these teachers, because she believes the children are able, makes them work real hard because she knows they can and the message that gets through is, She thinks I can. She is tough. Here is another teacher who also believes the children are able, but she says to them, "You know that is an interesting idea, why don't you take the rest of the afternoon to work on it by yourself?" She is a softy. Now here are two widely different methods, both of them used by good teachers. The important question is not what they are doing but the message that is conveyed by what they are doing, and the message comes from their beliefs, not what they did. In each case the same message gets through, "She thinks I can, she has confidence in me. She believes I am able." The important question we have to look at is the message that is conveyed by what people do rather than the things which they say.

There is an old Indian saying, "What you do speaks so loudly, I can't hear what you say." And that is true; the beliefs you have betray you in spite of yourself. Not long ago I was listening to a psychiatrist who was talking about the difficulties he had with some kinds of patients who came to his office. "I don't seem to be getting the kind of results that you people are getting," he said. "I believe in the same kind of therapy that you do. I believe in the dignity and integrity of my clients and I believe that the client ought to be helped to find his own answers," and so on. Then, when he was through with all this, he said, "I have great difficulty in making my patients understand." His real belief shows in spite of the fact that he knows the right words to say. His behavior is a function of the belief system which he has.

In research after research the good helpers all turn out to believe people are able and dependable and friendly and worthy and dignified and persons of integrity and value. The poor come out on the other side of that picture. You might ask yourself, do I really believe that people are really dependable?

RANDY—GRADE OF A
Jacqueline Murphy

Randy is a bright-eyed, enthusiastic, not very quick, but not easily frustrated eleven-year-old boy. He works carefully, slowly, methodically. He trys very hard. He seems to accept his slower mind philosophically. He said to me once, "You don't have to be smart to be good at everything. I'm great at baseball!" But there is in him a strong, clear desire to do better—to star. The things he does to his satisfaction delight him—he beams.

One time I gave him an A in history. His work was very ordinary, perhaps 'worth' a C, but he did the best he could. Carefully. And when I was making out those report cards and thought of how happy it would make him to get an A in something—probably the only A he would ever get in his school life—when I imagined his face brightening, the excitement and joy and pride, the decision made itself.

I watched him out of the corner of my eye as I was handing out the report cards, anticipating his reaction. His hand shot up excitedly after he glanced over his card. "Miss Murphy!" "Yes, Randy?" "Miss Murphy, but how'd I get to be so smart?"

He looked both genuinely puzzled and delighted. I felt warm and good. I don't know who was more delighted, he or I. And I was again reminded of how Randy viewed himself as intellectually inferior.

"You worked hard, Randy. You deserved that A." He looked down at his report card, beaming.

I will never forget that look.

TEACHER WHO RECOGNIZED YOUNG LOST STUDENT*
Arthur Combs

In one of the schools in the outskirts of Atlanta a very lovely girl was teaching the first grade. This young woman had beautiful long hair which

---

*From Arthur W. Combs. "The Human Aspect of Administration." *Educational Leadership,* November 1970, *28*(2), 197-205. Reprinted with permission of the Association for Supervision and Curriculum Development and Arthur W. Combs. Copyright © 1970 by the Association for Supervision and Curriculum Development.

she was accustomed to wearing in a pony tail down to the middle of her back. She wore her hair this way the first three days of the school year. Then, on Thursday, she decided to do it differently. She did it up in a bun on top of her head, and went to teach her first grade. Well, one of her little boys came, looked in her room, and did not recognize his teacher. That sometimes happens when a woman changes her hairdo. So the little boy was lost, all by himself out in the hall.

Soon, along came a supervisor who said, "What's the trouble?" He said, "I can't find my teacher." The supervisor then asked "What's your teacher's name?" Well, he did not know, so she said, "What room are you in?" but he did not know that either. He had looked in there and it was not the right place. So she said, "Well, come on. Let's see if we can find her," and they started down the hall together, the little boy and the supervisor, hand in hand. She opened the doors of several rooms without much luck. Finally, they came to the room where this young woman was teaching. As they opened the door the young teacher turned, saw the supervisor with the little boy standing in the doorway and said, "Why, Joey, it's so good to see you, son. We were wondering where you were. Do come in. We've missed you so." The little boy pulled out of the supervisor's hand and threw himself into the teacher's arms. She gave him a hug, a pat on the fanny, and he trotted to his seat.

While the supervisor was telling me this story, she and I were riding along in a car. She said to me, "Art, I said a prayer for that teacher, she knew what was important. She thought little boys were important!" We got to kicking this around; suppose she had not thought little boys were important, suppose she thought supervisors were important? In that case she would have said, "Why, good morning, Miss K., we've been hoping you would come and see us, haven't we, boys and girls?" And the little boy would have been ignored. Or she might have thought that the lesson was important. In that case she would have said, "Well, Joey, for heaven's sakes, where have you been? Come in here and get to work." Or she might have thought that the discipline was important. In that case she would have said, "Joey, you know very well when you are late you must go to the office and get a permit. Now run right down there and get it." But she didn't. She behaved in terms of what she believed was important, and so it is for each of us.

References and suggested readings

Adelman, H. "An Interactional View of Causality." *Academic Therapy*, 1970, *6*, 43-52.

Arnold, R. "The Achievements of Boys and Girls Taught by Men and Women Teachers." *Elementary School Journal*, 1968, *68*, 367-371.

Arnold, W., Glaser, N., and Ernst, L. *Teacher Move Analysis*. Dubuque, Iowa: Kendall/Hunt Publishing Company, 1971.

Barr, R. *Values and Youth*. Washington, D. C.: National Council for the Social Studies, 1971.

Beez, W. V. "Influence of Biased Psychological Reports on Teacher Behavior and Pupil Performance." In Morrison, A., and McIntyre, D. (Eds.) *The Social Psychology of Teaching.* Baltimore, Md.: Penguin Books, Inc., 1972.

Brophy, J., and Good, T. *Teacher-Student Relationships—Causes and Consequences*. New York: Holt, Rinehart and Winston, Inc., 1974.

Childhood Education. "The Poor Scholar's Soliloquy." *Childhood Education*, January 1944, *20*, 219-22.

Combs, A. "The Human Aspect of Administration." *Educational Leadership*, November, 1970, *28*, 197-205.

Cullum, A. The Geranium on the Window Sill Just Died But Teacher You Went Right on. New York: Harlin Quist Book, 1973.

Dion, D., Berscheid, E., and Walster, E. "What Is Beautiful Is Good." *Journal of Personality and Social Psychology.* 1972, *24*, 285-290.

Feshback, N. "Student Teacher Preferences of Elementary School Pupils Varying in Personality Characteristics." *Journal of Educational Psychology*, 1969, *60*, 126-132.

Fink, A., and Semmel, M. *Indiana Behavior Management System II*. Bloomington, Ind.: Center for Innovation in Teaching the Handicapped, 1971.

Flanagan, J. *Test of General Ability: Technical Report*. Chicago: Science Research Associates, Inc., 1960.

Flanders, N. *Teacher Influences, Pupil Attitudes, and Achievement*. Washington, D. C.: U. S. Department of Health, Education, and Welfare, Office of Education, 1965.

Flanders, N. *Analyzing Teaching Behavior*. Boston: Addison-Wesley Publishing Co., Inc., 1970.

Fleming, E., and Anttonen, R. "Teacher Expectancy or My Fair Lady." *American Educational Research Journal*, 1971, *8*, 241-252.

Galloway, C. "Teacher Nonverbal Communication." *Educational Leadership,* October 1966, *24,* 55-63.

Galloway, C. "Nonverbal Communication." *Theory Into Practice* (Columbus, Ohio: College of Education, The Ohio State University), December 1968, *7,* 172-175.

Galloway, C. "Body Language." *Today's Education,* December 1972, *61,* 45-46, 62.

Good, T. "Which Pupils Do Teachers Call On?" *Elementary School Journal,* 1970, *70,* 190-198.

Hall, B. *Values Clarification as Learning Process.* San Diego: Pennant Educational Materials, 1973.

Handy, R. *Value Theory and the Behavioral Sciences.* Springfield, Ill.: Charles C Thomas, Publisher, 1969.

Hargreaves, D. "Teacher-pupil Relations in a Streamed Secondary School." In Morrison, A., and McIntyre, D. (Eds.). *The Social Psychology of Teaching.* Baltimore, Md.: Penguin Books Inc., 1972.

Harmin, M. *Clarifying Values Through Subject Matter.* Minneapolis: Winston Press, 1973.

Hawley, R. *Human Values in the Classroom: Teaching for Personal and Social Growth.* Amherst, Mass.: Education Research Associates, 1973.

Hawley, R., and Hawley, I. *Human Values in the Classroom: A Handbook for Teachers.* New York: Hart Publishing Co., Inc., 1975.

Hughes, M. *Assessment of the Quality of Teaching in Elementary Schools.* Salt Lake City: University of Utah Press, 1959.

Hughes, M. "Development of the Means for the Assessment of the Quality of Teaching in Elementary Schools." *Cooperative Research Project No. 353, U. S. Office of Education.* Salt Lake City: University of Utah Press, 1959.

Jackson, G., and Cosca, G. "The Inequality of Educational Opportunity in the Southwest: An Observational Study of Ethnically Mixed Classrooms." *American Educational Research Journal,* 1974, *11,* 219-229.

Keogh, B., and Becker, L. "Early Detections of Learning Problems: Questions, Cautions, and Guidelines." *Exceptional Children,* 1973, *40,* 5-11.

Leacock, E. *Teaching and Learning in City Schools.* New York: Basic Books, Inc., Publishers, 1969.

Medley, C. "Experiences with the OSCAR Technique." *Journal of Teacher Education,* 1963, *14,* 267-273.

Medley, D., and Klein, A. "Measuring Classroom Behavior with a Pupil-Reaction Inventory." *Elementary School Journal,* 1957, *57*(6), 315-319.

Medley, D., and Mitzel, H. "A Technique for Measuring Classroom Behavior." *Journal of Educational Psychology,* 1958, *49,* 86-92.

Mitzer, J. "Cipher In The Snow." *N. E. A. Journal,* November 1964, *53,* 8-10.

Morrison, A., and McIntyre, D. *Teachers and Teaching.* Baltimore: Penguin Books, Inc., 1969.

Palardy, J. "What Teachers Believe—What Children Achieve." *Elementary School Journal,* 1969, *69,* 370-374.

Perkins, H. "A Procedure for Assessing the Classroom Behavior of Students and Teachers." *American Education Research Journal,* 1964, *1,* 249-260.

Raths, L. *Values and Teaching.* Columbus, Ohio: Charles E. Merrill Publishing Company, 1966.

Rosenthal, R., and Jacobson, L. *Pygmalion in the Classroom.* New York: Holt, Rinehart and Winston, Inc., 1968.

Rothbart, M., Dalfen, S. S., and Barnett, R. "Effects of a Teacher's Expectancy on Student-Teacher Interaction." *Journal of Educational Psychology,* 1971, *62*(1), 49-54.

Rubin, R., and Balow, B. "Learning and Behavior Disorders: A Longitudinal Study." *Exceptional Children,* 1971, *38,* 293-298.

Rucker, W. *Human Values in Education.* Dubuque, Iowa: Kendall/Hunt Publishing Company, 1969.

Schmuck, R. "Some Relationships of Peer Liking Patterns in the Classroom to Pupil Attitudes and Achievement." *School Review,* 1963, *71,* 337-359.

Schultz, E., Heuchert, C., and Stampf, S. *Pain and Joy in School.* Champaign, Ill.: Research Press, 1973.

Simon, S., and Clark, J. *More Values Clarification: Strategies for the Classroom.* San Diego: Pennant Educational Materials, 1974.

Simon, S., Howe, L., and Kirschenbaum, H. *Values Clarification: Handbook of Practical Strategies for Teachers and Students.* New York: Hart Publishing Company, Inc., 1972.

Simpson, B. *Becoming Aware of Values.* San Diego: Pennant Educational Materials, 1973.

Soar, R., Soar, R., and Ragosta, M. *The Florida Climate and Control System.* Gainesville, Fla.: Institute for Development of Human Resources, College of Education, University of Florida, 1971.

Theory Into Practice, October 1971, vol. 10. (Columbus, Ohio: The Ohio State University. Entire issue is devoted to nonverbal communication.)

White, N. J. "I Taught Them All." *The Clearing House,* November 1937, *12,* 151, 192.

Williams, F., Whitehead, J., and Miller, L. "Relations Between Language, Attitudes, and Teacher Expectancy." *American Educational Research Journal,* 1972, *9,* 263-277.

APPENDIX A

Captioned films for the deaf

The following annotated listing of captioned films are representative of titles that are available. The collection of films numbers more than 600, and to include the entire list would take too much space; therefore, only representative titles have been included.*

They may be obtained through the school's resource/intinerant teacher of the hearing impaired, the state instructional materials center for the hearing impaired, or the state department of special education.

The following abbreviations are used in describing these films:

1. CFD number (for example, CFD 83)—this number should be used when ordering the film
2. B & W or Color—black and white or color
3. Min.—length of film in minutes
4. P—primary
   I—intermediate
   J—junior high
   S—senior high
   A—adult

AIR POLLUTION

CFD 53C   Color   9½ min.   I–A
Presents the origins and effects of air pollution and explains the steps that are being taken to control it. The film stresses that all living things depend on clean air.

AIRCRAFT MACHINISTS

CFD 252   B & W   14 min.   J–S
Describes the vast amount of handwork necessary to build giant passenger jets: shows the labor involved from the first strut to the flight. Points out the growing area of employment in this industry.

*Taken from *Catalog of Captioned Films for the Deaf,* Bureau of Education for the Handicapped, U. S. Office of Education, Division of Educational Services, Media Services and Captioned Films.

ANIMALS IN AUTUMN

CFD 89   B & W   11 min.   P–I
Shows typical autumn activities of various animals, including deer, foxes, rabbits, ground squirrels, raccoons, coldblooded animals, birds, and insects as they search for food, build homes, and prepare to migrate or hibernate in winter.

ARTIFICIAL RESPIRATION

CFD 465   Color   8 min.   A
Two methods of artificial respiration, mouth-to-mouth breathing and the Sylvester method, are explained in this film.

BANKS AND CREDIT

CFD 339   Color   11 min.   J–S
Shows the nature and activities of a commerical bank; defines credit, showing how it is created, transferred, and put to work by the bank to serve the community. Illustrates how deposits help supply funds.

BELGIUM AND THE NETHERLANDS: LANDS AND PEOPLES

CFD 99   B & W   11 min.   I
A survey of the low countries showing how their culture and economy are affected by environmental factors such as easy access to the North Sea, dense population, and large coal resources.

BUTTERFLY—LIFE CYCLE OF AN INSECT

CFD 107   B & W   8 min.   I
Uses environmental sounds and close-up photographs to follow the development of a monarch butterfly as it goes through the stages from egg to larva, to pupa, to adult.

COUNTRY MOUSE AND CITY MOUSE, THE

CFD 4   B & W   8 min.   P
An animated film that tells the Aesop fable about the adventures of the country mouse who visits his city cousin, pointing to the age-old maxim that travel may be fun, but home is the best place.

CURIOUS GEORGE RIDES A BIKE

CFD 116   Color   10 min.   P
The adventures of a little monkey who is given
a bicycle by his friend, the man in the yellow hat.
An iconographic film.

EARS AND HEARING, THE

CFD 458   Color   22 min.   A
Shows the structure and functions of the human
ear and demonstrates how the ear transmits sound
waves to the brain. Describes how hearing aids
and surgery may improve the hearing of some
people.

ELECTRICITY: PRINCIPLES OF SAFETY

CFD 120   B & W   11 min.   J–S
Shows the hazards of electricity and their causes.
Overloaded or short circuits can cause fires.
Shows that a proper knowledge of electricity can
prevent bodily harm.

FORCES: COMPOSITION AND RESOLUTION

CFD 126   B & W   11 min.   S
Presents a simple example of forces acting in a
straight line at a single point. Defines forces as
vector quantities and illustrates how components
and resultants may be determined graphically.

GRAVITY: HOW IT EFFECTS US

CFD 13   B & W   14 min.   I–J
The film graphically depicts the importance of
gravity by showing how it affects our daily activities, the earth in the universe, and its effects
on an imaginary space traveler. Galileo's and
Newton's experiments are shown.

HITLER: ANATOMY OF A DICTATORSHIP

CFD 545   B & W   22 min.   S–A
To the German nation, torn by economic, political, and spiritual crises, Adolf Hitler promised
strong leadership and a policy of revenge against
supposed enemies. Through newsreel clips, the
viewers will see Hitler's rapid rise to power and
his eventual defeat by the Allies, after he produced an unmatched record of dictatorial bru-
tality.

HOW TO CHANGE A CHEMICAL REACTION

CFD 280   B & W   28 min.   I–J
A chemical reaction occurs when several solutions
are combined and either a gas is diffused or the
solutions change color. How to effect further
chemical change through temperature or con-
centration is also described.

HOW YOUR BLOOD CIRCULATES

CFD 274   B & W   28 min.   I–J
Examines the heart of a calf; uses a model of the
human heart to explain how it functions. Demonstrates how to make a simple stethoscope.

JOHNNY APPLESEED: A LEGEND OF
FRONTIER LIFE

CFD 150   B & W   15 min.   I–J
Depicts the life of Johnny Appleseed. Describes
his work in spreading the word of God and
encouraging the cultivation of apple trees
throughout Pennsylvania and the Ohio terri-
tory.

KNOW YOUR LIBRARY

CFD 153   B & W   11 min.   J
A young girl discovers the value of the library,
showing how to use the card catalog, to find
books classified by the Dewey Decimal System,
and to use reference materials such as an encyclopedia and the *Reader's Guide to Periodical Literature*.

MAN WITHOUT A COUNTRY

CFD 63   B & W   25 min.   J–A
A dramatization of the book by the same title.
The story is told by a judge to a group of new
citizens to help them develop a sense of loyalty
to their adopted country.

METRIC SYSTEM, THE

CFD 332   Color   13 min.   S
Defines the basic metric units of length, volume,
and weight as a set of units with easy-to-re-
member interrelationships. Points out its advantages and shows how to convert from English
to metric and vice versa.

MIDNIGHT RIDE OF PAUL REVERE, THE

CFD 23   B & W   11 min.   I–S
Tells the story of Paul Revere's ride by dramatizing the action and comparing the story
with the one told in Longfellow's poem. Re-
creates episodes of April 18, discussing the significance of Paul Revere's ride.

NAVAJO SILVERSMITH

CFD 302   Color   11 min.   I
Pictures the Navajo Indian as a master of a
very delicate craft, silversmithing. It bridges a
span of years by showing how objects of another
century were made. The scene is set in the rugged
land where the Navajos live.

PEOPLE ARE DIFFERENT AND ALIKE

CFD 410   B & W   11 min.   I

Illustrates that all people need friendship and love, food, and a place to live and that they want an education, fun, and happiness. Points out that people are more alike than different.

READING IMPROVEMENT: VOCABULARY SKILLS

CFD 406   Color   11 min.   I

Suggests specific vocabulary-building skills and exercises that are helpful in increasing reading effectiveness. Designed to develop students' desire to increase their vocabulary.

ROCKY MOUNTAIN AREA: BACKBONE OF THE NATION

CFD 70   B & W   16 min.   I–J

Discusses ways in which the Rocky Mountains serve the nation, with resources for mining, grazing, irrigation farming, hydroelectric power, lumbering, and tourism and the need for using natural resources wisely.

SCANDINAVIA—NORWAY, SWEDEN, DENMARK

CFD 71   B & W   22 min.   I–J

Discusses the cultural ties and physical geography of the Scandinavian countries; describes the contrasts in regional patterns of living, natural resources, and types of industrial development.

ST. LAWRENCE SEAWAY, THE

CFD 27   B & W   17 min.   S

Explains what the St. Lawrence Seaway is, what it looks like, how it was built, and how it works. Indicates some of the many changes the seaway has brought about in the world, pointing out how it has affected world trade.

TRACK AND FIELD EVENTS FOR GIRLS: TRACK EVENTS, PART I

CFD 571   Color   22 min.   I–A

Covers the track events in girl's competition—sprints, middle-distance and distance runs, hurdles, and relays. It presents each event in overall performance and then breaks down each event to analyze specific techniques and forms.

UGLY DUCKLING, THE

CFD 35   B & W   10 min.   P

Follows the misfortunes of the unwanted ugly duckling who finally grows into a beautiful swan. Filmed in Europe from Hans Christian Andersen's famous fairy tale.

WAR OF 1812, THE

CFD 187   B & W   15 min.   J–S

Covers the highlights of the military and naval action in the main theaters of The War of 1812 and discusses the conduct of the British and their impressment of American sailors as a cause of the war.

APPENDIX B

National organizations/services for the hearing impaired

Acoustical Society of America
335 E. 45th St.
New York, New York 10017

American Foundation for the Blind, Inc.
Services for Deaf-Blind Persons
15 W. 16th St.
New York, New York 10011

American Speech and Hearing Assn.
9030 Old Georgetown Rd.
Washington, DC 20014

Better Hearing Institute
1430 K St., N.W., #800
Washington, DC 20005

The Canadian Hearing Society
60 Bedford Rd.
Toronto, Ontario, Canada M5R 2K2

C.H.E.A.R., Inc.
P.O. Box 2000-871 McLean Ave.
Yonkers, New York 10704

Deafness Research Foundation
366 Madison Ave.
New York, New York 10017

Ear Research Institute
2130 W. 3rd St.
Los Angeles, California 90057

Easter Seal Research Foundation
National Easter Seal Society for Crippled
  Children and Adults
2023 W. Ogden Ave.
Chicago, Illinois 60612

National Assn. of Hearing & Speech Action
814 Thayer Ave.
Silver Springs, Maryland 20910

National Hearing Aid Society
23261 Grand River Ave.
Detroit, Michigan 48219

American Academy of Ophthalmology
  and Otolaryngology
15 2nd St., S.W.
Rochester, Minnesota 55901

American Board of Otolaryngology
W. P. Work, Secy.
1301 E. Ann St.
Ann Arbor, Michigan 48104

American College of Surgeons, Dept. of
  Otorhinolaryngology
55 E. Erie St.
Chicago, Illinois 60611

American Laryngological Assn.
J. F. Daly, Secy.
566 1st Ave.
New York, New York 10016

The American Laryngological, Rhinological &
  Otological Soc., Inc.
Lankenau Medical Bldg.
Philadelphia, Pennsylvania 19151

American Medical Assn. Section Council on
  Otorhinolaryngology
Richard B. Carley, M.D., Secy.
Central Medical Bldg.
393 N. Dunlap
St. Paul, Minnesota 55104

American Otological Society
G. Dekle Taylor, M.D., Secy.
221 Marshall Taylor Doctors Bldg.
Jacksonville, Florida 32207

American Rhinologic Society
Pat A. Barelli, M.D., Secy.
4177 Broadway
Kansas City, Missouri 64111

Society of University Otolaryngologists
ENT Dept.
Univ. of Michigan School of Medicine
Ann Arbor, Michigan 48104

PROFESSIONAL ORGANIZATIONS AND CENTERS OF INFORMATION ON DEAFNESS

Alexander Graham Bell Assn. for the Deaf, Inc.
Richard W. Flint, Pres.
George W. Fellendorf, Exec. Dir.
3417 Volta Pl., N.W.
Washington, D.C. 20007

Oral Deaf Adults Section (ODAS)
International Parents' Organization (IPO)
Daniel P. Griffin, Jr., Pres.
American Organization for the Education of
the Hearing Impaired

**Conference of Executives of American Schools
for the Deaf**
Howard M. Quigley, Exec. Secy.
5034 Wisconsin Ave., N.W.
Washington, D.C. 20016

Council for Exceptional Children
1920 Association Drive
Reston, Virginia 22091

   State-Federal Information Clearinghouse for
   Exceptional Children (SFICEC)
   CEC Information Center on Exceptional
   Children
   Dr. Don Erickson, Dir.

**Educators of Professional Personnel for the
Hearing Impaired (EPPHI)**
Teachers College, Columbia University
Dr. Ann M. Mulholland, Pres.
Department of Special Education Box 223
New York, New York 10027

Executive Audial Rehabilitation Society (EARS)
Box 1820
Corpus Christi, Texas 78403

Gallaudet College Alumni Association
1021 Leo Way
Oakland, California 84611

**Information Center for Hearing, Speech, and
Disorders of Human Communication**
Wood Basic Sci. Bldg.
The Johns Hopkins Medical Institutions
725 N. Wolfe St.
Baltimore, Maryland 21205

National Association of the Deaf
814 Thayer Ave.
Silver Springs, Maryland 20910

**National Association of State Directors of
Special Education, Inc.**
1201 16th St., N.W., Suite 301-C
Washington, D.C. 20036

**National Catholic Educational Association
Special Education Department**
1 DuPont Circle, Suite 350
Washington, D.C. 20036

**National Center on Educational Media &
Materials for the Handicapped**
Ohio St. Univ., 220 W. 12th Ave.
Columbus, Ohio 43210

National Education Association
Project to Improve Language Instruction to Deaf
Children
1201 16th St., N.W.
Washington, D.C. 20036

APPENDIX C*

Sources of materials for the visually impaired

As mentioned in Chapter 4, the resource/itinerant teacher of the visually impaired will have considerable information concerning the sources of materials that the teacher may need. If for some reason, however, such a resource person is not available to assist in acquiring materials, the following listing of sources of materials should be helpful.

The teacher's first attempt to obtain materials should be directed at the local school district's director of special education or to the individual serving the visually impaired. Another source of information would be the state education department—consultant for the visually impaired.

Many states have organized a state center to coordinate resources and educational materials of public and private state and national agencies that have specialized materials for the visually impaired. Individual states that provide state-wide service for the coordination of special materials are listed below.

California Clearinghouse/Depository
721 Capitol Mall
Sacramento, California 95814

Colorado Instructional Materials Center for the Visually Handicapped (CIMC/VH)
State Library Bldg.
1362 Lincoln St.
Denver, Colorado 80203

Connecticut Board of Education and Services for the Blind
170 Ridge Rd.
Wethersfield, Connecticut 06109

---

*Adapted from Schrotberger, W. B. "Sources of Materials for the Visually Handicapped." In *Handbook for Teachers of the Visually Handicapped,* Louisville, Ky.: American Printing House for the Blind, 1974.

Florida Instructional Materials Center for the Visually Handicapped
1407 E. Columbus Dr.
Tampa, Florida 33605

Hawaii Department of Education
Honolulu District Office
1037 S. Beretania St.
Honolulu, Hawaii 96814

Illinois Instructional Materials Services for the Visually Impaired
1020 S. Spring St.
Springfield, Illinois 62706

Indiana Division of Special Education
108 State Office Bldg.
Indianapolis, Indiana 46204

Iowa Commission for the Blind
Fourth and Keosauqua
Des Moines, Iowa 50309

Kansas Department of Education
Division of Special Education
120 E. 10th St.
Topeka, Kansas 66612

Louisiana Learning Resources System
Vocational Education Center
18th St.
Lafayette, Louisiana 70501

Maine Department of Health and Welfare
Division of Eye Care
32 Winthrop St.
Augusta, Maine 04330

Massachusetts Department of Education
Library for the Visually Handicapped
271 Boylston St.
West Boylston, Massachusetts 01583

Michigan Department of Education
Box 20
Lansing, Michigan 48902

Montana Office of the Superintendent of Public Instruction
Division of Special Education
State Capitol
Helena, Montana 59601

Nebraska Instructional Material Center for the Visually Handicapped
Nebraska School for the Blind
Nebraska City, Nebraska 68410

Nevada Department of Education
Heroes Memorial Bldg.
Carson City, Nevada 89701

New Hampshire Materials Center for the Visually Handicapped
870 Hayward St.
Manchester, New Hampshire 03103

New Jersey Commission for the Blind and Visually Impaired
1100 Raymond Blvd.
Newark, New Jersey 07102

North Carolina State Department of Public Instruction
Division of Special Education
Raleigh, North Carolina 27602

Ohio Central Registry
Ohio School for the Blind
5220 N. High St.
Columbus, Ohio 43214

Oregon Board of Education
942 Lancaster Dr., N.E.
Salem, Oregon 97310

Pennsylvania Department of Education
Bureau of Special Education
Box 911
Harrisburg, Pennsylvania 17126

Texas Education Agency
201 E. 11th St.
Austin, Texas 78701

Virginia Commission for the Visually Handicapped
Education Services Department
3003 Parkwood Ave.
Richmond, Virginia 23221

Wisconsin Instructional Material Center for the Visually Handicapped
1700 W. State St.
Janesville, Wisconsin 53545

Partially seeing students may often need materials in enlarged type for academic or recreational pursuits. The following listing of public and private agencies may be helpful in obtaining large type materials:

Albert Whitman Company
(Recreational large type)
560 W. Lake St.
Chicago, Illinois 60606

American Bible Society
(Bibles and religious literature)
1865 Broadway
New York, New York 10023

American Printing House for the Blind
(National organization for the production of literature and the manufacture of educational aids for visually handicapped)
1839 Frankfort Ave.
Louisville, Kentucky 40206

Bell and Howell Company
(Microfilm enlargement, catalog available)
Micro Photo Division
Duopage Department
1700 Shaw
Cleveland, Ohio 44112

Charles Scribner
(Recreational)
Large Type Editions
597 5th Ave.
New York, New York 10017

Children Press
(Children's books)
1224 W. Van Buren St.
Chicago, Illinois 60607

Children's Press, Inc.
(Type sizes ranging from 10 pt. to 30 pt.)
Jackson Blvd. and Racine Ave.
Chicago, Illinois 60607

Christian Record Braille Foundation, Inc.
(Publishes books and magazines for all age levels in large print)
4444 S. 42nd St.
Lincoln, Nebraska 68506

Dakota Microfilm Co.
(Microfilm enlargement, catalog available)
501 N. Dale St.
St. Paul, Minneosta 55103

Dakota Microfilm Co.
(Textbook, catalog available)
345 N. Orange St.
Orlando, Florida 32801

Economy Blueprint & Supply Co.
(Microfilm enlargement, catalog available)
123 S. LaBrea Ave.
Los Angeles, California 90036

G. K. Hall
(Large type, recreational, textbooks)
70 Lincoln St.
Boston, Massachusetts 02111

Guide for Large Print Books, Inc.
(Recreational)
211 E. 43rd St.
New York, New York 10017

Harper & Row
(Harper Crest large type editions)
49 E. 33rd St.
New York, New York 10022

J. B. Lippincott Company
(Recreational; elementary and secondary)
E. Washington Square
Philadelphia, Pennsylvania 19105

Jewish Braille Institute of America, Inc.
(Maintains circulating large type library)
110 E. 13th St.
New York, New York 10016

Keith Jennison Books
(Recreational)
575 Lexington Ave.
New York, New York 10022

Lanewood Press
(Recreational and textbooks)
729 Boylston St.
Boston, Massachusetts 02116

Lutheran Braille Workers, Inc.
(Provides religious and educational materials in large print in English and 16 other languages)
11735 Peach Tree Circle
Yucaipa, California 92399

Lutheran Library for the Blind
(Operates free lending library of materials in large print)
3558 S. Jefferson Ave.
St. Louis, Missouri 63118

The Macmillan Co.
(Recreational reading)
866 3rd Ave.
New York, New York 10022

Microfilm Business Systems Co.
(Microfilm enlargement, catalog available)
5810 W. Adams Blvd.
Los Angeles, California 90016

Microfilm Company of California
(Microfilm enlargement, catalog available)
Library Reproduction Service
1977 S. Los Angeles St.
Los Angeles, California 90011

National Association for the Visually Handicapped, Inc.
(Produces and distributes large print, 18 pt.; reading materials on request)
3201 Balboa St.
San Francisco, California 94121

National Braille Press, Inc.
(Provides, on request, large print materials)
88 St. Stephen St.
Boston, Massachusetts 02115

Random House, Inc.
(Recreational, secondary)
457 Madison Ave.
New York, New York 10022

Stanwix House
(Textbooks)
3020 Chartiers Ave.
Pittsburgh, Pennsylvania 15204

Ulverscoft Large Print Books
(Nearly 200 titles)
Oscar B. Stiskin
P.O. Box 3055
Stamford, Connecticut 06905

University Microfilms, Inc.
(Microfilm enlargement, catalog available)
Enlarge Editions Service
313 N. 1st St.
Ann Arbor, Michigan 48107

Viking Press, Inc.
(Recreational)
625 Madison Ave.
New York, New York 10022

Volunteer Transcribing Services
(Microfilm enlargement, catalog available)
617 Oregon Ave.
San Mateo, California 94402

Walker and Company
(Recreational)
720 5th Ave.
New York, New York 10019

William Morrow
(Childrens books, good list with point type listed, recreational)
105 Madison Ave.
New York, New York 10016

Xavier Society for the Blind
(Maintains free lending library of hand-transcribed large type books of primarily, but not exclusively, religious materials)
154 E. 23rd St.
New York, New York 10010

Xerox Corporation
(Microfilm enlargement, catalog available)
Box 33
P.O. Box 33
Grand Central Station
New York, New York 10017

APPENDIX D

National organizations concerning the crippled and other health impaired

American Academy of Pediatrics
1801 Hinman Ave.
Evanston, Illinois 60204

American Association for Rehabilitation Therapy
P.O. Box 93
North Little Rock, Arkansas 72116

American Cancer Society
219 E. 42nd St.
New York, New York 10017

American Corrective Therapy Association
1030 Jefferson Ave.
Memphis, Tennessee 38104

American Corrective Therapy Association, Inc.
811 St. Margaret's Rd.
Chillicothe, Ohio 45601

American Diabetes Association
18 E. 48th St.
New York, New York 10017

American Epilepsy Society
Department of Neurology
University of Minnesota
Box 341, Mayo Building
Minneapolis, Minnesota 55455

American Heart Association
44 E. 23rd St.
New York, New York 10016

American Lung Association
1790 Broadway
New York, New York 10019

American Medical Association
535 N. Dearborn St.
Chicago, Illinois 60610

American Nurses' Association
2420 Pershing Rd.
Kansas City, Missouri 64108

American Occupational Therapy
6000 Executive Blvd.
Rockville, Maryland 20852

American Public Health Association
1015 18th St., N.W.
Washington, D.C. 20036

American Physical Therapy Association
1156 15th St., N.W.
Washington, D.C. 20005

American Rehabilitation Counseling Association
1607 New Hampshire Ave., N.W.
Washington, D.C. 20009

American Rheumatism Association
1212 Avenue of the Americas
New York, New York 10036

American Speech and Hearing Association
9030 Old Georgetown Rd.
Bethesda, Maryland 20014

Arthritis Foundation
1212 Avenue of the Americas
New York, New York 10036

Association of Handicapped Artists
(Information and advice about handicapped
   artists)
1034 Rand Building
Buffalo, New York 14203

Closer Look
1828 L. Street, N.W.
Washington, D.C. 20036

Conference of Lung Association
Staff
1740 Broadway
New York, New York 10019

Council for Exceptional Children
1920 Association Dr.
Reston, Virginia 22091

Directory for Exceptional Children
Porter Sargent, Publisher
11 Beacon St.
Boston, Massachusetts 02108

Disability Insurance Training Council
(Information about insurance for the handi-
capped)
P.O. Box 276
Hartland, Wisconsin 53029

Federal Association for Epilepsy
1729 F. St., N.W.
Washington, D.C. 20006

Foundation for Child Development
345 E. 46th St.
New York, New York 10017

Goodwill Industries of America, Inc.
9200 Wisconsin Ave.
Washington, D.C. 20014

Heart and Lung Foundation
1025 5th Ave.
New York, New York 10028

Hemophilia Research, Inc.
30 Broad St.
New York, New York 10004

**International Society for Rehabilitation of the
  Disabled**
219 E. 44th St.
New York, New York 10017

Leukemia Society, Inc.
211 E. 43rd St.
New York, New York 10017

Muscular Dystrophy Association of America
810 7th Ave.
New York, New York 10019

Myasthenia Gravis Foundation
230 Park Ave.
New York, New York 10017

National Amputee Foundation
12–45 150th St.
Whitestone, New York 11357

National Association for Retarded Citizens
386 Park Ave., S.
New York, New York 10016

National Cancer Foundation
1 Park Ave.
New York, New York 10016

National Cystic Fibrosis Research Foundation
3379 Peachtree Rd., N.E.
Atlanta, Georgia 30326

**National Easter Seal Society for Crippled
  Children and Adults**
2023 W. Ogden Ave.
Chicago, Illinois 60612

National Epilepsy League
203 N. Wabash Ave.
Chicago, Illinois 60601

National Foundation for Infantile Paralysis
Box 2000
White Plains, New York 10602

National Genetics Foundation
250 W. 57th St.
New York, New York 10019

National Heart Institute
9600 Rockville Pike
Building 31, Room 5A50
Bethesda, Maryland 20014

National Hemophilia Foundation
25 W. 39th St.
New York, New York 10018

**National Institute of Arthritis and Metabolic
  Disease**
Bethesda, Maryland 20014

National Kidney Foundation
116 E. 27th St.
New York, New York 10016

National Multiple Sclerosis Society
257 Park Ave., S.
New York, New York 10010

National Paraplegia Foundation
333 N. Michigan Ave.
Chicago, Illinois 60601

Parkinson's Disease Foundation
640 W. 168th St.
New York, New York 10032

**Society for the Rehabilitation of the Facially
  Disfigured**
550 1st Ave.
New York, New York 10016

Tuberculosis Welfare League
155 W. 72nd St.
New York, New York 10023

United Cerebral Palsy Association
66 E. 34th St.
New York, New York 10016

United Epilepsy Association
111 W. 57th St.
New York, New York 10019

Volta Speech Association for the Deaf
1537 35th Street, N.W.
Washington, D.C. 20007

APPENDIX E
Pupil behavior rating scale

The Pupil Behavior Rating Scale reprinted here first appeared in *Learning Disabilities: Educational Strategies* (Gearheart, The C. V. Mosby Co., 1973). It is an adaptation of a scale developed under a U. S. Public Health Service research grant and used in the Aurora Public Schools, Aurora, Colorado. Since 1973, it has appeared in other publications and has demonstrated its value in continued use. It is similar to other rating scales in use in the elementary schools and is to be completed by the classroom teacher. Children are "rated" in five major areas of learning and behavior in comparison to their classmates; thus this scale is most effective after a teacher has worked with a group of children for several weeks, or preferably, several months.

Completion of this scale leads to an objectification of the classroom teacher's observations of children in her class, with the student-screening profile indicating relative performance in five major areas and twenty-four subareas. Low ratings on this scale *do not* indicate the presence of a learning disability. They do indicate that the pupil's performance should be further investigated and evaluated. The various possibilities that might be indicated by low ratings may be illustrated by considering an actual case in which a first grade child rated quite low in section I, auditory comprehension and listening, and section II, spoken language. This little girl appeared more capable in other areas of first grade work than in reading and, in contrast to the low ratings in sections I and II, had very high ratings in parts of section III, orientation, and all of section V, motor. Her school performance was erratic; that is, she did very well in some tasks and was relatively low in others. In many ways she sounded like a learning disabled child—perhaps one with auditory perceptual problems. However, after completing the rating scale and noting the low areas, her teacher discovered that she had been absent during the week in which the audiologist had completed hearing screening with her class. Upon referral, it was learned that she had a borderline mild/moderate hearing loss, but because she was quite intelligent (a fact discovered after completing individual intelligence testing), she was able to compensate for her loss to a considerable extent, thus it had not been discovered. It was also discovered that her hearing loss was slowly becoming more severe, but medical intervention helped reduce the loss and stopped the deterioration.

In this case, the Pupil Behavior Rating Scale was a "failure" in discovering a learning disability, but was a real success in assisting in educational assessment and amelioration (in this instance, medical amelioration). The Pupil Behavior Rating Scale, and others like it, has been used most in screening for children with learning disabilities, but in the process has been highly valuable in providing a meaningful point of focus for further investigative efforts on behalf of children other than the learning disabled. Low scores on such scales indicate two things—they indicate we should look further (with certain children) and they indicated where the focus of our investigation should be.

PUPIL BEHAVIOR RATING SCALE*
Instruction manual

One of the most important techniques for diagnosis in learning disabilities is the Pupil Behavior Rating Scale. This scale is used to assess areas of behavior that cannot be measured by standardized group screening tests. Therefore your careful rating of individual pupils is necessary.

You are asked to rate each child on these five areas of learning and behavior:

I. Auditory comprehension and listening

In this section, you evaluate the pupil as to his ability to understand, follow, and comprehend spoken language in the classroom. Four aspects of comprehension of language activities are to be evaluated.

II. Spoken language

The child's oral speaking abilities are evaluated through the five aspects comprising this section. Use of language in the classroom and ability to use vocabulary and language in story form are basic to this ability.

III. Orientation

The child's awareness of himself in relation to his environment is considered in the four aspects of learning that make up this section. You are to rate the child on the extent to which he has attained time concepts, knowledge of direction, and concepts of relationships.

IV. Behavior

The eight aspects of behavior comprising this section relate to the child's manner of participation in the classroom. Self-discipline in relation to himself (that is, ability to attend) as well as in relation to others is critical to your rating in this section.

V. Motor

The final section pertains to the child's balance, general coordination, and use of hands in classroom activities. Three types of motor ability are to be rated: general coordination, balance, and manual dexterity. Rate each type independently because a child may have no motor difficulties, only one type of difficulty, or any combination of those listed.

---

*Adapted from a project developed under Research Grant, USPHS Contract 108-65-42, Bureau of Neurological and Sensory Diseases.

Name_____No._____   School_____Grade_____

Sex_____Date_____   Teacher_____

PUPIL BEHAVIOR RATING SCALE*

1	2	3	4	5

I. Auditory comprehension and listening

Ability to follow directions

1	2	3	4	5
Always confused; cannot or is unable to follow directions	Usually follows simple oral directions but often needs individual help	Follows directions that are familiar and/or not complex	Remembers and follows extended directions	Unusually skillful in remembering and following directions

Comprehension of class discussion

1	2	3	4	5
Always inattentive and/or unable to follow and understand discussions	Listens but rarely comprehends well; mind often wanders from discussion	Listens and follows discussions according to age and grade	Understands well and benefits from discussions	Becomes involved and shows unusual understanding of material discussed

Ability to retain orally given information

1	2	3	4	5
Almost total lack of recall; poor memory	Retains simple ideas and procedures if repeated often	Average retention of materials; adequate memory for age and grade	Remembers procedures and information from various sources; good immediate and delayed recall	Superior memory for both details and content

Comprehension of word meanings

1	2	3	4	5
Extremely immature level of understanding	Fails to grasp simple word meanings; misunderstands words at grade level	Good grasp of grade level vocabulary for age and grade	Understands all grade level vocabulary as well as higher level word meanings	Superior understanding of vocabulary; understands many abstract words

II. Spoken language

Ability to speak in complete sentences using accurate sentence structure

1	2	3	4	5
Always uses incomplete sentences with grammatical errors	Frequently uses incomplete sentences and/or numerous grammatical errors	Uses correct grammar; few errors of omission or incorrect use of prepositions, verb tense, pronouns	Above-average oral language; rarely makes grammatical errors	Always speaks in grammatically correct sentences

*Adapted from a project developed under Research Grant, USPHS Contract 108-65-42, Bureau of Neurological and Sensory Diseases.

Continued.

PUPIL BEHAVIOR RATING SCALE—cont'd

1	2	3	4	5
II. Spoken language—cont'd				
Vocabulary ability				
Always uses immature or improper vocabulary	Limited vocabulary including primarily simple nouns; few precise, descriptive words	Adequate vocabulary for age and grade	Above-average vocabulary; uses numerous precise descriptive words	High level vocabulary; always uses precise words to convey message; uses abstraction
Ability to recall words				
Unable to call forth the exact word	Often gropes for words to express himself	Occasionally searches for correct word but adequate for age and grade	Above-average ability; rarely hesitates on a word	Always speaks well; never hesitates or substitutes words
Ability to formulate ideas from isolated facts				
Unable to relate isolated facts	Has difficulty relating isolated facts; ideas are incomplete and scattered	Usually relates facts into meaningful ideas; adequate for age and grade	Relates facts and ideas well	Outstanding ability in relating facts appropriately
Ability to tell stories and relate experiences				
Unable to tell a comprehensible story	Has difficulty relating ideas in logical sequence	Average ability to tell stories	Above average; uses logical sequence	Exceptional ability to relate ideas in a logical meaningful manner
III. Orientation				
Promptness				
Lacks grasp of meaning of time; always late or confused	Poor time concept; tends to dawdle; often late	Average understanding of time for age and grade	Prompt; late only with good reason	Very skillful at handling schedules; plans and organizes well
Spatial orientation				
Always confused; unable to navigate around classroom or school, playground or neighborhood	Frequently gets lost in relatively familiar surroundings	Can maneuver in familiar locations; average for age and grade	Above-average ability; rarely lost or confused	Never lost; adapts to new locations, situations; places
Judgment of relationships: big, little; far, close; light, heavy				
Judgments of relationships very inadequate	Makes elementary judgments successfully	Average ability in relation to age and grade	Accurate judgments but does not generalize to new situations	Unusually precise judgments; generalizes them to new situations and experiences

PUPIL BEHAVIOR RATING SCALE—cont'd

1	2	3	4	5
III. Orientation—cont'd				
Learning directions				
Highly confused; unable to distinguish directions as right, left, north, and south	Sometimes exhibits directional confusion	Average, uses R vs. L, N-S-E-W	Good sense of direction; seldom confused	Excellent sense of direction
IV. Behavior				
Cooperation				
Continually disrupts classroom; unable to inhibit responses	Frequently demands spotlight; often speaks out of turn	Waits his turn; average for age and grade	Cooperates well; above average	Cooperates without adult encouragement
Attention				
Is never attentive; very distractible	Rarely listens; attention frequently wanders	Attends adequately for age and grade	Above average; almost always attends	Always attends to important aspects; long attention span
Ability to organize				
Is highly disorganized; very slovenly	Often disorganized in manner of working; inexact, careless	Maintains average organization of work; careful	Above-average ability to organize and complete work; consistent	Always completes assignments in a highly organized and meticulous manner
Ability to cope with new situations: parties, trips, unanticipated changes in routine				
Becomes extremely excitable; totally lacking in self-control	Often overreacts; new situations disturbing	Adapts adequately for age and grade	Adapts easily and quickly with self-confidence	Excellent adaptation, utilizing initiative and independence
Social acceptance				
Avoided by others	Tolerated by others	Liked by others; average for age and grade	Well liked by others	Sought by others
Acceptance of responsibility				
Rejects responsibility; never initiates activities	Avoids responsibility; limited acceptance of role for age	Accepts responsibility; adequate for age and grade	Enjoys responsibility; above average; frequently takes initiative or volunteers	Seeks responsibility; almost always takes initiative with enthusiasm
Completion of assignments				
Never finishes, even with guidance	Seldom finishes, even with guidance	Average ability to follow through on assignments	Above-average ability to complete assignments	Always completes assignments without supervision

Continued.

PUPIL BEHAVIOR RATING SCALE—cont'd

1	2	3	4	5

IV. Bchavior—cont'd

Tactfulness

1	2	3	4	5
Always rude	Usually disregards other's feelings	Average tactfulness; occasionally socially inappropriate	Above-average tactfulness; rarely socially inappropriate	Always tactful; never socially inappropriate

V. Motor

General coordination: running, climbing, hopping, walking

1	2	3	4	5
Very poorly coordinated; clumsy	Below-average coordination; awkward	Average coordination for age	Above-average coordination; does well in these activities	Exceptional ability; excels in this area

Balance

1	2	3	4	5
Very poor balance	Below-average falls frequently	Average balance for age; not outstanding but adequate equilibrium	Above-average; does well in activities requiring balance	Exceptional ability; excels in balancing

Ability to manipulate utensils and equipment; manual dexterity

1	2	3	4	5
Very poor in manual manipulation	Awkward in manual dexterity	Adequate dexterity for age; manipulates well	Above-average manual dexterity	Almost perfect performance; readily manipulates new equipment

STUDENT SCREENING PROFILE

Date of birth_____

Name_____ Sex_____ Date_____

School_____ Grade or level_____ Teacher_____

FOR OFFICE USE ONLY—DO NOT WRITE ON THIS SIDE

I. Auditory comprehension and listing

   A. Ability to follow directions
      1   2   3   4   5   A._____

   B. Comprehension of class discussion
      1   2   3   4   5   B._____

   C. Ability to retain information
      1   2   3   4   5   C._____

   D. Comprehension of word meanings
      1   2   3   4   5   D._____ Total I_____

STUDENT SCREENING PROFILE—cont'd

II. **Spoken language**

    A. Ability to speak in sentences   A._____
        1   2   3   4   5

    B. Vocabulary ability   B._____
        1   2   3   4   5

    C. Ability to recall words   C._____
        1   2   3   4   5

    D. Ability to formulate ideas   D._____
        1   2   3   4   5

    E. Ability to tell stories   E._____   Total II_____
        1   2   3   4   5

III. **Orientation**

    A. Promptness   A._____
        1   2   3   4   5

    B. Spatial orientation   B._____
        1   2   3   4   5

    C. Judgment of relationships   C._____
        1   2   3   4   5

    D. Learning directions   D._____   Total III_____
        1   2   3   4   5

IV. **Behavior**

    A. Cooperation   A._____
        1   2   3   4   5

    B. Attention   B._____
        1   2   3   4   5

    C. Ability to organize   C._____
        1   2   3   4   5

    D. Ability to cope with new situations   D._____
        1   2   3   4   5

    E. Social acceptance   E._____
        1   2   3   4   5

    F. Acceptance of responsibility   F._____
        1   2   3   4   5

    G. Completion of assignments   G._____
        1   2   3   4   5

    H. Tactfulness   H._____   Total IV_____
        1   2   3   4   5

Continued.

STUDENT SCREENING PROFILE—cont'd

V. Motor

    A. General coordination
        1   2   3   4   5   A._____

    B. Balance
        1   2   3   4   5   B._____

    C. Manipulative skills
        1   2   3   4   5   C._____   Total V_____

APPENDIX F
Annotated bibliography of books about handicapped individuals

The following annotated listing of books written for children may be very helpful in providing information about handicapped individuals and their adjustment. It is arranged on the basis of the type of handicap, with the last section offering general titles that may be of interest. Some of the selections relate to adults, others are concerned with school-aged children, whereas others relate to animals. Age ranges are provided to assist in determining the approximate reading level.

CRIPPLING CONDITIONS

MINE FOR KEEPS

Sally, crippled with cerebral palsy, has many fears about returning home after five years in a school for the handicapped. Understanding parents and teachers help her discover that other children have similar fears. Training a dog brings her new friendships and a chance to encourage other handicapped children. (Ages 9–11)

BY: Jean Little
PUBLISHER: Little, Brown and Company, 1962

THE DOOR IN THE WALL

Robin, son of a great lord in Medieval England, is crippled by an illness. The brothers in a monastery teach him to strengthen his hands and arms through wood carving and swimming so that he is able to serve his King courageously in ways other than riding into battle. (Ages 10–12)

BY: Marguerite DeAngile
PUBLISHER: Doubleday & Company, Inc., 1949

ON THE MOVE

After becoming involved with other handicapped youth, a formerly sheltered paraplegic girl realizes that she can also learn to lead an independent life. (Ages 8–13)

BY: Harriet May Savitz
PUBLISHER: The John Day Company, 1973

IT'S A MILE FROM HERE TO GLORY

Early MacLaren is the school's star runner until a freak accident almost cripples him completely. Early's fight back toward health and toward the realization that being a person is more important than being a star is what this fast-moving sports book is really all about. (Ages 9–13)

BY: Robert C. Lee
PUBLISHER: Little, Brown and Company, 1972

SPRING BEGINS IN MARCH

Meg is the youngest of the Copeland family. She is the family clown turned rebel. Meg shares a room with her handicapped sister who has learned to make the best of her physical disabilities. The story tells about Meg's problems in dealing with her family and school situation. (Ages 10–12)

BY: Jean Little
PUBLISHER: Little, Brown and Company, 1966

SCREWBALL

Mike's polio-crippled arm makes him poor at baseball and earns him the unkind nickname of "Screwball." But his skill and sportsmanship in building a racer win him a respected place with his family and friends. (Ages 11–13)

BY: Alberta Armer
PUBLISHER: World Publishing Company, 1963

WHEELS FOR GINNY'S CHARIOT

After Ginny is paralyzed in an automobile accident, wise parents and teachers help her accept a wheelchair existence and find that she can be happy, useful, loved, and loving as she was before her accident. (Ages 11–13)

BY: Earline W. Luis and Barbara F. Millar
PUBLISHER: Dodd, Mead & Company, 1966

LET THE BALLOON GO

John has cerebral palsy and is spastic. This book tells of the day when he decides that grown-ups are not going to say "you can't do it" anymore. (Ages 11–15)

BY: Ivan Southall

PUBLISHER: St. Martin's Press, 1968

LET THE BALLOON GO

A story about a spastic cerebral palsied child's rebellion against the unfair restrictions placed on his life and his effort to achieve independence. (Ages 9–16)

BY: Ivan Southall

PUBLISHER: St. Martin's Press, 1968

THE F.D.R. STORY

The life, career, struggles, and triumphs of the man who, after a crippling polio attack, became our thirty-second president. (Ages 11–14)

BY: Catherine Owens Peare

PUBLISHER: Thomas Y. Crowell Company, 1962

TALL AND PROUD

Gail is struck down by polio and her recovery is almost slowed to a halt until a horse brings back her desire to walk. Together, the girl and horse triumph over fear and pain. (Ages 12–16)

BY: Vian Smith

PUBLISHER: Doubleday & Company, Inc., 1966

KAREN

This touching account by the mother of a child suffering from spastic cerebral palsy is to be recommended not only for its warm, realistic portrayal of the emotional trauma involved, but also for its factual explanation of this exceptionality and of what parents can do for such a child. (Ages 14 and up)

BY: Marie Killilea

PUBLISHER: Prentice-Hall, Inc., 1962

LEARNING DISABILITIES/ AUTISTIC LIKE

DIBS

A classic writing that relates to a young "autistic like" child named Dibs. Miss Axline records her weekly play therapy sessions with a gifted, rejected little boy. (Ages 14 and up)

BY: Virginia Axline

PUBLISHER: Houghton Mifflin Company, 1964

PLEASE DON'T SAY HELLO

This book helps to explain the phenomenon of infantile autism to young people through the story of 9-year-old Eddie, the most unusual new arrival to the neighborhood. This deeply moving story makes a strong plea for acceptance of autistic and other exceptional children. (Ages 7–13)

BY: Phyllis Gold

PUBLISHER: Behavioral Publications, Inc., 1974

I NEVER PROMISED YOU A ROSE GARDEN

The story of Deborah and her conflict in the world of reality that opposed her world. Every aspect of hospital life is shown through the experiences of a pretty, bright, autistic teenager. (Ages 14 and up)

BY: Hannah Green

PUBLISHER: Holt, Rinehart and Winston, Inc., 1964

SUE ELLEN

Sue Ellen has a learning disability and is surprised and happy with her new special class. A touching story of a child who is finally given the opportunity to learn. (Ages 9–14)

BY: Edith Hunter

PUBLISHER: Houghton Mifflin Company, 1969

ONE LITTLE GIRL

Because she is somewhat retarded, grown-ups call Laurie a "slow child." Laurie learns that she is only slow in doing some things. (Ages 7–13)

BY: Joan Fassler

PUBLISHER: Behavioral Publications, Inc., 1968

SPEECH

THE SKATING RINK

Tucker is silent most of the time because he is embarrassed by his stuttering. He is rescued from silence and ridicule by the owner of the new skating rink. (Ages 11 and up)

BY: Mildred Lee

PUBLISHER: The Seabury Press, Inc., 1969

HOW YOU TALK

This book tells how we use different parts of our mouth to talk. It explains the speech process and discusses the fact that some children speak incorrectly but should not be laughed at. (Ages 5–9)

BY: Paul Showers

PUBLISHER: Thomas Y. Crowell Company, 1966

HEARING IMPAIRED

DAVID IN SILENCE

David, born deaf in a small town in England, is harassed by children of his own age. His efforts to make friends results in disaster. Eventually, he proves his competence and courage after a hair-raising trip through an abandoned tunnel and finds acceptance and friendship. (Ages 10–12)
BY: Veronica Robinson
PUBLISHER: J. B. Lippincott Company, 1966

MARTIN RIDES THE MOOR

A boy who loses his hearing in a swimming accident learns to live with his disability after he reluctantly accepts the gift of a moor pony and later takes all the responsibility for its care and training. (Ages 9–11)
BY: Vian Smith
PUBLISHER: Doubleday & Company, Inc., 1965

GALLAUDET, FRIEND OF THE DEAF

Biography of the man who was instrumental in the education of the deaf in America. (Ages 10–12)
BY: Etta DeGering
PUBLISHER: David McKay Co., Inc., 1964

BURNISH ME BRIGHT

A story of friendship between Auguste, a deaf mute, and Monsieur Hilaire, a mime. Through mime, Auguste is accepted by the village and becomes very close to Monsieur Hilaire. (Ages 11–14)
BY: Julia Cunningham
PUBLISHER: Pantheon Books, Inc., 1970

LISA AND HER SOUNDLESS WORLD

This unique children's book represents a new approach to teaching nondeaf children about their deaf peers, while at the same time teaching deaf children how they can successfully participate in the social environment. (Ages 8–13)
BY: Edna A. Levine
PUBLISHER: Behavioral Publications, Inc., 1974

MENTAL RETARDATION

OUR JIMMY

A father talks with his two children about their younger brother who is retarded, explains his special needs and explains ways in which they can help him learn. A warm and loving book for parents and children. (Ages 5–8)
BY: Ruth K. Doorly and Kenneth Boudreau
PUBLISHER: Service Associates, 1967

THE BLUE ROSE

Emotionally moving photographs of Jenny, a young retarded girl. The accompanying descriptive text probes the world of a retarded child.
BY: Gerda Klein; with photographs by Norma Holt
PUBLISHER: Lawrence Hill & Company, Pubs., Inc., 1974

DON'T TAKE TEDDY

Afraid that his retarded brother, Teddy, will be taken away because he accidently injured a boy, 13-year-old Mikkel runs away with him to a mountain cottage. The relief of safety becomes hysteria when Teddy becomes painfully ill. (Ages 11–13)
BY: Bobbie Friis Baastad
PUBLISHER: Charles Scribner's Sons, 1967

A RACEHORSE FOR ANDY

This sensitive portrayal of a retarded boy's desire to be included in his friend's games is well drawn. (Ages 9–15)
BY: Patricia Wrightson
PUBLISHER: Harcourt, Brace, and World, Inc., 1968

A GIRL LIKE TRACY

Kathy feels responsible for her retarded older sister who has been overprotected by their parents. She helps her sister learn simple skills and self-respect in a sheltered workshop and, thereby, frees herself to live her own life. (Ages 12–13)
BY: Caroline Crane
PUBLISHER: David McKay Co., Inc., 1966

LONG SHOT FOR PAUL

Story of a retarded boy whose brother teaches him to play basketball and encourages him to join a team. Paul works hard and is finally accepted by the team and wins a game for them. (Ages 8–13)
BY: Matt Christopher
PUBLISHER: Little, Brown and Company, 1966

LISTEN, LISSA!

Melissa is a candy-striper who becomes deeply involved with a neighbor child who is retarded.

Through her concern for Artie, she becomes involved with other retarded children. The story also reveals the anguish a family goes through as they decide to institutionalize their retarded son. (Ages 13 and up)
BY: Earlene W. Luis and Barbara F. Millar
PUBLISHER: Dodd, Mead & Company, 1968

TAKE WING

When Laurel finally is relieved of taking care of her retarded brother, she finds a new world of friends and activities open to her. Her brother gets the help that he needs, and Laurel realizes that although she loves him, she can't protect her brother forever. (Ages 9–14)
BY: Jean Little
PUBLISHER: Little, Brown and Company, 1968

THE CHILD WHO NEVER GREW

A moving account of a parent's personal experience in rearing a severely retarded child. Miss Buck has successfully portrayed the problems of many parents of retarded children. (Ages 14 and up)
BY: Pearl Buck
PUBLISHER: The John Day Company, Inc., 1950

FLOWERS FOR ALGERNON

This book describes an experiment whereby Charlie Gordon's IQ is raised from 79 to 185 in about three months. However, the change would not be permanent and Charlie knew it. He described day by day the burnout and the regression, and then finally he returned to his old job at Donner's bakery. (Ages 14 and up)
BY: Daniel Keyes
PUBLISHER: Harcourt, Brace and World, Inc., 1959

CHRISTMAS IN PURGATORY: A PHOTOGRAPHIC ESSAY ON MENTAL RETARDATION

This is a pictorial study of visits to the restricted wards of five state institutions for the mentally retarded. It shows living conditions and the problems of policies, programs, personnel, and philosophy. It concludes with refreshing scenes from a well-run institution. (Ages 14 and up)
BY: N. J. Rockleigh
PUBLISHER: Allyn & Bacon, Inc., 1966

THE WILD BOY OF AVEYRON

This book tells the story of Victor. Victor was a wild boy who was found in the woods of southern France. He was taken in by a doctor and was supposedly civilized by him. (Ages 16 and up)
BY: J. Itard and G. Gaspard
PUBLISHER: Appleton-Century-Crofts, 1962

VISUALLY IMPAIRED

STEVIE'S OTHER EYE

A blind boy learns about the outside world and teaches something to his sighted companions. He proves that he can do many of the things they can do and earns their respect and admiration. (Ages 7–10)
BY: Lois Eddy
PUBLISHER: McDoccell, 1962

ABOUT GLASSES FOR GLADYS

After getting glasses that are just right, Gladys no longer is teased by her classmates about her nearsighted way of reading. (Ages 7–9)
BY: Mark K. Ericsson
PUBLISHER: Melmont Publishers, 1962

WINDOWS FOR ROSEMARY

Blind from birth, Rosemary enjoys all ordinary childhood activities because her parents' loving, unsentimental attitude towards her gives her a sense of security and independence. Her sighted brother is a good friend. (Ages 8–10)
BY: Marguerite Vance
PUBLISHER: E. P. Dutton & Co., Inc., 1956

DEAD END BLUFF

Despite his blindness, Quig wants to be as much like other boys as he can be, but an overprotective father prevents this. A summer job tests and proves his capabilities and also shows his father he can climb and swim like other boys. Both Quig and his family discover which obstacles he can surmount and which he cannot. (Ages 9–11)
BY: Elizabeth Wetheridge
PUBLISHER: Atheneum Publishers, 1966

MARY LOW AND JOHNNY: AN ADVENTURE IN SEEING

When Mary Low befriends her blind young neighbor, he helps her with her problems and together they brighten life for each other and for their friends—a story that emphasizes the importance of not treating the handicapped with pity. (Ages 9–11)
BY: Mildred Hart and Noel McQueen
PUBLISHER: Franklin Watts, Inc., 1963

THE STORY OF MY LIFE

The story of Helen Keller and how she fought the great struggle that liberated her from a dark and soundless world. (Ages 11–16)
BY: Helen Keller
PUBLISHER: Doubleday & Company, Inc., 1954

HELEN KELLER'S TEACHER

The story of Anne Sullivan, the woman who finally broke through the silence and darkness that surrounded Helen Keller to discover an exciting, intelligent girl. (Ages 9–15)
BY: Mickie Davidson
PUBLISHER: Scholastic Book Services, 1966

SEEING FINGERS, LOUIS BRAILLE

This is the story of how a French inventor of a system of reading for the blind adjusted to his own disability. (Ages 9–12)
BY: Etta DeGering
PUBLISHER: David McKay Co., Inc., 1963

THE BLIND CONNEMARA

The beautiful white pony is going blind. Rhonda knows that a sightless horse is dangerous to himself and his rider. She cannot stand the thought he might have to be put away. When "Pony" is given to her, she is overjoyed. With patience and devotion she begins to gain his trust and to teach him to move with confidence again. (Ages 11–13)
BY: G. W. Anderson
PUBLISHER: Macmillan, Inc., 1968

THE CAY

This is the story of Philip, a boy who loses his sight from a blow to the head. He and Timothy find themselves cast on an island after the freighter on which they were traveling is torpedoed. It tells of their struggle for survival and of Phillip's efforts to adjust to his blindness and overcome a learned prejudice of black people. (Ages 11–13)
BY: Theodore Taylor
PUBLISHER: Doubleday & Company, Inc., 1969

FINDING MY WAY

An autobiography. A well-known author gives a gripping account of her day-to-day experiences, learning to live with total blindness, continuing her career, and leading a full life. (Ages 11–13)
BY: Borgheld Dahl
PUBLISHER: E. P. Dutton & Co., Inc., 1962

TRIUMPH OF THE SEEING EYE

A blind man writes of the history and workings of the *seeing eye* and explains the great love between a seeing-eye dog and his master. (Ages 11 and up)
BY: Peter Putnam
PUBLISHER: Harper & Row, Publishers, 1963

A LIGHT IN THE DARK

The story of Samuel Gridley Howe, who directed the Perkins Institution for the Blind in 1831 and also helped found a school for education of deaf mutes. (Ages 8–17)
BY: Milton Meltzer
PUBLISHER: Thomas Y. Crowell Company, 1964

TOUCH OF LIGHT

The story of Louis Braille and how he developed an alphabet for the blind. (Ages 8–13)
BY: Anne E. Neimark
PUBLISHER: Harcourt, Brace and World, Inc., 1970

TO CATCH AN ANGEL

An autobiography writen by a man who was blinded at the age of 5, yet proceeded to become a great scholar, fine wrestler, and finally an associate professor, all through his leonine determination. (Ages 14 and up)
BY: Robert Russell
PUBLISHER: Vanguard Press, Inc., 1962

LIGHT A SINGLE CANDLE

A young girl finds she must face a very different way of living when she loses her sight at 14. The greatest challenges are in the attitudes of other people, rather than in her physical handicap. (Ages 11–15)
BY: Beverly Butler
PUBLISHER: Dodd, Mead & Company, 1965

LOUIS BRAILLE: WINDOWS FOR THE BLIND

A biography of the famous man who developed an alphabet for the blind. (Ages 12 and up)
BY: Alvin J. Kugelmass
PUBLISHER: Julian Messner, 1951

YOUNG LOUIS BRAILLE

Louis Braille in his childhood and some of the events that led to his life's work with the blind are described in this book. (Ages 12–17)
BY: Clare Abrahall
PUBLISHER: Roy Publishers, Inc., 1965

TEACHER OF THE BLIND: SAMUEL GRIDLEY HOWE

An exciting story of the achievement of a famous teacher of the blind. (Ages 12 and up)
BY: Katherine E. Wilkie and Elizabeth R. Mosler
PUBLISHER: Julian Messner, 1965

FOLLOW MY LEADER

Story of an 11-year-old boy who is blinded in an accident and how he overcomes his blindness with the use of a seeing-eye dog. (Ages 9–13)
BY: James B. Garfield
PUBLISHER: The Viking Press, Inc., 1967

HELEN KELLER

An execellent book that tells the courageous story of Helen Keller and her teacher, Anne Sullivan. (Ages 8–11)
BY: Margaret Davidson
PUBLISHER: Hastings House, Publishers, Inc., 1970

GENERAL

CHILD OF THE SILENT NIGHT

The story of Laura Bridgman who suffered an illness that left her blind and deaf. She is sent to the Perkins Institute, where she is taught to see and hear. (Ages 8–13)
BY: Edith Fisher Hunter
PUBLISHER: Yearling Books, 1963

CHALLENGED BY HANDICAP: ADVENTURES IN COURAGE

A collection of stories about handicapped people and their courage in fighting against all obstacles as they try to lead fulfilling lives. (Ages 9–13)
BY: Richard Little
PUBLISHER: Reilly and Lee, 1971

TAKE WING

The story emphasizes the problems of shyness and difficulty in making friends. (Ages 5–14)
BY: Jean Little
PUBLISHER: Little, Brown and Company, 1968

HOME FROM FAR

A deeply moving account of Jenny and her family facing the terrible loss of her twin brother, Michael, who had been killed in an automobile accident. Suddenly, Jenny was not "one of the MacGregor twins" any longer. Jenny's parents decided it was time to help, not just Jenny, but all of the family, with courage and understanding. (Ages 10–12)
BY: Jean Little
PUBLISHER: Little, Brown and Company, 1965

THE SMALLEST BOY IN THE CLASS

A little boy, nicknamed "Tiny" by his classmates, proves to himself and to them that size is not a real measure of worth. An easy to read book. (Ages 6–8)
BY: Gerrold Beim
PUBLISHER: Marrow, 1949

KATE

Story about Emily, who wrote a character sketch of her best friend, Kate. It told everything about her except that she was Jewish. For Kate, it was a year of insight and discovery of learning as much about others as she does about herself. (Ages 10–12)
BY: Jean Little
PUBLISHER: Harper & Row, Publishers, 1971

KRISTY'S COURAGE

Kristy's scarred face and blurred speech, resulting from an automobile accident, are difficult handicaps. She has to cope with schoolmates who tease her cruelly, but she keeps her troubles to herself. When her mother comes home with a new baby, Kristy finally turns to the hospital for help, but it is her own courage which eventually overcomes her difficulties. (Ages 10–12)
BY: Bobbie Friis Baastad
PUBLISHER: Harcourt Brace Jovanovich, Inc., 1965

ONE LITTLE BOY

This is the story of 8-year-old Kenneth, who had an asthma problem and many problems with his mother and father. The book is narrated by the consulting psychologist who helped Kenneth understand his deep-rooted feelings, and it can help all of us better understand the minds of troubled children. (Ages 14 and up)
BY: Dorothy Baruch
PUBLISHER: Julian Press, Inc., 1952

JENNIFER JEAN, THE CROSS-EYED QUEEN

Story of a cross-eyed girl and how she avoids ridicule even when her eyes are in the process of being straightened. She has to wear glasses and a patch. (Ages 5–13)
BY: Phyllis Naylor
PUBLISHER: Lerner Publications Company, 1967

SOUNDER

A black sharecropper, his family, and his dog transcend great affliction in this poignant story of cruelty and dignity, tragedy and courage. (Ages 11–13)

BY: William H. Armstrong

PUBLISHER: Harper & Row, Publishers, 1969

IN A MIRROR

Perceptive story of a college girl who hid her sensitive spirit under the burden of overweight. As she grows in maturity and reaches out to friendship, she finds satisfaction in her own world. (Ages 12–14)

BY: Mary Stolz

PUBLISHER: Harper & Row, Publishers, 1953

DON'T WORRY DEAR

Jenny is a little girl who sucks her thumb, wets her bed, and stutters on some of her words. Surrounded by the warmth and acceptance of a loving family, she is given an opportunity to outgrow these habits at her own pace and gradually manages to overcome them all. (Ages 7–12)

BY: Joan Fassler

PUBLISHER: Behavioral Publication, Inc., 1971

THE LITTLEST RABBIT

Story of the littlest rabbit and how prejudice is shown against him. He grows up and protects other little rabbits. (Ages 5–10)

BY: Robert Kraus

PUBLISHER: Harper & Row, Publishers, 1961

TALL TINA

Tina is not too self-conscious about being tall until she is teased by a new classmate. It tells of her different approaches to dealing with the problem and ends with a lesson on empathy and how some differences can have value. (Ages 6–9)

BY: Muriel Stanek

PUBLISHER: Whitman Books, 1970

ABOUT HANDICAPS

An interesting story that explains "extraordinary ways that ordinary children between 3 and 8 years of age attempt to make sense of difficult events in their lives." The story is about a boy and his friend with cerebral palsy. It is well written, and the photographs are excellent. (Ages 11–adult)

BY: Sara Bonnett Stein

PUBLISHER: Walker and Co., 1974

INDEX

Combs, A., 198, 199
Communication, process of, 39
Concept development, 34
Conceptualize, ability to
  of mentally handicapped, 118
  programming for, 139-140
Continuum of services, 22-23, 24, 30
Contract(s)
  examples, 160-168
  guidelines, 159
  minicontracts, 159-160
  systematic suspension, 167-168
  weekly academic, 159-160
Contractures, 83
Control braces, 87
Cooperative plan, 25-27
Coordination problems of learning disabled, 115
Corrective braces, 87
Cosca, G., 184
Council for Exceptional Children, 10

Counseling students and parents, 47, 68, 90, 171
Cratty, B., 137
Crippled and other health impaired, medical and
    technological advances, 74
Crisis teacher, 170
Crutches, purpose, care, and maintenance of, 87
Cullum, A., 178-179
Cursive writing, value in Fernald approach, 130

D

Dalfen, S., 183
Deaf; *see* Hearing impaired
Decibel, definition of, 35
Decker, J. L., 77
Degrees of hearing impairment, 35-36
Delayed speech, 100-101
  causes for, 100
Delivery systems, 18, 23
Devereux School Behavior Rating Scale, 147
Deviant behavior, nature of, 144-145
Diabetes, 78-80
  coma, 79
  identification of, 78
  insulin reaction, 79
Dictionary skills for hearing impaired, 41
Diagnosis and prescription in learning disabilities
    program, 29, 120-121
Diagnosogenic theory in stuttering, 103
Diagnostic-prescriptive center for children with
    learning disabilities, 119-122
  diagnosis and prescription, 120-121
  learning lab, 121
  parent conferences, 120
  placement committee, 120
  screening/assessment in, 119-120
Diana v. *State Board of Education,* 13-14
Dion, D., 184
Disabilities, nonspecific, 125
Distance vision, 52
Distortion, as a speech articulation problem, 97
Dog guide, 61
Dreikurs, R., 154, 157
Duchenne Muscular Dystrophy, 86
Dunn, Lloyd, 13
Dyslexia, 126

E

Earaches, 38
Early history, treatment of handicapped, 4-6
Egland, G., 94, 98, 101
Einstein, A., 100
Electronic travel devices, 61
Elementary and Secondary Education Act of 1965,
    12, 21
Emotionally disturbed; *see* Troubled children
Environmental sounds, intensity, 35
l'Epee, Abbé de, 5
Epilepsy, 80-82
  educational implications, 81-82
  identification, 80-81
Epilepsy Foundation of America, 81-82
Equal educational opportunity, 30
Equalizing education, 18
Ernst, L., 188-189
Evaluation, hearing impaired, 35, 43
Examination, audiometric, 35
Eye, medical information, 69
Eye specialists, 53, 57

F

Fatigue, hearing impaired, 42
Fernald, G., 124
  approach recommended by Myklebust, 133
  VAKT approaches, 129-132
Feshback, N., 184
Filmstrips, 43
Fink, A., 189
Flander, N., 187
Flanders' classroom interaction analysis, 187-188
Flannigan's Test of General Ability, 183
Flexibility disorders in speech, 102
Florida, legislation, 20
Free public education, rights of the handicapped,
    15
Freed, A., 156
Freudian hypotheses, as basis for stuttering causa-
    tion, 103
Frustration, low tolerance for
  of the mentally handicapped, 117
  programming for, 137-138
Frustration theory in stuttering, 103

G

Galloway, C., 188
Generalize, ability to
  of the mentally handicapped, 118
  programming for, 139-140
Georgia, legislation, 21
Gestures, facial and body, 40-41
Ghetto language, 99
Gillingham, A., 124
Glad notes, examples of, 151-152
Glad phone calls, 150-152
Glaser, N., 188-189
Glasser, W., 154, 157
Glasses, 24
Good, T., 184, 185
Gordon, T., 153
Grading, 43
Grand mal seizure, 80-82
Group meetings, 157-159
    academic planning meetings, 157

WITHDRAWN